Heidegger
and
Science

Current Continental Research
is co-published by
The Center for Advanced Research
in Phenomenology
and
University Press of America, Inc.

EDITORIAL BOARD

Lester Embree, *Chairman*
Duquesne University

Edward G. Ballard
  Tulane University

José Huertas-Jourda
  Wilfred Laurier
  University

Joseph J. Kockelmans
  The Pennsylvania State
  University

William McKenna
  Miami University

Algis Mickunas
  Ohio University

J.N. Mohanty
  University of
  Oklahoma

Thomas M. Seebohm
  Johannes Guttenberg-
  Universität, Mainz

Richard M. Zaner
  Vanderbilt University

CURRENT CONTINENTAL RESEARCH 207

Joseph J. Kockelmans

HEIDEGGER AND SCIENCE

1985

Center for Advanced Research in Phenomenology
& University Press of America, Washington, D.C.

Copyright © 1985 by

The Center for Advanced Research in Phenomenology, Inc.

University Press of America,™ Inc.

4720 Boston Way
Lanham, MD 20706

3 Henrietta Street
London WC2E 8LU England

All rights reserved

Printed in the United States of America

Library of Congress Cataloging in Publication Data

Kockelmans, Joseph J., 1923-
  Heidegger and science.

  (Current continental research ; 207)
  "This book which developed out of a series of lectures
on philosophy and natural science at Duquesne University
in April of 1979 and a seminar on the philosophy of
science at the Pennsylvania State University"—Pref.
  Bibliography: p.
  Includes index.
  1. Heidegger, Martin, 1889-1976. 2. Science—
Philosophy—History—20th century. I. Title. II. Series.
B3279.H49K625   1985   193   84-29171
ISBN 0-8191-4561-0 (alk. paper)
ISBN 0-8191-4562-9 (pbk. : alk. paper)

All University Press of America books are produced on acid-free
paper which exceeds the minimum standards set by the National
Historical Publications and Records Commission.

Contents

Acknowledgments	ix
Preface	xi

Introduction: PHILOSOPHY OF SCIENCE AND
              ONTOLOGY OF SCIENCE

A.	Science and the Modern Era	1
B.	Science, Foundational Research, and Philosophy of Science	3
C.	Recent Developments in Philosophy of Science. Logic and the History of Science	7
D.	Leading Schools and Trends in Philosophy of Science Today	10
E.	Philosophy of Science: The Place of Hermeneutic Phenomenology	14
F.	Heidegger and the Philosophy of Science	17

Part I: HEIDEGGER'S BACKGROUND.
ON THE MEANING OF HERMENEUTIC PHENOMENOLOGY

Chapter I: HEIDEGGER'S INTRODUCTION TO THE SCIENCES
           AND THE PHILOSOPHY OF SCIENCE OF HIS TIME   21

1: Heidegger's Education	21
2: From Dilthey's Personalistic Psychology via Husserl's Phenomenology to Heidegger's Analytic of Dasein	27
a. Origin and Development of Phenomenological Research	27
b. The Basic Discoveries of Phenomenology	31
c. Critical Evaluation of Husserl's Transcendental Phenomenology	35
3: Note on the "Geisteswissenschaften"	41

Chapter II: HERMENEUTIC PHENOMENOLOGY AS
            THE METHOD OF THE ANALYTIC OF DASEIN   48

4: On the Necessity, Structure, and Priority of the Question of Being	49
5: On the Scientific Character of Philosophy. Heidegger's Concern with Method	53

6:	Destructive Retrieve and Hermeneutic Phenomenology	59
7:	Heidegger's Conception of Phenomenology	62

    a. Phenomenology. The Meaning of the Term   62
    b. Hermeneutic Phenomenology   66
    c. Heidegger's Later Philosophy.
       Husserl and Heidegger   69

Chapter III: BEING-IN-THE-WORLD AND
              THE HERMENEUTIC CHARACTER OF
              MAN'S UNDERSTANDING AS SUCH   72

8:	Dasein, Ek-sistence, Being-in-the-World	72
9:	Concern and Theoretical Knowledge	74
10:	Heidegger's Conception of "Verstehen"	78
11:	Interpretative Understanding and the Hermeneutic Circle	85
12:	Dasein and Reality. Neither Realism nor Idealism	88
13:	On Truth	93
14:	Note on Regional Ontologies	102

    a. Husserl's Original Conception of
       Regional Ontologies   102
    b. Regional Ontologies and Empirical Sciences   109
    c. Heidegger's Critique of Husserl's
       Transcendental Phenomenology   113

      Part II: HEIDEGGER'S CONCEPTION OF THE SCIENCES

Chapter IV: TOWARD THE ESSENCE OF EMPIRICAL SCIENCE   117

15:	From Concernfully Dealing with ("praxis") to Theory	118
16:	Thematization. Thematization is Objectivation	124
17:	On the Relationship between Foundational Research in a Science and Philosophy	130

    a. The Limit of the Self-Founding of
       Every Science   130
    b. The Foundation of Science, Regional Ontology,
       and Fundamental Ontology   131

18:	Science and Other Forms of Rational Discourse	133

Chapter V: TOWARD AN ONTOLOGY OF THE MODERN
            SCIENCES OF NATURE   139

19:	Origin and Meaning of the Modern Mathematical Sciences of Nature	140

    a. Modern vs. Ancient and Medieval Science   140

	b. The Mathematical. On the Meaning of "mathesis"	142
	c. The Mathematical Character of Modern Natural Science. Newton's First Law	143
	d. The Difference between the Greek and the Modern Experience of Nature	145
	e. The Essence of the Mathematical Projection. Galileo's Free Fall Experiment	148

20: Toward the Essence of the Modern Science of Nature — 152

    a. Natural Science is Research — 153
    b. Natural Science proceeds according to Methods — 155
    c. Natural Science is Enterprise, System, and Institution — 157

21: Modern Natural Science as the Theory of What is Real — 162
22: Natural Science and Technology — 173
23: Science and Metaphysics in the Modern Era: The Metaphysical Meaning of the Mathematical — 177

Chapter VI: HISTORY AND HISTORIOLOGY. HEIDEGGER'S UNDERSTANDING OF THE "GEISTESWISSENSCHAFTEN" — 190

24: The Science of "History" within the Context of Hermeneutic Phenomenology — 190

25: The Eksistential Source of Historiology in Dasein's Historicity — 196

26: Toward a Comprehensive Theory of our Knowledge of History — 201

Chapter VII: HERMENEUTIC PHENOMENOLOGY AND THE HUMAN SCIENCES — 210

27: Why did Heidegger not Explicitly Focus on the Human Sciences? — 210
28: Objectifying Thematization in the Human Sciences — 220
29: Descriptive and Interpretative Human Sciences On the Methods to be Employed in the Descriptive Component of Each Human Science — 228
30: Interpretative Sciences of Man and Methods to be Used There — 231
31: The Canons of Hermeneutics and Interpretative Social Science — 236

Epilogue

    1: Two Forms of Thinking. Thoughtlessness
       the Dominant Characteristic of our Epoch   249

    2: The Threat of Nihilism   250

    3: The Danger of the Atomic Age   252

Abbreviations   256

Notes   257

Bibliography   283

Index of Names   299

Index of Topics   302

ACKNOWLEDGMENTS

Some of the material contained in this book appeared in different form in various journals and anthologies. Thus I wish to thank editors and publishers for their permissions to make use of sections of the following articles and book chapters:
"Phenomenology and the Critique of the Scientific Tradition," *Essays in Memory of Aron Gurwitsch*, ed., Lester E. Embree (Washington, D.C.: Center for Advanced Research in Phenomenology & University Press of America, 1984); "Destructive Retrieve and Hermeneutic Phenomenology," *Research in Phenomenology*, 7(1977), pp. 106-137; "Science and Discipline: Some Historical and Critical Reflections," *Interdisciplinarity and Higher Education*, ed. Joseph J. Kockelmans (University Park, PA: The Pennsylvania State University Press, 1979), pp. 17-24; "Reflections on Social Theory," *Human Studies*, 1(1978), pp. 1-15; "Some Reflections on the Meaning and Function of Interpretative Sociology," *Tijdschrift voor Filosofie*, 42(1980), pp. 294-324; "Toward an Interpretative or Hermeneutical Social Science," *Graduate Faculty Philosophical Journal*, 5(1975), pp. 73-96; "Hermeneutic Phenomenology and the Science of History," *Phänomenologische Forschungen*, 2(1976), pp. 130-179; and chapters 8 and 9 of my book, *Martin Heidegger: A First Introduction to His Philosophy* (Pittsburgh, PA: Duquesne University Press, 1965).

x

Preface

In this book which developed out of a series of lectures on philosophy and natural science at Duquesne University in April of 1979 and a seminar on the philosophy of science at The Pennsylvania State University, I wish to make an effort to give a systematic explanation of Heidegger's reflections on the sciences. In view of the fact that Heidegger himself never developed a systematic "philosophy of science," in some instances I shall attempt to go beyond the claims one can make on the basis of texts by Heidegger himself which explicitly deal with pertinent issues. In those cases I shall try to apply insights and ideas developed in his works to issues and problems which as such he himself did not address. This is relevant particularly for the domain of the human sciences.

In his reflections on the sciences Heidegger always makes a distinction between the *natural* and the *historical* sciences; as far as I know the distinction between the *natural* and the *social* sciences that is commonly made in the Anglo-American literature, is never made by Heidegger. As we shall see later (in chapter VII), there are several reasons that can be given for this fact, the most important of which are the neo-Kantian world in which Heidegger was introduced to this complex problem domain and the structure of most institutions of higher learning in Europe during the first quarter of this century.

Be this as it may, Heidegger took his point of departure for reflections on the sciences in a context which was influenced in part by a tradition that goes back to Plato and Aristotle, partly by Kant and the neo-Kantian tradition (Rickert, Dilthey), and partly by Husserl's phenomenology. With his "teachers" Dilthey, Rickert, and Husserl, Heidegger always makes a distinction between the natural and the historical sciences. This distinction had been debated systematically in the literature that deals with the sciences that use hermeneutic methods.[1] It is to be noted that this debate had taken place during a time in which empirical psychology, anthropology, economics, sociology, political science, etc., did not yet exist *as empirical sciences* in the modern sense of this term. It seems to me that the change in our entire conception of the sciences that lies behind the shift from a distinction between the natural and the historical sciences to a distinction between the natural and the social sciences, hides one of the basic problems which are the cause of much misunderstanding about the meaning and function of science among the various schools in philosophy of science today.

In his reflections on the sciences Heidegger is not concerned directly with logical, epistemological, methodological, historical, psychological, sociological, or political considerations. His major concern in this regard has always been to develop an ontology of the sciences that focusses primarily on the meaning and function of the sciences in our contemporary world. Thus Heidegger discusses mainly questions such as: Precisely what is science? How do the sciences relate to philosophy? In what sense can one claim that for modern man the sciences constitute a viable road toward the truth? Precisely what do the sciences teach us about what is real? What is the meaning and function of science in our contemporary world? How do the sciences affect the manner in which we think about ourselves and about the world in which we live? How does science affect religion, morality, the arts? etc.

As far as the so-called formal sciences (logic and mathematics) as well as the linguistic sciences are concerned, Heidegger has written extensively only on the science of logic and on grammar. These publications belong to the period that precedes *Being and Time*. I have decided not to discuss Heidegger's position in regard to logic and speculative grammar in this book in view of the fact that Heidegger later never explicitly returned to the issues that had occupied him before 1919.[2] It is true that in his later work Heidegger very often speaks about logic and language; but these reflections do not belong to what one commonly understands by philosophy of logic and philosophy of language.[3]

In this book I shall thus focus first on Heidegger's conception of the empirical sciences. In that chapter I hope to describe the basic ideas which Heidegger developed concerning the empirical sciences without yet making an explicit distinction between the natural, the historical, and the human sciences. In the subsequent chapters I plan to apply the general insights gained in this way first to the natural sciences and to mathematical physics in particular, and then to the historical sciences. Finally I hope to turn to the question of whether and how Heidegger's conception of the empirical sciences perhaps can be applied to what we now commonly call the behavioral and the social sciences.

I shall preface these reflections on the sciences with an introductory part in which I shall discuss those ideas and insights that are immediately pertinent to the manner in which Heidegger deals with the sciences. These ideas and insights are derived mainly from *Being and Time* and other works of the same period.

Several sections contained in this book appeared in a slightly different form in some of my other publications which I have listed in the bibliography. In all cases I have referred to these publications and made a special effort to revise the original material carefully and to adapt the ideas developed there to the present, systematic context.

                                      Joseph J. Kockelmans

                                      The Pennsylvania State University

INTRODUCTION

PHILOSOPHY OF SCIENCE
AND
ONTOLOGY OF SCIENCE

A. SCIENCE AND THE MODERN ERA

The empirical sciences constitute an essential dimension of our modern world.[1] This is the reason why the meaning and function of the empirical sciences cannot be fully understood except within the general framework of an effort to come to a better understanding of our modern world, taken as a whole. Thus here, too, we encounter already at the very beginning the hermeneutical circle, a circle which makes it necessary to constantly move from part to whole and from whole to part.

The modern world obviously has many other "regions"; in this connection it may suffice to mention the following dimensions of our world: religion, morality, the arts, our social institutions, the political dimension, and education. To come to a full understanding of the meaning and function of science our efforts will, therefore, necessarily lead us to the question of precisely how the development of the empirical sciences has affected our conception of, and the manner in which we relate to, these other dimensions of our world.

From the experiences we have had with the sciences and with the technological projects which they have made possible, it is clear that the influence of the sciences on the world as well as on most of its dimensions has had both positive and negative sides. It is impossible to come to a full understanding of the meaning and function of the empirical sciences if one is not willing to look very carefully at both of these aspects. It would be difficult, if not simply impossible, to deny the positive dimension of the sciences. In each science new vistas have been opened up and each empirical science has shown us many new and unexpected possibilities. Yet it is clear also that in every science modern man has become confronted with often unexpected problems, difficulties, and dangers.

Now it is not possible to look at both the positive and negative dimensions of the empirical sciences if it is not made clear first from what broad *ontological* perspective one is to look at the sciences. If one looks at the empirical sciences merely from a logical, linguistic, methodological, or epistemological point of view, these influences of the sciences will neither be fully realized, nor fully understood and evaluated. This is the main reason why an ontological view or perspective on the sciences is so important: precisely what is empirical science (in light of the many other human options and possibilities in the "cognitive" order), precisely what are its prospects, and what are its limits?

From the Renaissance and certainly from the Enlightenment onwards it has always been assumed without question that science, and the scientific method in particular, constitute the genuine and true approaches to the truth, regardless of what one is to understand here by "truth," and regardless of what kinds of truths one is looking for. This conception gradually led to the view that whatever comes from our heritage, tradition, and all non-scientific human efforts (such as religion, morality, the arts, the socio-political *praxis*, etc.) is to be subjected to the judgment of reason as reason itself has been understood from the perspective of science and method.

Anyone who questions this "blind" belief in science and method is automatically taken to have a negative stance in regard to the sciences and, thus, implicitly at least to promote occultism, irrationalism, and in the final analysis, nihilism. Yet it is difficult to understand why adopting a questioning attitude in this case is necessarily to be identified with negativism. Most people feel that it is correct to question religious, moral, social, and political conceptions; yet many seem to think that it is inappropriate to question the sciences, i.e., to ask questions about the positive and negative aspects of our engagement in the empirical sciences. It is often alleged that anyone who dares to ask questions about the empirical sciences is somehow afraid to learn the "genuine" truth about the convictions that have come to to use from our heritage.

And so it is of great importance from the very start to stipulate clearly that in Heidegger's view the sciences undoubtedly belong among the greatest achievements of modern Western man. Once this has been made clear, it is then important to realize that the sciences, like all other human achievements, share in the finitude, the temporality, and historicity of man. Thus it remains important to ask the question of precisely what science is, how it is to be related to all the other orientations of man toward the world, what its prospects and what its limits are, what kinds of contributions the sciences can make to meaningful discourse about religious, moral, aesthetic, social, political, and educational issues, and what the areas are in which, in this regard, one may not expect a positive contribution from the sciences, simply because of the fact that one appears to run into issues which lie far beyond the competence of the scientific method.

Today we find ourselves in an era of complete scientization: in the religious domain nothing can be accepted that cannot be legitimated scientifically; in many instances philosophical reflections on moral and aesthetic issues are replaced by psychological and sociological investigations about certain aspects of these issues; Habermas in my view correctly speaks of a scientization of the entire political domain; several authors have complained about the scientization of our educational framework. To make the claim that such a universal scientization is unwarranted and dangerous is not tantamount to promoting anti-rationalism. To make such a claim merely means that one finally begins to take the sciences very seriously, and that one is willing to make a systematic effort to discover precisely where one may expect positive contributions from the sciences and precisely where one will have to turn to other forms of "rational" discourse.

Whatever one may think about these issues, it is of the greatest importance to continuously keep in mind that in his ontological concern with the sciences, Heidegger was not guided by a basic mistrust of the sciences; rather he was always engaged in a serious effort to stake out their positive possibilities. I plan to return to these issues in some of the chapters to follow.

B. SCIENCE, FOUNDATIONAL RESEARCH, AND PHILOSOPHY OF SCIENCE[2]

If one looks at the sciences from a formal point of view, one could say that the sciences, taken in an objective sense, are the intentional correlates of a special kind of theoretical knowledge which must be characterized by its systematic and methodical character and its typical sense of critique. In their scientific activities the scientists select the steps to be taken with great care and evaluate their outcome on the basis of precisely formulated criteria, principles, and methods. The criteria, principles, and methods which they employ are determined in such a manner that it is continually possible to expand the realm of knowledge in a systematic fashion, even though this process of growth often goes through "revolutionary" stages.

The principles which are used to organize a realm of investigation and the insights which are pertinent to it, the criteria of validity, as well as the relevant research methods are, as a rule at least, taken from a domain outside the scientific discipline proper, but constitute nonetheless an integral part of the development of the scientific knowledge itself. Most of these criteria, principles, and methods are at first to a large extent implicit in a given piece of scientific research and usually remain unexamined for some time. At a later stage they are made explicit, critically analyzed and examined, and ultimately subjected to a rigorous process of validation and justification. At first, each science begins with a number of ideas, criteria, principles, and methods which are put to work in regard to a certain realm of phenomena. At that stage of the development of a science these ideas, criteria, principles, and methods still have the character of being presuppositions.

At a later stage these presuppositions are then made the subject matter of critical analysis and investigation in so-called foundational research. In this second type of research once again ideas, criteria, principles, and methods are put to work; in a later phase they, too, can be made the subject matter of a new type of foundational research. Thus even foundational research is never more than of relative validity. It tries to explain and justify presuppositions in the light of more fundamental assumptions, without being capable of ever reaching a final stage, a realm of "absolutes" of some kind. For many centuries both philosophers and scientists were convinced that the final justification of the assumptions made in scientific research was to be given by philosophy. I shall return to this issue in section 17 below.

During that same period in history no sharp distinction between science and philosophy was ever made. After the middle of the 19th Century, science and philosophy grew apart, and it is now generally accepted that some distinction between the two must be made, although there is little agreement on the question of how one should conceive of the distinction and the grounds on which it ultimately rests. Most philosophers and scientists today agree that the sciences constitute a legitimate subject matter for philosophical reflection, but here again there is no universal agreement on the question of how the expression "philosophy of science" is to be understood. According to some, philosophy of science is concerned with all the legitimate problems with which the phenomenon "science" confronts us today. Most authors who write on philosophy of science, however, apply the term in a more limited sense and use it to refer to those reflections which have to do with logical, methodological, and epistemological aspects of the sciences only. Of the latter some will claim explicitly that these are the only problems which should be dealt with in philosophy as far as the sciences are concerned, whereas others will leave room for problems of a more ontological nature which, they feel, should be dealt with in philosophy, but not in philosophy of science proper.

Finally, there are several philosophers and scientists today who share the opinion that research on the foundations of the sciences is an integral part of each science, and that the thesis according to which one of the functions and tasks of philosophy of science consists in clarifying and justifying the foundations of the sciences rests on a misconception of the meaning of both science and philosophy. Obviously it does not follow from this view that the historical development of the sciences no longer confronts philosophy with important and fundamental problems; yet these problems have no immediate connection with the foundations of the sciences, if the latter expression is understood in a limited and technical sense. According to these authors the sciences themselves are really autonomous, and science and science alone is capable of dealing with its own foundational problems. The problems which the sciences pose to philosophy are of a quite different nature and all of them center around the basic question of the meaning and function of science in our world: What is science? How does it relate to religion, morality, art? What is the precise relationship between science and action, between science and the socio-political practice? How can one explain the relationship between scientific constructs and the "structures" of the things which they try to explain? What are the implications of the intrinsic historicity of the sciences? Do the sciences have a "teleological" orientation? In what sense can one speak of progress in science? What are the limits of scientific knowledge? Whereas foundational questions are formulated and examined with the help of methodological, logical, and mathematical procedures in a general epistemology, the latter questions are of a strictly philosophical nature and, thus, cannot be adequately dealt with except on the basis of a general ontology.

In the realm of the empirical sciences physics occupies a privileged place, not only because of the impressive results to which its research has led over the centuries, but also because of the fact that physics more than any other empirical science shows us in what the typical scientificity of the empirical sciences precisely consists. Contrary to the formal sciences which discover their own subject matters while constructing them, physical research is oriented toward the natural beings that are given in experience, and, in the final analysis, toward the ontic universe as directly or indirectly given through perception. Physics tries to explain the ontic universe with the help of theoretical constructions which are analogous to those constructed in the formal sciences and which, to a high degree, are mathematical in character.

The basic problem encountered in the empirical sciences is the question of precisely how these two basic elements, the experiential component and the formal theory, are to be related to one another. The history of these sciences has shown clearly that one cannot account for this relationship in terms of some theory of induction, in that scientific theories are not the result of a generalizing process that takes its point of departure from individual cases. A scientific theory is the result of an intellectual, "creative" process which may have been suggested by empirically established relationships, or may have been structured with the help of models discovered through experience, but which essentially is independent of these activities, and is guided by organizing principles of a purely formal nature. But if the theoretical part of an empirical discipline is indeed not directly given through perception, and in this sense is a priori, then one must ask the question of how such an a priori construct can be used to explain real physical phenomena.

Many authors, following ideas suggested by Carnap and other members of the Vienna Circle, believed that this basic problem can be solved by a careful logical analysis of the language of physics. Yet according to others this attempt to solve this basic problem failed because it appeared to be impossible in principle to formulate a criterion of empirical significance, as presupposed in this approach. That is why some authors have tried to avoid this difficulty by assuming that a certain model is to be constructed to mediate between the purely formal structures and the data of observation and experiment. Most recently, however, several authors have pointed in a totally different direction for an answer to this problem by suggesting a "structuralist" approach to theories of empirical science.

In the pages to come we shall return to most of the issues raised here. Suffice it to state now that hermeneutic phenomenology is not concerned with epistemological, logical, or methodological issues posed by the sciences. In its view these reflections which make use of meta-physical assumptions (metascience) and are immediately related to the foundations of each science, are important, but as such they are not ontological in character and can be undertaken successfully only by scientists. Yet hermeneutic phenomenology maintains that there is an essential difference between science and philosophy and that philosophical reflections on the sciences are an integral part of philosophy's basic concern, as we shall see in Section E of this introduction.

C. RECENT DEVELOPMENTS IN PHILOSOPHY OF SCIENCE. LOGIC AND HISTORY OF SCIENCE[3]

For almost 300 years most scientists and philosophers have assumed that the history of the sciences exhibits a process of continuous growth and development; this process encompasses more and more phenomena and it brings us continuously closer to the truth about things. According to this conception, science also determines what is to count as genuine knowledge; all other forms of knowledge are to be evaluated in the light of the norms established by and for science. Furthermore, the pursuit of scientific knowledge is altogether autonomous; it is in no way answerable to outside norms. Since the beginning of the twentieth century this "optimistic" view of science has been questioned by some historians and philosophers, and it is now rejected by many philosophers and historians of science.[4]

The ideal of knowledge which this classical, predominantly empiricist and positivist, conception of science offered, was one in which method occupied the central place; it was commonly accepted that method is the only road that leads to the truth. Yet in order for the application of methods to be effective, scientific knowledge must be based on experience and all of its claims must be rated by a universally accepted means of testing.

If the scientists in their research keep this ideal in mind, their scientific knowledge is neither subjective nor just personal, but rather objective and value-free.[5]

Today many scientists, philosophers, and historians of science are convinced that this simplistic conception of science is unacceptable, because it cannot account for the manner in which science develops over time. Science does not grow merely by means of a process of accumulation. For in addition to the accumulation of observed facts and laws, there is equally a basic transformation of theories, and of their fundamental principles and concepts.

In philosophy of science this new view of science originated from ideas first formulated by Duhem and Meyerson, on the one hand, and by Popper and Kuhn on the other. These authors themselves had been inspired by a more accurate knowledge of the history of science as well as by the development which had taken place in the natural sciences after 1890. As for the latter, what is important here is the fact that both the theory of relativity and quantum mechanics do not fit into a cumulative conception of science (they are more like evolutionary mutations) and that the new scientific theories do not necessarily imply a complete rejection of older theories. What is meant by the last claim is particularly clear in the case of the general theory of relativity. For by 1920 most leading scientists had accepted the general theory of relativity as a definitive achievement in modern physics. Yet most practicing scientists, depending upon the types of questions they were concerned with, continued to make an effective use of Newton's mechanics, Maxwell's and Hertz's electrodynamics, and Einstein's special theory of relativity. Theoretically, one argued that the special theory of relativity is a limiting case of the general theory of relativity, whereas classical physics in its dual form is a limiting case of the special theory of relativity. Yet it is true that within the special theory of relativity one maintains a conception of gravity which is explicitly rejected in the general theory of relativity, whereas in classical physics one maintains a conception of space and time that is explicitly rejected in the special theory of relativity. Thus, even though mathematically it is possible to relate the various theories in a meaningful way by showing that and under what conditions one theory may be taken to be a limiting case of a more encompassing theory, it is true also that logically these different theories are incommensurable.[6]

Popper was one of the first to explicitly attack the classical view of science by convincingly showing that no scientific theory can ever be definitively verified; the most one can do is try to show that a proposed theory has not yet been definitively falsified.[7] Later Kuhn was able to show that from a historical point of view science develops in such a way that one must make a distinction between periods of normal science and periods of scientific revolutions. Kuhn drew the conclusion from this view that science is not oriented toward a *telos* and that science, thus, does not progressively approach "the truth"; furthermore, he argued, strictly speaking one can no longer speak about progress in science, because in periods of scientific revolutions the two competing theories (the old one and the new one) are logically incommensurable.[8] Popper and Lakatos later strongly objected to this view and argued that in a certain sense science approaches more and more the true conception about things and that history of science, thus, does not describe a process which is inherently irrational.[9] At a later stage of the development Sneed and Stegmüller tried to show that the facts upon which Kuhn and Lakatos based their claims can be interpreted in such a manner that the history of science shows us a process that is not irrational, and that the conceptions of science promoted by Carnap and Kuhn are not really contradictory.[10]

In a recent book, *Critique of Scientific Reason*, Hübner has tried to show that scientific endeavors are inherently historical efforts which depend to a considerable degree on the historical situation in which they developed.[11] In view of the fact that not "facts," generalizations, and laws, but theories constitute the very "essence" of modern science, and theories furthermore are to be formulated in concrete historical situations, it is impossible to understand the genuine meaning of modern science on the basis of logical and epistemological analyses alone. Furthermore, every theory is to some extent a priori in regard to the realm of phenomena for which it is developed. Finally, theories are neither true nor false; they are or are not adequate in regard to the phenomena to be explained, and their adequacy depends on a variety of factors, only very few of which can be evaluated strictly logically; coherence and simplicity are some of the criteria scientists do indeed apply; but in addition there is the question of relevance and fertility, and the problem of precisely how theories relate to the entire cognitive framework accepted by the members of a community at a given moment in time.

Thus the assessment of science is often a difficult and controversial affair. Yet the historical development of science is not necessarily an irrational process. For this assessment can make use of certain regulative principles, even though these principles may not always be the same for different scientific communities in different periods of time. Scientific theories are and always will be provisional. Thus it is incorrect to assume that, even purely ideally, in the future one will one day be able to formulate a theory which is ultimate and, thus, the true one. Nor is it correct to describe scientific progress in terms of a progressive approach to the truth. However, this does not mean that it would not be meaningful to speak about truth in connection with scientific theories. Theories may certainly be said to be true; but in that case one means that they are true from the a priori perspective that they inherently imply; they are not true in an absolute sense, precisely because that a priori perspective may change one day for very good reasons.

In other words, all forms of man's understanding, including our scientific ones, are really no more than justifiable forms of interpretation, developed on the basis of certain assumptions. This entails that empirical science is not the one and only road toward "the" truth. Philosophy, furthermore, cannot be reduced to a critical reflection on the sciences alone, and even less to a logic or methodology of empirical science. Yet it is true, also, that no solution for the problems with which the empirical sciences confront us will be found by an appeal to classical metaphysics.

D. LEADING SCHOOLS AND TRENDS IN PHILOSOPHY OF SCIENCE TODAY[12]

Philosophy of science constitutes a very fertile domain in contemporary philosophy. During the past fifty years a great number of books and articles have been published in this area. This vast literature must make a confusing impression on those who do not concern themselves regularly with philosophical issues relevant to their own research interests. Many different views on the sciences are proposed today and many of these views seem, at first sight at least, to be mutually exclusive. Obviously, it is not impossible to reduce these different views to a relatively small number of basic trends such as the logical, the historical, the epistemological, the socio-political, the phenomenological, the ontological trend, etc. But even if one does make these

PHILOSOPHY OF SCIENCE AND ONTOLOGY OF SCIENCE

distinctions, it still is the case that it is not easy to bring all the ideas that are now being proposed in these different trends to some form of harmonious synthesis.

To bring some rhyme and reason to this vast domain of literature it is important that one realizes that each individual science is really a very complex phenomenon that indeed can be approached legitimately from several perspectives. In each case there are particular scientists who decided to become members of the community of scholars in a certain field of study. This community of scholars finds itself in a scientific "paradigm" in which there is a relatively clear distinction between the phenomena that are already known scientifically and those that are still to be investigated further. In addition, the community of scholars which shares this "paradigm," finds itself to be part of a scientific tradition, and the meaning and function of its scientific activities appear somehow to be codetermined by the origin and development of this very tradition itself. In its research efforts the community and all its members are guided by typically "scientific values," but they are equally influenced by a number of "extra-scientific values;" as for the latter, they may be economic, social, political, psychological, "professional," etc. Employing the basic theories and laws implied in the governing paradigm to a carefully defined realm of phenomena, these scientists engage in research practices according to carefully formulated principles and methods, equally implied in the paradigm. The results of their scientific efforts can be formulated in statements that are rationally related to one another by means of logical procedures and can, thus, be made the subject of logical investigations. Sometimes the community of scholars encounters "unexpected" difficulties; one then re-examines all assumptions made and makes changes in the basic theories and laws wherever such changes appear to be necessary and meaningful. Finally, the insights gained through research are often employed in technology or in our social practice. This application sometimes leads to "progress," but it often also imples problems and confronts us with questionable options.

Thus it is obvious that the sciences themselves invite us to engage in a number of different but related sets of reflections; today the following kinds of reflections can be distinguished: historical, logical, sociological, psychological, methodological, epistemological, ethical, and ontological reflections. These different sets of reflections are all developed for very good reasons. Furthermore, they need not at all exclude one another in view of the fact that the complexity of the phenomenon itself is partly responsible for the multiplicity of the ideas that are now being proposed.

Thus the philosopher who critically reflects on the sciences can focus on different aspects with which each science confront us. In light of what is to be said about the aspect of science with which Heidegger was concerned mainly, it is of some importance to characterize the most important of these aspects briefly.

1) First there is the specific kind of activity in which the individual scientists as members of a scientific community engage in regard to a given set of relatively clearly defined phenomena; correlatively there is the specific manner in which as a result of these activities these phenomena, as given in our pre-scientific experience, change over into scientific objects; in contemporary philosophy this dimension is examined predominantly by phenomenologists (Husserl, Heidegger, Merleau-Ponty).

2) Next we must mention the various influences that operate in a scientific community and may range from purely theoretical and scientific concerns with what is really the case in a given domain, to economic and socio-political influences; this dimension is examined mainly by neo-Marxist philosophers, the members of the Frankfurt school, and by some of Popper's followers (Adorno, Habermas, Dahrendorf, Weinberg, Radnitzky).

3) Then we have the theoretical framework from which a scientific community approaches the given set of phenomena and which constitutes the core of the scientific "paradigm" to which the community of scholars subscribes, as well as the so-called "paradigm shifts" which in such communities may occur over time; this dimension is discussed widely by almost all philosophers who concern themselves with the history of the sciences (Popper, Lakatos, Kuhn, Feyerabend, Sneed, Stegmüller).

4) Another aspect of the sciences that must be mentioned here is the systematicity of the claims to which the scientific research ultimately is to lead. This dimension is studied mainly by logicians such as Carnap, Nagel, Hempel, Stegmüller, etc. Yet this dimension is also examined in a "transcendental logic" by all authors whose ideas have been influenced by Kant and the neo-Kantian tradition.

5) Next we have the relationship between scientific claims and the phenomena which they try to explain, and the processes

PHILOSOPHY OF SCIENCE AND ONTOLOGY OF SCIENCE

of verification or falsification involved in each case (Popper, Lakatos, Musgrave, Kuhn).
6) Another set of issues that is often discussed today is closely connected with the difficult problems which flow from the fact that each scientific theory develops in a historical and social context which to some degree codetermines the formulation and, thus, also the meaning of scientific theories (Toulmin, Merton, Hübner).
7) Furthermore, there is the complex problematic connected with any attempt to apply scientific insights to technology and to our social practice (Habermas, Apel, Mumford, Ellul, Radnitzky).
8) The relationship between our scientific claims and the meaning which the phenomena to which these claims relate may have, independent of the scientific approach itself, constitutes the focal point for another set of reflections on the sciences; yet this distinction and this relationship are important mainly in the realm of those sciences that concern themselves with human beings and their world; the issues relevant here are addressed predominantly by hermeneutic philosophers since Dilthey and Weber.
9) Finally there is the complex relationship between the scientific approach to the phenomena on the one hand and the aesthetic, moral, cultural, and religious approaches to the same phenomena on the other (Kant, Heidegger, Hübner, etc.)

Yet, as we mentioned before, it is obviously true that although these various approaches need not really conflict with one another, one will also not come to the "true" view on the matter by simply adding them together. All of these perspectives are to be rethought carefully from a perspective that is concerned mainly with basic ontological issues, i.e., issues of meaning and truth. These issues imply questions about what it really means to be a human being; why human beings engage in scientific activities; what constitutes the scientificity of our scientific endeavors; how purely scientific and theoretical activities relate to all of man's other possible involvements with the world, things, and fellowmen; how theoretical frameworks from which the phenomena in each domain are to be examined, precisely are constituted; in what sense scientific claims are true; what their exact meaning really is; etc.

In the chapters to come I shall make an effort to deal with these issues from the perspective of Heidegger's thought. But before turning to a systematic treatment of his ideas on these issues, I shall first try to locate Heidegger's concern with the sciences within the large domain of research that has just been described. In so doing I shall say a few words first on the place of phenomenology and hermeneutic phenomenology within contemporary philosophy of science as a whole.

E. PHILOSOPHY OF SCIENCE: THE PLACE OF HERMENEUTIC PHENOMENOLOGY

It is well-known that phenomenologists have sometimes been reproached for making critical remarks about the sciences. Hence the objection often raised against phenomenology as a whole is that it takes too negative an attitude toward science. This objection to the phenomenological movement is often substantiated by reference to Husserl's critique of science in "Philosophy as a Rigorous Science" and *The Crisis of European Sciences*, Heidegger's criticism of logic, "calculative thinking," and technology, and Merleau-Ponty's claims about the sciences in *Phenomenology of Perception* and *The Visible and the Invisible*.[13]

On closer inspection, however, it is difficult to understand how this claim could possibly be true. For Husserl was a mathematician and physicist who, in addition, had an excellent training in psychology under Brentano, Wundt, Paulsen, and Stumpf.[14] Heidegger for some time studied modern physics and history at the University of Freiburg. Finally, Merleau-Ponty was a professor of child psychology during one period of his career.[15]

What is true in regard to this claim is that phenomenology from the very start has objected to a one-sided naturalistic and objectivistic interpretation of the sciences. What phenomenology objects to is not science itself but the implicit philosophical self-understanding of modern science. Thus what phenomenology criticizes is not science itself, but scientism; not empirical research and its achievements, but the positivistic interpretation of science. What is true also is that phenomenology from the very beginning has objected to the idea that the sciences of man are somehow to be reduced to the natural sciences. Thus what is being criticized here is not the sciences of man themselves, but merely their reductionist interpretation in behaviorism and positivist sociology and anthropology.

What phenomenologists during the first part of this century were concerned with was not a criticism of science, but rather a critique of scientific knowledge, the latter expression to be understood in the sense of Kant. This critique is necessary if one is to understand the genuine and true meaning of scientific claims as well as the limits that are intrinsic to empirical research. Such a "transcendental" concern is not a denial of science, but precisely presupposes its existence and legitimacy. In their critique of modern science phenomenologists had to take a critical stance in regard to the leading interpretations of the meaning and function of science, and since the latter part of the 19th century this interpretation has been positivism. By "positivism" I mean here any philosophical view that in one sense or another holds that (1) science teaches us the real and genuine truth about things and the world in which we live, and (2) that genuine science should not be contaminated by metaphysics.

From the very beginning phenomenologists have tried to understand the underlying assumptions from which scientists view the phenomena which they have selected for study. In their investigations about the sciences they were guided by the following question: how is one to understand the precise meaning of scientific claims in light of the fact that they were formulated from a carefully chosen perspective from which a given community of scholars views a certain realm of phenomena? For the phenomenologist the scientific conceptions of world are obviously legitimate and important. Yet, on the other hand, it is equally clear that every scientific claim is a claim that is made from a limited perspective, from a limited a priori synthesis. This is the reason why we must say that no science could ever claim to have discovered *the* all-encompassing, exhaustive, and final truth about anything. Each science may claim that it has discovered and disclosed a true view on a domain of phenomena from a perspective that (in principle at least) rests on clearly formulated and justifiable assumptions. Given this fact, it is then also clear at once why, according to all phenomenologists, no science could ever claim to be a substitute for philosophy.

Yet this does not mean that the sciences have nothing to say that is relevant to the world in which we live and for that matter to philosophy. It does not entail either that the sciences do not confront philosophy with important and often even grave issues. It is well known that the natural sciences first, the historical and linguistic sciences next, and the so-called behavioral and social sciences today, have done just that. It is the entire network of issues and problems with which the sciences confront us, that makes a philosophical reflection on the sciences necessary.

We have just seen that most contemporary philosophers and scientists who are actually involved in philosophical reflections on the sciences define philosophy of science as the logic, epistemology, and methodology of the sciences. For a phenomenologist it is important to realize that in so doing these authors are in perfect harmony with philosophy of science's own history. For the majority of the works on philosophy of science published since 1786 were written either from a Kantian and neo-Kantian or from an empiricist point of view. According to both perspectives the main purpose of the philosophy of knowledge in general and of the philosophy of the sciences in particular consists in clarifying the epistemological, logical, and methodological problems with which scientific research confronts us.

Evidently this is not to say that there is not a vast difference between the philosophies of science written by Kant, Herschel, Whewell, and Mill, on the one hand, and the philosophies of science developed by the leading philosophers and scientists who today concern themselves with these issues, on the other.[16] That there is a relatively great difference between the first treatises on philosophy of science and those that are written today is, in my view, due not so much to a difference of opinion about the nature and the function of philosophy of science, as to the following four factors: (1) the profound changes in the empiricist, positivist, and neo-Kantian conceptions of philosophy under the influence of the philosophical views propagated by the Vienna Circle, Russell, Husserl, Heidegger, and the later Wittgenstein, among others; (2) the important influence of modern logic on the method and language of the sciences as well as on the method and language of philosophy of science; (3) the very important changes in the modern sciences themselves, notably in physics and biology; and (4) the origin and development of the human sciences.

At any rate, the research projects in contemporary philosophy of science have branched out in different directions so that today epistemological, logical, historical, psychological, sociological, and political investigations are to be distinguished. Although these research efforts have not always been very successful, it is nonetheless fair to say that contemporary philosophy of science has substantially contributed to our understanding of the sciences.

Thus when phenomenologists in the twentieth century entered the scene to join empiricists, neo-Kantians, positivists, logical empiricists, and analytic philosophers, it certainly was not with the pretention of offering the one and only approach to the sciences to the exclusion of all other approaches, as some of their followers sometimes have suggested. Such an attitude would have been absurd and would have constituted a blunt denial of philosophy of science's entire history. To be sure, phenomenology from the very start offered a very severe criticism of some of the presuppositions of other philosophical views, just as these other views rejected basic insights brought to the fore by phenomenology. But no one can rightly claim that the work done in philosophy of science over the past 200 years is meaningless.

When phenomenology, therefore, stepped onto the scene in philosophy of science, it was not with the pretention of knowing everything and, in consequence, having to criticize all that had been said before. The only pretention a phenomenologist could legitimately have was one of contributing something positive to the work that had already been done. Such positive contributions were suggested in several areas: (1) the life-world issue discussed by Husserl, (2) the relationship between philosophy and science and between their respective subject matters, an issue on which almost all phenomenologists have focussed, and (3) the ontological foundation of the sciences and, thus, also of all epistemological, logical, and methodological conceptions, an area to which Heidegger in particular has paid special attention. It is mainly this last issue that will be examined in detail in the sections to follow.

F. HEIDEGGER AND PHILOSOPHY OF SCIENCE

Heidegger was never a scientist, nor did he ever devote a substantial amount of his time to a careful and detailed study of the sciences. Yet for two years he studied physics and he also devoted himself for some time to the study of historiography at the University of Freiburg. Furthermore, throughout his long career as a teacher he kept close contact with the leading scientists of his time (theologians, historians, physicists, biologists, psychologists, etc.). Professor Carl von Weizsäcker reports on one of the meetings which Heidegger had with Heisenberg and the biologist Victor von Weizsäcker. In this report it becomes clear that Heidegger had a remarkable knowledge of both physics and biology and that he was able to conduct a penetrating discussion on important topics with leading scientists.[17]

Furthermore, Heidegger was never seriously concerned with logical and methodological questions posed by the sciences and he never claimed to have a sophisticated knowledge of these large areas in the domain of the "philosophy of science." His basic question was one of what the engagement in modern science gradually has come to mean to Western man and how it has affected the manner in which he thinks, acts, and lives.

The question as to whether or not a philosophy of the empirical sciences can be found in Heidegger's works is answered in different ways by different authors. In his essay "Heidegger's Critique of Science," W. Richardson writes: "On the longest day he ever lived, Heidegger could never be called a philosopher of science."[18] On the other hand H. Seigfried states that "Heidegger's *Being and Time* has to be recognized and discussed as a treatise in the philosophy of science in a strict, though not parochial sense, a philosophy of science which resembles in many ways the so-called 'new' philosophy of science advanced by Feyerabend, Polanyi, Hanson, Kuhn, and others."[19] It seems to me that to some degree both these claims are correct. Depending upon the question of how one defines the expression "philosophy of science" the former question can be answered positively or negatively.

In view of the fact that this issue in my opinion is of great importance for a proper understanding of Heidegger's conception of philosophy and its relation to the empirical sciences, it will be necessary to describe Heidegger's position in this regard as carefully as possible. I plan to return to this issue in section 6 below. Suffice it for now to state that it is indeed true that between 1914 and 1935 Heidegger strongly stressed the scientific character of philosophy. Furthermore, it is true also that Heidegger was then convinced that with respect to the foundations of the empirical sciences philosophy has a very important role to play. Yet to say this is not tantamount to claiming that Heidegger's philosophy during that period was really no more than a philosophy of science. This is the reason why I basically agree with Richardson: Heidegger never developed a philosophy of science in the common sense of this expression, although it is true that many ideas can be found in his works which are invaluable for a comprehensive philosophy of science which does not limit itself to logical reflections only. This is what I hope to show in the pages to follow.

PART I

HEIDEGGER'S BACKGROUND
ON THE MEANING OF
HERMEMEUTIC PHENOMENOLOGY

CHAPTER I

HEIDEGGER'S INTRODUCTION TO THE SCIENCES AND TO THE PHILOSOPHY OF SCIENCE OF HIS TIME

1: HEIDEGGER'S EDUCATION[1]

Martin Heidegger (1889-1976) is one of the greatest philosophers of the twentieth century. From 1927 until his death he enjoyed a world-wide reputation. Yet relatively little is known about his private life and personality. He himself was always reticent on personal matters and his devoted friends and pupils have until now reverently respected his silence on these matters. The few data on his life and personality mentioned in most studies about Heidegger's thought are not always reliable and often they are even conflicting with respect to important matters. In the pages to follow I shall limit myself to a few observations on Heidegger's intellectual development to the degree that they are relevant to the present task.

Heidegger was born in Messkirch (Baden) in 1889. After attending the village school of Messkirch he enrolled at the Gymnasium of Constanz. Later he moved to a Gymnasium in Freiburg, where he completed his studies in 1909. The most likely reason for attending these schools was Heidegger's intention to study for the priesthood, an intention about which he changed his mind in 1911. According to his own testimony, during the six years at the Gymnasium he "acquired everything that was to be of lasting value."[2] Here he learned Greek, Latin, and French, in addition to history, mathematics, and the natural sciences. It was here also that he first came in contact with Hölderlin. Finally, it was here that he first became acquainted with philosophy, which eventually would become the subject of his main interest.

In 1907 his friend and advisor, Father Conrad Gröber, then pastor of Trinity Church in Constanz but later archbishop of Freiburg, gave Heidegger a copy of Brentano's *On the Several Senses of Being in Aristotle* which set Heidegger on his life-long search for the meaning of Being. If that which is in being has several meanings as Aristotle claims, what then does Being itself mean in its unity?[3]

In 1909 Heidegger enrolled at the Albert Ludwig University in Freiburg where at first he studied theology and philosophy. After he had definitively abandoned the idea of becoming a priest, he applied himself for some time to mathematics and physics, but finally decided to devote his life to the study of philosophy.

While still a student in philosophy, Heidegger published a short article on epistemology, "The Problem of Reality in Modern Philosophy."[4] In this article he did not yet express a personal viewpoint, but rather confined himself to defending the kind of realism propagated by Geyser, Messer, and Külpe against a form of psychologism that rejected all metaphysics. At that time there was no trace yet of any influence of the thoughts of Nietzsche, Kierkegaard, and Dilthey. In his doctoral dissertation, *The Theory of Judgment in Psychologism*,[5] which he wrote under the mentorship of A. Schneider, Heidegger abandoned the traditional standpoint which he had adopted earlier; he also explicitly then took distance from Brentano's philosophy with which he had familiarized himself; yet even then he had not yet arrived at a genuinely personal position.

Because of his frail health, Heidegger was at first exempted from military service until 1917; his work at the post office left him enough time to continue his studies. In 1915 he completed his second book, *Duns Scotus' Doctrine of Categories and Meaning*,[6] which he subsequently presented as his second thesis (*Habilitationsschrift*). This book was based mainly on the *Grammatica Speculativa* which at first had been attributed to Duns Scotus; in 1926 Grabmann was able to show, however, that this work was really written by Thomas of Ehrfurt.

Although Heidegger had written his dissertation under the direction of Schneider, the influence of H. Rickert was nonetheless already quite noticeable in his first major work. Under the latter's guidance he then wrote his *Habilitationsschrift*. Yet when Husserl came to Freiburg in 1916, his influence overshadowed that of Rickert from then on. As a matter of fact, Heidegger had tried to read Husserl's *Logical Investigations*[7] during his first semester in Freiburg, because at that time he thought that

Husserl's work could help him find a way to approach the question of Being which Brentano's book on Aristotle had aroused in him. Gradually, however, he began to realize that whereas phenomenology, merely taken as a philosophical method, might help him articulate the various modes of Being, Husserl's turn toward transcendental idealism led in a direction which seemed to be unacceptable. "He had already begun to see that not consciousness, as in Husserl, but rather *aletheia*, as in the Greeks, was the central issue for philosophy."[8]

Yet this obviously was not the end of the relationship between Heidegger and Husserl. For from 1916 on Heidegger worked closely with Husserl and in 1920 he even became his assistant. In 1923 Heidegger moved to Marburg; but even there he kept in contact with Husserl, although the basic differences between their approach to philosophical issues had begun to manifest themselves ever more clearly and also, on the part of Husserl, ever more painfully.

Sheehan mentions a number of other thinkers to whom Heidegger paid careful attention during the period between 1911 and 1916.[9] First of all, there are the French thinkers Maurice Blondel, Henri Duméry, and Felix Ravaisson. Then there was the influence of the Catholic theologian Carl Braig who inspired Heidegger through his treatise *On Being: An Outline of Ontology*;[10] this book introduced Heidegger to the concept of the onto-theological structure of metaphysics; it also suggested to him the importance of the etymology of fundamental concepts, and explained to him the limitations of scholasticism and the important possibilities opened up by German idealism, notably by the work of Schelling and Hegel. But during the same years Heidegger also discovered the works of Dostoevsky, Rilke, Trakl, and George on the one hand, and Kierkegaard and Nietzsche on the other.

After Heidegger had received the right to teach as a *Privatdozent* he began immediately to give lectures on Parmenides, Kant, Fichte, and Aristotle. In 1917, however, he was drafted for military service and in 1918 he was sent to Verdun where he was active in the meteorological service. After returning from the front he continued to teach in Freiburg, partly on Christian authors such as St. Paul and St. Augustine, but partly also on philosophers such as Aristotle, Descartes, and Husserl. Yet in all of his studies he employed the phenomenological method. By phenomenology Heidegger, however, did not understand Husserl's transcendental idealism, but rather a very personal interpretation of Husserl's phenomenology along strictly methodical lines.

Between 1916 and 1927 Heidegger published virtually nothing. In 1917 he wrote his "Anmerkungen zu Karl Jaspers 'Philosophie der Weltanschauungen'," but this essay was not published until 1973.[11] Also, in 1922 he composed an essay which was meant to be the introduction to a book on Aristotle. This, too, was not published at the time, although a version of it was sent to Marburg in connection with the fact that Husserl had strongly recommended Heidegger for a position there as a *professor extraordinarius*. But, as we have seen, during the same period (1916-1927) Heidegger gave an impressive series of lectures and seminars, many of which are currently being prepared for publication.

From these lectures we have now received a clearer idea of Heidegger's philosophical development as well as of the genesis of *Being and Time*, particularly between 1923 and 1926. Heidegger himself has given us a remarkable, detailed description of his development in the lecture course which in 1925 was delivered in Marburg under the title *Prolegomena zur Geschichte des Zeitbegriffs*.[12] I plan to summarize the main ideas developed there shortly; but before doing so I wish to make a few comments on Heidegger's attitude in regard to both Husserl and Dilthey, as we find it in *Being and Time*, and with which we thus have been familiar for a long time.

During his formative years as well as during his years in Marburg, Heidegger's attitude towards both Dilthey and Husserl was always very positive. Yet Heidegger soon developed into a very independent and creative, critical thinker so that this positive attitude did not at all imply that he just followed these thinkers in a purely passive manner. He learned from them and would not hesitate to call himself their student; yet from the beginning he demanded for himself the right to go his own way.

In *Being and Time* Heidegger explicitly gives credit to Husserl for the influence which the latter exerted on him as far as the "scientific" conception of philosophy and philosophy's method are concerned.[13]

Dilthey's name occurs quite regularly in *Being and Time* and on a few occasions Heidegger's language clearly suggests the great respect he had for Dilthey's thought. On three occasions Heidegger discusses ideas from Dilthey in detail. In section 43 he speaks about the question of whether the reality of the external world can be proven. Heidegger explicitly refers there to Dilthey's essay, "Beiträge zur Lösung der Frage vom Ursprung unseres Glaubens an die Realität der Aussenwelt und seinem

Recht," of 1890.[14] In the first part of section 43 Heidegger shows that "the scandal of philosophy" is not, as Kant thought, to be found in the fact that as yet no proof for the existence of the real world has been given, but rather that such proofs are expected and attempted again and again. In his view, even if one were to conclude that the Being-present-at-hand of things outside of us is to be accepted merely on faith, as both Kant and Dilthey had suggested, one still fails to surmount the perversion of the problem to which Heidegger tries to point here. For then one still assumes that such a proof is possible. This inappropriate approach to the genuine problem is thus still endorsed if one limits himself to a *"faith"* in the reality and shows or states that one can rightly maintain it. For even then one is still in principle demanding a proof and trying to satisfy this demand.[15]

In the second part of section 43 Heidegger returns to Dilthey's essay. There he admits that the reality of the world can be characterized phenomenologically within certain limits without any explicit ek-sistential-ontological basis or foundation. "This is what Dilthey has attempted in the article mentioned above. He holds that the real gets experienced in impulse and will, and that reality is resistance, or, more exactly, the character of resisting. He then works out the phenomenon of resistance analytically. This is the positive contribution of his article . . . But he is kept from working out the analysis of this phenomenon correctly by the epistemological problematic of reality."[16] The "principle of phenomenality" prevents Dilthey from coming to an ontological interpretation of the Being of consciousness. This prevents him from seeing the Being-relationship which consciousness bears to the real. "That this has not been done, depends ultimately on the fact that Dilthey has left 'life' standing in such a manner that it is ontologically undifferentiated; and of course 'life' is something which one cannot go back 'behind'."[17] Yet, Heidegger concludes, the fact that Dilthey can be refuted epistemologically, does not mean that one could not employ what is positive in his analyses.[18]

In a footnote which pertains to section 50 of *Being and Time* Heidegger observes that Dilthey who was primarily concerned with an ontology of life, could not fail to recognize how intimately life is connected with death and how "the bounding of our eksistence by death is always decisive for our understanding of life."[19]

Heidegger returns to Dilthey explicitly in his reflections on historicity. In section 72 he writes that the "researches of Dilthey were, for their part, pioneering work; but today's generation has not as yet made them its own. In the following analysis the issue is solely one of furthering their adoption."[20]

In section 74 Heidegger employs Dilthey's conception of generation and refers to Dilthey's essay, "Uber das Studium der Geschichte der Wissenschaften vom Menschen, der Gesellschaft und dem Staat," of 1875.[21]

In section 77 Heidegger once more remarks that he is in the process of appropriating the labors of Dilthey.[22] He then gives an overview of Dilthey's work insofar as it is relevant to Heidegger's own concern in *Being and Time*.[23] He admits that such a presentation is very inadequate in regard to the problems which moved Dilthey's own thinking. In a footnote, pertaining to p. 399, Heidegger writes that a systematic presentation of Dilthey's ideas is no longer necessary after G. Misch's concrete presentation of Dilthey in vol. V of the *Gesamtausgabe*. Heidegger then discusses remarks of Graf von Yorck. He finally concludes that these remarks show how his own analytic of Dasein is resolved "to foster the spirit of Count Yorck in the service of Dilthey's work."[24]

Yet for our present purposes the most interesting place where Heidegger discusses Dilthey's ideas in *Being and Time*, is section 10 where he tries to establish the difference between his analytic of Dasein and the various sciences of man from biology to anthropology, and explains why he wishes to avoid such expressions as "man" and "life." In this context Heidegger writes that Dilthey conceived of life as a kind of Being which ontologically he did not make into an explicit theme of investigation. Starting from life as a whole, Dilthey tried to understand its expressions in their structural and developmental interconnections. His "geisteswissenschaftliche Psychologie" is no longer atomistic and, thus, Dilthey no longer tried to piece life together from different parts; rather he focused on life as a whole and spoke of *Gestalten*. The philosophical relevance of these investigations, however, is to be found elsewhere, namely in the fact that Dilthey was indeed on his way toward the question of "life" as such. Yet even in the work in which he tried to find the way to a genuinely personalistic psychology, the problematic itself, as well as the set of basic concepts used, was still very limited. These limitations are found also in the world of Bergson and in the treatises of all other personalistic philosophers such as Scheler. In Heidegger's view both Husserl and Scheler have given us a very penetrating, phenomenological interpretation of the phenomenon of personality, which, in each case, took its point of departure in ideas of

ORIGIN OF THE ANALYTIC OF DASEIN 27

Dilthey. Yet they, too, never addressed the question of the very Being of Dasein itself.[25]

In the pages to come I shall focus on these claims and in so doing I shall make use of the Marburg lectures, particularly the *Prolegomena zur Geschichte des Zeitbegriffs*. Toward the end of these reflections I wish to make a few brief comments on the origin and the development of the *Geisteswissenschaften* to which Heidegger explicitly refers in the *Prolegomena*. In my view these comments are necessary in light of the confusion with which the discussion about the *Geisteswissenschaften* has been affected from the very beginning.

2: FROM DILTHEY'S PERSONALISTIC PSYCHOLOGY VIA HUSSERL'S PHENOMENOLOGY TO HEIDEGGER'S ANALYTIC OF DASEIN

a. ORIGIN AND DEVELOPMENT OF PHENOMENOLOGICAL RESEARCH

In his *Prolegomena zur Geschichte des Zeitbegriffs* Heidegger explicitly locates his own thinking within the philosophical climate as he found it during the first quarter of this century. This brings him rather quickly to such thinkers as Brentano, Dilthey, and Husserl. It is in this larger context that Heidegger makes the claim that he sees a close connection between the attempts of these authors to overcome naturalism and psychologism in philosophy by means of the development of a new, personalistic psychology, an effort to which Scheler also tried to make an important contribution, and his own efforts to develop an analytic of Dasein, which was to combine ideas of Kant's transcendental analytic, Husserl's phenomenology, and Dilthey's conception of hermeneutics.[26]

In his lecture course, which was delivered in Marburg in the summer of 1925, Heidegger never really did come to the basic issue referred to by the title of the course, namely the history of the concept of time. Originally the *Prolegomena*, whose subtitle was listed as "Prolegomena Towards a Phenomenology of History and Nature," was to have contained three major parts: (1) The analysis of the phenomenon of time and the formation of the concept of time; (2) the disclosure of the concept of time; and (3) the working out of the horizon for the question concerning Being as such and concerning the Being of history and nature in particular. The first part was to have consisted of three major sections: (a) the preparatory description of the field, in which the phenomenon of time becomes manifest; (b) the discovery of time itself; (c) the conceptual interpretation of the discovery of time. The first section which consists of eighteen subsections runs somewhat parallel to the first forty-four sections of *Being and Time*, whereas the second section appears to be the first draft of the most important divisions of sections 45 through 83 of *Being and Time*; The third section, on the other hand, was not presented in the lecture course and is not included in the published work either. The same is obviously true for part two, which was to concern itself with the history of the concept of time in Bergson, Kant, Newton, and Aristotle. Finally, as we have seen, part three was to treat the question concerning the meaning of Being in general and the question concerning the meaning of Being of history and nature in particular; this part is missing also.[27]

The three parts mentioned were preceded by a brief, introductory orientation which is called the preparatory part; it concerns itself with reflections on the method of these investigations, i.e., phenomenology. It consists of three chapters: (1) the origin and the first impact of phenomenological research; (2) the fundamental discoveries of phenomenology, its basic principle, and an explanation of its name; and (3) Heidegger's own conception of phenomenology and a criticism of Husserl's and Scheler's interpretations of this method.[28]

In chapter one of the introductory part Heidegger briefly describes the position in which philosophy found itself during the second part of the nineteenth century and particularly focuses on positivism, neo-Kantianism, Dilthey's criticism of positivism, the trivialization of Dilthey's basic concern by both Windelband and Rickert, and finally, in great detail, Brentano's and Husserl's efforts to come to a genuinely scientific philosophy by means of a psychology of a new kind.[29]

The *Prolegomena* begin thus with a brief reflection on the crisis in which the modern sciences found themselves in the beginning of this century. At that time it was quite common in Germany to divide the sciences into two basic groups: the sciences of nature and the sciences of history. For Heidegger, the basic question with which the sciences of nature and history are confronted is the following: how can one bring the things themselves, about which one asks questions in these sciences, to manifest themselves in an original experience?[30] This is the reason why Heidegger wants to make an effort in this lecture

ORIGIN OF THE ANALYTIC OF DASEIN

course to bring the original mode of Being of nature and history to light.[31] This explains at once the subtitle of the course: prolegomena towards the phenomenology of history and nature.[32]

In the introduction to the course Heidegger then explains that in a phenomenology of history and nature the concept of time is to play the leading part so that a phenomenology of history and nature must use as its guiding clue the history of the concept of time.[33] Heidegger explicitly admits that at first sight this seems very strange; yet, he argues, one should realize that in our scientific concerns with both nature and history the concept of time indeed does play an essential role, insofar as the measurement of time and chronology presuppose that things and events are to be taken as being in or within time; furthermore, we constantly use time to make a distinction between the various modes of Being of such beings as temporal, extra-temporal, and supra-temporal entities. Thus Heidegger can conclude that the concept of time is not just like any other concept; rather it is very closely related to the basic question of philosophy, namely the question concerning the Being of beings.[34]

In other words, the history of the concept of time is the history of the discovery of time and the history of its conceptual interpretation; that is to say, this history consists in the question concerning the Being of beings; it is the history of the efforts to reveal the Being of beings.[35] However, in view of the fact that the history of these efforts to some extent at least is the history of man's inability to pose the question concerning the meaning of Being in a genuinely radical manner (Kant) and to develop this question anew as far as its first and fundamental basis is concerned, it is impossible in these investigations to proceed either strictly historically or strictly thematically or systematically. What is needed, therefore, is a phenomenological approach which both criticizes and retrieves our entire philosophical heritage.[36]

Heidegger then describes that he shares Dilthey's view according to which the philosophical theory of the sciences which was oriented primarily toward Kant, is fundamentally incomplete, because it limits itself to the natural sciences only, to the sciences of nature. There is an important group of disciplines which do not belong among these sciences of nature, namely the historical sciences. Already in 1870 Dilthey was convinced that Kant's work was to be complemented by a theory of historical reason.[37] Even as a young man Dilthey saw immediately that Mill's efforts to apply the methods of the natural sciences to the historical disciplines is impossible. In Dilthey's opinion, furthermore, it is impossible to develop a positive theory of the historical sciences except by starting from a careful ontological analysis of what constitutes the subject matter of these sciences; Dilthey calls all of this by one word: life.[38] This led him to develop a new type of "psychology" to be understood as a new science of consciousness. This science was meant to be not a natural nor an epistemological science, but rather an attempt to unfold life itself as that with which the historical sciences concern themselves. Yet, in Heidegger's opinion, the permanent achievement of Dilthey is not to be found in his contributions to the theory of the sciences, but rather in his effort to come to a philosophical understanding of the reality of what is historical and from there to an explanation of the nature and the possibility of interpretation.[39]

Heidegger, however, also admits that Dilthey remained within the problematic of his time and in his *Introduction to the Historical Sciences* remained within the domain of an epistemological concern.[40] It should be noted that Heidegger had already determined that for him the term *Geisteswissenschaften* indeed has the same meaning as the term "the sciences of culture" or "the historical sciences."[41]

In the next section Heidegger discusses the question of why Windelband and Rickert misunderstood and even trivialized Dilthey's basic concern,[42] and then in the last section turns to the efforts of Brentano[43] and Husserl[44] to lay the foundations of a truly scientific philosophy and to determine the part a new type of psychology in their opinion had to play in these efforts. As for Husserl, Heidegger very briefly describes his education in mathematics under Weierstrass and in philosophy under Paulsen. He then characterizes the influence which first Brentano and later Stumpf exerted on his development. After a brief comment on the meaning of Husserl's earlier works in philosophy of mathematics, Heidegger then turns to Husserl's *Logical Investigations*, in which Husserl explicitly rejected psychologism and developed his phenomenological theory of knowledge for the first time. This work influenced the philosophical views of Dilthey, Lipps, and Heidegger himself. Natorp wrote a review of the first volume of the book, but did not bother to review the second volume. Heidegger attributes the fact that the book at first drew little attention to Husserl's own remark that phenomenology is really a descriptive psychology. Husserl corrected the false impression suggested by this expression in 1903, but at first this, too, was not very successful. Finally, Heidegger describes the importance of the second volume of *Logical Investigations* for a general theory of knowledge. In his view, Husserl's work is not really a theory of knowledge, but rather a reflection on the essence of human knowledge as such.

Heidegger concludes this part of his reflections on Husserl by praising the *Logical Investigations* for its thoroughness and originality. In passing he makes two very interesting remarks which in his opinion are relevant to all treatises that are phenomenological in character: (1) It is usually impossible just to derive some results from them taken in isolation; in such treatises everything appears to belong together and the way according to which the ideas have been reached is almost as important as the content itself. (2) Usually it is impossible to summarize a phenomenological study; one has to work his way through the analyses and ask time and again whether one indeed "sees" what is being argued for, and whether it would be possible to reject or to contradict it.[45]

b. THE BASIC DISCOVERIES OF PHENOMENOLOGY

Heidegger next discusses three basic phenomenological themes at greater length: intentionality, categorical intuition, and Husserl's conception of the a priori. By means of a section which is devoted to the principle of evidence as employed in Husserl's phenomenology, Heidegger then proceeds to explain what he understands by phenomenology by taking the word "phenomenology" itself as his guiding clue. In a final chapter he then criticizes Husserl's transcendental idealist phenomenology systematically, using Husserl's *Ideas*, volume one, as his point of departure.[46]

As far as the concept of intentionality is concerned, Heidegger first states that Husserl received the ideas from Brentano, but instead of using it in a sense which is affected by metaphysical presuppositions, as Brentano had done in a context which was concerned mainly with epistemological issues,[47] Husserl tried to show that intentionality is a basic structure of every experience as such. Every original experience is a being-oriented-toward-something. One sees this most clearly in our acts of perception, at least as long as one takes perception as it gives itself immediately, namely as a form of concerning oneself with something. Perception is thus intentional, regardless of whether the "object" is present *realiter* or not. Perception is inherently an orienting-one-self-toward-something; usually we are oriented towards things that are real; sometimes we merely believe or think that we are concerned with real things; sometimes we suffer from mere hallucinations. But in all cases, when there is an issue of perception, then there is an issue of being-oriented-toward-something, genuinely or allegedly. Usually we have the means at our disposal to decide which one of these modes is really the case. Heidegger uses the example of perceiving "this chair here in the class-room" to clarify the point.[48]

In the next section Heidegger observes that Rickert misunderstood both Brentano and Husserl and tried to interpret perception by means of the taking of a position in regard to a certain cognitive value; he thus really rejected the concept of intentionality in Husserl's sense. Rickert was led to this view by his prejudice that presentation is true knowledge only when it has the form of an explicit judgment. In his view, only in the latter case is there a question of true knowledge.[49]

The ideal of intentionality as such and the idea that perception is perception of something, are obviously still formal and empty. Heidegger, therefore, tries to show now, with Husserl, that what is perceived in perception is the thing itself, this thing in my everyday world, this real thing of nature, this thing, taken as such, i.e., as it is given in perception. I can unfold it in its main characteristics in a manner which is intersubjectively verifiable. What is perceived, is the perceived thing itself which has hardness and extension, which occupies space, has color and shape, and which can be used for this or that purpose, etc.[50]

Heidegger then shows, again following Husserl, that in perception the thing is given as perceived, i.e., as being presented in its bodily-being-present-here-and-now. To be given in bodily presence is a privileged mode in which things are given in themselves. In perception, contrary to the presentation by means of an image of some kind, the being is present bodily, here and now. Furthermore, each thing given in perception is given in the form of perspectives (*Abschattungen*).[51]

Finally, Heidegger shows with Husserl that intention and that-which-is-intended by it (*intentio* and *intentum*) essentially belong together, and that the perspectivity of the perceived thing "logically" leads to a process of fulfillment, so that intentionality is not the last word, but only the starting point for an entire domain, or field, of thematic reflections, in which the concepts of noesis and noema play important parts. Heidegger concludes these reflections by stressing the point that in

ORIGIN OF THE ANALYTIC OF DASEIN 33

Husserl's view one should not concern himself in these cases with an interpretation of the *data*, but rather one should stick and adhere to what gives itself immediately in its bodily reality by means of a certain perspective. According to Heidegger, however, it may very well be that in approaching perception in this manner we are already on a wrong path. Is it not the case that perception, so understood, is already an abstraction, something which we encounter only in a purely theoretical and analytic attitude? Is our primary contact with the things not always one of concernful dealing-with? It should be noted here that the term intentionality as well as that of perception no longer occur in *Being and Time*.[52]

Heidegger then engages in a long reflection on categorial intuition. The main issue here is to show that a radical empiricist position, according to which the immediately given is nothing but a set of isolated sense data ("patches of blue") is unacceptable. By intuition is meant here the immediate presentation of a being in its bodily reality; a simple grasping of what is bodily given, taken just as it manifests itself. In other words, intuition as meant here has nothing to do with what Bergson and Schutz understood by this term.[53]

Heidegger next focuses on Husserl's ideas about fulfillment and identification. In his view, these ideas are of vital importance in view of the fact that all perception is perception by means of perspectives. Now for Husserl, identification is a process of fulfillment which leads to a point where the thing indeed is itself shown to be present (*eine ausweisende Erfüllung*). Where one has such a fulfillment one may speak of evidence. Thus evidence is the result of an identifying fulfillment. If the process of identification reaches the point where there is no longer a difference between the intended thing and the shown thing, we speak of truth. The being-true of an act of perception thus consists in the fact that this identity has been established with evidence. In that case we may even speak of truth in a double sense: the being-true of the act and the being-true of the perceived thing insofar as the latter makes the act of perception true (*wahrmachend*). A thing which makes our perception true, is, if taken as such, also said to be true, to be "real"; it is simply said "to be."[54]

Finally, Heidegger shows how the relationship between being and being-true is to be broadened, when acts other than perceptual acts are taken into consideration. He also explains how this conception of truth can be expanded so as to include the truth of judgments and statements (logic). Heidegger finally concludes these reflections by very briefly indicating why this approach to the truth, which overlooks some essential elements of the Greek conception of truth, is really inadequate. Heidegger discusses this issue in much greater detail later in section forty-four of *Being and Time* and particularly in the lecture *On the Essence of Truth*.[55]

After these considerations which focus mainly on evidence, certainty, and truth, Heidegger turns to Husserl's conception of the relationship between intuition and expression as Husserl had unfolded this in the second volume of his *Logical Investigations*. Heidegger first stresses the importance of Husserl's effort to show that statements constitute the main subject matter of logic. He then describes Husserl's efforts to relate intuition with expression; this obviously implies some conception of the meaning and function of language. Husserl does not explicitly unfold this conception of language, but rather tries to show how claims formulated in statements can be shown to be true on the basis of what is given in perceptual acts, mediately or immediately. It is here where Husserl convincingly refutes naive empiricism. Heidegger mentions only those elements that are essential to give his students a first impression of Husserl's achievements in the sixth logical investigation.[56]

Finally, Husserl's attempt to deal with the problem of universals is analyzed in detail; Heidegger focuses here on Husserl's interpretation of Kant's conception of synthesis and on Husserl's original idea of ideation (*Wesensschau*).[57] Heidegger particularly stresses the importance of these discoveries by Husserl and refutes the misinterpretation of this view by some authors, while also mentioning the influence of these ideas on Scheler and Lask. In Heidegger's view Husserl's work in this area has made it possible to see the genuine meaning of the a priori. Yet a proper understanding of this view also shows immediately why phenomenology is inherently ontology; as a matter of fact, scientific ontology is nothing but phenomenology.[58]

The next section is devoted to a brief reflection on the original meaning of the a priori. Heidegger claims again that Husserl's phenomenology here, too, made an important contribution to the clarification of the concept of the a priori, even though it is the case that in Husserl's interpretation this concept still remains unduly affected by certain conceptions of the tradition. Heidegger briefly sketches the history of this concept, its origin in Plato where it still has an ontological meaning, its development in modern philosophy where in Kant the a priori becomes a characteritic of the sphere of the subject. In Heidegger's opinion, phenomenology has given the concept an ontological meaning again: it becomes again a characteristic of Being and thus is primarily not a characteristic of man's comportment.[59]

c. CRITICAL EVALUATION OF HUSSERL'S TRANSCENDENTAL PHENOMENOLOGY

Heidegger finally, in chapter three, turns to a critical reflection on Husserl's phenomenology. In his opinion, phenomenology has made a lasting contribution to philosophy because of its doctrine of intentionality, its conception of the possibility of the categorical intuition, and its discovery of the original meaning of the a priori. Yet in his opinion the phenomenology of Husserl and Scheler left several important issues unexamined and made several unacceptable assumptions.

For Husserl the field in which phenomenology operates is the domain of pure consciousness; in Heidegger's opinion it is not difficult to show that in the detailed articulation of the phenomenological field four basic theses concerning pure consciousness are presupposed which are really untenable: namely that (1) consciousness is immanent Being, (2) consciousness is absolute Being, (3) consciousness is given in such a manner that it appears as something which does not need any other being in order to be what it is (*nulla re indiget ad existendum*), and (4) consciousness is given as pure Being. But what is even more important is the fact that Husserl did not realize the arbitrariness of these assumptions, because he neglected to ask the question concerning the mode of Being of the intentional as such. In the detailed discussion about intentionality, taken as the thematic field of phenomenology, the question concerning the mode of Being of that which is intentional remained unexplained.[60]

Yet according to Heidegger, the greatest neglect on the part of Husserl and Scheler consisted in the fact that they did not explicitly raise the question concerning the meaning of Being itself and the mode of Being of man. One could obviously ask here whether such questions indeed are to be asked in philosophy, and whether it would indeed not be adequate just to determine the "what" of Being as well as its multiple meanings. Heidegger refutes this objection by explaining that in the order of knowledge questions of whether and why are no ultimate criteria. In his view, to ask the question concerning the mode of Being of that which is intentional is possible and necessary. Let us not forget that in his own exposition of the thematic field of phenomenology, i.e., pure consciousness, Husserl himself tried to resolve the questions mentioned in an ontological manner. In the first volume of *Ideas* (1913) Husserl wrote: "The theory of categories must start entirely from this most radical of all ontological distinctions--being as consciousness and being as something which becomes *manifested* in consciousness, "transcendent" being-- which, as we see, can be attained in its purity and appreciated only by the method of the phenomenological reduction."[61] And it is not only the case that the basic distinction within Being is found with the discovery of the pure consciousness itself; but it is also the case that the reduction has no other task than to determine and elucidate this ontological distinction within Being (*diesen Seinsunterschied*). In Heidegger's view, it is thus rather peculiar that Husserl here claims to find the most radical distinction in Being without explicitly asking the question concerning the Being of beings as such.[62] If we further ask the question of what Husserl understands by Being, i.e., that in regard to which he makes the distinction in Being between absolute Being (=consciousness) and reality,[63] then we wait in vain for an answer and are puzzled by the fact that Husserl does not even pose the question.[64] Thus in his effort to justify the fundamental distinction between Being as pure consciousness and Being as reality Husserl "does not even ask about the mode of Being itself of the elements that are being distinguished . . . and fundamentally not about that which directs the entire distinction between distinct modes of being as such--about the meaning of Being. From this it is clear, that the question about Being is not just an arbitrary and a merely possible question; rather it is the most urgent question in the strictest sense of phenomenology itself . . ."[65]

Husserl's phenomenology thus neglects basically to reflect on the mode of Being of that which was supposed to be its fundamental theme: the intentional comportment itself and that which is given in it. One will obviously ask how this could be possible. How could phenomenology be so unphenomenological as to neglect to examine the question concerning the Being of its own fundamental theme? Does phenomenology perhaps not somewhere ask the question about the mode of Being of the intentional? Does this question not emerge with necessity when one asks the question of how phenomenology is to be distinguished from psychology?[66]

We all know that Husserl's phenomenology developed from Brentano's conception of psychology. To distinguish this new kind of psychology from the naturalistic psychology of his time, Husserl had to speak about the mode of Being of the psychic acts with which the new psychology had to concern itself. To determine the Being of these acts as such it was thus obviously impossible to remain within the naturalistic attitude, because in that attitude these acts are not taken as such, but merely as "appendices" of material things.[67]

Husserl's phenomenology thus severely criticized naturalism in psychology as well as the tendency to believe that philosophical problems can be resolved by a natural psychology (psychologism). In so doing he continued the work already started by Dilthey. In his own scientific treatises Dilthey gradually tried to move away from a psychology which takes man merely as a thing of nature and studies him as such, which thus tries to explain man and tries to construct him on the basis of laws of genesis which were discovered elsewhere but were later claimed to be of universal applicability. Instead Dilthey tried to understand man as a living person who acts in history; he thus tried to describe him and articulate his mode of Being (*beschreibend und zergliedernd*). One recognizes here immediately the tendency to develop a new kind of psychology, a personalistic psychology.[68]

Heidegger is convinced that Dilthey was also the first who fully understood the deeper intentions of phenomenology. Already in the 1860s Dilthey was on the way to somehow develop a new type of psychology which conceives of man in a primary fashion just as he eksists in history as an acting person. The first results of these efforts can be found in *Ideen über eine beschreibende und zergliedernde Psychologie* (1894) and in *Über vergleichende Psychologie: Beiträge zum Studium der Individualität* (1895-1896).[69]

After the publication of Husserl's *Logical Investigations* (1900-1901) Dilthey immediately returned to these efforts and made an explicit attempt to employ the phenomenological method. The first results of these renewed efforts can be found in a short fragment, entitled "Studien zur Grundlegung der Geisteswissenschaften" of 1905 as well as in *Der Aufbau der geschichtlichen Welt in den Geisteswissenschaften* of 1910.[70] In Heidegger's opinion the ideas which Dilthey developed in chapter seven of his own *Ideen* remain of lasting value; in his view, both Husserl and Scheler accepted some of the basic theses which Dilthey developed there concerning the structure of psychic life, and then tried to develop them phenomenologically in greater detail. Among these theses Heidegger mentions two in particular: (1) each person finds himself in a definite selfsameness always related to a world upon which he or she exerts an influence while at the same time being influenced by it; and this is so not only in acts of will, feeling, or reflection, but always and in every respect; (2) the whole of a person's life is in each situation something that constantly is in a state of development. Yet, in Heidegger's view, in that work Dilthey still tried to develop these theses with the help of the traditional psychology of his time. According to Heidegger, what is truly important in these investigations is not so much the conceptual articulation, but rather the opening-up of new horizons for the question concerning the Being of man's actions and, in the final analysis, of the Being of man as such.[71]

Husserl, in turn, tried later to develop Dilthey's efforts to project a new, personalistic psychology. The first results of this can be found in Husserl's *Logos*-article, "Philosophy as a Rigorous Science" of 1911.[72] In this article Husserl makes an effort to define the meaning of pure consciousness in opposition to the Being of physical nature; physical nature is described there as that which is transcendent, whereas pure consciousness is portrayed as that which is given immanently. In Heidegger's opinion, from the manner in which Husserl articulates the meaning of immanent Being it is clear that for him Being is nothing but true Being, i.e., objectivity, i.e., Being which is true only for a theoretical, scientific consciousness. The issue for Husserl is not the specific mode of Being of consciousness or of man's experiences, but rather their being the privileged object for an objective science of consciousness. In other words, Husserl characterizes consciousness with respect to its Being primarily through the meaning of a possible scientific objectivity, but not directly through its own specific mode of Being which before and antecedent to any possible scientific objectivation itself already has its own proper meaning.[73]

Heidegger then quotes a long passage from the *Logos*-article in which Husserl states that all psychic phenomena are unities of a fundamentally different kind than the things of nature. According to their essence, natural things are given through perspectives (*Abschattungen*); psychic phenomena are never given in this way. A man's body is given through perspectives; but this cannot be said of a human being and most certainly not of his personality, character, etc. But although Husserl here thus explicitly claims that psychic phenomena are of a fundamentally

ORIGIN OF THE ANALYTIC OF DASEIN

different nature than natural things, it is nonetheless still the case, Heidegger observes, that the mode of Being of the psychic phenomena as such remains undetermined.[74]

In the second volume of *Ideas* Husserl made a deliberate effort to develop a genuine, personalistic psychology in a more systematic manner. At that time, (1912 ff.) these ideas, however, were not published. Yet Husserl gave the manuscript to several of his students who then made an effort to develop these ideas further.[75] Husserl himself, too, returned regularly to the issue and between 1913 and 1925 he made several efforts to develop a personalistic psychology systematically, notably in lectures which he gave in Freiburg from 1916 onwards under the title "Nature and Spirit."

Heidegger also mentions the lecture course on phenomenological psychology of 1925 and notes that Husserl's ideas at that time still were in a developmental stage. He, therefore, decided to refrain from further criticism, because he realized that most of his criticism might very well no longer be relevant.[76] Heidegger admits that he is no longer fully informed about Husserl's conception on these matters and adds to this that he has reasons to believe that Husserl made a serious effort to meet the criticism which he himself had formulated in regard to Husserl's position with respect to these issues. Heidegger finally states that it should be understood that in these matters Husserl obviously is the teacher whereas he himself still considers himself to be the disciple.[77]

Yet, according to Heidegger, even in the second volume of *Ideas* and also in his later lectures Husserl ultimately failed to determine the mode of Being of man and that of all psychic phenomena. As a matter of fact, Heidegger even believes that Husserl's approach to psychic phenomena, as we find it in his own efforts to develop a personalistic psychology, precisely precludes access to the very mode of Being of these phenomena. His intention to develop a personalistic psychology with the help of the phenomenological method must obviously be applauded. Yet his efforts, just as also the efforts of Dilthey, remain stuck in a fundamental manner in the classical problematic. In Husserl's personalistic psychology the Being of the person is not truly experienced as such. Furthermore, Husserl's access to the Being of the person is defined as immanent reflection and as the *inspectio sui* of those experiences to which all theses about absolute givenness can be reduced. The subject matter of this *inspectio sui* is no longer the person, but rather his actions; and the mode of Being of these actions remains completely undetermined. Finally, Heidegger argues, both Scheler and Husserl maintain the classical conception of man which is expressed in the famous definition: *homo, animal rationale*. It is indeed true that Husserl no longer conceives of man in terms of a natural thing; yet man still is a wordly reality which as transcendent being must be constituted in absolute consciousness.[78]

Thus here, too, Husserl does not really go beyond Dilthey even though it is the case that Husserl's analyses are superior to those of Dilthey. Yet from another point of view Dilthey's reflections are of superior quality. It may be the case that Dilthey, too, never asked the question concerning the meaning of Being; yet in Heidegger's view one should realize that Dilthey did not have the means to do so and that the tendency to do so was most certainly alive in him.[79]

Heidegger finally concludes these reflections with the observation that his investigations have shown that in all these questions about that which is intentional, psychical, about consciousness, experience, life, man, reason, spirit, person, ego, subject, etc., we still continue to encounter the old definition of man: man is a rational animal. It is not difficult to show that this definition does not flow from experiences which are oriented toward the very Being of man as such, but rather from experiences which focus on man as a mundane thing that just is present at hand.[80]

Even Scheler who in 1928 certainly was one of the most influential philosophers and whose basic concern at that time certainly was oriented toward the development of a philosophical anthropology which was to clarify the genuine position of man within the cosmos, continued to focus on the traditional conception of man, expressed in the classical definition. Influenced by Dilthey and Bergson, Scheler certainly already came much closer to the basic question; yet in his work, too, the question concerning the Being of man remained unanswered.[81]

If we are to lay the foundations for a genuine theory of the sciences of nature and history we thus must turn to a more radical reflection on the Being of man. In Heidegger's opinion such a radical reflection can be found in an analytic of Dasein which itself constantly remains oriented toward the question concerning the meaning of Being itself. It is such an analytic of Dasein which he finally would present in his *magnum opus, Being and Time* (1927).

3: NOTE ON THE *GEISTESWISSENSCHAFTEN*[82]

The discussion about the *Geisteswissenschaften* has been affected with serious problems and ambiguities from the very beginning. This state of affairs reflects itself in the difficulties which surround the use of the term. It is rather a strange situation that after more than one hundred years there is still no common agreement on how to translate this term; even the "history" of the term is rather paradoxical.

There are people who are convinced that there is no good equivalent in English for the German expression. This is true obviously only in a certain sense. Since the German expression itself is an 18th century creation, one wonders why one did not create an analogous neologism in English. The expression "the sciences of the spirit" would have been the obvious translation of the German term.

There are several reasons why it has been difficult to find a good English equivalent for the German term. One of these reasons is the fact that the German term is used by different authors with a different meaning so that the term has various shades of meaning which cannot be all captured by one single English expression. Another obvious reason is to be found in the fact that the extension of the term continues to change over time. And finally there is the fact that the term reminds us of romanticism and German idealism.

Although the term *Geisteswissenschaft* was already used in the 18th century by different authors it would not receive its modern meaning until the middle of the 19th century. It seems that the term was used first as a German translation of the technical term *pneumatologia*, a term first employed to refer to a theological discipline. Later it was sometimes used in the sense of "philosophy" or as a technical term for a branch of metaphysics. The first one to use the term for a set of sciences or disciplines which are not concerned with nature, but rather with the objective spirit or culture was probably Calinich. The term was soon employed regularly as a technical term in the middle of the 19th century to refer to a group of disciplines which from a methodical, systematic, and epistemological point of view were thought to constitute a unity and which with respect to subject matter and methods to be used can be determined by opposing them to the natural sciences.

Yet the term was at first used predominantly in the context of German idealism, where always a sharp distinction had been made between philosophy and science, on the one hand, and within the sciences between the sciences of nature and the sciences of the spirit (or culture) on the other. Originally it was assumed quite generally that the *Geisteswissenschaften* had both a practical and a normative character. Later when the *Geisteswissenschaften* began to fall apart in a number of relatively independent, individual disciplines, this idea was given up. The term was then used merely to refer to the historical and literary or philological disciplines which by means of interpretation try to explain and understand all manifestations of the human spirit in a manner which is strictly "value free." Among the manifestations of the human spirit to be studied by the *Geisteswissenschaften* one understood then myth, religion, morality, law, art, literature, and all other linguistic "expressions," signs, symbols, or traces. These manifestations can be taken to refer to a society's heritage or tradition as well as to a society's actual world. At that time it was quite generally assumed by many that all of these disciplines have in common that they make use of both hermeneutic and critical methods. In both the idealist and the neo-Kantian traditions in philosophy various authors have tried to lay the foundation for this group of sciences or disciplines and among these the work of Dilthey occupies a privileged position.

Some English authors have tried to translate the expression *Geisteswissenschaften* by the term moral science. J. Schiel, who translated Mill's *Logic* into German, had indeed used the German term for Mill's term "the moral sciences." Yet from the discussion by most 19th century authors who were concerned with laying the foundation of the *Geisteswissenschaften*, it is obvious that this is not a good choice, because the empiricist expression "the moral sciences" includes certain philosophical disciplines which are not covered by the German term. Other authors speak of the *humanities*, the *human studies*, or the *humanistic studies*. This, too, is not a fortunate choice in that these terms are usually used in an educational, not in an ontological or in an epistemological and methodological context. Obviously, it cannot be denied that part of the ambiguity of the discussion regarding the *Geisteswissenschaften* is indeed the result of the fact that in the concern with and the discussion about the *Geisteswissenschaften*, the educational dimension did play an important part in the opinion of some authors, to say the least.

In the German language it was, and to some degree still is, quite common to speak about the distinction between the natural sciences and the *Geisteswissenschaften*. In the English language such a distinction is very seldom used, certainly not in treatises on the philosophy of science. But it is common to make a distinction between the natural and the social sciences, or the human sciences, the sciences of man, etc. Yet it seems to me that the proposal to employ the term "human sciences" for the term "*Geisteswissenschaften,*" is also unfortunate. There is no doubt about the fact that in the 19th century the term *Geisteswissenschaften* at first did not include the behavioral and the social sciences. Dilthey in particular explicitly excluded psychology and sociology from the domain of the *Geisteswissenschaften.* Furthermore, most 19th century authors employed the term to refer to the cultural sciences, the sciences of the objective spirit, and notably to the historical and philological disciplines, only. Regardless of what one thinks about this very issue, it certainly illustrates clearly the complexity of the basic problem and the ambiguity with which the discussion about the *Geisteswissenschaften* has become clouded. Underlying the dispute about the issue is the question of the precise ontological, epistemological, and methodological status of both psychology and sociology, but equally of anthropology, economics, the study of law, the sciences of religion, etc. It is well known that in this regard psychology has been the focal point of a great number of authors since 1880, and that the question concerning the precise relationship between sociology on the one hand, and history and practical philosophy on the other, has never been resolved to everyone's satisfaction. I am aware of the fact that even mentioning these issues makes many authors very uneasy; yet it is the case that these and many other issues of this kind have played a part in the discussion about the *Geisteswissenschaften.*

One of the first authors who expressed the idea that it is necessary to develop a completely new type of science in addition to the flourishing natural sciences, and which was to concern itself with the human reality, was Vico. In his view, the natural sciences which make extensive use of mathematics and logic, are guided by broad logical principles; a *scienze nova* is to be developed which makes use of a new type of logic to be developed by means of some combination of ideas taken from philosophy, philology, and history. After Vico's death several people have tried to materialize this idea concretely. Hegel is said to have been the first one to have succeeded in this task. Yet after Hegel's death it became clear quite soon that Hegel's position is really unacceptable, not only because of the metaphysical assumptions which it implies and the closure which it demands, but also because of the fact that his system was in plain contradiction with the actual state of affairs and certain insights brought to light by various sciences. Thus the scientific study of the "whole" of the spirit soon fell apart into a number of disciplines which epistemologically and methodologically appeared to be heterogeneous. Thus a new search for a unity among these disciplines appeared to be necessary. Several authors tried to give an account of the epistemological status and the methodological problems of these sciences from a number of different philosophical perspectives, but none of these attempts was successful. It was during this period that the term *Geisteswissenschaften* was introduced to refer to these disciplines. But, as we noted already from the very beginning, the meaning of the expression was rather ambiguous and the extension of the term varied from author to author or from school to school.

It is important to realize here that the discussion about the *Geisteswissenschaften* originated in a very complex and often confusing world. The term began to circulate as a technical term at a time when the Churches had already lost their influence on the greater part of the intelligentsia; a time when the same Churches began to lose their influence on the rapidly developing "labor force"; a time in which the structure of most Western societies changed drastically and moved from being agrarian to becoming industrial societies; a time of great political turmoil on the national and international scene; a time in which both theology and philosophy began to lose their classical positions in the entire educational framework of the West; a time in which the ideas of the enlightenment became an integral part of every scholar's "general education"; when the structure and the function of the university began to change substantially; when ever more new disciplines were added to the curriculum, each searching for independence, recognition, and power; a time in which German idealism began to become ever more severely criticized, Nietzsche began to develop his conception of modern nihilism and began to think of ways to overcome it without having to return to classical "Platonism," Comte proposed his *philosophie positive*, and Lotze introduced what later would become known as value philosophy and axiology; a period finally in which for the first time attempts were made to develop strictly empirical sciences of man and society.

It is obviously very difficult to evaluate the influence of these and other important factors on society, on the structure and function of our Western educational system as a whole, and on the meaning and function of the university in particular, and the impact of all of this on the manner in which the various authors began to conceive of the meaning and function of the *Geisteswissenschaften*. Yet it can perhaps explain why in some schools of thought which were critical of the idealist perspective, other terms were introduced to refer to this group of disciplines, such as *Kulturwissenschaften, Gesellschaftswissenschaften,* or *Geschichtswissenschaften*. These new terms, in turn, point to another source of confusion and ambiguity, already mentioned earlier. Some of these expressions suggest that the behavioral and social sciences (at least to some extent) also belong to the *Geisteswissenschaften*, whereas others suggest that they are to be excluded. Finally, this can perhaps explain why in the philosophical discussion about the foundation of the *Geisteswissenschaften* some authors preferred to remain within the framework of thought that via Hegel goes back to Vico, whereas others tried to consider the basic issues from a perspective that was basically Cartesian in origin and which, thus, stressed the sharp distinction between nature and mind or spirit, emphasized the need for the *Geisteswissenschaften* methodologically and epistemologically to "imitate" the natural sciences, maintain a "value-free" attitude, and generally speaking dissolve the normative criteria of the tradition for the distinction between different branches of learning and research.

We have already pointed out that in the 18th and 19th centuries the university went through rather drastic changes. Gradually many new sciences and disciplines were introduced. Soon it became clear that the classical Greek conception of the "division" of the sciences was inadequate. The distinction between theoretical and practical sciences on the one hand and the "division" of the theoretical sciences in different philosophical branches on the other appeared totally inadequate to give an account of the situation which had developed over time. This generally accepted conviction made it possible for the *Geisteswissenschaften* to find their way into the university as independent disciplines. At first only the philological and historical sciences were included in the *Geisteswissenschaften*. Later other sciences of man were added to these "core" disciplines.

Once different *Geisteswissenschaften* had developed and once they had found their way into the university through their affiliation with the philosophical faculty, the question of their foundation was raised systematically. Since the latter part of the 19th century two questions have been debated heavily: (a) are the

Geisteswissenschaften indeed independent disciplines or sciences; and (b) how are they to be distinguished from the natural sciences?

After the efforts of Pascal (who distinguished an *esprit geometrique* from an *esprit de finesse*) and Vico, both of whose efforts were really independent from the Cartesian framework of thought, new efforts developed in the 19th century all of which assumed the distinction between nature and consciousness. Comte and Mill argued that the *Geisteswissenschaften* must also employ empirical methods, whereas Boeckh, Droysen, and Dilthey thought this to be impossible. The two leading schools in neo-Kantianism adopted the latter point of view. Cohen and Natorp suggested that ethics should be the "logic" of the *Geisteswissenschaften*, whereas Windelband and Rickert tried to account for an independent "logic" of the *Geisteswissenschaften* via the opposition between law and event and the distinction between nomothetic and ideographic methods.

The most important effort to clarify the foundations of the *Geisteswissenschaften* (which Rickert and Windelband call the cultural sciences) was at that time given by Dilthey in his critique of historical reason. Dilthey stressed the distinction, introduced first by Droysen, between understanding and explaining, and still tried to understand the *Geisteswissenschaften* in a normative sense as general sciences of action (*allgemeine Handlungswissenschaften*). The language of the *Geisteswissenschaften* does thus not limit itself to describing historical facts; that language also formulates nomological-theoretical as well as practical statements. Thus Dilthey attributes to the methodical understanding and explanation of the witnesses of the past that have been handed down, a practical intention, namely the task to found rationally individual and social actions which are relevant to the present and the future.

It is quite understandable that in the discussion about the *"Geisteswissenschaften"* those who were primarily concerned with *Bildung*, formation, and education tended to conceive of the term in a rather broad sense, to maintain a rather close relationship between the *Geisteswissenschaften* and philosophy, and thus to give the relevant disciplines a predominantly normative character. On the other hand, those concerned with research who wanted to compete with the leading scientists in the realm of the natural sciences, and tried hard to become accepted among their predominantly unphilosophical, "scientifically" and sometimes even positivistically oriented colleagues in the "genuine" sciences, tended to define the term in a rather narrow sense (linguistic and historical sciences only) and focused primarily on the epistemological and methodological dimensions of the *Geisteswissenschaften*, i.e., on the methods to be used there as well as the manner in which one can philosophically account for these methods. It is thus understandable that toward the end of the century when the confusion had reached extreme proportions, Dilthey could turn to the question of precisely how the *Geisteswissenschaften*, which are essentially different from the sciences of nature, can receive a foundation which is analogous to the foundation which Kant in his *Critique of Pure Reason* had given to the physical sciences. The methodically oriented scholars were obviously not blind to the fact that *Bildung*, formation, and education cannot be replaced by scientific research in a number of limited areas; they were of the opinion that the traditional *humaniora* and particularly philosophy would have to take care of the typically educational aspect of someone's training as a specialist in some area or other. Dilthey's concern with the *Geisteswissenschaften* was inspired by this problematic, also.

It is obviously impossible in this context to elaborate on Dilthey's philosophical reflections on the meaning and function of the *Geisteswissenschaften*. I must refer here to the secondary literature. Suffice it to mention the fact that Dilthey's investigation inspired a great number of scholars and invited them to concern themselves with the "foundation" of these sciences. In this connection not only the work of Count von Yorck, Husserl, Heidegger, Gadamer, and Ricoeur are to be mentioned, but equally the work of a number of philosophers who devoted their efforts to research in the area of philosophical anthropology since the time of Scheler.[83]

As far as Heidegger is concerned, we have seen that he employs the term *"Geisteswissenschaften"* in a rather narrow sense for the historical sciences, only. I shall deal with his contribution to the discussion on the most important issues raised here in chapters VI and VII.

CHAPTER II

HERMENEUTIC PHENOMENOLOGY AS THE METHOD OF THE ANALYTIC OF DASEIN

In the preceding chapter we have followed Heidegger in his development between 1909 when he entered the University of Freiberg to 1926 when he completed *Being and Time* in the form in which we now have it. We have dwelt particularly on Heidegger's relation to both Dilthey and Husserl in order to show how Heidegger, starting with Dilthey's reflection on the need for a new personalistic psychology, was led via Husserl's phenomenology to his own conception of an analytic of Dasein. We have already shown there also that within the domain of the sciences as a whole Heidegger, following Dilthey and Husserl and, thus, the entire neo-Kantian tradition in which they developed and matured, makes a clear distinction between the natural and the historical sciences. Furthermore, with the same philosophical tradition he maintains a rather sharp distinction between philosophy and the sciences, although he defends this distinction on grounds that are quite different from those proposed by either Dilthey or Husserl. Finally, it is understood that this distinction between philosophy and the sciences should not be taken in the sense of a separation. For such a separation is in Heidegger's opinion impossible and it would certainly be very detrimental to both science and philosophy, if one were to make an effort to keep them separate.

Finally, we have shown that in Heidegger's view philosophy has to play an important part in the foundation of the natural and the historical sciences. In this respect Heidegger was also influenced by Dilthey and Husserl, insofar as he was convinced that in order to do so adequately philosophy itself has to be

THE QUESTION OF BEING   49

strictly scientific, and that in order to become scientific, philosophy is to make use of the phenomenological method.

In order to be able to explain Heidegger's position in regard to the natural and the historical sciences more adequately, a few introductory remarks which focus on the hermeneutic character of phenomenology are necessary. In the sections to follow, however, I shall mention only those ideas which I take to be essential to understand Heidegger's position in regard to those sciences.

4: ON THE NECESSITY, STRUCTURE, AND PRIORITY OF THE QUESTION OF BEING

Being and Time, still the most important of Heidegger's works, was written in Marburg. In this book Heidegger applies "hermeneutic phenomenology" to the analytic of man's Being and carefully explains the sense in which this new expression is to be understood. In his opinion philosophy's main concern is to be found in the question concerning the meaning of Being (*Sein*). This question is to be dealt with in ontology, but such an ontology is to be prepared for by a fundamental ontology which must take the form of an existential analytic of man's mode of Being, to be understood as Being-in-the-world. It is in this fundamental ontology in particular that the hermeneutic-phenomenological method is to be used.

It was Heidegger's original intention in *Sein und Zeit* to offer two different conceptions of phenomenology, the first of a preliminary nature (found in section 7),[1] and a more definitive one under the heading "the idea of phenomenology." In view of the fact that the definitive conception has never been published, the preliminary outline is still one of Heidegger's most explicit formulations of his conception of phenomenology.[2]

At the very outset Heidegger makes it clear in *Being and Time* that what is to be understood by "hermeneutic phenomenology" is not identical with what Husserl meant by his transcendental phenomenology. He explicitly claims the right to develop the idea of phenomenology as suggested by Husserl in his own way beyond the stage to which it had been brought by Husserl himself. On the other hand, it is clear also, that Heidegger sees in Husserl's phenomenology the indispensable foundation for such a further development.[3] Although Heidegger does not explicitly mention this in *Being and Time*, it is clear implicitly, as well as from other documents, that the main reason he was unable to follow Husserl more closely is to be found in Husserl's transcendental idealism which in Heidegger's view is necessarily connected with Husserl's conception of the transcendental reduction and his idea that the ultimate source of all meaning is to be found in a transcendental subjectivity which as such is originally worldless.[4] This explains why Heidegger tries to conceive of man's mode of Being in terms of "Being-in-the-world." It explains also why Heidegger usually quotes Husserl's *Logical Investigations* (1900), but seldom mentions his main work, *Ideas* (1913).[5]

The second reason that Heidegger changed Husserl's conception of phenomenology is to be found in his concern with hermeneutics. In *On the Way to Language* (1959)[6] Heidegger tells us that he had his first experience with the word "hermeneutics" during his study of theology when he learned that hermeneutics is the method of interpreting the Scriptures. Later he found the term in Dilthey who had taken it from the theological writings of Schleiermacher for whom hermeneutics is the "art" by which one correctly understands the writings of an author. Between 1923 and 1927 Heidegger gradually became acquainted with hermeneutics in its different meanings and applications; this study led him to the idea of conceiving of "hermeneutics" in a more radical way and to substitute for Husserl's transcendental phenomenology a hermenetic phenomenology. It is of some importance to note here that according to Heidegger's own testimony his interest in hermeneutics originated from his concern with and knowledge of theology, and that without this knowledge of theology he would never have found the way to his hermeneutic phenomenology as developed in *Being and Time*. It is important to note here also that between 1923 and 1928 Heidegger was in close contact with Rudolf Bultmann and that the subject matter of their regular discussions often was the problem of hermeneutics.[7]

In the pages to follow I wish to describe briefly how Heidegger defines his conception of "hermeneutic phenomenology," in order then to elucidate this description with some topics vital to Heidegger's philosophy as a whole. However, it seems necessary first to say a few words about Heidegger's conception of the meaning of philosophy and the basic problems with which he feels it should concern itself.

According to Heidegger, as we have just seen, the focal point of philosophy is to be found in the question concerning the meaning of Being (*Sein*).[8] It is his conviction that the question concerning the meaning of Being has been forgotten. Everyone seems to be of the opinion today that an inquiry into the very meaning of Being is not necessary. This opinion, however, rests

THE QUESTION OF BEING

upon a misunderstanding which may have its origin in one of the following prejudices. Some philosophers argue that Being is the most universal concept and that for that very reason it cannot be explained with the help of other concepts. Heidegger remarks here that if it were true that Being is the most universal concept, then Being could not possibly be the clearest concept. It is rather the darkest of all, as the history of philosophy convincingly proves. It has been maintained, secondly, that the concept of Being is undefinable in principle; if Being is the most universal concept, then it cannot be defined by means of genus and specifying difference. According to Heidegger this cannot mean that Being no longer offers any problems to philosophy. From this remarks we can infer only that Being cannot have the character of a being (*Seiendes*); it is not a thing of some kind. That is why one cannot apply here the conception of definition as presented in traditional logic. Thirdly, it is generally held that Being is of all concepts the one that is self-evident; for, whenever we know something or make an assertion about it, some use is necessarily made of the concept of Being. According to Heidegger this fact manifests only that we already live in a preontological understanding of Being; it does not solve the Being question. For if it did, philosophy would be superfluous altogether. Heidegger concludes from these brief reflections that the Being question not only lacks an answer, but that the question itself is obscure and still without any direction. That is why we must first try to work out a way of adequately formulating it.[9]

Every question implies a looking-for or seeking. Every seeking is guided beforehand by what is sought. Every inquiry is a knowing seeking for a being both with regard to the fact that it is and with regard to what it is. Every inquiry about something implies: (1) that which is asked about, (2) that which is interrogated, and (3) that which is to be found out by the asking.

Thus if we ask the question concerning the meaning of Being, that which is to be found out is "the meaning of Being," that which is asked about is Being. All of this presupposes that the meaning of Being must already be available to us in some way when we ask the question. Since Being constitutes what is asked about, and Being means the Being of beings, the beings themselves turn out to be that which is to be interrogated. They must be questioned in regard to their Being. But among all beings the questioner himself occupies a privileged position. That is why to work out the question of Being we must make this being, the inquirer himself, transparent in his own mode of Being. The very asking of the Being question itself is a mode of Being of a determinate being; and as such this being receives its essential character from what is inquired about, namely Being. This being which each of us himself is, and which implies inquiring as one of the possibilities of its own mode of Being, Heidegger calls Dasein. Thus he concludes, if we wish to formulate the Being question explicitly, we must first give a proper explication of this particular being itself, namely Dasein, with respect to its own mode of Being.[10] There-Being (Dasein) is not just one being among others. As a being it is distinguished from all other beings by the fact that, in its very Being, this Being itself is an issue and a task for it. This implies that Dasein constitutively has a relationship toward that mode of Being. Thus there is some way in which Dasein understands itself in its own Being. It is characteristic of this being that together with its own mode of Being, Being itself is also somehow disclosed to it. That is why a radical investigation concerning the meaning of Being must take its point of departure in a fundamental ontology, that is in an analytic of Dasein's mode of Being.

I have brought up Heidegger's concern for the question concerning the meaning of Being for two reasons. First of all, it is an undeniable fact that Heidegger's philosophy as a whole centers around this question and, thus, cannot be properly understood except from this particular perspective. Secondly, however, the preceding exposition clearly shows how Heidegger's thought is hermeneutical through and through. The Being question is approached from the viewpoint of the hermeneutic circle; and the hermeneutic circle is employed again where Heidegger approaches the question concerning the very Being of man himself. As we shall see, the hermeneutic circle is vital to every important problem that is dealt with in *Being and Time*. This is evidenced from the fact that Heidegger, when he first formulates his approach to the Being question, explicitly mentions that his approach is circular, although this approach does not imply any form of circular reasoning.[11] At a later stage in the book he illustrates his view as follows. "Any interpretation which is to contribute understanding, must already have understood what is to be interpreted."[12] There he points out again that although his approach is somehow circular in the hermeneutic sense of the term, it is not open to criticism from the point of view of logic. The reason is that his approach is not a deductive approach. Summarizing his position he writes: "But if we are to obtain an ontologically clarified idea of Being in general, must we not do so by first working out that understanding of Being which belongs to Dasein? . . . Does it not then become altogether patent in the end that this problem of fundamental ontology which we have broached, is one which moves in a 'circle'?"[13] In dealing with this objection Heidegger points to the fact that what is called a circle here belongs to the very essence and the distinctive character of understanding as such.

In the sections to follow I shall return to Heidegger's conception of understanding (*Verstehen*) as well as to his ideas concerning the meaning and function of the hermeneutic circle. However, in order to be able to place these considerations in their proper perspective we must turn firs to Heidegger's conception of the method of ontology.

5: ON THE SCIENTIFIC CHARACTER OF PHILOSOPHY. HEIDEGGER'S CONCERN WITH METHOD.

We have seen that in Heidegger's view the science which concerns itself with the question concerning the meaning of Being, i.e., the truth of Being, is ontology. This science must take its point of departure in an analytic of Dasein's Being; ontology is thus to be founded upon fundamental ontology. In developing such a fundamental ontology Heidegger orients himself explicitly toward the transcendental doctrine of method proposed in Kant's *Critique of Pure Reason*.[14] Thus the real meaning of *Being and Time* can be understood only if the book is taken in the context of investigations which have a transcendental and methodical task; in other words, the transcendental, methodical problematic is an essential part of Heidegger's fundamental ontology. Dasein is described there as that being which brings about the transcendental phenomenological constitution of the Being of the beings; the constitution of the a priori synthesis and the projection of all beings upon the transcendental horizon of the truth of Being constitutes the very mode of Being of Dasein and its transcendence.[15]

The transcendental methodical task of fundamental ontology explains why reflections on method occupy such an important place in Heidegger's earlier works. The expression "methodical" appears more than 40 times in *Being and Time*, and it also occurs time and again in *The Basic Problems of Phenomenology* and *Kant and the Problem of Metaphysics*. Yet Heidegger never carefully defined what he means by method. It appears that the relation between method and "the thing itself" is of prime importance and that this relationship itself is taken to be a fundamental, methodical, ontological problem. The correct method can be found only by means of a "pure ontological methodology."[16] This means that the method used must first unfold the "thing itself" in such a manner that the "thing itself" so revealed can then make a methodology possible which is capable of showing the foundation of the actual method used. In *Prolegomena zur Geschichte des Zeitbegriffs*, *Being and Time*, and *The Basic Problems of Phenomenology*, Heidegger gives us a preliminary description of the phenomenological method and in all these works he promises to develop a more definitive description and a justification of this method.[17] Thus the earlier works were not only written according to the phenomenological method, but they were also intended to contain a justification of this method in a general methodology. This brings Heidegger's concern very close to Kant's efforts in the *Critique of Pure Reason*. This must be explained briefly. In so doing I shall first make a few remarks on Heidegger's position in *Being and Time*.

From the way in which in *Being and Time* Heidegger determines both subject matter and method of ontology it is clear that he is trying to find and justify a personal stance in regard to the entire philosophical tradition. In the manner of the Western tradition since Plato, Heidegger subscribes to the view that ontology is a science. Like Descartes he defines the scientificity of ontology by means of the method to be employed.[18] With the entire modern tradition he admits that in a science, that which counts is not what other thinkers have already thought, but that which can be methodically justified in regard to the "things themselves" to be studied in that science.[19] Heidegger even seems to join Descartes, Kant, and Husserl in their negative evaluation of philosophy's history, when he speaks about the need for a destruction of the traditional content of ancient ontology.[20] Finally, Heidegger is fully aware of the intimate relationship between method and subject matter in ontology and, thus, seems to subscribe to the view that it is incorrect to conceive of method in a purely instrumental fashion. This intimate relationship appears to imply that the explicitation of the immediately given is to be mediated by what is already somehow implicitly contained in what is given immediately, without, however, being explicitly thematized there.[21]

Yet at the same time Heidegger makes it abundantly clear that he does not share any of these views without major modification.

Ontology is a "science," indeed, but it is a science whose scientificity has nothing in common with either the formal or the empirical sciences.[22] Secondly, although it is true that as a science ontology is to be defined in its scientificity by means of the method to be employed, yet this method cannot possibly be conceived of as consisting in deduction (Descartes) or description (Husserl). Rather this method is to be conceived of as being both transcendental and hermeneutic.[23] It is true, also, that no philosopher can think without both explicitly standing in a tradition and taking a critical stance in regard to that tradition. Yet this critical attitude is not a rejection of the tradition, but rather a destructive retrieve of what is worth being thought about in that tradition.[24] Finally, although it is true that method and content are intimately intertwined in ontology and that the mediation of the immediately given presupposes that what guides the explicitation takes its clues from what is already somehow present in the immediately given, the latter is not to be found in some anticipation of Hegel's absolute truth, but rather in the finite "truth of Being" which functions as the necessary synthesis a priori in all finite understanding.

Thus in philosophy it is impossible to develop a method independent from the subject matter to be disclosed by the method. Any genuine method is based on viewing, in advance and in the appropriate manner, the basic constitution of the "object" to be disclosed and of the domain within which it is to be found. Thus any genuinely methodical consideration which is not just an empty discussion of techniques, must give information about the kind of Being of the being which is to be taken as the theme.[25] In the positive sciences this information follows with necessity from the a priori synthesis which each science "freely" projects;[26] in ontology this information is to be derived from that peculiar synthesis which as the comprehension of Being is constitutive of Dasein.[27] This is the reason why in philosophy every effort to deal with the method of philosophy itself implies a dilemma: this effort comes either too early or too late. For strictly speaking the method of ontology can be determined adequately only after the process of thought has reached its destination and its subject matter has been articulated. Yet, on the other hand, it is precisely this process of thought which is to be conducted methodically.[28] Solving this dilemma is one of the basic problems of every philosophy which concerns itself explicitly with its method. Somehow the basic problems must be solved at the very beginning and yet they cannot be solved definitively except at the end.

Thus at the beginning one can do no more than make some provisional and suggestive remarks; these are then to be reconsidered toward the end of the philosophical reflection.[29] Heidegger justifies this way of proceeding by means of a reference to the hermeneutic character of all finite understanding and to the hermeneutic circle which all research about ontological issues appears to imply.[30]

Concern for method and methodology has been a characteristic of modern philosophy since Descartes. In view of the fact that the deductive method in principle is incapable of clarifying the basic axioms of any given deductive system, from the very beginning there was the question of whether it would be possible to develop a new science which as *prima philosophia* could give an ultimate foundation to some basic insights from which then all of our theoretical knowledge could be derived according to principles and laws.

Since all rationalist and empiricist attempts in this direction had failed, Kant in his *Critique of Pure Reason* attempted to provide a theoretical framework which would lay the foundation for philosophy as well as for all other sciences. Thus the *Critique* does not contain the system of science, but is concerned primarily with its method.[31] The possibility of scientific knowledge is explained only when reason can develop for itself a method which will both guide and bind reason itself in all of its theoretical endeavors. This implies that the method to be developed must be of a totally different nature than the methods employed in the formal and empirical disciplines; thus the new method cannot be either analytic or empirical. According to Kant the great discovery of the modern age from which philosophy and science must learn a lesson is that "reason has insights only into that which it produces after a plan of its own."[32] What is needed then in Kant's view is a transcendental logic, a philosophical reflection on the projective achievement of reason by which reason provides itself with an a priori framework which is the necessary condition of our theoretical knowledge of all objects.

What is completely new in this view is not the reference to the fact that there is to be an a priori of some kind, but the fact that in the question concerning our knowledge a priori the stress is placed on method, which alone can guarantee the necessity and universality of all of our scientific insights. In Kant's view only the proper application of the "transcendental" method is capable of closing the gap between subject and object to which Descartes has pointed and which both rationalism and empiricism had been unable to bridge. Knowledge of objects is possible only if the transcendental method is capable of showing that the objectivity of the object is projected in advance by reason itself. In the final analysis the projection of this objectivity is the reason why all of our theoretical knowledge constitutes a harmonious unity and can be developed into a system.[33]

Between Fichte and Husserl various forms of transcendental philosophy were developed. They all have Kant's basic concern in common and share his view that there is to be a highest principle of all synthetic judgments a priori which has fundamental implications for the systematicity of all genuine knowledge. The difference between the various forms of transcendental philosophy is to be found in the concrete manner in which each author or group of authors has tried to conceive of the a priori synthesis and the principle which founds its unity.[34]

From his earliest works it is clear that between 1914 and 1930 Heidegger conceived of himself as one who was seriously concerned with the development of transcendental philosophy in the sense of Kant, the neo-Kantians, and Husserl. Thus it was to be expected that in the first sections of *Being and Time* one would find an attempt by Heidegger to formulate his own position in regard to the basic problems of transcendental philosophy, even though it would not be stated explicitly in so many words.[35]

Heidegger defends the same view in *The Basic Problems of Phenomenology*. In this work he attempts to formulate the fundamental problems of phenomenology, to elaborate on these problems, and to bring them somewhat closer to a solution. For the concept of phenomenology must be developed from that which phenomenology makes into its theme, and from the manner in which it examines its subject matter. Yet, in order to be able to discover the fundamental problems mentioned, it is necessary to begin with a provisional conception of phenomenology. A critical reflection on the conceptions of phenomenology proposed by Kant, Hegel, and Husserl shows that one can assert provisionally that phenomenology is not a philosophical science among others; it is neither, as some have thought, the propaedeutic science for all other philosophical sciences; the expression "phenomenology" rather is the title for the method of scientific philosophy as such.[36]

From this perspective it is then clear at once that the explanation of the idea of phenomenology is identical with the explanation of the concept of scientific philosophy. Although the expression "scientific philosophy" is really a pleonasm, it is nevertheless advisable to use the adjective "scientific" explicitly, in view of the fact that since the nineteenth century certain conceptions of philosophy have been proposed which deny the scientific character of philosophy. Thus today it is important to distinguish the scientific conception of philosophy from those conceptions in which it is claimed that philosophy is not a theoretical science, but rather attempts to provide us with a conception of world and with practical wisdom. After a brief reflection on the latter conception of philosophy and a short explanation of his own conviction that the task of philosophy cannot possibly consist in the development of a *Weltanschauung*, Heidegger notes with emphasis that anyone who conceives of philosophy in terms of the formation of a conception of world, cannot appeal to Kant; for Kant accepts only a philosophy which has the character of being a true science. The main reason why in Heidegger's own view philosophy cannot have the task of developing a conception of world is to be found in the fact that every such conception is ontic in character and, thus, must lead to a positing science.[37]

But if philosophy does not concern itself with beings, does this mean that it is concerned with nothing? No; for every meaningful concern with beings implies some understanding of Being, although at first this form of understanding does not imply that we also already have an explicit concept of Being. Yet this implicit understanding of Being can be made explicit and this is the task of philosophy. Being is even the genuine and only theme of philosophy. This is a thesis which one finds defended in philosophy's history time and again.

Philosophy is not a science of beings, but the science of Being itself; thus it is inherently ontology. To elucidate the fundamental problems of phenomenology is therefore tantamount to giving a foundation for the claim that philosophy is the science of Being, and to giving an explanation of how it can be such a science. Philosophy is the theoretical and conceptual interpretation of Being, its structures, and its possibilities. All other sciences concern themselves with beings; and they do so in such a manner that in each case a certain domain of beings is already pregiven as such. What for a given science is to be understood by being is in each case posited in advance so that all non-philosophical sciences, including the mathematical sciences, are positing and thus positive sciences. Philosophy cannot posit in advance what is to be understood by Being; instead it must try to discover what is meant by Being, from what something like Being is to be understood, and how our understanding of Being itself is even possible at all.[38]

6: DESTRUCTIVE RETRIEVE AND HERMENEUTIC PHENOMENOLOGY

In the Introduction to *Being and Time*, after indicating that ontology is concerned with the Being question and is to be prepared by a fundamental ontology which takes the concrete form of an analytic of Dasein's mode of Being, Heidegger turns next to the question concerning "the right way of access" to the primary subject of investigation, namely Dasein. He stresses the point that this problem is a very difficult one, because Dasein is to be taken as something already accessible to itself and as something yet to be understood. We must thus be able to explain how and why Dasein itself can be grasped immediately, although the kind of Being which it possesses is not to be presented just as immediately, but rather is to be mediated by explanation and interpretation.[39]

Dasein is in such a way that it is capable of understanding its own Being; yet it has the tendency to do so in terms of those beings toward which it comports itself proximally. And this means that its "categorial structure" remains to some degree concealed. Thus the philosophical interpretation of Dasein's mode of Being is confronted with very peculiar difficulties. Furthermore, Dasein has been made the subject of both philosophical and scientific investigations. Thus there are already many ways in which Dasein has been interpreted. It is not clear how all of these interpretations can go together. This complexity makes the problem of securing the right access which will lead to Dasein's Being even a more burning one. We have no right to resort dogmatically to constructions and to apply just any idea of Being to Dasein, however self-evident such an idea may be, nor may any of the "categories" which such an idea prescribes be forced upon Dasein without proper ontological consideration.[40]

In Heidegger's view temporality constitutes the meaning of Dasein's mode of Being.[41] Temporality is also the condition which makes historicity possible as a temporal mode of Being which Dasein itself possesses. Historicity stands here for the state of Being which is constitutive for Dasein's coming-to-pass as such. Dasein is *as* it already was and it is *what* it already was. Dasein *is* its past, not only in the sense that it possesses its own past as a kind of property which is still present-at-hand; Dasein is its past particularly in the way of its own Being which comes-to-pass out of its future on each occasion. Regardless of how Dasein is at a given time or how it may conceive of Being, it has grown up both into and in a traditional way of interpreting itself; in terms of this tradition it understands itself proximally and, to some degree at least, constantly. Its own past, which includes the past of its generation, is thus not something which just follows along after Dasein, but something which already goes ahead of it.[42]

But if Dasein itself as well as its own understanding are intrinsically historical, then the inquiry into the meaning of Being is to be characterized by historicity as well. The ownmost meaning of Being which belongs to the inquiry into Being as an historical inquiry, points to the necessity of inquiring into the history of that inquiry itself. Thus in working out the question concerning the meaning of Being one must take heed of this pointing, so that by positively making the past his own, he may bring himself into full possession of the very possibility of such inquiry.

When a philosopher turns to philosophy's own history he must realize that this tradition constitutes that from which he thinks as well as that from which he, to some degree at least, must try to move away. Yet Dasein is inclined to fall prey to its tradition. This tradition often keeps it from providing its own guidance whether in inquiring or in choosing. When a tradition overpowers one's own thinking it often conceals what it really tries to transmit. Dasein has the tendency to take what the tradition hands down to it as being self-evident. This blocks the access of those primordial sources from which the categories, concepts, and views handed down have been drawn. Dasein is in fact so caught in its own tradition that in philosophy it often confines its interest to the multiformity of the available standpoints of philosophical inquiry; but by this interest it seeks to hide the fact that it has no ground of its own to stand on. The state in which philosophy's concern about the Being question finds itself today, is the clearest evidence of this tendency.

Thus in the inquiry into the question concerning the meaning of Being one has to have a ground of his own and yet one's thought must carefully heed its own philosophical tradition. Both these demands are met in the "destructive retrieve." One must "destroy" in the tradition what is philosophically unjustifiable and maintain those primordial experiences from which any genuine philosophical insights ultimately flow. The meaning of the retrieve is not to shake off the philosophical tradition, but to stake out the positive possibilities of a tradition and keep it within its proper limits.[43] "By the retrieving of a fundamental problem we understand the disclosure of its original potentialities that long have lain hidden. By the elaboration of the potentialities, the problem is transformed and thus for the first time in its intrinsic content, conserved. To conserve a problem, however, means to retain free and awake all those inner forces that render this problem in its fundamental essence possible."[44]

It is obvious that in these reflections Heidegger takes a critical stance with respect to Descartes, Kant, and Husserl whose positions in regard to the philosophical tradition are too negative. In this regard Heidegger's position is closer to that adopted by Hegel. One major point in which he does not follow Hegel in this respect consists in the fact that Hegel saw the various philosophical perspectives developed in the past as elements of an organic unity or system and that, thus, some form of necessity is constitutive for "the life of the whole." In Heidegger's view, philosophy's history does not bind the philosopher who lives today with the necessity of the unbreakable laws of the Hegelian dialectic; rather, the philosophical tradition, like every other form of tradition, delivers and liberates man. The answer to a philosophically relevant question consists in man's authentic response to what in philosophy's history is already on the way to him. Such a response implies, at the same time, his willingness to listen to what is already said and the courage to take distance from what he has heard. This makes a certain criticism of the past necessary in philosophy. Yet such a criticism should not be understood as a break with the past, nor as a repudiation of philosophy's history, but as its adoption in the form of a transformation and adaptation to the requirements of the world in which we live and of what in this world has been handed down to us. Heidegger, thus, does not deny the necessity to re-think every "experience," to mediate it and transcend it. Yet he does deny that this should be done from the perspective of the absolute knowledge of the Absolute. In his opinion, each "experience" is to be mediated from the perspective of Being. It is in this finite perspective that man understands his own mode of Being in its full potentialities so that he can compare each mode of Being, present in each "experience," with the whole of possibilities and thus understand its genuine, limited meaning. Furthermore, it is within this finite perspective that one can "let things be seen from themselves and in themselves," because within this perspective, by projecting the things upon this a priori synthesis, one can show them in their full potentialities so that the concrete mode of givenness as found in a given "experience" can appear in its true and limited sense.[45]

Heidegger obviously maintains that the philosophical reflection should be methodical and critical. Although he rejects presuppositionlessness (Husserl) and absoluteness (Hegel), he does not reject method and rigor. The first, last, and constant task of our philosophical reflection is never to allow our pre-judgments to be dominated by merely arbitrary conceptions, but rather to make the relevant themes secure scientifically by working out our anticipatory conceptions in terms of "the things themselves."[46] In other words, the destructive retrieve is guided by a hermeneutic phenomenology which in each case allows for a careful comparison of the claims made by thinkers of the past with the "things" to be reflected upon.[47]

7: HEIDEGGER'S CONCEPTION OF PHENOMENOLOGY

a. PHENOMENOLOGY. THE MEANING OF THE TERM

As Heidegger sees it, the term "phenomenology" does not refer to a trend or school in philosophy, nor does it represent any particular standpoint or direction. The expression "phenomenology" signifies primarily a methodical conception. For this expression does not characterize the what of the objects of philosophical research, but rather the how of that research.[48]

The term "phenomenology" expresses a maxim which can be formulated as follows: "to the things themselves." As such it is opposed to all free-floating constructions and accidental findings. It is opposed to taking over any conceptions which seem only to have been demonstrated. Taken in this way the maxim appears to express something which is self-evident in that it expresses the fundamental principle of any scientific knowledge whatsoever. And although it is true that there is here indeed a kind of self-evidence, we nonetheless must try to bring it a bit closer to us in order more accurately to understand its genuine meaning.[49]

The expression "phenomenology" has two components: *phenomenon* and *logos*, both of which go back to Greek words. Taken superficially, the term "phenomenology" is formed like the words "theology," "biology," "sociology,"--expressions which can be translated as "science of God," "science of life," and "science of society." This would make phenomenology the "science of phenomena." Since this obviously cannot be the meaning of the expression, we should at this point try to specify first the precise meaning of the two components of the term, in order then to establish the meaning of the compound expression in which these two components are put together.[50]

The Greek expression *phainomenon*, to which the word "phenomenon" goes back, is derived from the verb *phainesthai*, which signifies "to show itself." Thus *phainomenon* means that which shows itself. *Phainesthai* itself comes from *phaino*, which means to bring to light. *Phaino* comes from the stem *pha-*, found in *phos*, the light, that which is bright, that wherein something can become manifest in itself. Thus we must keep in mind that the expression "phenomenon" signifies that which shows itself in itself, the manifest. The phenomena are the totality of what lies in the light of the day; the Greeks sometimes identified this simply with *ta onta*, the beings.

Now a being can show itself from itself in many ways, depending in each case on the kind of access one has to it. It is even possible for a being to show itself as something which in itself it is *not*. When it shows itself in this way it looks like something else, but it is not this being. This kind of showing-itself is what one calls "semblance." It is of importance to realize how phenomenon as that which shows itself and phenomenon as semblance are structurally interconnected. It is particularly important to observe that when phenomenon signifies "semblance," the primordial signification of the term (namely the phenomenon as the manifest) is already included as that upon which the second signification is founded. Furthermore, both are to be carefully distinguished from what is called "mere appearance." When we talk about a "mere appearance" we are not talking about something which shows itself, but about something which announces itself without showing itself from itself. What appears does *not* show itself, but it announces itself by means of something which shows itself immediately. What we call "indication," "symptom," "symbol," "sign," all of these have this basic formal structure of appearing, even though they differ among themselves in many other respects.

In spite of the fact that "appearing" is never a "showing itself from itself" in the sense of phenomenon, appearing is nonetheless possible only by reason of the showing-itself of something else, thus by means of a phenomenon in the proper sense of the term. But this phenomenon which helps to make possible the appearing, is not the appearing thing itself. Appearing is the announcing-itself through something that shows itself immediately. Thus phenomena are never mere appearances, though on the other hand every appearance is dependent upon a phenomenon.

In summary, both semblance and appearance are to be carefully distinguished from phenomenon as that which shows itself in itself and from itself. On the other hand, however, both semblance and appearance are founded upon phenomenon in the proper sense of the term, though in completely different ways. And thus, the confusion created by the multiplicity of "phenomena" to which we refer with the expressions "semblance," "appearance," "mere appearance," and "phenomenon," cannot be unravelled unless the concept of phenomenon is understood originally as that which shows itself in itself and from itself.[51]

Until now we have limited ourselves to defining the purely formal meaning of the term phenomenon in that we have not yet specified which entities we consider to be phenomena, and have left open the question of whether what shows itself in itself is a being, or rather some characteristic which a being might have in its Being. In order to be able to answer this question, Heidegger makes an explicit distinction between the ordinary and the phenomenological conception of phenomenon, both of which are then defined with an explicit reference to Kant. *Phenomenon in the ordinary sense* is any being which is accessible to us through our "empirical intuition." Formulated again within the perspective of the Kantian framework, *phenomenon in the phenomenological sense* of the term is that which already shows itself in the appearance as "prior to" the phenomenon in the ordinary sense and as accompanying it in every case. Even though it shows itself unthematically, it can nonetheless be brought to show itself thematically. Thus the phenomena of phenomenology are those beings which show themselves in themselves, i.e., Kant's forms of intuition. In other words, the phenomena in the phenomenological sense of the term refer to "the conditions of the possibility of the objects of all experience."[52] Be this as it may, in Heidegger's view before we are able to define the phenomenological meaning of the term "phenomenon" in greater detail we must first try to specify the signification of the term "logos."

In Plato and Aristotle the concept "logos" has many competing significations, none of which at first sight seems to be primordial. And yet the term has a basic meaning in the light of which all other and derivative meanings can be understood. One could say that the basic signification of *logos* is articulating discourse (*Rede*); but such a translation remains unjustified so long as we are unable to determine precisely what is meant by this expression. *Logos* is also translated as "judgment," "concept," "understanding," "mind," "definition," "ground," "relationship," and so on. But how can "articulating discourse" be so susceptible to modification that *logos* indeed can signify all the meanings listed here?

Logos is related to *legein* which means the same as *deloun*: to make manifest what one is talking about; and according to Aristotle this has the same meaning as *apophainesthai*. *Logos* lets something be seen (*phainesthai*), namely what the talk is about; and it does so for those who are somehow involved in this talking. *Logos* furthermore lets something be seen *apo-*: it lets us see something from the very thing the talk is about. In the *logos* as discourse (*apophansis*), what is said is drawn from what the talk is about, so that discursive communication, in what it says, makes manifest what the talk is about and makes it thus accessible to other people. And when in this context *logos* becomes fully concrete, then discoursing, as letting something be seen, has the character of speaking, of a proclamation in words, of an utterance in which something is sighted in each case.

Furthermore, because *logos* is letting something be seen, it can therefore be true or false. But it is of the greatest importance to realize here that in this connection truth cannot be understood in the sense of an agreement between what is and what is said. Such a conception of truth is by no means the primary one. The Greek word for truth is *aletheia* and this means unconcealment. The being-true of the *logos* as *aletheuein* means that the beings about which one is talking must be taken out of their original hiddenness; one must let them be seen as something unhidden (*a-lethes*); that is, the beings must be discovered. And similarly, "being-false" amounts to deceiving in the sense of covering-up: putting something in front of something else in such a way as to let the former be seen, thereby passing the latter off as something which it is not.[53]

Heidegger claims that from the interpretation of the words "phenomenon" and "logos" as just given, it becomes clear that there is an inner relationship between the things meant by these two words. The expression "phenomenology" may be formulated in Greek as *legein ta phainomena*; and since *legein* has the meaning of *apophainesthai*, phenomenology means *apophainesthai ta phainomena*: to let that which shows itself be seen from itself in the very way in which it shows itself. This is the formal meaning of the discipline which calls itself "phenomenology." Taken in this sense the term tries to express the same thing as the maxim we formulated earlier: to the things themselves.

The term "phenomenology" is certainly quite different in its meaning from expressions such as "theology" and "biology." These terms designate the objects of the respective sciences; they refer to the typical character of their contents. The term "phenomenology" neither designates the objects of its research, nor does it indicate the specific character of their contents. The word merely informs us about the how with which the subject matter of this discipline is to be exhibited and handled.[54]

b. HERMENEUTIC PHENOMENOLOGY

But what is it that phenomenology is to "let us see." We have seen already that this question must be answered if we are ever to be able to go from a purely formal conception of phenomenon to a phenomenological one. What is it, therefore, that by its very essence must be called a "phenomenon" in a distinctive sense? What is it that is necessarily the theme whenever we try to exhibit something explicitly? Obviously, it is something that proximally and for the most part does not show itself; it is something that lies hidden in contrast to that which proximally and for the most part does show itself. And at the same time it must be something that belongs to what thus shows itself, and it must belong to it so essentially as to constitute its very meaning and ground.

History of philosophy shows that what remains hidden in a specific sense, what relapses and gets covered up time and again, is not this or that being, nor this or that kind of beings, but rather the Being of these beings. This Being can even be covered up so extensively that it becomes forgotten and there is no longer any question which arises about it and its ultimate meaning. In other words, that which demands that it become a phenomenon, and which demands this in a distinctive sense and in terms of its ownmost content as a thing, is precisely that which phenomenological philosophy wants to make the very subject matter and theme of its own investigations. But if phenomenology is man's way of access to what is to be the very theme of ontology, it is clear that the phenomenological conception of "phenomenon" as that which shows itself refers to the Being of things, to its meaning, its modification, and its derivatives.[55]

With respect to its subject matter phenomenology is then the science of the Being of beings; it is in this sense that we could say phenomenology is ontology. But in explaining the task of ontology we have already referred to the necessity of a fundamental ontology which has to take the form of an existential analytic of man's Being as Being-in-the-world. This fundamental ontology must prepare our investigation of the question concerning the meaning of Being. In other words, that which phenomenology is concerned about first is the Being of man. Its first task is to let be seen the Being of man's Dasein, a Being that is concealed, that once was revealed and now has slipped back into oblivion, that is revealed now again but in a distorted fashion so that man's Dasein seems to be what in fact it is not. Now it is precisely inasmuch as Being is *not* seen that phenomenology is necessary. To permit man's Dasein to reveal itself of its own accord as that which it is and how it is, it must be submitted to a phenomenological analysis in order to lay the Being of Dasein out in full view. Such a laying-out necessarily takes the form of an interpretation; and that is why phenomenology essentially is hermeneutical.[56]

As we have noted before, hermeneutics is not a new word. It has its origin in biblical exegesis and has later been applied to the interpretation of the meaning of historical documents and works of art. But as the expression is used here by Heidegger it no longer refers to documents and results of symbolic expression, but to man's Being. What does it mean to interpret such a non-symbolic fact as man's Being? Interpretation aims at the meaning of things to be interpreted. It presupposes, therefore, that what is to be interpreted has meaning. Now Dasein has meaning which admits of interpretation. For, Dasein as ek-sistence is essentially related to its own mode of Being as that which continuously is at stake for it. The essence of man's Being consists in his "Being-toward." That toward which Dasein ek-sists consists primarily in its own possibilities. Hence in its orientation toward possibilities beyond itself Dasein is capable of interpretation. And Dasein is not only capable of such an interpretation, it also demands it. For just as Being has the tendency to fall into oblivion, so man's Being has an inherent tendency to degenerate, a decay which is characteristic of the everyday mode of Dasein from which hermeneutic phenomenology precisely must take its point of departure.[57] In other words, the phenomenology with the help of which the analytic of Dasein is to be developed, is hermeneutic, insofar as the letting-be-seen limits itself to Dasein only and exclusively insofar as Dasein is oriented toward the understanding of Being; thus it lets Dasein be seen only *as* that being which is essentially oriented toward Being itself.

But, Heidegger continues, to the extent that by disclosing the meaning of Being and the fundamental structures of Dasein phenomenology also exhibits the horizon for any further ontological investigation concerning those beings which do not have the mode of Being of Dasein itself, this hermeneutic also becomes a hermeneutic in the sense of working out the conditions on which the possibility of any ontological investigation rests. In other words, this hermeneutic must have the character of a transcendental science in the sense of Kant, insofar as it is concerned with the conditions of the possibility of any ontology whatsoever.

And finally, Heidegger concludes, insofar as Dasein, taken as that being which has the possibility of ek-sistence, finds itself in a position which is ontologically prior to every other being, hermeneutic, taken as the interpretation of Dasein's mode of Being, has also the specific meaning of being an analytic of the ek-sistentiality of Dasein's ek-sistence. In other words, the analytic of Dasein, taken as this hermeneutic, is a transcendental analytic which concerns itself not with man's scientific knowledge, but rather with the Being of Dasein taken as such. In Heidegger's own opinion this latter meaning is the sense which is philosophically primary.[58]

From what has been said, it should be clear that every hermeneutic interpretation depends on certain preconceptions, and that no interpretation is ever completely free from presuppositions. Hermeneutic interpretation has even all the earmarks of a logical circle. Since the anticipations of hermeneutics, however, are not determined by chance ideas, by popular conceptions, by so-called philosophical ideas, or by any other mere prejudices, but only and exclusively by the things themselves, this circle is not a vicious one.[59]

Heidegger concludes his explanation of the meaning of phenomenology by stating again that ontology and phenomenology are not two distinct philosophical disciplines among others. Both these terms characterize philosophy itself in regard to its subject matter and in its way of treating this subject matter. "Philosophy is universal phenomenological ontology and takes its departure from the hermeneutic of man's Dasein which, as an analytic of man's ek-sistence, has made fast the guiding-clue for all philosophical inquiry at the point where it arises and to which it returns."[60]

c. HEIDEGGER'S LATER PHILOSOPHY. HUSSERL AND HEIDEGGER.

In Heidegger's later publications the term "phenomenology" is no longer found. For many years a great number of commentators have drawn from this the conclusion that Heidegger had changed his mind and that his later "thought" can by no means be called phenomenological. That this way of looking at the matter is not correct became apparent from what is found in a few older documents which were recently published[61] as well as from what was written by Heidegger in a letter to Richardson.[62] In this letter Heidegger says that he has always maintained the following basic insights: (1) the fundamental problem of philosophy is the question concerning the meaning of Being; (2) this question is to be studied phenomenologically; (3) the phenomenological study of Being must take its starting point in a hermeneutic phenomenology of man's Being.[63] It has always been quite clear, he writes, that "the thing itself" which phenomenology is looking for, is not "intentional consciousness," nor the "transcendental ego," but the Being of beings. Since "phenomenology" in Husserl's sense was developed into a idealistic philosophical position rooted in and coming very close to the philosophies of Descartes, Kant, and Fichte, he decided not to use the expression "phenomenology" any longer, in order to avoid confusion and misunderstanding, although no fundamental change had taken place in his own basic outlook on philosophy's meaning and task.[64] All of this, however, obviously does not exclude the fact that Heidegger's understanding of the genuine meaning of hermeneutics has grown over a great number of years.[65]

Be this as it may, my brief description of Heidegger's view of phenomenology will undoubtedly have suggested to the reader that although Heidegger takes his point of departure in Husserl's phenomenology, his conception of phenomenology nevertheless differs radically from Husserl's original view. Yet, if one were to describe these two conceptions of phenomenology in greater detail, it would soon appear that the differences are not as great as a brief summary of both views might seem at first to suggest. One must not forget that notwithstanding the radical and essential differences which indeed do exist in regard to some issues, both Husserl and Heidegger share many basic insights, such as their conception of the meaning of intuition, analysis, and description, intentionality, constitution, and even the famous reduction. In my opinion the root of the differences in their views is to be found in the fact that Husserl extends the transcendental reduction so far as to include the "meditating ego itself," reducing it from a mundane ego to a transcendental subjectivity which as source of all meaning is originally world-less, whereas Heidegger believes that such a reduction is neither necessary nor possible. In a letter to Husserl, Heidegger makes the following illustrative remarks: "We agree that Being taken in the sense of what you call 'world' cannot be clarified in its transcendental constitution by means of a return to a being of the same kind."[66] The world must indeed be explained in its transcendental constitution by the human subjectivity, but this must not be taken as a world-less transcendental ego, but precisely as this concrete man in the world.[67] That is why the first task of philosophy consists in explaining that this being indeed is different from all other beings. "One must try to show that the mode of Being of man's Dasein is completely different from that of all other beings and that this mode of Being, as that which it is, precisely contains the possibility of the transcendental constitution. Transcendental constitution is a central possibility of the ek-sistence of the factical self. Thus, the concrete man is as such (e.g., as being) never a 'mundane real fact,' since man never is merely present-at-hand, but ek-sists. And the 'marvel' consists in this that the understanding of Dasein's ek-sistence makes the transcendental constitution of everything which is positive, possible."[68]

In other words, Husserl and Heidegger agree that the world is to be constituted. They disagree in that Heidegger, in opposition to Husserl, claims that, in constituting the world, man always finds the world already there, because it is a constitutive component of his own Being of which he always has already a pre-ontological understanding. This is the deepest reason why a hermeneutic phenomenology is to be substituted for Husserl's transcendental phenomenology.

With respect to the famous "*Kehre*" to which I referred at the beginning of this section, it seems reasonable to assume with Gethmann that the reversal refers not to a breach in Heidegger's thinking, but rather to a decisive characteristic of Heidegger's thought taken as a whole. The reversal refers to the necessity of thought's turning from a concern with Being from the perspective of Dasein to a concern with Being itself, i.e., to the coming-to-pass of Being's truth.[69] Furthermore, it is then also reasonable to assume that the reversal does not imply a denial of Heidegger's earlier investigations concerning the method of ontology. On the contrary, his concern with method is a necessary condition for the proper understanding of the meaning of the reversal. Yet it is true that Heidegger in his later philosophy no longer is concerned with the scientificity of philosophy, so that his concern with the method of thought is then to be understood from the perspective of the requirements that must be met by a form of thinking that makes a serious effort to listen to the saying of Being. Finally, it is reasonable to state that no one will properly understand what Heidegger means by "thought" if he does not first begin with a careful study of *Being and Time* which, as far as the question of method is concerned, constitutes Heidegger's attempt to come to an authentic stance in regard to the transcendental philosophies of both Kant and Husserl.[70] Yet one should note that if in the later works there appears the possibility of a thinking of the truth of Being which no longer thinks within the context of the categorial-ontological perspective of fundamental ontology, this thinking no longer can be called hermeneutical, although it can still be called phenomenological. But this does not change the fact that the later Heidegger obviously maintained the hermeneutic character of all human understanding.[71]

CHAPTER III

BEING-IN-THE-WORLD
AND
THE HERMENEUTIC CHARACTER OF
MAN'S UNDERSTANDING AS SUCH

In this chapter I wish to focus on a few themes developed in *Being and Time* with which the reader should be familiar if he is to understand Heidegger's conception of the natural and the historical sciences. Here, too, I shall limit myself to what seems essential to our present purpose. Thus I shall make a few observations on Heidegger's conception of the essence of man, the relationship between theoretical knowledge and concernful preoccupation, Heidegger's conception of understanding (*Verstehen*), and of the meaning and function of the hermeneutic circle, his view on the relation between realism and idealism, and his conception of truth. The choice of these themes will become understandable from the content of the chapters to follow. I plan to conclude this chapter with a brief reflection on regional ontologies.

8: DASEIN, EK-SISTENCE, BEING-IN-THE-WORLD

We have seen already that in Heidegger's view man has some comprehension of Being even before he poses the question of Being. In his most casual contacts with the things and with his fellowmen man experiences that these beings are sufficiently open to him so that he may realize that they are and somehow comprehend what they are. However, this radical comprehension of the Being of beings is for that reason not yet seized in clear concepts. This comprehension is still pre-conceptual and for the most part unarticulated. And yet it is this pre-conceptual comprehension of Being that makes the Being question possible. The task to be pursued in ontology in regard to the Being question can thus

DASEIN, EK-SISTENCE, BEING-IN-THE-WORLD

be reduced to this: what is the essence of the comprehension of Being which is obviously rooted so deeply in man's Being?[1]

It is this comprehension of Being that for Heidegger most profoundly characterizes man. "Man is a being who is immersed among beings in such a way that the beings which he is not, as well as the being that he is himself, have already become constantly manifest to him."[2] This fact explains why Heidegger prefers to designate the questioner by a term which suggests this unique privilege, namely Dasein, the There-Being. Dasein is to be understood here ontologically, not in an anthropological manner. Dasein is to be understood as an irruption into the totality of beings by reason of which these beings as beings become manifest.[3] In other words, Dasein is the *There* of Being among beings. It lets beings be; it makes them manifest, rendering all encounters with them possible. Correlative to the referential dependence of Dasein on beings, there is a dependence of beings on Dasein such that it allows them to be manifest. In letting beings be, Dasein does not create things, but only discovers them as what they really are. If it is by the irruption of Dasein among beings that these become manifest, then there is no difficulty in understanding how Dasein lets these beings be. In letting them be (manifest), it liberates them from concealment and places them in the non-concealment (*aletheia*), and thus renders them free.

The comprehension of Being which is the most profound characteristic of man, is not to be understood in terms of a kind of theoretical knowledge; it belongs to the very mode of Being of man that he is capable of comprehending Being. In other words, the comprehending relationship to Being constitutes the very ontological structure of Dasein. Heidegger refers to this ontological structure with the expression "eksistence." This term is to be understood here literally and expresses the fact that Dasein stands-out; as an eksisting subject Dasein places itself outside itself in the world; Dasein stands out toward the things in the world and toward the world itself. That is why Heidegger also uses the expression: Being-in-the-world. As eksistent man is *lumen naturale*: he originates meaning in everything he does, by letting things be what they are.[4] In view of the fact that in comprehending the Being of beings Dasein passes beyond the beings to Being itself, Heidegger also uses the expression "transcendence" instead of eksistence. "What is transcended is precisely and uniquely the beings themselves, every being that can be and become unhidden to Dasein, hence even, and indeed most of all, that being which eksists as itself."⁵ Thus it is in transcendence that the comprehension of the Being of beings is achieved.⁶ Transcendence is the coming-to-pass of our ontological understanding. This coming-to-pass is inherently finite as well as temporal. It continues dynamically but it is never completed.

The finitude of man's transcendence can be made explicit by pointing to the fact that Dasein dwells in the midst of beings and is engaged in continual comportment with them. Dasein is essentially referred to beings. It is dependent upon them and can never completely become their master. In most cases Dasein is even lost in its commerce with beings. Heidegger refers to this aspect of Dasein's finitude with the term "fallenness." But Dasein is even less powerful with regard to itself. Dasein is not the source of its own Being; rather it finds itself as an already eksisting being, immersed in its original situation as a comprehension of the Being of beings. Thus its origin as well as its destiny are obscure.⁷ Heidegger refers to this aspects of man's finitude with the expression "thrownness." Finally, because Dasein in its comprehending of Being, in which the innermost ground of Dasein consists, is so profoundly finite, its own eksistence hides within itself a need of its own: the need for a continued comprehension in order that it be itself, in order that it eksists. The essence of this being lies in its to-be; Dasein's eksistence comprises equally the power and the compulsion to be as well as the comprehension of Being.⁸

9: CONCERN AND THEORETICAL KNOWLEDGE

We have seen that Dasein as Being-in-the-world is a being which in its very Being comports itself understandingly towards that Being. Furthermore, Dasein is also a being which in each case I myself am. Ipseity belongs to any eksisting Dasein and belongs to it as the condition which makes authenticity and inauthenticity possible. In each case Dasein eksists either authentically or inauthentically depending upon whether it cares for its own genuine self or loses itself in the world of intramundane things. But both of these possibilities are grounded in that mode of Being which was called Being-in-the-world.

In the compound expression "Being-in-the-world" which stands here nonetheless for a unitary phenomenon, the word "in" does not indicate any spatial relationship. Man is not in the world as the table is in the room. The word "in" rather has the meaning here of "being familiar with" or "being accustomed to." Thus

CONCERN AND THEORETICAL KNOWLEDGE 75

Dasein is, essentially seen, familiar with the world and this Being-alongside-the-world means concretely and factically that Dasein is normally absorbed in the world (fallenness). Dasein's factical mode of Being is such that its Being-in-the-world has always dispersed itself or even split itself up into definite ways of Being-in. The multiplicity of these ways can be clarified by the following examples: having to do with, producing, attending, looking after, accomplishing, evincing, interrogating, considering, discussing, determining, etc. All these ways of Being-in have concern (*Besorgen*) as their common kind of Being. All concrete forms of Being-in can be characterized generally as forms of concern.

Classical philosophy almost without exception has assumed that knowing the world theoretically is the original and basic mode of Dasein's concern; and Dasein itself according to its own facticity shares this view, namely that knowing the world is the fundamental mode of its own Being-in-the-world. The ontological structure of Dasein, namely its Being-in-the-world, was never explicitly explained either in classical philosophy or in Dasein's everyday understanding. That is why many people have thought of knowledge in terms of a relation which exists between one entity (the world) and another entity (the soul or the mind), both according to their own modes of Being understood as merely present-at-hand. Thus, in every metaphysics of knowledge a subject-object-opposition is presupposed. For what is more obvious than that in knowledge a "subject" is related to an "object"? Thus, the encompassing phenomenon of Being-in-the-world has for the most part been represented exclusively by one single example: knowing the world theoretically. Because knowing has been given the priority here, our understanding of Dasein's mode of Being was led astray. That is why we must show now that knowing-the-world is really a founded mode of Dasein's Being-in.[9]

In traditional epistemology there is first given a being called "nature"; this being is given proximally as that which becomes known. Knowing as such is not to be found in this entity. Knowing belongs solely to those entities who know. But even in these entities, namely human beings, knowing is not present-at-hand and externally ascertainable as bodily properties are. Now, inasmuch as knowing belongs to these entities, it must be inside of them. But if knowing is proximally and really inside, the problem concerning the relation between subject and object emerges immediately. For only then can the problem arise of how this knowing subject comes out of its inner "sphere" into one which is "other and external," of how knowing can have any object at all, and of how one must think of the object itself so that eventually the subject knows it without needing to venture a leap into another sphere. But in any of the numerous varieties which this approach may take, the question of the kind of Being which belongs to this knowing subject is left entirely unasked, although whenever its knowing is examined, its manner of Being is already included tacitly in one's theme. Of course, we are sometimes assured that we are certainly not thinking of the subject's "inside" and its "inner sphere" as a sort of "box." But when one asks for the positive signification of this "inside" or immanence in which knowing is proximally enclosed, then silence reigns. And no matter how this inner sphere may be interpreted, if one does no more than ask how knowing makes its way "out of" it and achieves "transcendence," it becomes evident that the knowing which presents such enigmas will remain problematic unless one has previously clarified how it is and what it is.

With this kind of approach one remains blind to what is already tacitly implied even when one takes the phenomenon of knowing as one's theme in the most provisional manner: namely, that knowing is a mode of Being of Dasein taken as Being-in-the-world, and is founded ontically upon this state of Being.

If we now ask the question of what shows itself in the phenomenal findings about knowing, we must keep in mind that knowing is grounded beforehand in a Being-already-alongside-the-world, which is essentially constitutive for Dasein's Being. Proximally, this Being-already-alongside is not just a fixed staring at something that is purely present-at-hand. Being-in-the-world, as concern, is fascinated by the world with which it is concerned. If knowing is to be possible as a way of determining the nature of the present-at-hand by observing it, then there must first be a deficiency in our having-to-do with the world concernfully. When concern withdraws from any kind of producing, manipulating, etc., it puts itself into what is now the sole remaining mode of Being-in, the mode of just sojourning-alongside and dwelling-upon. This manner of Being toward the world is one which lets us encounter beings within-the-world purely in the way they look (*in ihrem Aussehen--eidos*). On the basis of this manner of Being and just as a mode of it, looking explicitly at that which we encounter is possible. Looking at something in this way is a definite way of taking up a direction towards something. It takes over a viewpoint in advance from the entity which it encounters. Such looking-at enters the mode of dwelling autonomously alongside beings within the world. In this kind of dwelling as holding-oneself-back from any manipulation or utilization, the perception of the present-at-hand is consummated. Perception is consummated when one addresses oneself to something and discusses it as such. This amounts to interpretation in the broadest sense which implies determination and expression with the help of propositions. But in all these cases knowing is not to be conceived of as a procedure by which a subject provides itself with representations of something which remain stored up inside as having been thus definitely appropriated, and with regard to which the question is to be put of how they agree with actual reality.

When Dasein directs itself toward something and grasps it, it does not somehow first go out from an inner sphere in which it has been proximally encapsulated, but its primary manner of Being is such that it is always "outside," alongside beings which it encounters and which belong to the world already discovered. And furthermore, the perceiving of what is known is not a process of returning with one's booty to the inner box of consciousness after one has gone out in order to grasp it. Even in perceiving, retaining, and preserving, Dasein which knows, remains outside, and it does so as Dasein. In knowing, Dasein achieves a new status of Being towards the world which has already been discovered in Dasein itself. This new possibility of Being can develop autonomously; it can become a task to be accomplished in the different sciences. But a commercium of the subject with a world does not get created for the first time by knowing, nor does it arise from some way in which the world acts upon a subject. Knowing the world is a mode of Dasein's Being which is founded upon its Being-in-the-world.[10]

In this passage Heidegger really accomplishes two different but closely related things which are of vital importance for a correct understanding of man. First of all, he tries to show that knowing-the-world-theoretically is a derivative mode of man's Being-in-the-world. If knowing-the-world is a special mode of our Being-in-the-world, then it can be shown easily that the subject-object-opposition is not a fundamental datum of our immediate experience. This opposition comes about merely on the level of reflection. Furthermore, if the subject-object opposition is not fundamental, it is easy to show that the famous epistemological problem with which Descartes and Kant struggled is really a pseudo-problem.

But in addition to this first thesis, namely that theoretically knowing-the-world is only one particular mode of Dasein's concern for the world, Heidegger also tries to show that in man's primordial concern with the world there is found a kind of "knowledge" which is quite different from what we normally call "knowledge," namely theoretical and scientific knowledge. Heidegger shows the difference between our concernfully knowing the world and our theoretical knowledge of the world not only from the viewpoint of man's approach to the world, but also from the viewpoint of the world itself. He carefully analyzes the difference which undeniably exists between the world of Dasein's everyday concern and the derivative world as found in the sciences. The primordial world has its center in Dasein itself and originally coincides with our personal environment (*Umwelt*) insofar as this is experienced in our concernful dealing with the things and our fellow-men in the world. Heidegger shows convincingly that the things found in our world are given primarily not as physical objects which are simply lying there "before our hands" (*vorhanden*), but as usable things or utensils of some kind, as equipment which refers to possible applications within a "practical" world and, thus, as "ready-to-hand" (*zuhanden*). Things of this kind inherently refer to one another and form systems of mutual references of meaning. World and things are very closely related here, and yet the world itself is not a thing, nor the sum of all things, but rather the totality of meaning toward which all equipment points by its very structure. What we call the world is the totality of all mutual reference-systems within which every thing is capable of appearing to man as having a determinate meaning (*Sinn*).[11]

10: HEIDEGGER'S CONCEPTION OF *VERSTEHEN*

We have just seen that according to Heidegger the relationship between man and world which manifests itself in man's concernful dealing with things, implies a kind of knowledge, but that this knowledge, originally at least, is not yet theoretical knowledge. In trying to explain man's primordial way of knowing, namely that which is inherent to Dasein's concern, Heidegger describes man's Being as a structural unity which implies three different elements: mood (*Befindlichkeit*), understanding (*Verstehen*), and *logos* (*Rede*). We must now turn to a brief reflection on two of these "eksistentials" which constitute Dasein's "There." An eksistential is thus a basic "category" of the mode of Being of man, taken as Dasein.

It is not easy to say what the ontological structure of "original mood" precisely is because our thematic knowledge of all that is connected with man's "emotional life" is rather vague. Undoubtedly, mood communicates to us something about our own mode of Being in relationship to the world. But it is difficult in each case to determine why one is disposed or "tuned" in a determinate way, and what this disposition tells us about ourselves and about the world. Original mood informs man about his position in the midst of things in the world. Different elements which can be distinguished are contained in this "insight." First of all, in his mood man is aware of his own being. Without wanting it, and without having chosen it freely, man is. His being appears to him as a being-thrown; he appears to himself as thrown among things. In mood, man not only becomes aware of the fact that he is, but also of the fact that he "has to be," that his being is to be realized by himself as a task.

Secondly, the determinate mood a man is in, depends on the modalities of the involvement which he always has with things in the world. Thus mood is an implicit, but continuous "judgment" regarding his own self-realization. Hence man can be disclosed to himself in a more primordial way through mood than through theoretical reflection. However, if it is true that man eksists and is as Being-in-the-world, then mood must also disclose to him his relationships with other men and with things.

Thirdly, it was previously mentioned that in his everyday concern man encounters intramundane things as emerging from the horizon of the world, taken as a referential totality. But this is possible only if the world has been disclosed as such beforehand. It is precisely because the world is given to man beforehand that it is possible for man to encounter intramundane things as such. This prior disclosedness of the world is constituted by one's mood; that man is openness in the direction of the "other" in the world is given to him in the most original way through that fundamental feeling of his "Being-there."[12]

Man not only possesses an eksistential possibility of being always in a mood, his mode of Being is determined equiprimordially by his understanding (*Verstehen*). Understanding is not to be conceived of here as a concrete mode of knowing, but precisely as that which makes all concrete modes of knowing possible. On the level of our everyday life this primordial understanding is always present in mood, and all understanding in its turn is connected with mood.

Thus, original understanding has not so much reference to this or that concrete thing or situation as to the mode of Being which is characteristic of man as Being-in-the-world. In original understanding the mode of Being characteristic of man manifests itself as "being-able-to . . ." However, man is not something present-at-hand that possesses its being-able-to . . . by way of an extra; he himself is primarily a being-able-to-be. This being-able-to-be, which is essential for man, has reference to all the various ways of his being concerned for others and with things, and of his concern with the world. But, in all this, man always realizes in one way or another his being-able-to-be in regard to himself and for the sake of himself.

Original understanding thus always pertains to Dasein's Being-in-the-world as a whole. That is why Dasein's moodful understanding brings to light not only man himself as being-able-to-be, but also the world as a referential totality. By revealing the world to man, his primordial understanding also gives him the possibility of encountering intramundane things in their own possibilities. That which originally was ready-to-hand is now explicitly discovered in its serviceability, usability, and so on.

Accordingly, primordial understanding always moves in a range of possibilities; it continuously endeavors to discover possibilities, because it possesses in itself the eksistential structure of a "project." In its primordial understanding Dasein projects itself onto its ultimate "for the sake of which"; but this self-projection necessarily implies at the same time--and equally primordially--a world projection. In his original understanding man thus opens himself in the direction of his own Being but, at the same time, also in the direction of the world. For this reason primordial understanding implies essentially an antecedent view, an anticipatory "sighting" of things, of fellowmen, of the world as a whole, and obviously also of his own mode of Being. To the extent that man's view is concerned with equipment, fellowmen, himself, or the world as a whole, this antecedent and anticipating "sight" can appear in different modalities. The important point here is to note that for Heidegger *Verstehen* implies, first of all, that the one who understands grasps by anticipation the structure of a being still to be encountered and, secondly, that during the encounter the grasp which was anticipated is explicitly achieved according to the predetermined plan as dictated by the primordial constitution of Dasein itself.[13]

Primordial understanding, which is inseparably connected with mood, always has the character of an anticipating,

HEIDEGGER'S CONCEPTION OF "VERSTEHEN" 81

interpretative conception in which Dasein discloses itself as being-able-to-be in the different modalities that are possible for it, modalities to which different possibilities correspond with respect to its equipment, fellowmen, or the world. But this interpretative conception is as such not yet explicitly articulated in understanding. However, it can develop in that direction by means of *Auslegung*, a term which means explanation as well as interpretation. In and through interpretative explanation Dasein's understanding appropriates comprehendingly that which is already understood by it. Interpretative explanation is the development of the possibilities that in anticipation were projected in understanding itself.[14]

What is meant here can perhaps be explained best by taking one's point of departure in man's everyday concernful dealing with things. Suppose we enter the workshop of a carpenter who is in the process of making a table. In his work, i.e., his concernful dealing with the intramundane things found in his workshop, the carpenter is guided by a certain kind of understanding to which Heidegger refers with the term "circumspection." His circumspection discovers the intramundane things in the shop by setting them apart and interpreting them. What originally was ready-to-hand circumspectively in its serviceability, i.e., in its "in order to," is to be set apart and to be taken *as* this or that. That which has been set apart in this way in regard to its in-order-to, thereby receives the structure of "something taken *as* something." To the circumspective question as to what this particular ready-to-hand thing may be, the circumspectively interpretative answer is that it serves such and such purpose. By explicitly pointing to what a thing is for, we do not simply designate that thing; what is so designated is understood as that as which we are to take that particular thing. This hermeneutic *as* constitutes the structure of the explicitness of each thing that is circumspectively understood. In other words, the hermeneutic *as* is the constitutive element of what Heidegger calls interpretative explanation. If in dealing with what is environmentally ready-to-hand we interpret it circumspectively, we take it, we "see" it *as* a hammer, the top of the table, the drawer. However, what is thus interpreted need not necessarily be taken apart in an explicit enunciation (*Aussage*). Any mere prepredicative using and thus "seeing" of what is ready-to-hand is in itself already something that understands interpretatively. The articulation of what is understood in the interpretation of each intramundane thing with the help of the guiding clue "something as something" is there before any explicit statement is made about it. Thus the hermeneutic *as* does not emerge for the first time in the explicit statements we make about things; the *as* gets merely expressed and enunciated in them.[15]

If we never perceive intramundane things which are ready-to-hand without already understanding and interpreting them, and if all perception lets us circumspectively encounter something *as* something, does this not mean that at first something purely present-at-hand is experienced and is later interpreted as a hammer, a top, a table? Evidently this is not the case. Man's interpretation does not throw meaning over some naked thing that is merely present-at-hand, nor does it place a value on it. The intramundane thing that is encountered as this or as that in our original understanding, which is characteristic of our concernful dealing with things, already possesses a reference that is implicitly contained in our co-understanding of the world; that is why we can articulate and interpret it as this or as that. In our original understanding that which is ready-to-hand is always already understood from a totality of references which we call our "world"; but this relationship between what is ready-to-hand and the world need not be grasped explicitly in a thematic interpretation and explanation, although such an interpretative explanation is evidently, in principle, always possible. If such a thematic interpretation occurs, it is always on the basis of our original understanding. Thus we may say that the fact that we "have" intramundane things, that we take and "see" them in this way or in another, and "conceive" of them on the basis of our interpretation of them, must be founded in an earlier "having," an earlier "seeing," and an earlier "conception," all of which are constitutive for our original understanding. Heidegger refers to this fact with the expression: our *hermeneutic situation*. Since the hermeneutic situation plays an important role in his conception of the hermeneutic circle, I shall return to it in the next section.[16]

We have seen that in the pro-ject (*Ent-wurf*) characteristic of our original understanding, a thing becomes disclosed in its possibilities. The character of these possibilities corresponds in each case to the mode of Being of the thing which is so understood. Intramundane things are necessarily projected upon the world, i.e., upon a whole context of meaning, a totality of references to which Dasein's concern as Being-in-the-world has been tied in advance. When an intramundane thing is discovered and comes to be understood, we say that it has meaning. But what is understood is, strictly speaking, not the meaning but the thing itself. Meaning is that in which the intelligibility of something maintains itself. Thus, meaning is that which can be articulated in the disclosure of man's understanding. The concept of meaning contains the formal framework of what necessarily belongs to that which can be articulated by our interpretative understanding. Meaning is a project's "upon-which," which can be structured by our understanding and from which each thing *as* this or that can be understood. Meaning is therefore the intentional correlate of the disclosedness which necessarily belongs to our original understanding. Thus, strictly speaking, only the mode of Being characteristic of Dasein "has" meaning insofar as the disclosedness of Being-in-the-world can be "filled" by the things which are discoverable in that disclosedness. In other words, there can be a question of meaning only within the dialogue between Dasein and the things in the world. This is also why in each understanding of the world, Dasein's eksistence is co-understood and *vice versa*.[17]

All interpretative explanation is rooted in the original understanding characteristic of Dasein's concern. That which is articulated in interpretative explanation and thus was already predelineated in the original understanding as something which can be articulated, is what Heidegger calls "meaning." Insofar as enunciation, as a derivative mode of interpretative explanation, is also grounded in our primordial understanding, it too has meaning; but this meaning cannot be defined as that which is found in Dasein's enunciation along with the enunciating act.

An explicit analysis of our enunciations or statements can take different directions. One can focus first on the fact that enunciations have three different, but closely related functions: they point out something, they attribute something to something, and they communicate something to someone. Heidegger analyzes these three functions carefully and points out that in each case he adheres strictly to the original meaning of *logos* as *apophansis*, i.e., as letting things be seen from themselves, as letting something which was already somehow manifest be seen in its further determinateness, and letting someone see with us what we have pointed out by determining it. Secondly, he strongly stresses the point that in pointing-out, attributing, and communicating we refer to the things themselves and not to representations of them taken either as represented things or as the psychic states of the person who utters the enunciation.[18]

In the second place, one can try to show how in an enunciating act the structure of the hermeneutic *as*, which is constitutive for our understanding and interpretative explanation, becomes modified by the enunciating act. In his attempt to explain this aspect of the issue Heidegger states that enunciation is a derivative mode of interpretative explanation because the latter does not come about originally in a theoretical, predicative judgment, but is already present in our concernful dealing with things. The problem is one of identifying the modification through which enunciation originates from our concernful, interpretative understanding. In our primordial concern an intended thing is ready-to-hand as a piece of equipment. If this thing becomes the object of enunciation, then along with the enunciation a modification of the character of the intentional orientation must first be enacted. The ready-to-hand with which we were originally concerned in our practical achievements changes now into something about which we are going to enunciate something. The necessary condition for this is that we orient ourselves intentionally in that which is ready-to-hand toward a certain presence-at-hand. Through this new way of looking-at, which we have mentioned earlier, that which at first was ready-to-hand becomes now concealed as ready-to-hand. Within the discovering of a thing's presence-at-hand, which at the same time is the concealing of its readiness-to-hand, the thing which is encountered as present-at-hand becomes determined as present-at-hand in such and such a manner. Only at this moment are we given any access to "properties" or the like, which evidently are drawn from that which is present-at-hand as such.

In other words the hermeneutic *as* structure which we have already met in explanation, undergoes a typical modification in enunciation. The hermeneutic *as*, whose function was to appropriate what was understood, no longer refers to the totality of references within which our primordial concern comes about. As far as its possibilities for further articulation are concerned, the hermeneutic *as* is now cut off from the referential totality that constitutes the world of my concern, and is pushed back into the homogeneous domain of what is merely present-at-hand. Therefore, the apophantic *as* characteristic of the enunciation has as its function only the determining letting be seen of what is present-at-hand. This leveling of the hermeneutic *as* characteristic of circumspective, interpretative explanation, to the apophantic *as* in which something is determined in its presence-at-hand is the specifying characteristic of our enunciations. For it is only in this way that the possibility of a pointing-out which merely "looks at" comes about.[19]

It is to be noted that between our concernful understanding of what is ready-to-hand (in which the interpretative explanation, as it were, is still implicit) and the extreme opposite, namely the purely theoretical enunciation of what is merely present-at-hand (in which our interpretative explanation is clearly articulated) there are many intermediate forms. A careful analysis of these forms is of great importance for philosophy of language, but need not occupy us here.

Concluding these reflections we may say that in Heidegger's opinion all understanding (*Verstehen*) is interpretation. The interpretation may be implicit as in our concernful dealing with things, or explicit as in our interpretative explanation and enunciation. The deepest root of the hermeneutic character of all human understanding is to be found in the fact that all understanding necessarily takes place in the hermeneutic situation. For Dasein, understanding is impossible except on the basis of a fore-having, a fore-sight, and a fore-conception because of the fact that its transcendence is inherently finite and temporal. Furthermore, Heidegger argues, anyone who wishes to give a justification for his interpretation must do so by clarifying the "presuppositions" which are inherent in the hermeneutic situation, both in a basic experience of the thing to be disclosed, and in terms of such an experience.[20]

11: INTERPRETATIVE UNDERSTANDING AND THE HERMENEUTIC CIRCLE

Most logicians adopt a negative attitude in regard to the circle as a mode of thought. Their attitude is completely justified as long as one limits himself to a circle occurring in a formal argument or to the circle in our defining of concepts. Those who adopt a more positive attitude in regard to the circle usually limit its use to cases in which a study is to be made of phenomena which appear to imply antinomic oppositions. If opposites are to be overcome and, thus, some identification is to be accomplished, the combination of the antinomic elements can generally be attempted from the viewpoint of one member as well as from that of the other; then circular propositions often emerge. We have seen that in Heidegger's case the circle becomes a structural element of each human act of understanding as such. The hermeneutic circle is an inherent element of any attempt to interpretatively understand phenomena. For the interpretative explanation of phenomena is possible only insofar as the one who understands brings with him from his own point of view a certain preunderstanding of this phenomenon and of the context in which it manifests itself. By interpreting the new phenomenon from this perspective, an understanding of this phenomenon can be achieved which in turn will change and deepen the original perspective from which the interpretation was made. Here insights which Schleiermacher had suggested in connection with the question concerning the conditions of text interpretation are applied by Heidegger to the act of human understanding as such and to man's philosophic understanding in particular.[21]

Already on the very first pages of *Being and Time* Heidegger brings up the hermeneutic circle as an essential element of philosophical discourse. There he states that he wishes to work out the question concerning the meaning of Being, but that this can be done only by first giving a proper explanation of a being, namely Dasein, with regard to its mode of Being. After making this statement he continues: "Is there not, however, a manifest circularity in such an undertaking? If we must first define a thing *in its Being*, and if we want to formulate the question of Being *only on this basis*, what is this but going in a circle?"[22] Heidegger points out first that there is no circle at all in formulating his basic concern as he has described it. For one can determine the mode of Being characteristic of a thing without having an explicit concept of the meaning of Being at one's disposal. For if this were not the case, no ontological knowledge would ever have been possible. But the fact that there has been such knowledge cannot be denied. In all ontology "Being" has obviously been presupposed, but not as a concept at one's disposal. "The presupposing of Being has the character of taking a look at it beforehand, so that in the light of it the things presented to us get provisionally articulated in their Being. This guiding activity of taking a (provisional) look at Being arises from the average understanding of Being in which we always operate and which in the end belongs to the essential constitution of Dasein itself."[23]

On several occasions in *Being and Time* Heidegger returns to the problems which the hermeneutic circle seems to cause. We have already pointed to the fact that in Heidegger's view any genuine act of understanding implies interpretation, and that interpretation is impossible except on the basis of certain "presuppositions." As we have seen, these presuppositions which constitute the hermeneutic situation, are characterized by the technical terms "fore-having," "fore-sight," and "fore-conception."

INTERPRETATIVE UNDERSTANDING

Anyone who tries to understand a human phenomenon, necessarily presupposes a totality of meaning or "world" within which, in his view, this phenomenon can appear as meaningful (fore-having). Secondly, he assumes a certain point of view which fixes that with regard to which what is to be understood is to be interpreted (fore-sight). Finally, one tries to articulate one's understanding of that phenomenon with the help of concepts which are either drawn from the phenomenon itself, or are forced upon it, as it were, from the outside. In either case, the interpretative understanding has already decided for a definite way of conceiving of it (fore-conception).[24] The important point, in Heidegger's view, is that such an interpretation is never a presuppositionless apprehending of something presented to us. True, our interpretation does not "constitute" the meaning things and phenomena have for us; but it is true that the meaning of things receives its structure and articulation from our fore-having, fore-sight, and fore-conception.[25]

One of the basic characteristics of philosophical discourse is that, although it itself, too, is subject to the hermeneutic situation, it conceives of its task as to clarify and give a foundation to the totality of the presuppositions which constitute our hermeneutic situation in each case. But if this is indeed so, then it is obvious that philosophy itself will again encounter the circle. As Heidegger sees it, if the problematic of fundamental ontology is to have its hermeneutic situation clarified, one has to ask the question of whether its method implies a circular argument. One could argue that using a type of circular interpretation implies that one presupposes the idea of Being and that Dasein's Being gets interpreted accordingly, so that then the idea of Being may be obtained from it. Heidegger does not deny that in his analysis he presupposed some understanding of Dasein's Being and of Being itself, but he denies that this process implies positing one or more propositions from which further propositions about Dasein's Being and Being itself are to be deduced. On the contrary, "this presupposing has the character of an understanding projection," this projection makes possible an interpretation which lets "that which is to be interpreted put itself into words for the very first time, so that it may decide of its own accord whether as the being which it is, it has the state of Being as which it has been disclosed in the projection as far as its formal aspects are concerned." In other words in an eksistential analytic one cannot but avoid the logical circle and a circular proof for the simple reason that such an analysis does not do any proving at all by the rules of logic. Furthermore Dasein is primordially constituted by care; but as such it is already ahead of itself. It has in every case already projected itself upon definite possibilities; and in such eksistential projections it has, in a pre-ontological manner, also projected its own mode of Being and Being itself. And yet, Heidegger continues, we object to the circle not only on logical grounds, we also object to it in that it seems contrary to our common sense conception of what it means to "understand something." But, he continues,

> [w]hen one speaks about the "circle" in understanding, one expresses the failure to recognize two things: (1) that understanding as such makes up a basic kind of Dasein's Being, and (2) that this Being is constituted as care. To deny the circle . . . means finally to reinforce this failure. We must rather endeavor to leap into the "circle," primordially and wholly, so that even at the start of the analysis of Dasein we make sure that we have a full view of Dasein's circular Being. If, in the ontology of Dasein, we take our departure, from a worldless "I" in order to provide this "I" with an object and an ontologically baseless relation to that object, then we have presupposed not too much, but *too little* [Husserl]. If we make a problem of "life," and then just occasionally we have regard for death too, our view is *too short-sighted* [Dilthey]. The object we have taken as our theme is artificially and dogmatically curtailed if "in the first instance" we restrict ourselves to a "theoretical subject," in order that we may then round it out "on the practical side" by tacking on an "ethic." This may suffice to clarify the eksistential meaning of the hermeneutic situation of a primordial analytic of Dasein.[26]

It seems to me that in those passages Heidegger has shown not only that the hermeneutic circle is essential to all ontological inquiry, but also that this circle does not have to lead to relativism in that ontology makes it its task to clarify, and give a radical foundation to, the totality of presuppositions which constitute our hermeneutic situation in each case.

12: DASEIN AND REALITY: NEITHER REALISM NOR IDEALISM

In classical metaphysics, the understanding of Being was, according to Heidegger, oriented onesidedly to the mode of Being

DASEIN AND REALITY

of innerworldly beings. Furthermore, too much attention was paid there to what is present-at-hand--to such an extent even that being was identified with thing (*res*). Thus, being acquired the sense of reality (a term derived from the word "*res*"). Since Dasein was considered there in the same perspective, it too was conceived like all other beings, as a real thing that is merely present-at-hand.[27] In this way the concept of reality received a peculiar priority over all other concepts in the ontological problems with which classical metaphysics concerned itself.

This priority, in turn, had several important consequences for classical metaphysics. First of all, Dasein's own mode of Being could no longer correctly be understood. Furthermore, the problematic of Being was forced into an entirely wrong direction because classical metaphysics did not start from a primordially given phenomenon.

Moreover, in the problem of reality several issues were mixed and thereby confused. (1) Those beings which supposedly transcend consciousness, are they indeed actually real? (2) Can we adequately prove the reality of the "external world"? (3) To what extent can this being, insofar as it is real, be known in its being-in-itself? (4) What is the profound meaning of this being called "reality"?

From an ontological point of view the last of these questions is undoubtedly the most important one. Nevertheless it has never been clearly formulated because it has always been associated with the problem of the external world. That this could happen is, although objectionable, quite understandable. For the analysis and description of reality are obviously possible only if Dasein has an appropriate access to reality. Now, according to the commonly accepted view, philosophy has long held that reality can be understood only and exclusively by theoretical knowledge which, as we have just seen, takes place "in" consciousness. Thus, insofar as reality has the character of being something independent of consciousness and of something in itself, the question of the meaning of reality becomes necessarily linked with the question of whether reality can be independent of consciousness, and whether consciousness is able to transcend itself and to know the real world the way it is "in itself." The possibility of an adequate ontological analysis of reality, therefore, depended for centuries upon how far that which is supposed to transcend itself (namely consciousness) has been clarified in its own mode of Being. In the attempt to do so consciousness was quite arbitrarily understood as a "thinking substance," so that the radical clarification of consciousness was to be identified with the radical clarification of consciousness' knowledge.[28]

In the problem of knowledge, traditional metaphysics since Descartes has always separated subject and object. It is, however, not difficult to understand that whoever adopts such a point of view must, sooner or later, in some way or other, hit upon Descartes' epistemological problem. For whoever conceives of the world as independent of man necessarily throws man back upon himself. If one then speaks of knowledge of the world, he must interpret such knowledge as a special process taking place "within" consciousness. And the more univocally one maintains that knowledge is really "inside" consciousness and has by no means the same kind of Being as the intramundane things, the more reasonable and urgent the question concerning the clarification of the relationship between subject and object appears to become. For only then can the problem arise of how this knowing subject is able to come out of its inner sphere into another which is "external" to it, and of how one must think of the object itself so that the subject is able to know it without having to take a jump into that other sphere. But in all of the numerous varieties which this approach has taken, in the rationalist as well as in the empiricist tradition, the question concerning the mode of Being characteristic of the knowing subject, that is consciousness or mind, has been left entirely unasked, as we have seen already. Furthermore, one is also confronted with the question of how one can show that this process "inside" man can give reliable knowledge about the "outside world." The existence of this world, finally, is simply postulated without any justification whatsoever.

On the other hand, if knowing is viewed as a way of Being-in-the-world, then it does not have to be interpreted as a process in which the subject makes "representations" of "outside" things that are kept "inside" himself. And the question of how these "representations" can agree with reality then becomes a meaningless question.[29] Moreover, the questions of whether there really is a world and whether its reality can be proven, become, likewise, meaningless as questions asked by Dasein whose mode of Being is Being-in-the-world. And who else but Dasein could possibly ask such questions or try to answer them?[30]

The confusion of what one wants to prove with what one does prove, and with the means to carry out the proof, manifests itself very clearly in Kant's "Refutation of Idealism." According to Kant, it is a scandal of philosophy that the cogent proof for the existence of things outside us has not yet been delivered. But

DASEIN AND REALITY

for Heidegger, the basic error of all attempts to find such a proof lies in the fact that they start from the supposition that man is originally "world-less" and that he, therefore, has to assure himself somehow of the world's existence in and through philosophical reflection. Being-in-the-world then becomes something that is based on opinion, reasoning, belief, or some kind of "knowing already," whereas all knowledge is precisely a mode of Dasein's Being, based on Being-in-the-world.

Accordingly, the problem of reality as the question of whether there is an "outside world" reveals itself as an impossible question, not because its consequences lead to insurmountable difficulties, but because the beings themselves considered in that question exclude such a problematic. One does not have to prove that and why there is an "outside world," but one has to explain why Dasein as Being-in-the-world tends first to bury the "outside world" epistemologically, in order then to prove its existence. Heidegger feels that the explanation for this state of affairs is to be found in Dasein's fallenness, for in fallenness Dasein's primary understanding of Being is diverted to beings which are already there.[31]

Heidegger's standpoint is in agreement with that of realism insofar as it does not deny in any way that innerworldly beings are there; but it is in disagreement with it insofar as realism thinks that the reality of the world can and must be proved. In principle, Heidegger even has a measure of preference for the standpoint of idealism because idealism clearly realizes that Being cannot be explained in terms of beings. However, even though Being cannot be explained in terms beings, we still have the obligation to investigate the Being of consciousness, the question of the mode of Being of the *res cogitans*. Only because Being is "in consciousness," i.e., is understandable by Dasein, can Dasein understand and conceptualize such characteristics as the independence of Being, its "in itself" so to speak, its reality.

If, then, idealism amounts to realizing that Being cannot be understood and explained in terms of beings, that Being is "transcendental" with respect to every being, then idealism offers the only possibility to posit the problem in a genuinely philosophical manner. But in that case Aristotle was just as much an idealist as Kant. If, however, on the other hand, idealism amounts to reducing all Being to a subject or a consciousness, then idealism is just as naive as the most superficial form of realism.[32]

Accordingly, we must conclude that the problem of reality, no matter how it is approached, is to be included in Dasein's eksistential analysis as an ontological problem, and not merely as an epistemological issue. If the term "reality" indicates the Being of the innerworldly beings, the *res* that is just there (and it would be very difficult to assign any other sense to it), then, as far as the analysis of Dasein's mode of Being which is called "knowing" is concerned, this means that the innerworldly beings can be ontologically understood only when the phenomenon of the world's worldlihood is explained. But this worldlihood is based on the phenomenon of the world, which, itself, as an essential aspect of the structure of Being-in-the-world, belongs to Dasein's fundamental constitution. Being-in-the-world, in turn, is ontologically tied up with the structural totality of Dasein's own mode of Being, which is to be characterized as care.

These reflections outline the foundations and horizons which must be clarified if an analysis of "reality" is to be possible.[33] As an ontological term, "reality" refers to innerworldly beings. If it is used only to signify this way of Being, then "merely being present-at-hand" and "being ready-to-hand" function as the modes of reality. No matter how one conceives of the mode of Being of "nature," all modes of Being of the innerworldly beings are ontologically founded in the worldlihood of the world and, consequently, in the phenomenon of Being-in-the-world itself.

Thus it follows that reality has no priority among the modes of Being of innerworldly beings and that reality is a mode of Being which is not even suited to characterize the world and Dasein. On the level of the interconnection of the beings in their ontological foundation and on the level of any possible categorial and eksistential explicitation, reality refers back to the phenomenon of care.

The statement that reality is ontologically rooted in Dasein's Being does not mean that an innerworldly being can be what it is in itself only when, and only as long as, Dasein eksists. Of course, it is true that only as long as Dasein is, i.e., as long as the understanding of Being is ontically possible, "is there" (*gibt es*) Being. If no Dasein eksists, "independence" "is" not either, nor "is" there an "in itself." In such a case, these expressions are neither understandable nor not understandable, since innerworldly beings can then neither be discovered nor lie hidden. In other words, one can say neither that they are, nor that they are not.

Accordingly, the dependence of Being (not the dependence of innerworldly beings) on the understanding of Being by Dasein, i.e., the dependence of reality (not the dependence of real beings) on care, intends to express only that beings as beings become accessible only when there is understanding of Being by Dasein. But now, since there are in fact beings that have Dasein's mode of Being, the understanding of Being is possible as a being.[34]

13: ON TRUTH

According to Heidegger, the fundamental question of what truth is can be approached in different ways, depending on one's point of departure. Because of the important discoveries that can be made by approaching truth from more than one point of view, Heidegger has incorporated the most important of these approaches in *Being and Time*. He starts there from what the analytic of Dasein's mode of Being has already disclosed and then concludes that precisely the phenomenon of truth is that which constitutes Dasein as Dasein. The phenomenological analysis of Dasein as Being-in-the-world and eksistence appears to lead of necessity to the essence of truth, and in this essence of truth Dasein's own mode of Being finds its radical explanation.

Heidegger comes to a similar conclusion in *On the Essence of Truth*[35] by a different and shorter way. Here he explicitly starts from the traditional definition of truth (which was also briefly discussed in *Being and Time*) as the conformity of intellect and thing (*adaequatio intellectus et rei*). After asking what precisely is to be understood by conformity, he tries to determine there how, ultimately, this conformity is intrinsically possible. Finally, he attempts to give a definitive foundation to this possibility.

In his latest works Heidegger endeavors to clarify the essence of truth from the history of the "clearing" of Being (*die Lichtungsgeschichte des Seins*),[36] i.e., from the essence of that to which, in the course of history, truth has led in the fields of science, art, technology, and philosophy.

The reflections on truth contained in *Being and Time* can be interpreted in two entirely different ways, insofar as Heidegger's conception of truth in 1927 still contained unresolved problems. One could conclude from the text of *Being and Time* that, according to Heidegger, the ultimate foundation of truth lies in Dasein's eksistence. However, reading the same text from the perspective of the *Letter on Humanism*,[37] it appears that Being itself is the ultimate foundation of truth, although this point is not yet explicitly made in *Being and Time* or in *On the Essence of Truth*.[38]

According to Heidegger, philosophy since Parmenides has tried to connect truth closely with Being. Aristotle, too, did not distinguish between searching for truth and investigating Being.[39] The famous conception of truth, which is traditionally attributed to Aristotle, however, seems to have been formulated first by Isaac Israeli. It can be formulated in the following two theses: (1) the place of truth is judgment; and (2) the essence of truth lies in the conformity of judgment and object or thing. This conception has, according to Heidegger, been maintained until the present, without any serious opposition. Not only did medieval scholasticism take over this view, but Descartes and Kant also adhered to it, though with some reservations and changes.[40]

Husserl, too, never doubted the classical definition of truth; he accepted it as correct, although he gave it a different interpretation, probably without even being explicitly aware of this. The meaning and function of the classical definition of truth in Husserl's works were different from those it had in classical philosophy, as is evident from the fact that in this matter Husserl did not distinguish between intellectual knowledge and sense knowledge, and did not hold that the judgment alone is the true locus of truth. Of course, Husserl accepted that truth is also encountered in the judgment; but according to him, this judgment is rooted in a pre-predicative experience in which the contrast between sense knowledge and intellectual knowledge is already transcended and in which the problem of truth announces itself already in a primordial way. According to Husserl, the problem of truth on the level of pre-predicative experience is more complicated because the notions of "presence" and "evidence," which are essentially allied to the notion of truth, are not univocal notions. Nevertheless, he maintained the classical definition of truth on this level also, although, because of the above mentioned analogy, its meaning differs from the one Aristotle had given to it.[41]

Heidegger agrees with the main lines of Husserl's position in this matter, but adds that Husserl limited himself to a theory of truth, although in addition an ontology should have been provided to give a foundation of this theory. In *On the Essence of Truth* Heidegger says that the crucial problem about truth does not lie in the question of which things, which judgments, or which acts are in fact true, or even in precisely what kinds of truths one has to distinguish from one another. The primary task, he claims, is to define truth as truth.[42] Undoubtedly, the question of the different levels of truth, its eternity, its necessity, its absoluteness or its contingent character, etc., are of great importance also, and they have to be discussed in any coherent theory of truth; but all this is not possible until a foundation has been provided by an ontological doctrine of truth as truth.

From the different ways in which man gives expression to the idea of truth Heidegger concludes that the classical definition of truth is undoubtedly meaningful. Truth is the "conformity" between thing and intellect. If one speaks of true gold, one intends to say that a certain piece of metal is really gold, i.e., that it corresponds to the notion we have formed about genuine gold (*adaequatio rei ad intellectum*, conformity of the thing with an intellect). On the other hand, we also call a judgment true, namely when it corresponds to the thing which is judged (*adaequatio intellectus ad rem*, conformity of the intellect with the thing). Thus Heidegger does not reject the scholastic conception of ontological and logical (or epistemological) truth. According to scholasticism, all knowledge has to be in harmony with the things, and these, in the last analysis, have to be in harmony with the ideas that God had about them when He created them. Hence logical truth has to be connected with ontological truth. However, one should keep in mind that in these two cases there is a question of two different intellects and, strictly speaking, also of two different things.[43]

Later the reference to the divine intellect was omitted, but otherwise the scholastic conception was maintained in its original form. Kant and Hegel also spoke about logical truth as conformity of the intellect with the thing, and about ontological truth as conformity of the things with the intellect. According to Kant, the truth of the object is constituted by the transcendental subject, while our empirical knowledge is governed by the objects. In Hegel these two aspects of truth became inseparable, and one is only an abstract phase of the other. Yet the idea of conformity continued to define the essence of truth.[44]

If, as it is generally done, one conceives of consciousness as being identical with representation, the problems of truth become insoluble, as is clear from the history of epistemology. Husserl was right when he argued that the classical definition of truth is meaningful only when one regards consciousness to be intentional. Yet Husserl did not go far enough because in the final analysis it is impossible to define truth in any way whatsoever without implying an interpretation of the Being of the beings. If one does not accurately indicate what intellect (Dasein) and thing (*res*) are in themselves, any theory of truth remains empty and certainly without a radical foundation.[45] Moreover, the classical conception of truth contains a series of implicit positions in regard to untruth and error, which should have been made explicit and then also justified. Thus it is clear that the classical theory of truth, even in the sense in which Husserl corrected it, requires an ontology of truth for its foundation.[46] This ontology can best be presented by starting from the classical conception of truth.

What exactly is meant by the conformity upon which this view is based? Its explanation will immediately lead us to the ontological presuppositions upon which this view rests. The conformity in question is obviously an analogous notion. We say, for example, that two silver dollars are equal or in conformity with each other; on the other hand, in my true judgment I am in conformity with the object of my judgment. In the first case there is a conformity between two objects based upon their participation in one and the same form. In the second case there is no question of two material objects, but of one material thing and a statement about it. How then can one speak here of conformity? One could say that the judgment refers to "itself" in the piece of silver insofar as the judgment represents the object under a certain aspect, just as it is.[47]

Closer investigation, however, shows that this form of presentation has nothing to do with a representation by means of signs or images (*repraesentatio*), but means that one places a thing as it is before oneself (*appraesentatio*). In the judgment I intend and aim at something other than the I. In this intending, this other, to the extent that it is "tended to," and under the formal aspect in which it is "tended to," is presented by me to myself and finds itself now before me, that is, it is constituted as an object. This objectivation is not the same in all cases; but it varies according to different kinds of judgments. This point, however, need not concern us at present.

Every judgment and every statement related to a real thing which they present as it actually is, call forth a special form of human behavior which characterizes Dasein's mode of Being and distinguishes its mode of Being from that of all other beings. This behavior is essentially tied up with reality in an intentional and transcendental manner. But one cannot give a meaning to the real if it is not first made present to man and if man has not first placed it before himself and if he does not let it rise before him. This, however, presupposes that man is openness, both to things and to himself, i.e., that man is Dasein, Being-in-the-world, eksistence. In this perspective, representation, as a supposedly essential element of every form of finite knowledge, makes no sense at all. Thus we see that Heidegger expressly returns here to Husserl's idea of intentionality, but interprets it in a different manner.⁴⁸ Accordingly, Heidegger accepts the correctness of the classical definition of truth as Husserl tried to interpret it, but he claims that this view of truth necessarily implies a certain vision of the mode of Being of man. He attempts to clarify this "vision" first⁴⁹ and then goes on to draw attention to other aspects of the issue. ⁵⁰

In Heidegger's view, a statement or a claim is true, if and only if, it reveals and uncovers a thing just as it is. A true statement reveals the thing as it is in itself; it asserts and lets the thing be seen (*apophansis*) in its uncoveredness. In the process of confirmation the thing is made to show itself in its selfsameness; the confirmation shows that the thing itself which now shows itself immediately is indeed just as it was revealed in the statement or the claim.

This implies that being-true is being as uncovering; my claim is true to the degree that it reveals and uncovers. At first sight, this seems strange and rather arbitrary. Yet on closer inspection it appears not to be as arbitrary as it seems to be; Heraclitus already had suggested this idea and the Greek word for truth, namely *a-letheia*, also suggests the same idea. By "translating" *aletheia* by un-hidden-ness or non-concealment, no word mysticism is intended; rather philosophical reflection must make an effort to preserve the saying power of the most basic and elementary words; it must make an effort to say how things in fact are, *phrazon hopos echei*, as Heraclitus says. Furthermore, also in this case the task of the philosopher is not to shake off the tradition, but to retrieve it and to appropriate it in a primordial manner. ⁵¹

But what is more, to be as uncovering and revealing is not only characteristic for my claims; it is first of all characteristic for Dasein as such; Dasein is *lumen naturale*. ⁵² The uncovering of my claims has its eksistential, ontological foundation in the uncovering of me as Dasein. Uncovering or revealing is a mode of Being for Dasein as Being-in-the-world. Dasein can reveal in many ways, in circumspection, in theoretical viewing, in the scientific way of thematizing things, etc. In these different modes of Being things become uncovered and revealed. Thus Dasein, as revealing, is true in a primordial sense; things insofar as they are revealed are true in a secondary sense. The uncoveredness (*Entdecktheit*) of the beings within the world is grounded in the uncoveredness of the world in Dasein's own *Da*. Thus the disclosedness (*Erschlossenheit*) of the world is related to the disclosing which is intrinsic in Dasein's own Being-in, taken as moodness, understanding, and logos. Dasein's own disclosedness is the most primordial phenomenon of the truth. Everything else is true to the degree that Dasein discloses it. Only Dasein itself is "in the truth."[53]

That Dasein is in the truth means from an eksistential point of view many things. First it means that disclosedness belongs to Dasein's mode of Being essentially; it is because Dasein is as disclosedness that beings can become disclosed. Thus Dasein is in the full sense of the term the natural light. Yet since Dasein is thrown, this disclosedness is inherently factical; this means that in each case it is my disclosing. Furthermore, to Dasein's mode of Being belongs projection; Dasein can project itself authentically or inauthentically; the same is true for Dasein's projection of the innerworldly beings. Finally, Dasein is lost in fallenness; thus Dasein can equally be in untruth; the beings are then disguised and shown in the mode of semblance.[54]

It is then essential that Dasein must explicitly appropriate what has already been uncovered, defend it against semblance and disguise, and assure itself of its own uncoveredness again and again. Thus uncoveredness must always be wrested from the beings by a kind of robbery; the beings are to be brought from hiddenness into the open of non-concealment. Also, the fact that Dasein is a thrown projection explains why Dasein is both in truth and in untruth.

Finally, one should observe here that the truth of our claims originates from Dasein's disclosedness. In other words, the truth of our claims is a derivative modification of truth taken as Dasein's revealing, so that the phenomenon of agreement or conformity is also derivative in character.[55] This thesis runs parallel to a thesis we mentioned earlier to the effect that the hermeneutic *as* always proceeds the apophantic *as*; only the latter accounts for the theoretical explanation of the structure of the truth.[56] --But let us now return to the manner in which Heidegger relates truth and freedom.

If it is true, Heidegger states, that our judgments are directed to the things about which they attempt to say something, then one has to ask why our judgments, as well as our entire knowledge, can and must accept the real as their norm. Why does man "consent" to adjust himself radically to the beings in his knowledge, his actions, and his entire behavior? Why does he subject himself to the beings in order to derive from them the substance and the norm of what he knows and does?

Strictly speaking, one cannot really ask the question in this way, because we are confronted with the fact that man does indeed obey the real and that the beings do constitute the norm that governs his knowledge and behavior. It is better therefore to ask under what conditions such an attitude is possible. The answer is that it is possible because man is free. For, if our behavior adjusts itself to the beings, if it meets them as they are, then "the beings taken as they are" have to be the norm that governs the open being, namely Dasein, that faces them. Remaining what they are, things present themselves as they are, and this within the domain of that "open" whose openness is not created by Dasein's representation, but merely is taken over by it as a possible referential system. This "open" is for Heidegger the world as the necessary horizon within whose limits every concrete being can be truly brought to light by man.[57]

Man is essentially and primordially related to this always already given "open," the world, and in each concrete form of behavior this fundamental relation is, as it were, actualized.[58] In this actualization man relates himself to the beings which, as being-present and manifest, are experienced as such. "What is thus, and solely in the strict sense, made manifest was experienced early in Western thought as that 'which is present' (*ousia*) and has long been called being."[59]

Because man is open to himself and to the world as the "open," and ultimately because man is primordially open to Being as the unconcealed, man is able to make particular things manifest as these particular things, that is, as they are. The judgments and the statements that follow these judgments, must be governed by the beings that have become manifest in this manner. It is clear, therefore, that neither judgment nor statement can be the original *locus* of truth. The essential *locus* of truth lies in the primordial relation in which beings become disclosed as they are. Dasein's openness is a necessary condition for this primordial relation. This openness must be regarded as the proper characteristic of freedom, so that we can conclude that "the essence of truth is freedom."[60]

In spite of the explanation given, this assertion may still seem strange. One could say, of course, that man must be free in order to be able to perform a certain action and therefore also free to make a representative statement and, thus, to agree to or to disagree with a "truth." But the above mentioned assertion claims that freedom is the essence of truth. By essence is meant here the basis of the inner possibility of whatever is accepted and generally admitted as known. But in the idea of freedom one does not think of truth and even less of the essence of truth. Moreover, it seems that, by making freedom the essence of truth, truth is left to man's discretion. Such a surrender of truth to man's discretion fundamentally undermines truth by basing it on the subjectivity of the human subject.

These and other similar objections, however, proceed from assumptions that are foreign to what Heidegger really wants to say. The reason for the confusion lies in the fact that the objectors tenaciously cling to certain prejudices concerning the essence of freedom. They assume that freedom is primarily a characteristic of man, that the essence of freedom is immediately evident, and that everyone knows at once what man is. One of these prejudices is to be examined more closely here.[61]

The term "freedom is usually taken to mean the possibility to choose, "the random ability to go this way or that in our choice."[62] Although it cannot be denied that freedom is to be found also in choice, the essence of freedom does not lie there. Freedom means essentially the absence of necessity together with a certain autonomy. Freedom means primordially that way of Being which enables man to liberate himself from "nature's" grasp. This negative aspect of freedom, however, contains also a positive side. In my power to escape from the grasp of facticity, the positive possibility of my fundamental openness reveals itself equiprimordially and, by virtue of this openness, I can orientate myself to the world and to my own possibilities in regard to the innerworldly beings. This freedom is primordially not a characteristic of man's activity, but, as Being-in-the-world, Dasein is openness; it transcends being necessitated and has the positive possibility to transcend and to project. Primordially, therefore, freedom indicates the Being of man.[63]

To explain the relationship between truth and freedom we must return to the classical definition of truth which is to be given an ontological foundation. We have seen that the *locus* of truth is not primordially in the judgment[64] but in Dasein's eksistence itself. The conformity between judgment and reality has been drawn from concealment. For this purpose a certain light is needed; this is the light of Dasein's eksistence which itself is openness. "Insofar as Dasein is its disclosedness essentially and, as disclosed, discloses and uncovers, it is essentially true."[65] Taken in his essence, man is openness and a light to himself; but equiprimordially he is openness and light with respect to other beings. As eksistence, Dasein is a natural light, a *lumen naturale*. Primordially disclosed, Dasein, taken as eksistence, is equiprimordially disclosing and thereby giving rise to meaning.[66]

The truth of the judgment presupposes truth as unconcealedness of the beings and the truth of human eksistence taken as that which discovers things; and these two presuppose man's fundamental openness. Hence, the truth of judgment ultimately presupposes that man is "in the truth."[67] "What is primarily 'true'--that is, un-covering--is Dasein."[68] The task of Dasein lies in "taking beings out of their concealedness and letting them be seen in their unconcealedness [their un-coveredness]."[69]

The untruth of the judgment can also be considered in the same way. The being untrue of a judgment presupposes man's being untrue, i.e., the being uprooted of his eksistence.[70] This being uprooted means that man no longer stands in truth as unconcealedness, but stands in semblance (*Schein*). Reality does not remain completely concealed here but, although it is to some extent disclosed, it is distorted in one way or another. Thus the untrue judgment merely explicates Dasein's standing in semblance.[71]

Truth in the most primordial sense of the word is, therefore, an eksistential of Dasein's own mode of Being. Thus we must conclude that "Dasein, as constituted by disclosedness, is essentially in the truth. Disclosedness is a mode of Being that is essential to Dasein. 'There is' (*es gibt*) truth only insofar as Dasein is and so long as Dasein is. Beings are discovered only when Dasein is; and they are disclosed only as long as it is."[72]

Does it follow from this that all truth is merely subjective? If by "subjective" one understands the idea that all truth, by virtue of its own essential way of Being, is relative to Dasein's Being, then this question must undoubtedly be answered in the affirmative. If, however, "subjective" is taken to mean "left to the subject's discretion," then the answer must be negative, because "dis-covering . . . places the dis-covering Dasein face to face with the beings themselves."[73] Dis-covery aims precisely at the beings as they are, and every judgment and statement likewise aims at these beings as they are. The intended being itself shows itself as it is in itself, i.e., it shows "that it, in its self-sameness, is just as it gets pointed out, dis-covered, in the statement as being."[74] As ek-sistence, Dasein discloses reality itself; it lets the beings be for itself as they are.

"Letting be" sometimes means that one wants to renounce something, but in the present context it means precisely the opposite. "Letting be" here means to let the beings be as they genuinely are. It implies also that one wishes to have something to do with the beings, not in order to protect, cultivate, or conserve them, but only to let them truly be what they are. This "letting be" takes things from concealedness, it brings them to light and makes them participate in the truth of Being.[75] This "having something to do with beings" in order to bring them to light does not become absorbed in beings. On the contrary, it unfolds itself precisely in making room for the beings in order that they can reveal themselves as what they are themselves and precisely as they are, and in order that subsequently our judgments and statements can find their norm in them.

If both truth and freedom are nothing but expressions of Dasein's own mode of Being then it is evident that the essence of truth can lie precisely in freedom taken as openness. "The essence of freedom, seen from the viewpoint of the essence of truth, shows itself as the 'bringing out' of beings into unconcealedness."[76] It also becomes evident then that the *locus* of truth is not in the judgment, but in that which makes judgments and statements possible, i.e., in primordial understanding and fundamental moodness.[77]

In Heidegger's own view, these few remarks about truth do by no means exhaust this rich and important subject. As he sees it, at this point of the analysis it is not yet possible to offer a definitive solution for the most important problems. Such solutions become possible only after the basic problem of ontology, i.e., the question of the meaning of Being itself, has been discussed. Yet what has been said here about truth is adequate to understand Heidegger's position in regard to the sciences provided one constantly keeps in mind that in the coming-to-pass of the truth of Being, Being itself occupies the privileged position.

14: NOTE ON REGIONAL ONTOLOGIES

a. HUSSERL'S ORIGINAL CONCEPTION OF REGIONAL ONTOLOGIES

On several occasions Heidegger mentions regional ontologies. For him these are forms of scientific discourse that focus on the

REGIONAL ONTOLOGIES

ontological assumptions made in the various empirical sciences. Let us take one case to see how Heidegger conceives of these ontologies and how in his view they are related to both the empirical sciences on the one hand and to the ontological concern with the meaning of Being as such on the other.

In section 3 of *Being and Time* Heidegger tried to establish the ontological priority of the question of Being. One of the claims he made there is that strictly ontological inquiry is more primordial than all ontical inquiry of the positive, i.e., empirical sciences. He writes in this passage that

> . . . [the] question of Being aims therefore at ascertaining the a priori conditions not only for the possibility of the sciences which examine beings as beings of such and such a type, and, in so doing, already operate with an understanding of Being, but also for the possibility of those ontologies themselves which are prior to the ontical sciences and which provide their foundations.[78]

Heidegger refers here to Husserl's conception of regional ontologies which, in Husserl's view, are to mediate between transcendental phenomenology and the empirical sciences. Although Heidegger does not share Husserl's position completely, the essence of Husserl's position is nonetheless maintained by him. This makes it necessary to say a few words about Husserl's view and about the question of in how far Heidegger's position is different from Husserl's.

Husserl mentioned "regional ontologies" in the first volume of *Ideas* (1913),[79] but the view developed there was already anticipated in the second volume of *Logical Investigations* (1901).[80] In the third volume of *Ideas* (written in 1912) Husserl for the first time explicitly applied his view on regional ontologies to "eidetic" psychology (=phenomenological psychology) whose necessity and nature was already briefly indicated in the first volume of the same work.[81] It seems to me that Husserl has maintained these ideas on "regional ontologies" in general, and on eidetic or phenomenological psychology as a particular regional ontology among others in particular, in all of his later writings, at least as far as the essence of this conception is concerned.[82]

However, between 1913 and 1925 Husserl must gradually have come to the conclusion that his original conception was incomplete and in some details incorrect. The first evidence of this change of view is found in the lectures on phenomenological psychology (1925). In this work, which was posthumously published in 1962, Husserl for the first time mentions a "general ontology of the world of our immediate experience"[83] which logically must precede all regional ontologies. In the same book Husserl also makes a distinction between "the world of our immediate experience" and the world in which we live our everyday life.[84] Finally, in his last publications, *Crisis* (1936), Husserl no longer uses the expression "the world of our immediate experience" but instead focusses on the function which investigations concerning the lifeworld (*Lebenswelt*) have in regard to transcendental phenomenology.[85] It seems to me, however, that even then Husserl maintained the view that a "general ontology of the world of our immediate experience" must be accepted as the necessary starting point for the regional ontologies in general, and for phenomenological psychology in particular.

It must be admitted that Husserl's view on the epistemological status of the regional ontologies and their relationships to the empirical sciences on the one hand, and to philosophy taken as transcendental phenomenology on the other, is rather intricate and not without serious difficulties. I wish to discuss two of these difficulties briefly in that they immediately relate to Husserl's position in regard to the regional ontologies that are related to the empirical sciences of man.

According to Landgrebe, in 1913 Husserl considered the regional ontologies to be philosophical sciences.[86] Although I do not deny that Landgrebe can point to a number of pertinent arguments for his thesis, I nonetheless believe that his view cannot possibly be correct in that there is too much textual evidence to the contrary. Already in *The Idea of Phenomenology* (1907) Husserl characterized the difference between the philosophical and the non-philosophical disciplines by pointing to the fundamental difference that exists between the philosophical and the natural attitudes and, in the same book, the regional ontologies are explicitly classed under the sciences of the natural attitude.[87] In a note of 1916[88] referring to the first lecture of the lecture series, *The Idea of Phenomenology*, Husserl adds the material ontologies and makes again the explicit remark that all these ontologies belong to the realm of the "natural" sciences, that is to say to the sciences of the natural attitude. That Husserl in 1913 was of the same opinion is not only clear from the remark with which he concludes his "logical investigations,"[89] but especially from the passage in which he explicitly says that the formal ontologies as well as the material ontologies must be "disconnected" by the phenomenological reduction.[90] Here Husserl even goes so far as to claim "the absolute independence of

REGIONAL ONTOLOGIES

phenomenology from all sciences, including the eidetic sciences," that is from the formal and material ontologies; this claim is motivated by the "philosophical functions" which phenomenological philosophy has to perform.[91] In the third volume of *Ideen*, which according to the editor, Marly Biemel, was written in first draft in 1912,[92] Husserl says that it is one of the most important tasks of phenomenological philosophy to give the eidetic, regional ontologies their ultimate foundation.[93] This point is explained there in the following way.

It cannot be denied that transcendental phenomenology and the group of ontologies taken as a whole partly overlap. For, the essential task of transcendental phenomenology consists in carefully examining the beings or entities which form the objects of the different forms of our experience in regard to their modes of being given, and in clarifying in what phenomenological context these different modes of reality become constituted as unities of meaning. And this holds true in particular for the regional categories of all regions of beings or entities: material things, geometrical entities, our body, our psychic life, our social life, etc. Analogously the same thing can be said for the formal entities of formal ontology (*mathesis universalis*). But if it is true that all these entities according to their essential structures belong immediately to the subject matter of transcendental phenomenology itself and if, on the other hand, it is true also that the fundamental concepts and axioms in which we express our intuitive insight into the very essences of these beings and entities form the very subject matter of the different regional ontologies, then it is again clear that regional ontologies "somehow" belong to phenomenology. However, it then also becomes clear that it is of the greatest importance to examine carefully whether statements and propositions which equally occur in phenomenology and in one or another ontology, really have the same meaning, even if we disregard the results of the transcendental reduction which is characteristic of transcendental phenomenology only.

One has to keep in mind here that formal and material ontologies are dogmatic sciences in which the subject matter of each science is taken in its particular existential status and becomes examined in regard to its essential structures, that is to say, structures which belong to it in unconditioned necessity and generality. Phenomenology, on the other hand, is not a dogmatic but a transcendental science; as such it deals with the ultimate fundaments and matrices of all knowledge; that is why it and it alone is able to clarify the still problematic foundations of all dogmatic sciences.[94] From this it becomes clear that the term "phenomenological" can be used in a strict and in a broader sense; taken in the strict sense of the term, "phenomenological" exclusively applies to the transcendental investigations concerning that realm of Being which is opened up by the transcendental reduction; taken in a broader sense, the term "phenomenological" can be applied to the investigations of the ontological sciences provided these sciences are taken as ultimately founded in transcendental phenomenology.[95]

In order to explain the difference between transcendental phenomenology and regional ontologies, in Husserl's view, the following remarks could also be very helpful. Regional ontologies are evidently sciences of essences; they have to deal with the essential structures and relationships which govern a certain region of Being. In so doing they try to find out how things are and what in truth pertains to them as such, in unconditioned necessity and generality;[96] in other words they try to formulate "eidetic existential" judgments concerning the essences of the things they are dealing with. Ontological sciences thus are essentially directed toward beings, toward certain domains of beings determined by the different regions, and try to bring to light their mode of Being as far as their essential, necessary, and universal structures are concerned.[97] Phenomenology, on the other hand, deals with transcendental consciousness and with its transcendental occurrences inasfar as these can be examined in immediate intuition and eidetic generality. In so doing transcendental phenomenology, among other things, has also to deal with the same essences and essential structures which form the subject matter of the regional ontologies. Phenomenology, however, is not interested in the question of how things are and of what genuinely and truly belongs to them in unconditioned generality and necessity; phenomenology asks about our consciousness of things and about the different modes of conscious acts in and through which those things can manifest themselves to consciousness and as such are constituted by it. In other words, the same things which form the subject matter of regional ontologies are also studied by transcendental phenomenology not as beings, but only as correlates of conscious acts, as *noemata* of corresponding *noeses*, both of which are taken in eidetic necessity and unconditioned generality.[98]

The second difficulty connected with Husserl's view is caused by the fact that it is not very clear how he thinks "the world of our immediate experience" is to be related to what he calls the "life-world."

In 1913 Husserl was of the opinion that the Being-structure on which the various material ontologies focus their attention is not always the same: different regions of beings are differently constituted and cannot, therefore, be described with the help of the same categories. Certainly one can universally apply the categories "thing," "object," "relation," etc., but the structure which is expressed in these concepts common to all regions of beings, is merely formal. Therefore, the concept "object in general" is not the supreme genus of which the basic concepts of the different material ontologies are to be the various species.

At the time *Ideen* was written Husserl had not yet developed a general material ontology of the world of our immediate experience as such. We also fail to find there the later idea that the subject matters of all regional ontologies must be justified from the point of view of such a general material ontology of the world of our immediate experience. Originally Husserl seems to have felt that these different subject matters are already somehow predelineated in our pre-scientific experience and thus, via the empirical sciences studying these "regions," can be taken from it. In his later view, however, Husserl maintains what he had said earlier about formal ontology. The concept of "regional ontology" is equally maintained in its original meaning, but with the introduction of the "newcomer," the general ontology of the world of our immediate experience, all the relationships between regional ontologies and the corresponding empirical sciences change radically.[99] Husserl's description of the "world of our immediate experience" as found in *Phänomenologische Psychologie* (1925) shows a great resemblance to his later description of the life-world (1936).[100] And yet in 1925 Husserl made an explicit distinction between "the world of our immediate experience" and the "life-world" whereas what in *Crisis* is called life-world seems to be identical with what in *Phänomenologische Psychologie* is called "the world of our immediate experience."[101] Let us briefly indicate the development which took place in Husserl's thought between 1925 and 1936.

In 1925 Husserl gave the following description of the two basic expressions involved. The world of our immediate experience is the world which each of us immediately encounters in his experience. That is to say, this world includes only and exclusively what is immediately perceived at each concrete moment with the exclusion of any interpretation of the immediately given data;

it is what we "passively" find present to us in its bodily selfhood, and is to be taken, therefore, as completely deprived of any layer of meaning which refers to our own active appreciation and understanding. It is obvious that it will be difficult, if possible at all, to describe such a world.[102] For it seems that such an experience of world has been realized only by the very first human beings in the very beginning of their lives as humans.

Still in 1925 Husserl opposes to this world what he calls "the world in which we live our everyday life." This is the world in which we constantly live and in which we encounter houses, furniture, fields, gardens, tools, pictures, institutions, and above all human beings.[103] Thus Husserl refers here to our "cultural world" which surrounds us and in which the meaning of all things is already determined to a very large extent by our culture, including the sciences and technology. It is obvious that this "life-world" is very different from the "life-world" of primitive people, whereas the "world of our immediate experience" is the same for all human beings of all times. Drüe is of the opinion that the life-world as found in *Crisis* is of exactly the same content as the "life-world" described in *Phänomenologische Psychologie* and thus that in 1936 Husserl abandoned the idea of a "world of our immediate experience."[104] I have tried to show elsewhere why I think that this view is incorrect. In my opinion in *Crisis* Husserl distinguishes between the life-world taken as we encounter it in our everyday life, and the original life-world. It is the latter which Husserl mainly wishes to discuss in *Crisis*, but this original life-world is precisely what was formerly called the "world of our immediate experience." My main reason for defending this view is that without the distinction just mentioned many passages of Husserl's text become incomprehensible and contradictory, and that it seems impossible to come to a genuine understanding of the reductive procedures explicitly described in *Crisis*.[105] I shall give just one example.

In *Crisis* Husserl says that the general ontology of the lifeworld must concern itself with the general, unchanging structure of that world and with its essential characteristics. In elaborating this point he states that this science need not be limited to the life-world of Western man, but can include the life-worlds of other cultures. As a matter of fact we need not limit ourselves to actual existing cultures, or cultures that have actually existed at some time. We can even concern ourselves with possible lifeworlds. While comparing one life-world with another we can gradually rid ourselves of the actual and factual aspects involved in each concrete case. We can try to approach purely possible life-worlds by means of the method of free variation, and thus achieve an understanding of the essential and necessary aspects of any life-world whatsoever. In this approach we place all the cultural aspects of a given cultural community between brackets (reduction); we leave out of consideration all those typical cultural aspects that give this culture its particular physiognomy; and thus we make the original world of our immediate experience appear. We, therefore, can consider this science to be an ontology of the life-world as such, provided that we understand life-world to mean here a possible world of man's immediate, intersubjective experience.[106]

I have discussed these issues here in some detail, not because I think they are important in themselves, but merely because they relate immediately to our main topic of discussion. For from what has been said it is more than clear that in Husserl's view a phenomenology of the life-world, regardless of whether one takes it in the sense of transcendental phenomenology or in the sense of a mundane phenomenology, is not immediately relevant to the empirical study of human phenomena. I shall return to this in the pages to follow.

b. REGIONAL ONTOLOGIES AND EMPIRICAL SCIENCES.

In the preceding pages the expression "regional ontologies" has been used regularly. We must now try to come to a better understanding of precisely what this expression stands for in Husserl's view.

In 1913 Husserl adopted the point of view that in its many directions the world which we encounter in our everyday life has already become the object of scientific determinations in which all that is found in our pre-scientific and daily experience merely in a vague and naive way, is grasped in precise concepts and explanatory theories. Each science has its own domain of investigation, but it is not able to furnish this domain for itself; this domain is already pre-given to it in advance insofar as in our pre-scientific experience the beings immediately manifest themselves as being distinguishable from and comparable to one another.

Our pre-scientific experience precedes all empirical sciences and predelineates their different domains of investigation. We have seen that Husserl calls the totality of objects that each science investigates in its own typical way, a region. Thus he speaks, for instance, of the region of physical nature, the region of psychic phenomena, the region of social phenomena, etc. What all the objects of a certain region have in common and, therefore, what characterizes them is, according to Husserl, fixed in the categories which are germane to each region. Together they constitute the regional categories, or the fundamental and basic concepts, of that region. In these basic concepts are found all the region's presuppositions under which each multiplicity of beings which are immediately given in our pre-scientific experience can be conceived of and understood as belonging together in such a way that they can become the object and theme of one or other empirical science. Because these basic concepts constitute the typical mode of intelligibility and, therefore, also the specific object-character of the objects of the different sciences, the sciences in which the categories of a determinate region are discovered, are called regional ontologies. That is why every empirical science which is engaged in the scientific investigation of a determinate domain of beings is to be founded in a regional ontology in which the basic concepts of this science are to be explained in a radical way.[107]

When Husserl now claims that every empirical science is to be founded in a regional ontology, this evidently does not mean that the regional ontologies should have to precede the empirical sciences. On the contrary, it is Husserl's view that regional ontologies can be built up only by starting from a subsequent reflection on the conditions under which such a domain of beings could ever be delineated. Regional ontologies make explicit what in unconditioned generality and necessity must belong to a certain object if it really is to be the object of investigation of the correlative empirical science. That is to say, regional ontologies must determine and describe the essential structures of every possible object of the different empirical sciences which deal with the entities belonging to the region in question. That is why Husserl also speaks of eidetic sciences in contradistinction to the sciences of fact, the empirical sciences. On the other hand, however, it follows from the preceding reflections that, although it is true that the regional ontologies come after the corresponding empirical sciences in the order to time, nevertheless, as eidetic sciences they precede those sciences *de jure*.

In *Ideas* (1913) a formal ontology which makes abstraction from all the regional distinctions of the different objects, is put ahead of the regional ontologies.[108] It is the science which deals with the formal idea "object-in-general." Its task consists in the

REGIONAL ONTOLOGIES

study of the conditions under which anything whatsoever can be a legitimate subject matter of man's thought and science, and under which, therefore, this object can be examined and described by every science. The fundamental concept or the basic category of formal ontology thus consists in the empty concept "object-in-general." Although, on the one hand, one could say that this formal ontology is a branch of logic taken as universal analytic, it is, on the other hand, true also that it comprises the whole *mathesis universalis* (= formal logic, arithmetic, pure analysis, set theory, etc.).[109]

The regional or material ontologies try to investigate all the conditions which from the point of view of their subject-matters are necessarily presupposed in the different empirical sciences. They have to focus attention on the *eidos*, that is, the universally operative and necessary essence of the objects of the empirical sciences. It is these essences of the different objects of the empirical sciences which are investigated in formal ontology in the reduced form of "object-in-general." The subject matter of formal ontology, therefore, does not consist in the class of essences, but in a mere "essence-form,"[110] that is to say, "an essence which in the manner of an empty form fits all possible essences, and which in its formal universality has the highest material generalities subordinated to it."[111] However, the formal region is not on a par with the material regions; "it is properly speaking not a region at all, but the pure form of region in general only."[112] Formal ontology, therefore, investigates a completely new dimension of Being, namely the necessary conditions of "being-object."[113]

Thus it is Husserl's idea that the Being-structure on which the material ontologies focus all their attention, is not everywhere the same: different regions of beings have a different constitution and cannot, therefore, be described with the help of the same categories.[114] Certainly, one can universally apply the categories "object," "relation," etc., but the structure which is expressed in these concepts common to all regions of being, is merely formal. Therefore, the concept of "object in general" is *not* the supreme genus of which the basic concepts of the different material ontologies are to be the various species. The categories that express the material being-structure which, for instance, defines nature as nature, psychic phenomena as psychic phenomena, social phenomena as social phenomena, etc., are not mere specifications of formal categories; that is to say, they are not the result of the addition of a *differentia specifica* to a *genus proximum*. This is why Husserl stresses the difference between genus and form, between generalization and formalization, and between specialization and deformalization.[115]

The careful reader will have observed that in 1913 Husserl adopted the point of view that although each empirical science has its own domain of investigation, it is not capable of furnishing this domain for itself; this domain is already pre-given in our pre-scientific experiences. In 1925 Husserl introduced the general ontology of the world of our immediate experience mainly for the purpose of critically examining the question of precisely how the various regions of objects become constituted in our pre-scientific life and to determine the categories which all of these objects have in common, namely those which immediately pertain to their spatial and temporal determinations, their causal interrelationships, etc. However, once Husserl had seen the necessity, not only of a material ontology of nature as nature, of psychic life as psychic life, of society as society, etc., but first and foremost of a general ontology of the world of our immediate experience, it became clear to him that the subject matters of the different regional ontologies cannot be determined by taking one's starting point in the empirical sciences, but must be drawn precisely from this general, material ontology of the world of immediate experience. However, all that was said in 1913 about formal ontology as well as about the description of the meaning and function of the regional ontologies is maintained in 1925. Husserl thus merely adds a new discipline to the list, a discipline which in regard to the regional ontologies has a foundational function. It is to be noted here that in all these reflections Husserl was guided by ideas taken from Kant's *Critique of Pure Reason* on the one hand, and by his *Metaphysical Principles of the Natural Sciences* on the other.

Be this as it may, when Husserl uses the expression "regional ontology" he has in mind a discipline which tries scientifically to establish the essential elements and the invariable structures of the realms of beings which are examined empirically in the various empirical sciences. In other words, regional ontologies try to establish the necessary and sufficient conditions which a being or a group of beings must possess in order to be a valid subject matter of the corresponding empirical sciences. Regional ontologies, it is to be noted here, are not interested in beings taken as ontic entities, but in the meaning these beings have in the various intentional relationships which man can establish in regard to them. That is why the prime methods to be used in regional ontologies are intentional analysis and ideation.

c. HEIDEGGER'S CRITIQUE OF HUSSERL'S TRANSCENDENTAL PHENOMENOLOGY.

We have already seen some of the reasons that gradually led Heidegger to take distance from Husserl's transcendental phenomenology. In Heidegger's view Husserl basically remains within the metaphysical framework of German idealism. Heidegger wishes to "overcome" metaphysics by focussing on the finitude and historicity of all meaning. This was the main reason why in his philosophy Heidegger is concerned mainly with the coming-to-pass of the truth of Being. Thus not the transcendental subjectivity, but rather the truth of Being must be the central issue in genuine philosophical reflection. Furthermore, the human being is not to be understood exclusively in terms of being a consciousness, but rather as that being that stands out toward the truth of Being as this historically comes-to-presence to man and his world.

Yet all of these changes notwithstanding, Heidegger thought that Husserl's conception of regional ontologies can and should be maintained in his ontology. In his view, it is indeed the case that all empirical or positive sciences are as such unable to lay the foundations for the kind of research that they try to promote. Thus it is necessary to develop regional ontologies which provide the various empirical sciences with their proper foundations. The main task of these ontologies consists in the clarification of the precise mode of Being of the entities with which each empirical science concerns itself. Now in view of the fact that such disciplines are concerned with the mode of Being of various regions of entities, these ontologies themselves remain "blind and perverted from [their] ownmost aim, if they have not first adequately clarified the meaning of Being, and conceived of this clarification as their fundamental task."[116]

In other words, the basic ontological assumptions made by the regional ontologies themselves are to be clarified and founded in fundamental ontology and particularly in ontology proper. We have seen furthermore, that Heidegger also adopts a positive attitude in regard to the methods which Husserl attributes to regional ontologies. Yet in the case of empirical sciences that concern themselves with human beings, these phenomenological methods are to be reinterpreted into hermeneutic-phenomenological methods.

Part II

Heidegger's Conception of the Sciences

CHAPTER IV

TOWARD THE ESSENCE
OF
EMPIRICAL SCIENCE

Heidegger has written several times on issues that are immediately relevant to philosophical reflections on the empirical sciences, namely in *Being and Time*, in *Phänomenologische Interpretation von Kants Kritik der reinen Vernunft*, *What is a Thing?*, *Nietzsche*, *Vorträge and Aufsätze*, *Holzwege*, *Gelassenheit*, and *What is Called Thinking?*[1] This serious concern with the sciences is understandable in light of the fact that the prevalent world view in our contemporary Western civilization is largely controlled by the sciences. A philosophy that wants to make the fundamental philosophical problems its theme in a manner that appeals to modern man can hardly afford to ignore the sciences and their impact on ourselves and on the world in which we live. In these reflections on the sciences Heidegger proves himself a philosopher who is remarkably well informed about several sciences. Before definitively embarking on his philosophical career, Heidegger had spent several years in fruitful studies of mathematics, physics, history, and theology.[2]

The main questions which he raised with regard to the sciences are the well known problems of what science is, how a science becomes constituted, what is to be thought about its truth, certainty, and exactness, what relations there exist between science and technology, and especially what the relation is between the sciences and philosophy.

In the pages to come I shall make an effort to explain how Heidegger has tried to answer these questions as far as the empirical sciences are concerned. In so doing I shall focus first on ideas developed in the twenties. Toward the end of this chapter I shall then add some reflections on the basic ideas about the empirical sciences in Heidegger's later works. I plan to discuss Heidegger's conception of the relation between science and technology in chapter V.

In *Being and Time* Heidegger dealt with the empirical sciences in two different places. In Section 13 he wrote about our theoretical attitude and its impact on the empirical sciences with the intention of clarifying the "Being-in" of our Being-in-the-world. He tried to shed light on the primordial meaning of "Being-in" by contrasting our primordial mode of Being-in-the-world with our theoretical manner of Being-in-the-world, and by presenting the theoretical attitude and the empirical sciences as rooted in and derived from Dasein's primordial mode of Being-in-the-world. In Section 69 on the other hand Heidegger tried to explain the temporality of Being-in-the-world by showing how Dasein in its various modes of "Being-in" is temporal and temporalizing. Heidegger uses our scientific mode of "Being-in" there as an example. During the winter semester of 1927-1928, when *Being and Time* had just appeared, Heidegger gave a course on Kant's first *Critique* in which he particularly focused on how in each science the scientists objectify the entities with which they concern themselves in order then to show the relationship between a given empirical science, its corresponding regional ontology, and fundamental ontology.[3] In these reflections Heidegger employed ideas which he had developed during his first years in Marburg, if not earlier. I shall discuss the main ideas developed in these different sections by ordering them in a somewhat "systematic" fashion.

15: FROM "CONCERNFULLY DEALING WITH" (*PRAXIS*) TO THEORY

We have seen that according to Heidegger, theoretical knowledge is a special mode of Dasein's Being-in-the-world, but that theoretical knowledge is not the primary and privileged mode of Being of Dasein. Dasein's primary mode of Being consists rather in Dasein's concern with the beings that are within-the-world (*Besorgen*). These beings are encountered there first as utensils and pieces of equipment with which man is to concern himself. The kind of knowledge that is intrinsic in our effective concern with the beings that are within-the-world, however, is not theoretical in nature. Thus it is not a scientific kind of knowledge, either. One could perhaps say that this kind of knowledge is

FROM "DEALING-WITH" TO THEORY

prescientific. Furthermore, this kind of knowledge is obviously also still prephilosophical and, thus, preontological, even though our effective concern with the beings within-the-world implies already some understanding of their mode of Being. The worldliness of the world and the mode of Being characteristic of utensils and equipment remain still hidden in that kind of knowledge. In our concern with the beings that are within the world our comprehension of Being is still unthematic and preontological. This is the reason why our understanding of the mode of Being of the utensils as well as that of Dasein's own mode of Being remains unthematic and preontological, also.[4]

What has been said here is true for Dasein regardless of whether it actually concerns itself with the sciences or not. We must now try to come to a better understanding of how our scientific comportment, taken as a possible mode of Being of Dasein's eksistence, is to be related to Dasein's prescientific concern with the beings that are within-the-world, and how the former somehow originates from the latter.[5]

We must thus turn to the question of precisely how Dasein's concernful dealing with things changes into a merely looking at things in a purely theoretical manner. At first one might be inclined to think that this happens simply by abstaining from any kind of concernful dealing with things, i.e., by abstaining from every form of *praxis*. In that case, the origin of the theoretical attitude would consist essentially in the disappearance of all *praxis*. For those who consider the practical concern to be the primary and dominating mode of Being of Dasein, theory would appear to derive its ontological possibility from some kind of privation; one could perhaps say that for those people theory remains when *praxis* disappears.

It is hardly necessary to show that this view must be wrong. For first of all, every form of *praxis* at times implies a mere looking-at and, on the other hand, in many instances there can be no theory without *praxis*. It suffices to point to the technical views which are incorporated in the use of complicated measuring devices in contemporary science. Moreover, the practical handling of innerworldly beings requires a certain circumspection, understanding, and survey which ultimately become deliberation. It is precisely this "viewing" of things as equipment which must be changed if the theoretical attitude is to arise.

Accordingly, the theoretical attitude does not consist in abandoning the *praxis*, but rather in taking a second look at the things that are within-the-world which our concernful dealing regards as equipment, and in conceiving and projecting them as "being merely there." The scientific way of looking at the world, then, results from a shift in Dasein's attitude, which fundamentally modifies the primarily adopted view of the world. The things which initially were handled by Dasein within the framework of its primordial world now assume a different character. They lose their location in their original world and, henceforth, appear only in a place that is unrelated to Dasein and is without limitations.[6] "Looking-at," which is so characteristic of the theoretical attitude, always implies a new viewpoint and a new attitude with regard to the things that are present. This attitude, taken in advance, makes a certain specific aspect of the thus encountered beings the center of our attention.

Theoretical knowing is thus a "dwelling by" which includes a perceiving of, and an addressing oneself to, and a discussing of, something *as* something--briefly, an interpretation in the widest sense of the term. On the basis of this interpretation, perception becomes making-determinate. What is perceived in this way can also be pronounced and preserved in propositions.

Perception, too, is a mode of Being-in-the-world and need not be interpreted as a "procedure" by which a subject produces "representations" of something which then are stored "inside" and can give rise to the question of whether and how they are "in agreement" with reality. In its turning to something and grasping it, Dasein does not first come out of an "inner sphere" as from its shell but, by virtue of its primary mode of Being itself, it is always "outside with" an already encountered being that belongs to an already discovered world. Dasein, thus, does not leave an "inner sphere" when it "whilingly" is with the beings to be known theoretically and tries to determine them, but its "being outside with the object" is Dasein itself as Being-in-the-world theoretically and knowingly.

Likewise, the perceiving of what is known is not a returning to the "lockers" of consciousness loaded with "booty," after one has gone out to "gather" knowledge. Even in perceiving, retaining, and preserving, the knowing Dasein remains "outside" as Dasein. Even when I merely know, merely imagine, or merely remember some way in which the beings are interconnected, I am not less with them "outside" in the world than I was when I originally perceived them.

By knowing in a theoretical way, Dasein achieves a new "state of Being" with regard to the world already discovered in Dasein's basic mode of Being itself. This new power-to-be can

FROM "DEALING-WITH" TO THEORY   121

develop in an autonomous way and, as science, it can even take control over our Being-in-the-world. The subject's dealing with the world, however, is neither freshly created by theoretical knowledge, nor does it originate from an action of the world on the subject. Theoretical knowledge is a mode of Dasein based upon Being-in-the-world itself.[7]

The preceding remarks contain also a reply to the question about the eksistential conditions which make it possible for Dasein to eksist by way of theoretical knowing. Nevertheless, we must now explicitly reflect on this question in order to throw light on the temporal significance of the transition from the original *praxis* to theory and science. For this reason we must revert also to what was said about the circumspection which characterizes our everyday dealing with beings that are within-the-world.

As has already been shown, the origin of theory cannot be explained by simply declaring that theory is that which is left over when the *praxis* is abandoned. One of the reasons why the origin of theory cannot be explained in this way is the fact that the *praxis* itself always implies a certain way of viewing the beings that are within-the-world, which Heidegger calls circumspection. According to him, theory arises precisely because this "looking-at" the beings that are within-the-world is itself changed when there is a question of theory.

Circumspection is concerned with the referential relations that exist within a given equipmental totality. It is guided by a certain "survey" of this totality. The main characteristic of this survey is that it discloses a complex of involvements in which our concernful dealing with things is situated. In other worlds, this surveying is ultimately a function of the power-to-be that Dasein tries to realize.[8] By interpreting what it has seen through "deliberation," Dasein's surveying circumspection brings the beings that are within-the-world within its area of interest.[9]

The scheme according to which this deliberation takes place can be indicated by the conditional relation "if . . . then." For example, *if* this is to be made, *then* that has to be done first. *If* I want to build a house, *then* I must first buy bricks. By such circumspective deliberation Dasein becomes clearly aware of its situation in the world. Thus, circumspective deliberation does not intend to establish what the characteristics of things are, but to provide Dasein with the possibility of orienting itself within the world. Circumspective deliberation brings things closer to us; it is a way of "making present." This circumspective "making present" has several foundations.

In the first place, it presupposes the retention of a certain equipmental context, that is, a temporalization of the past, a bringing back of the past. In its circumspective deliberation Dasein is always already with a complex of equipment and materials which it discovered in its concernful dealing with the beings that are within-the-world.

Secondly, Dasein looks toward the realization of a certain possibility to which it tends. Thus, whatever Dasein does, realizes, or undertakes is conditioned by a "tending to" and is oriented toward an intended possibility. Therefore, the typical "making present" of circumspective deliberation is confined to bringing closer that which is discovered in a retentive "tending to."

Thirdly, Heidegger continues, the equipment and the material needed for doing something must already be known as such. But this knowing likewise implies necessarily a retention and a "tending to": a "tending to" because I can grasp bricks as bricks only in the perspective of the house that will be built of them; a retention because I can link bricks to the house which I intend to build only by returning to past events.

The condition which makes it possible that what has been projected in circumspective understanding can be brought closer in a "making present," lies in the unity of temporalization, i.e., in the way the present is rooted in the future and in "having-been."[10]

The importance of all this for the transition from the original *praxis* to theory and science can perhaps best be shown by way of an example. When I say of a hammer which I am now using, that it is too heavy for me, I want to say that the handling of that hammer requires too much effort on my part. In that case I regard the hammer as a tool which I use within a certain equipmental totality. I can also say, however, that the hammer weighs three pounds. In that case, I no longer consider the hammer in function of a definite role within this particular equipmental totality, but rather as a material thing that is subject to the law of gravity. Compared to the first sentence, the second sentence contains a shift in standpoint: the hammer has been detached from the whole within which it was handled and conceived; it is considered now merely as a material thing which is "simply there."

In this latter perspective it is no longer meaningful to say that the hammer is heavy or light; now the only meaningful statement is the one that expresses precisely how much the hammer weighs. This shift in standpoint is neither the result of the fact that we have actually ceased to wield the hammer, nor of the fact that we make abstraction from such possible handling of it. These two aspects are left out of consideration in a purely negative way. The only important point is that we have adopted an entirely new attitude in regard to the hammer, in virtue of which we acquire a new view of it. This viewpoint, in turn, leads to an entirely new type of understanding in which the hammer is regarded solely as a material thing that is "simply there."

Accordingly, there is a change in our understanding of the beings as beings, for the beings that are within-the-world are now divorced from their world; they are no longer conceived in their relation to the whole of the surrounding world (demundanization). When we say that the hammer weighs three pounds, we disregard not only its possible use, but also its location relative to a certain equipmental totality. Its actual and possible locations do not matter any more, for the hammer is no longer within the spatial and temporal world. We can also reverse this and say that its location has become a spatio-temporal moment, a "world point," which is in no way distinguished from any other such point.[11]

In this way the world is being stripped of its spatial determinations. The temporal aspect of the beings are also eliminated, since I no longer consider the hammer in the perspective of its use now, on the basis of an actual situation. The advantage of such a procedure is that from now on I am able to describe and determine with precision the structural moments of the "merely there." --We must now return to the question concerning the relevance of all of this for our effort to come to a better understanding of the essence of modern science.

An important characteristic of contemporary science can perhaps be seen in the fact that the sciences make the relevant beings appear only in that kind of objectivity which is constituted and maintained by the various scientific objectivations.[12] This point needs to be explained somewhat more in detail. As we have already seen, for Heidegger the primordial root and source of meaning is not found in a relationship of knowing but in a relationship of Being. Knowing is only a special, derivative mode of our Being-in-the-world. The characteristic feature of this way of Being-in-the-world is that Dasein confines itself to "looking at" the world without being totally involved and engaged in it.

This contemplative "looking at" always implies a *particular* attitude of Dasein toward the beings in the world; hence the beings that are encountered in this way are always seen from a *particular* viewpoint. Which aspect these beings will reveal to

Dasein in its theoretical attitude depends on the attitude Dasein will adopt in regard to them. By making that aspect the object of a critical and methodical inquiry, theoretical Dasein lays the foundation for a particular empirical science.

Accordingly, by his very attitude toward the things that are there, the man of science defines an area of the beings that are within-the-world as the domain of his object of study. This discovery and the precise delimitation of a well-defined domain is the first step of every scientific research. The assertion that the "object" of each of the sciences represents a well-defined domain is evident from the fact that the "object" prescribes a priori the way in which possible problems should arise. Every new phenomenon emerging in such a domain is examined as long as it fits into the normative object totality of the science in question.[13] The problem now is how this discovery and this delimitation of such an object domain is to take place.

16: THEMATIZATION. THEMATIZATION IS OBJECTIVATION

Heidegger thinks that in every theoretical, and a fortiori in every scientific, orientation toward the world, the scientific experience itself contains already a special thematization in which the object of knowledge is taken, constituted, and projected as its theme.[14] In this projection a certain domain of the beings is staked out, the approach to this domain is given its particular methodical direction, the structure of the conceptual and discursive explanation receives its orientation, and a specific language is constituted.

The thematization comprises the above mentioned primordial projection, the staking out of a definite object domain, the determination of the method as the approach to this domain, and the orientation of the conceptual structure and of the linguistic expression proper to this domain of research. The purpose of the thematization is to free the worldly beings or a particular group of beings in such a way that they can be the object of a purely theoretical discovery and therefore can be examined "objectively." Thematization thus is objectivation.

Heidegger, thus, demands that every science be "objective," that it adhere to the "facts"; but he refuses to admit that these facts can be completely "dehumanized" (scientism) or ought to be completely divorced from the world (idealism). The reason for this refusal is that the scientific subject also is a Being-in-the-world and as such continues to be at least partially involved in it.[15]

To clarify his position, Heidegger distinguishes between "Being available as equipment" of the beings within-the-world in our everyday concernful dealing and their "merely Being present at hand" when we assume the scientific attitude. He argues that just as our daily concern precedes our scientific "looking at," so also "Being available as equipment" precedes "merely Being present at hand."

Before we are able to conceive of something under a special aspect in a limiting and abstracting consideration, we must already have been confronted with this thing in its fullness in an all-embracing relation in which we were still totally involved.

Accordingly, the shift in standpoint of the theoretical scientist has an abstracting and limiting function, by virtue of which that which is primordially given is broken up in such a way that one aspect can be sharply illuminated. Thus every science, even in its scientific experience, is rooted in the a priori character of the formal aspect under which a group of things is considered in each case.

Everything else depends on this formal aspect: the foundations of scientific research, the methods, the language, the type of argumentation, the mode of intelligibility, and the typical conception of truth and certitude. Thus, at the root of every science we find a "making present" of the beings that are within-the-world. This "making present" differs from our everyday concern in that it aims solely at disclosing the beings in an "objective" way, i.e., as pure data of theoretical observation, as "merely being there."[16]

The ultimate material object of a science is the perceived real things. The task of science is to describe that which is so perceived as "merely present at hand," i.e., from the viewpoint of the ontic objectivation. Thus it follows that science is not only abstract in itself, but that its proper object also must always be something abstract. For reality, taken as "merely there" is only the correlate of a secondary intentionality which has its foundation in, and results from, our primordial intention which is our eksistence itself. If, then, in science we speak of reality as an object by itself, we envisage it from the start according to a dimension which is only virtually contained in perception, but with which it does not coincide completely.

In comparison to perceived reality, objective reality is an interpretation and an explanation but at the same time also an impoverishment. Science makes an objective aspect of the primordial perception explicit, but in doing so it turns away from the real beings taken in the full sense of the term, in order to discover and explain only one of their aspects. Since this aspect is indeed an aspect of the real, science remains theoretical knowledge of what is real. Accordingly, the explicitation, interpretation, and explanation of the purely objective side of the real leads to a specific meaning which truly belongs to these beings, but only from the viewpoint of its "merely Being present at hand." This meaning can be disclosed only by a method and by cognitive processes that correspond to the proper object.[17]

Thus both the prescientific and the scientific comportment to the beings constitute a form of knowing, i.e., a form of revealing that reveals what previously was still concealed and hidden, the uncovering of what formerly was still covered up, the disclosing of what before was closed over. Scientific knowledge is determined by the fact that eksisting Dasein gives itself as its own freely chosen task the revealment and disclosure of the beings which to some degree at least already are accessible to it, and it does so in such a manner that this is done for the sake of the beings' Being-discovered (*um seines Ethülltseins willen*). The free grasping of the possibility of such an unveiling (taken as a task of Dasein's eksistence) is, as the grasping of the unveiling of those beings, in itself also a freely binding-itself to the beings that are so to be unveiled as such. When Dasein gives itself this task, the beings themselves, taken as what they are and how they are, are taken freely as the only instances which from now on will regulate the investigating comportment. When Dasein commits itself to this kind of investigation, all practical aims and goals of this comportment which are oriented toward use and application of what is so unveiled and known must be suspended or at least deferred; in the same way, Heidegger continues, all limits fall away and disappear which may limit the investigation perhaps from a merely technical point of view; the entire effort is oriented rather toward the beings themselves and meant to bring them from concealment into the open and in this way "to give them their due," i.e., to let them be the beings which in themselves they are.[18] We must now ask the question of precisely what the essential structural moment is through which such a new comportment that is meant to do nothing but to unveil the beings for the sake of their own Being-unveiled, becomes constituted? Heidegger calls this comportment in which the scientific attitude becomes constituted, the objectivation (*Vergegenständlichung*). What is objectivation and what is the basic condition of its realization?

THEMATIZATION AND OBJECTIVATION 127

By objectivation, Heidegger continues, we mean the process in and through which we make something into an object. We can make an object only those beings that already somehow were beforehand. Yet beings need not become objects; they can be what they are without our objectivation. For a being to become an object does not mean that it now for the first time begins to be. Rather it means that this being, as the being that it is, now comes to stand before our knowing questioning to which it from now on will be answerable. From now on the beings stand opposite the questioning that tries to unveil them; and it is in this way because it is answerable to the question of what, how, and whence it is.[19]

Once the beings have become objectified, we are confronted with the task of showing and determining these beings in themselves which have been encountered from themselves in this standing opposite to us. Now all determining is a distinguishing, delineating; yet, at the same time, it also implies the effort to show that all of these determinations somehow belong together. In the unveilment of these beings they become delineated, comprehended, and understood. The concepts which are the result of such an unveilment of the beings must as far as their content is concerned, be shown and verified from the perspective of the beings that they signify and from which they have been derived. There are a great number of different domains of beings which can become the objects of scientific investigation. Depending on the essence of these beings, there is in each case a typical approach, a typical form of research, and correspondingly also in each case a different manner in which the basic concepts are formed, and a different manner in which proofs are given. Heidegger says that he is here unable to describe these different approaches and procedures in detail. He rather prefers to proceed at once to the second question raised above: what is the basic condition of the performance of the objectivation and precisely what is its result?

We have seen already that each comportment toward the beings is possible only on the basis of some pre-ontological understanding of the Being of these beings, even though this understanding remains in many instances completely implicit and, thus, cannot yet really be called a genuine understanding of the Being of these beings. Yet any time we concern ourselves with beings, we do so on the basis of a pre-ontological understanding of the Being of these beings. In the sciences certain beings must in each case as such become the object of unveilment and unveiling determination. In that case the main and primary task becomes the effort to bring these beings to light as the beings which they are. The realization of this task will, therefore, depend on the realization of the basic condition which belongs to every form of unveilment of the beings, i.e., on the effective understanding of their Being. In the sciences, in which these beings as such become objects of investigation, obviously an explicitly developed and articulated understanding of the beings' Being becomes necessary. In other words, the essence of the objectivation consists in the explicitly developed and articulated understanding of the Being of the beings in which the basic constitutive structure of the beings which are to become the objects of investigation, becomes understandable. To give some examples: the task of the historical objectivation of the beings as history implies necessarily an explicitly articulated understanding of that which belongs to history as such; all biological research necessarily implies some understanding of life, organism, etc. The more explicit and original our understanding of the beings' mode of Being is, the more adequate will the effort be in which the beings which are made the objects of research in the various sciences, will become unveiled.

Thus the genesis of a science comes-to-pass in the objectivation of a domain of beings, i.e., in the formation and structural development of the understanding of the conception of the mode of Being of the relevant beings. In this development the concepts which are to delineate what the historical as such is, what is truly characteristic for living things, etc., become articulated; in other words, in this process the basic concepts of a given science become unfolded and articulated. The articulation of the basic concepts also delineates in each case the ground and the foundation of the given discipline and its domain. The domain which in this way is delineated by the process of objectivation can now become the theme of investigation; the objectified whole can then be examined in different directions and established and defined as the object of investigation. Thus the thematization develops in each case on the basis of the relevant form of objectivation.

The entire process which we have tried to describe here usually takes place in a "naive" manner so that the researchers often are not explicitly aware of what is happening before their eyes, so to speak. Yet that the objectivation constitutes the essential process in the genesis of a given science, and that this process is nothing but the formation and articulation of the understanding of the basic mode of Being of the relevant beings

THEMATIZATION AND OBJECTIVATION 129

which are to become the theme of scientific investigation in a given science, can be shown unequivocally to be the case by means of a description of the genesis of the modern, mathematical science of nature. We shall return to this later and, thus, shall now merely indicate briefly in what sense this indeed is the case.[20]

What is decisive for the development of mathematical physics consists neither in its high esteem for the observation of the "facts," nor in its application of mathematics in determining the character of the natural processes and events; rather it consists in the manner in which nature itself is mathematically projected. In this projection something which is constantly present-at-hand, namely, the material beings, is discovered in advance in such a way that a certain horizon is opened up in which only what is somehow quantitatively determinable is further relevant (for instance, mass, motion, force, place, time, and so on). Only in the light of natural things that have been projected in this way can anything like a fact be found and set up for an experiment which will be regulated in terms of this projection. The foundation of a factual science was possible only because the early scientists understood that in principle there are no "bare facts."[21]

In the mathematical projection of nature, moreover, what is decisive is not primarily the mathematical as such, but the fact that such a projection discloses a certain *a priori*. Therefore, the paradigmatic character of mathematical physics does not consist in its exactness or in the fact that it is intersubjectively valid and binding for everyone. It consists rather in the fact that the beings which it takes as its theme are discovered consistently in harmony with the prior projection of their Being-structure. When the basic concepts of this way of understanding a mode of Being have been worked out in detail, the clues for its methods, the structure of its way of conceiving things, the possibility of truth, and certainty which belongs to it, the way in which things get founded and proved, the mode in which it is binding for everyone, and the way in which it is communicated, all of these are then determined. It is precisely the totality of all these items which constitutes the full eksistential meaning of a science.[22]

17: ON THE RELATIONSHIP BETWEEN FOUNDATIONAL RESEARCH IN A SCIENCE AND PHILOSOPHY

A science of beings is constituted by the objectifying thematization, i.e., by the basic act in which the ontological constitution of these beings which are to be delineated as the object domain of the relevant science becomes projected. But is such a "self-founding" already truly a foundation of that science? The answer to this question is "yes," insofar as each science receives its ground and research domain by the projection of the ontological structure of the beings which it examines. The answer must be "no," insofar as this projection in each science itself is in need of a future foundation. The foundation of the objectifying projection which projects the ontological structure and its domain and which, thus, is constitutive for every science, can, in and by that science itself, not be provided. But why is it that the projection of the ontological structure of the relevant domain of investigation which is achieved in and by every science, of necessity is intrinsically limited, and why does every science ask for a further foundation?[23]

a. THE LIMIT OF THE SELF-FOUNDING OF EVERY SCIENCE

In the projection of the ontological structure of a domain of beings (such as nature or history) we find reflections on what the beings of that domain are and how they are. The understanding of the mode of Being of these beings becomes to some degree explicit and one usually succeeds in articulating this understanding in clear concepts. The projection of the ontological structure of the region "nature" implies the determination of the basic concepts to be used in the study of this domain of beings: motion, body, place, time, etc. Yet the delineation and determination of the basic concepts to be used reach only as far as the task which a science sets itself, demands it. That means that the physicist, for instance, carefully defines what he understands by motion, place, and time, but he does not focus on the essence of motion, space, and time as such. For a physicist time is that in regard to which he measures motion.[24]

As long as the scientist concerns himself with the beings that belong to his domain of investigation, his research has a typical definiteness and certainty. Yet in reflections on what motion, place, and time might be, he often feels insecure in view of the fact that the methods he is used to, are of little help here. The result of this state of affairs is that most scientists refrain from reflections on such basic concepts as motion, place, and time. We see a similar attitude among biologists, anthropologists, philologists, and historians, the moment questions are raised about what life, historicity, language, etc., precisely are. In all cases it appears that the methods of the different sciences are incapable of dealing with such issues. Yet these questions are very important insofar as the development in a science is determined not so much by the discovery of facts, but by a new conception of the meaning of its basic concepts, i.e., by the change in our understanding of the ontological structure of the beings of the relevant domain.

It is thus clear in what sense the effort to give a science a foundation from within the science itself in part has to fail. The sciences use methods that are incapable of dealing with "foundational" issues, i.e., of dealing with questions about the genuine meaning of the basic concepts and with questions about the ground from which such basic concepts can be explained. The further foundation of the foundational work that takes place within each science, cannot be provided by the relevant science; yet this further foundation is the genuine and proper foundation of a science.[25]

b. THE FOUNDATION OF A SCIENCE, REGIONAL ONTOLOGY, AND FUNDAMENTAL ONTOLOGY

Heidegger finally turns to an effort to explain briefly the significance of the foundation that no science can give itself and for which it thus depends on another kind of theoretical knowledge.

We have seen that no science, using its own methods, can deal meaningfully with questions about the meaning of its own basic concepts. These basic concepts have to do not with the relations and interactions between the beings of a given domain, but rather with the ontological structure of the beings of that domain. The scientific methods employed in a science were developed to study the relations and interactions between the beings of a given domain, not to unfold the basic meaning of fundamental concepts which describe the mode of Being of the relevant beings. To unfold the basic meaning of fundamental concepts one cannot use methods which objectify beings, but rather one must employ methods which help us thematize the ontological structure of the beings of a given domain.[26]

We thus see that at the borderline of each science we find the need for a thematic reflection on the projection of the ontological structure of the beings of a relevant research domain in which the Being of these beings is articulated as such. The foundation of each science's self-foundation tries to change a pre-ontological understanding of Being into an ontological understanding. Such a foundational effort inquires thematically and systematically into the concepts of the mode of Being and the ontological structure of the relevant beings as such. Thus the deeper foundation described here is not added to a science from the outside, but consists in the explicit articulation and justification of the pre-ontological understanding of the Being of the relevant beings.

Now in view of the fact that each science has its own domain or region of beings which it makes its object of investigation, the relevant ontological reflection focuses in each case on the regional ontological structure which determines the mode of Being of the beings of a region. Thus to every science there belongs a certain regional ontology which as such it itself, however, is unable to develop.[27]

Yet in addition to all these regional ontologies we also need a general ontology which concerns itself with the mode of Being of all beings, regardless of whether they are made into objects of a given science. Heidegger calls this ontology fundamental ontology. In his view, ontology, provided it be taken in a universal and radical sense, is nothing but the essence of philosophy itself. Heidegger does not explain all of this in detail but limits himself to the observation that from the preceding reflection it should be clear by now that the foundation of every science leads to some kind of ontological research which, in turn, leads us to general ontology. Thus the foundation of the sciences has to take place in philosophy.[28]

In the philosophical reflections that focus on the ontological structure of the beings studied by the various sciences, one focuses on what the sciences themselves usually presuppose and thus on that which is *a priori* in regard to what the sciences themselves deal with.

Heidegger finally concludes these reflections by developing the following theses: (1) historically there always was a close relationship between science and philosophy; (2) the preceding reflections have shown that all sciences in their root and ground really are already philosophical; (3) yet explicit engagement in philosophical reflection is a matter of the highest personal freedom; (4) this is the reason why many scientists engage in their science without ever explicitly reflecting on their own science by means of philosophical investigations; for one can indeed engage in science without turning to philosophical reflection, just as one can practically and technically without turning to philosophical reflection.[29]

In conclusion we can thus say that the self-founding already present in every science needs a further and deeper foundation, because in each science there is a pre-ontological understanding of the Being of the relevant beings that must be accounted for even though each science itself is incapable of doing so. The deeper foundation of the self-foundation of each science is to take place in a relevant regional ontology. Regional ontologies themselves must again be founded in a fundamental ontology which constitutes the center of philosophy. Each science has within itself necessarily a latent, more or less developed and articulated ontology which supports and founds that science.[30] This ontology is to be founded in the last analysis by fundamental ontology.

18: SCIENCE AND OTHER FORMS OF RATIONAL DISCOURSE

If we understand by "culture" the realm in which the spiritual and creative activities of man are carried out, science together with its structure and organization is a part of our Western culture. Science ranks high among those achievements which modern man values. But as long as we take science merely in this sense we shall never be able to gauge the scope of its abiding presence among us. This is equally true for art; art is also mentioned as a part of our culture; and if we look at art merely from that point of view we experience again nothing of its mode of Being. Science is really no more a cultural activity than art is. Science is one way (and today this is the predominant and decisive way) in which all-that-is presents itself to us. The domain within which contemporary man moves and tries to maintain himself is fundamentally determined on an increasing scale by modern, Western science.

Over the past four centuries science has developed into such a power as could never have been met with on earth before. This power is now spreading over the entire earth. Since it seems to be a human creation, and since man seems to have brought it to its dominance, science seems to be totally under man's control, so that if he ever wished, he could destroy it. In fact this is not the case because a certain destiny reigns here which is more powerful than the free decision of an individual or group. Science appears to be more than a mere wanting-to-know on the part of man; and this something more hides itself from us as long as we look at science from the ordinary and common point of view. This other dimension is something which holds sway throughout all the sciences, but remains hidden to the sciences themselves. We shall not be able to bring this "something other" to the fore, if we do not first try to achieve adequate clarity about what science really is.

In view of the fact that the prevailing world view of our contemporary Western culture is largely controlled by the sciences, a philosophy which wishes to make the fundamental philosophical problems of the time its theme in a manner that appeals to modern man, can hardly afford to ignore the phenomenon "science." The main problems philosophy must raise in regard to the sciences are the well-known basic questions of what science really is; how it is constituted; what is to be thought about its truth, certainty, and exactness; what relationships exist between science and technology; and especially what the relationship between philosophy and the non-philosophical sciences should be.[31]

Science and philosophy are essentially different. One of the differences between these two forms of knowing can be found in the fact that the sciences as such do not "think radically," while philosophy is to be characterized precisely by the radicalism of its thinking. This fundamental difference, which at the same time implies a profound divergence in method, creates an unbridgeable gap between philosophy and science. Any attempt to pass from the one form of knowing to the other encounters insurmountable difficulties because no bridge over this abyss exists. Going from philosophy to science and vice versa can be accomplished only by a leap, an abrupt transition by a fundamental change of attitude.[32]

Scientists generally interpret such a statement as a belittling remark which, however, is in no way so intended. Philosophy does not mean to speak against science; on the contrary, it tries to act on behalf of the latter by attempting to reach clarity in regard to science's true nature. Science itself is unable to attain such clarity. For science also has another characteristic which becomes immediately evident when one tries to understand what science is; it consists in the fact that science cannot turn toward its own essence and the essence of its own subject matter. At any rate, the statement that science does not think radically does not mean that scientists do not think, or that philosophical thinking

SCIENCE AND OTHER FORMS OF RATIONAL DISCOURSE

is superior to scientific thinking, or even that philosophical thought should not pay attention to the sciences. As a rational being, every scientist can move onto various levels of thoughtful investigation and reflection, and often does so whenever he goes beyond his method to deal with problems flowing from the presuppositions of his science. Science is intimately related to thinking, even though a leap is necessary to move from the one to the other. For the unique and positive essence of each science as well as the essence and origin of its domain and its mode of knowing are inaccessible to the methods characteristic of that science, whereas both obviously are most worthy of thought.[33]

Thinking moves into the unthought of science, to the question of its mode of Being, without the assistance of logic and empirical methods, without the intention of formulating theories and ideas which directly would be scientifically relevant. Thinking is not a science, most certainly not the science of science (epistemology). The claim that science itself is unable to deal with its own essence and the mode of Being of its subject matter and that thought is able to move into the unthought of science is often taken by scientists as a sign that philosophy evaluates itself as superior to scientific thinking. We must take into account, however, that "philosophy" is aware of the fact that it has not yet been successful in trying to discover the essence of the mathematical, the physical, and the historical. Strictly speaking, it knows less in this regard than the sciences, in that for centuries the latter have lived up to their name by leading to genuine achievements within the limits imposed upon them by the methods they employ.[34]

Nevertheless it remains true that the sciences are one-sided in the sense that so long as they remain true to their own character, they are unable to reflect upon the essence of their own subject matter, as well as upon the mode of Being of their own objects. The impressive results which the sciences have accomplished within their own domains often caused scientists to overlook this one-sidedness. When the scientists begin their scientific investigations they always presuppose a certain realm of meaning which is "already there," whereas philosophy's major concern precisely consists in the radical questions that are immediately connected with the totality of all possible meaning of which we can now conceive.

A final characteristic of contemporary science can, as we have seen, be found in the fact that the sciences make things appear only as objects to be characterized by a certain kind of objectivity which in each case is constituted and maintained by the various objectifying thematizations. The sciences themselves do not and cannot make these various forms of objectivation into the explicit theme of investigation; philosophy, taken in the sense of meditating and reflecting thinking, finds here again something unthought in science that is worthy of being examined carefully.[35]

We have seen thus that one of the characteristics of modern science consists in the fact that science cannot turn toward the essence of its own subject matter. The historian who confines himself to purely historical methods can never discover what "the historical" is in itself, just as a mathematician is unable to explain the essence of "the mathematical" with purely mathematical methods. Biology already presupposes a certain realm of phenomena, that of the living things, which is to constitute its domain of objects. Classical physics presupposed as its domain of investigation the celestial and terrestrial bodies to the degree that their motions can be explained with the help of masses and forces within the overall framework of absolute space and time. In each case, the scope and the limits of the realms of the phenomena to be examined rested or rests on certain assumptions. This is true for every empirical science. The field in which a science moves is never grounded by that science itself. Every science rests on assumptions with regard to its domain of investigation which, in fact, are meta-physical positions that cannot be justified or even suitably thought by scientific concepts and scientific methods. When a scientist turns to these assumptions, he speaks no longer as a scientist but as a meta-physicist. Such a meta-physical deliberation on these assumptions is necessary if a science is to be genuine knowledge. The capacity to explain, predict, and control certain phenomena is a very important one; yet the application of methods does not necessarily lead to genuine understanding. A scientist must realize that there is an essential difference between science and meta-physics and that, thus, a leap must be made and not just a broadening of the ways of thought which he uses in his scientific research, if he is to clarify his basic assumptions. In other words, there is hidden in every science a higher form of knowledge upon which the value of that science appears to rest. As we have seen already, scientific research and meta-physical deliberation are bound together at an even more fundamental level. Historically it can be shown that both are grounded on a definite interpretation of the totality of meaning and a definite conception of the essence of truth, which

SCIENCE AND OTHER FORMS OF RATIONAL DISCOURSE

themselves are eminently worthy of being thought about. The very idea of the possibility of a scientifically founded world view, which confuses the function of meta-physics with that of science, emerges from the hidden source that constitutes the metaphysical essence of our entire modern age.[36]

The extra-scientific character of the reflections on the mode of Being of science should be even more evident. Yet it is commonly believed that someone competent in a science is also competent in a discourse about that science as a science. Physics itself is not a possible object of physical research and a physicist who acts as a physicist cannot make any statements about physics. In order to be able to reflect on a science as such, it is necessary to transcend that science and adopt a "transcendental" point of view. The history of science clearly shows that each science evokes such a "transcendental" deliberation on a continuous basis.[37]

Although the scientist is unable to think *scientifically* about his own science, he can certainly think *meta-physically* about the basic assumptions of his own science, and this can be done on different levels. Newton, Einstein, Bohr, and Heisenberg, in the basic ideas which they introduced, have been led to meta-physical decisions with regard to the fundamental concepts and principles of modern physics. Rather than merely thinking within the domain of physics, they have thought about it, delineating new directions for it and "creating new ways of asking questions and above all holding-out into that which is most worthy of questioning."[38]

But even these reflections on the fundamental assumptions of a particular science are not yet the highest possibility for thoughtful reflection. Far more important than the foundational crises of the individual sciences is the crisis of modern science as such which has led to the present fate of Western man. To deal with these issues in a meaningful manner a more radical form of thought is necessary, one which implies the "composure toward that which is most worthy of questioning."[39] For despite all the efforts to demarcate the essence of modern science, the fundamental issue involved here continues to remain unnoticed. It has been said that science is a cultural product of the creative activity of man; this may be true; yet it does not reveal the more fundamental issues that belong to the essence of modern science. The manner in which many people understand modern science suggests that science is the privileged and primordial way in which man is to comprehend all that is; at the same time, it obscures the progressively increasing domination which science exercises over modern man. There is a more profound destiny hidden in modern science than the common interpretation of science can account for. It will not do to characterize modern science by simply stating that science is something that man has made because of his curiosity and his desire to know.[40]

The essence of modern science is inextricably interwoven with the essence of modern metaphysics and that of modern technology. Thus a genuine meditating reflection on the essence of science is actually a reflection on our own age and its hidden orientation and direction. But particularly as far as this is concerned, thoughtlessness is a basic characteristic of modern man. This thoughtlessness is the result of a long process in which philosophy was gradually reduced to metaphysics and metaphysics subordinated to science and technology. True there were at no time such far-reaching plans, so many inquiries into so many areas, so much research carried on as passionately as today. It is true also that this kind of thinking has its great usefulness and even remains indispensable. Yet this calculative form of thinking is incapable of dealing with the *meaning* of the things and events it treats scientifically.[41] It is equally unable to guide modern man in the technical possibilities which modern science made available to him. Both modern science and technology have become powers that seem to go their own ways and, thus, have become modern man's "fate." If today we are to come to grips with our own destiny we shall have to turn to a form of thinking which is not calculating, but one that is characterized by "releasement toward things and openness to the mystery."[42]

These vague and as yet ambiguous assertions must be explained in more detail in what follows. There it will become clear from the very start that as far as science is concerned, our concern will not be with epistemological, logical, or methodological issues, but rather with ontological problems connected with the all-pervasive phenomenon "science." That such a concern does not include any immediate criticism of other approaches to science is obvious, although it is true that this view entails that a philosophy of science without this basic dimension remains incomplete.[43] We must now turn to the question of what all of this entails as far as the modern sciences of nature are concerned.

CHAPTER V

TOWARD AN ONTOLOGY
OF
THE MODERN SCIENCES OF NATURE

Between 1936 and 1959 Heidegger wrote a number of essays and lecture courses in which he raised issues that are immediately relevant to what I have called an "ontology of science." Of these essays and lecture courses the following are of prime importance: *What is a Thing?* (1935-1936), "The Era of the World as Picture," (1938), "Zur Erörterung der Gelassenheit," (1944-1945), *What is Called Thinking?* (1951-1952), "Science and Reflection," (1953), "The Question Concerning Technology," (1953), and *Gelassenheit* (1955).[1]

In each case Heidegger focussed on an important aspect or dimension of modern science in an effort to explain the coming-to-presence and abidance (*Wesen*) of modern science in our world, and its impact on the manner in which we think, act, work, and live. Whereas Heidegger in his earlier works made a clear distinction between reflections on the natural sciences and reflections on the historical sciences, in the later works the historical sciences are seldom mentioned as such. From 1936 on Heidegger appears to have been predominantly concerned with the scientificity of the empirical sciences and with their impact on our world.

In most of these texts Heidegger selects the modern science of nature as the paradigm with the help of whose genesis and historical development he then tries to clarify the basic theses which he tries to develop in each case. This is the reason why I have decided to distinguish Heidegger's concern with the modern science of nature from his reflections on other empirical sciences. Thus in this chapter I plan to focus on the genesis of mathematical physics; the behavioral, social, and historical sciences will be discussed in subsequent chapters.

In view of the fact that these reflections on physics form a closely knit unity I have made an effort to present what I take to be Heidegger's main concern in a systematic fashion. Yet I shall follow Heidegger's essays just mentioned rather closely; on a few occasions this procedure appeared to entail some overlap and repetition.

19: ORIGIN AND MEANING OF THE MODERN MATHEMATICAL SCIENCES OF NATURE

a. MODERN SCIENCE VS. ANCIENT AND MEDIEVAL SCIENCE

Heidegger begins his reflections on the natural sciences with the remark that he is concerned here with modern science, not with the Greek *episteme* or the medieval *doctrina* or *scientia*. For, Heidegger continues, it is important to realize that each of these conceptions of systematic knowledge that can be developed on the basis of principles and methods, has its own distinctive way of looking at, and asking questions about, "things" which, in turn, depend on their interpretation of the Being of things, their thingness.[2] In other words, there is an essential difference between modern science on the one hand, and Greek and medieval science on the other, and this basic difference is founded upon a different interpretation of the Being of the relevant beings. Thus it is not correct to describe the difference between modern and ancient science as a simple "paradigm change" within one existing and established discipline. This is also the reason why it is impossible to conceive of ancient and modern science as two forms of knowledge which differ in degree only and to claim that modern science has made great progress in comparison with ancient science.[3]

But even those who do admit that there is an essential difference between ancient and modern science have not been able to come to a common agreement on the manner in which the difference is to be determined in detail. According to some authors the difference between classical and modern science consists in this that modern science, in contradistinction to ancient and medieval science, starts from universal speculative propositions and concepts. In Heidegger's view, there is some truth to this claim, even though it is the case that ancient and medieval science did observe facts and that modern science employs universal concepts and propositions. Both ancient and modern sciences are concerned with facts and with universal concepts and statements; the contrast between them consists in the manner in which in each case the facts are conceived, and in the manner in which universal concepts and statements are established.[4]

The greatness of physics during the sixteenth and seventeenth centuries rests in part on the fact that most scientists were also philosophers. Thus they fully understood that there cannot be just mere facts; a fact is what it is only in light of the fundamental conception with which man in each case approaches the natural phenomena. Twentieth century positivism thinks that one can manage with facts alone and that basic concepts are just expedient means which one somehow needs, but with which in science one should not concern himself. Yet the leading scientists themselves today still do what the leading scientists of the 17th century did: the founders of atomic physics, Bohr and Heisenberg, still think in a thoroughly philosophical manner. This is the reason that they created new ways of asking questions and were able to find new ways to solve them.[5]

Other authors have tried to characterize the difference between the ancient and the new science by claiming that the latter, contrary to the former, uses experiments and proves its theses "experimentally." But to get information about things and events, experiments and tests were already used in both the Greek and the medieval world. For this kind of "experience" is implicit in all technical interaction with things in the various crafts as well as in the use of tools. Here, too, it is thus not so much the experiment or the test as such, but rather the manner in which experiment and test are set up, and the intention with which they are undertaken, that are different in both cases. In modern science in particular, the manner of experimentation is closely connected with the kind of conceptual determination of the facts which the thematizing projection makes possible, as well as with the typical hypotheses used in the effort to find meaningful answers for the questions that from that perspective can be asked in regard to those facts.[6]

Others, finally, have tried to characterize the difference between ancient and modern science by stating that the latter, contrary to the former, uses calculations and measurements. But one should not forget here that calculations and measurements were also used in ancient Greece and in the Middle Ages. It is again the specific manner in which both are being employed that is characteristic for modern science.[7]

Thus these three ways of characterizing the distinction between modern science on the one hand, and ancient and medieval science on the other, remain inadequate as long as one does not find the basic characteristic of modern science, i.e., that which explains why modern science comes-to-presence and abides the way it actually does, that which rules and determines the basic movement of modern science taken as such. As Heidegger sees it, this basic characteristic consists in the typical metaphysical projection of the thingness of the things in modern science. One can indeed say that this characteristic is intimately connected with the mathematical character of modern science, but it is then again essential that this characterization be properly understood. This manner of characterizing modern science is in harmony with an often quoted statement once made by Kant: "However, I maintain that in any particular doctrine of nature only as much genuine science can be found as there is mathematics to be found in it."[8]

b. THE MATHEMATICAL. ON THE MEANING OF "*MATHESIS*"

From the preceding it should be clear by now that the answer to the question of what is meant in this context by "mathematics" cannot be simply taken from the science "mathematics."[9] Heidegger explains that the word "mathematics" is derived from the Greek word *ta mathemata*. Originally this expression meant that which can be taught and learned. Thus the word "*mathesis*" originally meant the act of teaching and learning, as well as that which is taught and can be learned. Furthermore, Heidegger continues, teaching and learning must be taken here in a very broad sense, i.e., in a sense that is not yet connected with any "official" institution of learning or school. To fully understand what the Greeks meant by *ta mathemata*, Heidegger says, one must compare it with that from which they tried to distinguish it: the things insofar as they originate and come-to-presence from themselves (*ta phusika*), the things insofar as they are produced by man (*ta poioumena*), the things insofar as they can be used by man and are at his disposal (*ta chremata*), and the things insofar as man has to do with them, works on them, uses them, transforms them, looks at them, examines them, etc. (*ta pragmata*). The term *ta mathemata* thus refers to the things insofar as they can be learned, i.e., insofar as they can be understood in terms of something that one knows already.[10]

But what is meant here by learning? Inspired by Plato, Heidegger describes it as a becoming familiar with something that somehow one knows already. Learning is a taking cognizance of something that one knows already, a taking cognizance of

TOWARD AN ONTOLOGY OF THE SCIENCES OF NATURE   143

something as what one already knows it to be in advance. When someone shows you a particular bird, then what you see placed before you, becomes visible to you as what it is, because you know already in advance what a bird is. Speaking in general terms, one could say, therefore, that you learn something about a thing when you are able to understand it in terms of something that you know already. A student begins to learn something, not when he just takes over something that is offered to him, but when he experiences what he takes, as something which he himself already has. The most difficult learning consists in coming to know all the way what we already know somehow.[11]

Since mathematical numbers and relationships are most easily learned, this most familiar mathematical domain became "mathematics." But the essence of the mathematical does not lie in numbers of geometrical forms.

After what has been said, Heidegger continues, it will be clear that the claim that the basic characteristic of modern science consists in the mathematical, does not mean that modern science employs mathematics, even though modern science does often use mathematics, taken in the narrow sense of the term. Thus we must now show in what sense the foundation of modern thought is essentially mathematical in the broad sense indicated above.[12] To that end Heidegger turns to a brief reflection on Newton's *Principia*.

c. THE MATHEMATICAL CHARACTER OF MODERN NATURAL SCIENCE. NEWTON'S FIRST LAW

Modern thought did not come-to-presence all at once. Its origin is to be found in the later Scholasticism of the fifteenth century.[13] In the sixteenth century important discoveries were made by Copernicus, Kepler, Paracelsus, Agricola, and many others; yet in the same century the development also encountered a number of unexpected difficulties. It was not until the seventeenth century that the decisive foundations and clarifications of modern science were provided. The entire development found its culmination and its first systematic expression in Newton's major work, *Philosophiae Naturalis Principia Mathematica* (1686-1687), a work devoted to a careful study of the very first principles of natural science. In Heidegger's view, this work "was not only a culmination of preceding efforts, but at the same time the foundation for the succeeding natural science."[14] The book constitutes the foundation of modern science and at the same time sets the limits for its further development. When today we speak of classical physics we always mean the physics for which Newton's *Principia* laid the foundations. When Kant later speaks of "science" he always means Newton's physics; it is thus understandable that Kant's conception of the scientificity of science was deeply influenced by Newton's main work.

The book begins with a brief introductory section, entitled "Definitions." It contains Newton's definitions of quantity of matter (mass), quantity of motion (momentum), and various forces. Then Newton adds a scholion which contains some important statements about absolute and relative space, time, and motion. The next section is entitled "Axioms, or Laws of Motion," a section to which we shall return shortly. After this section the proper content of the work follows; it is divided into three large sections, two of which are concerned with the motions of bodies, whereas the third deals with the system of the world. Heidegger limits his reflections here to a few brief remarks on Newton's first law of motion, the principle of inertia.[15]

The first law states that "every body perseveres in its state of rest, or of uniform motion in a right line, unless it is compelled to change that state by forces impressed thereon."[16] In the Preface to the second edition which was published in 1713, while Newton was still alive, Cotes writes that this law was immediately accepted by all natural scientists.[17] The law was also accepted by virtually all scientists of the subsequent centuries. Today most students of nature do not puzzle over this law, either, and consider it to be more or less self-evident. Yet one hundred years before Newton put the law in this particular form, it was still completely unknown. Furthermore, the law was not really discovered by Newton, but perhaps by Galileo. It is important to note, however, that Galileo never formulated the law in general terms; this was done for the first time by Balliani. Descartes tried to give a metaphysical foundation for the law, whereas Leibniz employed it as a metaphysical principle. What interests us here is the question of precisely how the "mathematical," taken in the broad sense, becomes decisive in the application of this law.[18]

And yet, Heidegger continues, this law is not at all self-evident, and it was not self-evident in the seventeenth century, either. During the preceding two thousand years it was not only unknown, but it would then even have been taken to be meaningless. Its "discovery" and its formulation and establishment as the fundamental law of modern physics belong, in Heidegger's

TOWARD AN ONTOLOGY OF THE SCIENCES OF NATURE

opinion, among the greatest in human thought; it provides the ground for the turning from Ptolemy to Copernicus. It is true, though, that the law of inertia has had its predecessors, in Democritus' philosophy as well as, as we have just seen, in modern science. At any rate, Heidegger concludes, Kant was correct when, in regard to its discovery and formulation by Newton, he spoke about a fundamental fact in the history of thought.[19]

d. THE DIFFERENCE BETWEEN THE GREEK AND THE MODERN EXPERIENCE OF NATURE

The "scientific" conception of the universe that reigned in the West until the seventeenth century was determined by Plato and Aristotle. As far as the knowledge of nature is concerned, scientific thought was guided mainly by Aristotle's treatises on nature. In order to fully appreciate the true significance of the "revolution" articulated in Newton's first law, it will thus be necessary to briefly dwell on some of the basic conceptions of Aristotle. But before we can do so successfully, Heidegger says, we must first free ourselves from a prejudice that many scientists have against the physics of Aristotle. It has often been said by critics that Aristotle's propositions were merely an expression of conceptions which he just thought up, but which lacked any support in the things themselves. This is certainly not true for Aristotle himself, even though this may have been true for some of his commentators. In his treatise on the heavens Aristotle writes that physics wishes "to say that which corresponds to what shows itself as far as the beings themselves are concerned." Aristotle says there also that "the issue, which in the case of productive knowledge (*poietike episteme*) is the work or the product, in the scientific knowledge of nature is the unimpeachable evidence of perception as to each fact."[20]

We have seen that the Greeks distinguished different kinds of things; those that come-to-presence of themselves (*phusei*) were always carefully distinguished from the man-made things. Correspondingly they distinguished different kinds of knowledge; in the present case, theoretical and practical knowledge. The claim which Aristotle makes for the theoretical knowledge of natural things is in no way different from those which Newton made in the *Principia*.[21] To show this, Heidegger places his own translation of the last passage quoted from Aristotle next to a text from the second edition of the *Principia*. Aristotle wrote that "that at which productive knowledge comes to a halt (*telos*) and wherein from the beginning it takes its footing, is the work to be produced. That, however, in which the knowledge of nature takes its foothold, is that which shows itself of that which comes-to-presence of itself." On the other hand, in Book III, Newton lists as Rule IV: "In experimental philosophy we are to look upon the propositions inferred by general induction from phenomena as accurate or very nearly true, notwithstanding contrary hypotheses that may be imagined, till such times as other phenomena occur, by which they may either be made more accurate, or liable to exceptions." And yet, the similarity in basic attitude in regard to procedure notwithstanding, the fundamental position of Newton is substantially different from that of Aristotle. For that which is actually apprehended as appearing, and the manner in which it is interpreted, are by no means the same in each case.[22]

Both Aristotle and Newton agree that natural things are either in motion or at rest; this "fact" is given in direct experience. How bodies and their motions are to be conceived, and what relations they have to each other, is not directly given in experience; nor is it immediately evident what one is to think about these matters. The early Greeks conceived of the earth first as a large disc around which Okeanos floats; the heaven overarches the earth and turns around it. Later Plato, Aristotle, and Eudoxus, each in his own way, pictured the earth as a large ball that constitutes the center of everything. In view of the fact that in the period between 300 B.C. and 1500 A.D. Aristotle's conception of nature became dominant, Heidegger limits himself here to a brief description of Aristotle's doctrine of motion.

Aristotle distinguished different types of change (*metabole*), one of which is *kinesis kata topon*, change or motion according to place. For Newton this type of change is the proper motion of things. According to Aristotle, things move locally *kath'hauta*, from themselves. Every body itself has its own *arche kineseos*. For Aristotle each body moves naturally to that place which is proper for it: earthy bodies move downward, fiery bodies move upward, because the earthy things have their place below, the fiery things belong somewhere in the heaven. Thus each body has its proper place according to its "nature." If a body is not in its proper place, it is brought there by force, by "violence" (*biai*). Its not-being in its proper place is to be explained. All natural motions are motions in a straight line (*kinesis eutheia*); yet celestial bodies move in circular orbits; they move in "perfect" orbits because they are perfect bodies. Celestial movements are also eternal; on the other hand, all natural motions of sublunar

TOWARD AN ONTOLOGY OF THE SCIENCES OF NATURE   147

bodies come to an end, because they all have a natural *telos*. The motion of the celestial bodies in their regular orbits is a natural movement for them, and, thus, needs no explanation by means of extrinsic forces: these bodies do what they are supposed to do according to their "nature." Forces are necessary in cases where bodies do not move *phusei*, according to their nature. All forced motions must ultimately come to a stop.[23]

Heidegger points out here that it is important to realize that all these claims correspond distinctly to the common conception of people based on direct experience and observation: no body moves in a straight line, and the motion imparted to a sublunar body continues for some time and then ceases, passing over into a state of rest, whereas celestial bodies move without end.[24]

Contrary to this view of Aristotle, Newton formulated as the first law of motion that every body left to itself moves uniformly in a straight line: "Corpus omne quod a viribus impressis not cogitur, uniformiter in directum movetur." Let us try, Heidegger continues, to explain the peculiarity of this view step by step:

1) Every body: thus the distinction between sublunar, earthly bodies and celestial bodies is to be abolished; all natural bodies are essentially of the same kind.
2) Circular motion has no priority over motion in a straight line; motion in a straight line becomes fundamental; it and it alone needs no explanation.
3) There are no privileged places for different kinds of bodies. The place of a natural body is no longer the place where it belongs according to its nature; place is just a position of a body in relation to the positions of other bodies.
4) The motions themselves are no longer determined according to different natures, and the essence of force is determined by the fundamental law of motion. A moving body, left to itself, moves uniformly in a straight line for all eternity; a force is that whose impact results in a body's declination from rectilinear, uniform motion. The impressed force is the action exerted on a body in order to change its position of either being at rest or being in a uniform motion in a straight line (Definition IV). For Aristotle the moon moves in a circular orbit because for a perfect celestial body it is its nature to do so. For Newton, on the other hand, the moon should have moved in a straight line uniformly; the reason why it moves in a circular orbit is due to the gravitational force exerted by the earth.
5) Since the concept of place has change, motion is only seen

as a change of position. Motion is defined by means of distances that can be measured. In other words, motion is now defined as the amount of motion ("quantity of motion" is the expression which Newton uses). The same is true for mass and weight.

6) There is no essential difference between natural and forced motions; forced motion is now defined as the measure of the change of motion, i.e., as the measure of the motion's acceleration.

7) Nature no longer is the inner principle out of which the (natural) motion of a body necessarily follows; rather nature becomes the variety of the ways in which the relative positions of bodies can change, the manner in which they are present in space and time; space and time are domains of possible positional orders and determinations of order.

8) The manner of questioning nature changes completely; in a certain respect the manner in which Newton questions nature is even the opposite of the manner in which Aristotle addresses questions to nature.[25]

e. THE ESSENCE OF THE MATHEMATICAL PROJECTION. GALILEO'S FREE FALL EXPERIMENT

We must now try, Heidegger continues, to understand in what sense the mathematical becomes decisive in the application of Newton's first law. The law speaks about a body that is not compelled by impressed forces (*a viribus impressis non cogitur*). Where do we find such a body? There appear not to be any of such bodies. There is also no experiment which could ever bring such a body to direct perception. Thus even though modern science, in contrast to medieval science, was supposed to be based on experience, Newton's basic law of motion speaks of things that as such do not exist. The law requires a basic conception of things which is in contradiction with what everyday experience shows us. This fact tells us something important about the meaning of the "mathematical."

The mathematical, taken in the broad sense, rests on a claim which does not start with a determination of the things' thingness that is in harmony with experience, and yet lies at the base of every determination of the thing, makes them possible, and makes room for them. Such a basic conception of the things' thingness is neither necessary nor arbitrary.[26] It is not possible, Heidegger continues, in this context to describe the long controversy

TOWARD AN ONTOLOGY OF THE SCIENCES OF NATURE   149

controversy which finally led to a universal acceptance of the law, nor can we explain in detail why it required a basic change in the entire approach to natural things, and even the development of a fundamentally new mode of thought. Thus Heidegger limits himself to characterizing this controversy and the basic change it brought about with the help of an example.

According to the conception of Aristotle, heavy bodies fall downward; light bodies move upward. This is what according to their nature they are supposed to do. Furthermore, heavy bodies that are mixed with light bodies must fall more slowly than heavy bodies that are not mixed with light bodies; in other words, the more weight a body has the faster it will fall. On the other hand, Galileo had come to the conclusion that all bodies must fall with the same velocity. There is a story that Galileo performed a public experiment from the leaning tower of Pisa, involving bodies of different weights. Although the bodies did not arrive on the ground at exactly the same time, Galileo nonetheless maintained his position. His opponents, on the other hand, interpreted the outcome of the experiment in favor of their interpretation of Aristotle's theory. Because of this experiment, so the story goes, the opposition against Galileo increased to such an extent that he had to give up his position at the University and leave Pisa.[27] In Heidegger's opinion the following insight can be derived from this story.

Both Galileo and his opponents saw exactly the same "facts." Yet they gave a different interpretation of these facts. Thus the same events were made visible here in different ways. In other words, both parties thought something *along with* the same phenomena, something that according to their view was closely related to the very essence of body and the nature of its motions.[28] What Galileo thought along with the observed phenomena in advance concerning the motions of bodies of different weights was the a priori determination that the motion of *every* body is uniform, when every obstacle is removed, but that the motion of each body also changes uniformly when an equal force affects it.

In 1638 Galileo wrote in his *Discourses on Two New Sciences*: "I think here of a body thrown on a horizontal plane and every obstacle excluded . . . the motion of the body over this plane would be uniform and perpetual, if this plane were extended infinitely."[29] In this proposition by Galileo, which perhaps is the first formulation of Newton's first law, we find the expression: *mente concipio, I think in my mind* of something movable that is left to itself. Thus Galileo gave himself a cognition in advance about the determination of material things. There is here a prior comprehending of what should be essential to all bodies and their motions; all bodies are alike; there is no privileged motion; every place is like every other place; each moment in time is like any other; every force is to be determined by the change of motion which it causes. All determinations of bodies have one basic characteristic as their origin: each natural process is nothing but the space-time determination of the motions of certain point-masses. This basic feature also explains why "nature" is everywhere uniform.[30]

In Heidegger's opinion, we are now in a position in which we can grasp the essence of the mathematical more precisely. In the preceding pages we said only that it is the knowledge of things in which man gives to himself and from himself in advance what he himself takes a thing to be, thus giving himself what he already had before. We can now specify this insight with the help of the following points.

1) The mathematical, taken as thinking in one's mind in advance, is a projection of the thingness of the things which opens up a domain in which only things of a certain kind can henceforth show themselves.
2) In this projection there is posited in advance what things are taken to be and how they are to be evaluated. Such taking-for and evaluating are called in Greek *axioein*. The anticipated determinations which are implied in the projection, are called the *axiomata*. Newton thus correctly called the section in which he presents these essential determinations of all bodies: *axiomata*. Insofar as every science is expressed in statements, the cognition which is posited in the mathematical projection is of such a kind as to set things on their proper foundation *in advance*. Thus axioms are fundamental propositions *a priori*.
3) The mathematical projection is the anticipated conception of the essence of natural bodies. Thus the projection sketches out in advance the blueprint of the structure of every natural body as well as of its relation, to every other body.[31]
4) The blueprint at the same time provides the extention of the realm which, in the future, will eventually encompass all things of that kind. Nature thus no longer is an inner capacity of each body that determines its motion and rest, as Aristotle had claimed,[32] but rather "the realm of the uniform space-time context of motion," which is determined by the

axiomatic projection. In this way nature now becomes the closed totality of the motions of the spatio-temporally related point-masses.[33]

5) The realm of nature which is so axiomatically determined in outline by this projection, also requires for the bodies which belong to it, a mode of access or method that is appropriate to the so predetermined objects. Thus the mode of questioning and determining of natural bodies is now no longer ruled by traditional opinions and conceptions. Bodies have no qualities beyond those projected in the mathematical projection itself. Natural bodies are now only as what they show themselves to be, within this so projected realm. Their entire mode of being is now determined by space and time determinations, masses, and forces. How they show themselves is thus predetermined by the mathematical projection. Therefore, the projection also codetermines the manner in which the scientists perceive, experience, and study what shows itself. The projection posits in advance the conditions to which natural bodies must respond in one way or another. The medieval *experientia* in this way becomes the modern experiment. Modern science is experimental because it is mathematical. In other words, experimentation is necessary because of the *a priori* character of the mathematical projection.[34]

6) Because the projection establishes the uniformity of all bodies according to relations of space, time, mass, force, and motion, it also requires a universal and uniform measure, i.e., a numerical measurement. In this way, Newton's mathematical projection leads to the development and the application of a new kind of mathematics in the narrow sense of the term. Modern science did not arise because mathematics became an essential part of the study of nature. Rather, the fact that a particular kind of mathematics could every become an essential part of the study of nature is a consequence of the mathematical projection of nature. Analytic geometry (Descartes), infinitesimal calculus (Newton), and differential calculus (Leibniz) became possible and necessary on the ground of the basically mathematical character of modern thinking.[35]

In a brief note Heidegger explains that one would most certainly be mistaken if he were to assume that with this brief characterization of the mathematical he had already gained a clear picture of actual, mathematical physics. For in the preceding reflections only an outline of the basic elements has been given.

Several important questions remained undiscussed. Among them the question concerning the relationship between the mathematical in the narrow sense of the term and the intuitive, direct, perceptual experience of the relevant things as well as these things themselves, is probably the most important and the most complex one.[36]

20: TOWARD THE ESSENCE OF THE MODERN SCIENCES OF NATURE

In his essay "The Era of the World as Picture" Heidegger states that the modern sciences of nature constitute an integral part of our modern world; they are essential phenomena of the modern era. Each era of our history is grounded by metaphysics; each era is grounded by a specific interpretation of what-is and by a specific understanding of the truth. This metaphysical foundation dominates all the phenomena that are characteristic for a given age. As Heidegger sees it, the modern era has a number of different but closely related characteristics: modern science, machine technology, the fact that the arts move into the domain of aesthetics, the conviction that one can conceive of all human activities in terms of culture which itself is then understood as the realization of the highest values, and, finally, the complete dedivinization of the world in which Christendom, misunderstanding its true essence, has played an important role. Thus if one is to understand the essence of the modern era one must make an effort to come to a clear understanding of the conception of what is and of the interpretation of the truth that lies at the foundation of these phenomena. Let us limit ourselves here to a brief reflection on the meaning and function of natural science in the modern epoch. The questions which we must reflect on here are the following: (1) How does natural science come-to-presence in the modern era and precisely how does it abide there? (2) What conception of the beings and of the truth is underlying this conception? (3) What does the metaphysical ground which gives modern science its foundation, teach us about the essence of the modern era itself?[37] In the Appendixes to this essay Heidegger states that his main interest in asking these questions is to be found in the question concerning the meaning of Being; for in the final analysis, for philosophical reflection Being is that which is most worthy of questioning. In this chapter we shall not be able to follow Heidegger in his basic concern, however; instead we shall limit ourselves to what he has to say about the "essence" of the modern sciences of nature.[38]

Before one can answer the first question, one must keep in mind, as we have seen already, that the term "modern science" means something that is completely different from what the Greeks called *episteme* and also from what in the Middle Ages was called *doctrina* or *scientia*. Thus it makes no sense to state that modern science is more exact than Greek or medieval science; for Greek and medieval science could not be exact and did not need to be exact. It makes no sense either to claim that Galileo's doctrine of free falling bodies is true and that Aristotle's teaching according to which light bodies strive upwards, is false; for Aristotle's understanding of the essence of body and place and of their mutual relationships rests on a different metaphysical interpretation of what-is and, therefore, conditions a correspondingly different way of looking and of asking questions. Thus anyone who wishes to understand the essence of modern science must free himself from the habit of comparing the new science of nature with the physics of Aristotle and the medieval *philosophia naturalis*.[39]

a. NATURAL SCIENCE IS RESEARCH

According to Heidegger, the essence of modern science consists in this that it is research (*Forschung*). Research, if taken in its essence, contains two basic characteristics: it uses very typical research procedures and it limits its investigations to a clearly delineated realm of beings. The term "procedure" does not mean here "method," because every methodical manner of proceeding presupposes that there is already an open realm in which a science with its methodical procedures can move. The opening-up of such a well-defined realm of beings is precisely the fundamental operation of each form of research. The opening-up and the careful delineation of a determined realm of beings is brought about by a typical thematizing projection (*Entwurf*) by means of which the objects of each form of research become constituted so that a certain aspect of the things is taken as the exclusive theme of investigation. As we have seen, it is by such a thematizing projection that the realm of beings characteristic of a particular form of research becomes delineated, that the methodical procedures to be used in examining these beings from the relevant point of view become determined, and that the structure of the conceptual and discursive explanation acquires its first orientation. In other words, it is this fundamental thematizing projection which, in the final analysis, determines the rigor of scientific research. To explain what is meant here by the thematizing projection, Heidegger uses the example of modern mathematical physics which, in his view, is the earliest in the modern era and, at the same time, also the one that commonly is taken to be the normative one.[40]

We call modern physics mathematical because it makes use of a special kind of modern mathematics. Yet, Heidegger reminds us again, one should realize that modern physics can proceed mathematically only because it is already "mathematical" in a deeper sense. Taken in its original Greek meaning, "the mathematical" refers to that which man, in his theoretical reflections on beings as well as in his practical concern with things, knows already in advance.

By physics we understand the scientific knowledge of nature; in the modern era, physics is usually taken to be the scientific study of the motions of material bodies. When this modern kind of physics developed, it too, to the degree that it is inherently mathematical, had to take something beforehand as that which is already known. This stipulating of what is already known beforehand is nothing less than the thematizing projection of that which from then on, for the knowledge of nature which one was seeking for, would be nature. Modern mathematical physics is concerned with nothing except the closed totality of all spatio-temporally related moving mass-points. And as we have seen, in this blueprint of what is supposed to be nature, a number of important stipulations were incorporated: motion is nothing but change of place, there is no privileged motion and no privileged direction of motion, space has the property of isotropy, no point in time has a privileged position in regard to any other point in time, and finally every force must be defined by the motion it is capable of producing. Each process and each event in nature must be understood from the perspective of this blueprint of nature. The thematizing projection of nature receives the guarantee for its certainty from the fact that physical research, in all of its questioning steps, binds itself in advance to that outline of nature that the thematization itself has projected. The rigor of scientific research, thus, has in every science its own typical character which is determined in each case by the thematizing projection. The rigor of mathematical physics is exactitude.

An event can be considered to be an event of nature, if and only if, it is determined in advance as a spatio-temporal, kinetic magnitude. Such a determination can be established by means of processes of measurement and with the help of the numbers that result from these processes as well as with the calculations applied to them. However, Heidegger observes here again, mathematical physics is not exact because it measures and calculates; rather it must measure and calculate in that manner because its being-bound to its own realm of objects has the character of exactitude. The *Geisteswissenschaften*, on the other hand, and also the sciences that concern themselves with what Dilthey calls "life," must necessarily remain inexact if they are to remain rigorous, i.e., in harmony with the thematizing projection from which they flow.[41]

b. NATURAL SCIENCE PROCEEDS ACCORDING TO METHODS

Science, thus, becomes research (*Forschung*) through its thematizing projection and by securing this projection by proceeding rigorously. Thematizing projection and rigor, on the other hand, can develop into what they truly are only, if the scientists proceed according to methods. Proceeding according to methods constitutes the second characteristic of modern natural science, research with its two essential aspects being the first. For if the projected domain of investigation is to be thematized in its entirety, then it will be necessary to bring the entire domain to light in all its basic dimensions. Now the things of nature are in a constant change. The plenitude of the particularity of the "facts" of nature shows itself only within the horizon of the continuous becoming different of what is changeable. But we have seen already that it is precisely these "facts" which must be objectified. Science, therefore, in all its procedures must place before it the changing things in their change; thus it must bring motion to a stand-still and yet, at the same time, let the motion be as motion. The fact that these "facts" of nature remain identical to themselves, notwithstanding the continuity of their change, constitutes what Heidegger calls the *rule*, whereas the constancy of the change in the necessity of its course constitutes what he calls the *law*. It is therefore, in his view, only within the perspective of rule and law that the "facts of nature" become understandable as such. Scientific research of "facts" in the domain of nature, therefore, always implies the formulation and the verification of rules and laws.

The methodical procedures in and through which a domain of objects can be brought to light have the character of a clarification which clarifies something on the basis of something else that is clear already; thus they have the character of an elucidation. This elucidation always has two sides: on the one hand, it gives a foundation to something which is unknown by means of something that is known already, and, on the other hand, it verifies what is known already through that which at first was still unknown. In other words, this clarification is effected in and by investigations. In the natural sciences investigation always implies experimentation; the nature of the experiments is in each case determined by the character of the realm of "facts" to be investigated and by the goals to be achieved by the clarification. But, as we have seen, according to Heidegger modern physics does not become research because it performs experiments; rather experiments become possible where and only where our knowledge of nature has already changed into research. Modern physics can be experimental because it is essentially mathematical in the sense indicated.[42]

In the preceding section we have seen that according to Heidegger there is an essential difference between modern science on the one hand, and the Greek *episteme* and the medieval *doctrina* on the other. In Heidegger's view, neither the Greeks nor the medieval scientists did ever perform genuine experiments; they were simply unable to perform such experiments in view of the fact that neither *episteme* nor *doctrina* was science in the modern sense, i.e., science in the sense of research.

To be sure, Aristotle and Albert the Great knew what *empeiria* and *experientia* meant: the observation of things of nature, their properties, and their changes observed under various circumstances and conditions; such an observation, provided it be systematically performed, does indeed lead to knowledge of the manner in which things as a rule behave. It is true also that in their observations the Greek and medieval authors sometimes made use of measurements and measuring numbers; in several instances they even used certain instruments. And yet all of this was not yet an experiment in the modern sense of the term because the decisive factor, as far as modern research experiments are concerned, was still missing. We have an experiment in the modern sense of the term when one begins by laying down a law. To perform an experiment means to posit in advance a set of conditions according to which a given kinetic whole can be followed carefully in its necessary course and, thus, can be controlled in advance by our calculations.

TOWARD THE ESSENCE OF THE SCIENCES OF NATURE 157

In other words, an experiment in the modern sense is "suggested" and "governed" by certain laws which, in turn, point to the "facts" which eventually will verify or falsify these laws. Yet the laws which indeed do have the character of being hypotheses, are not arbitrary hypotheses; they are developed on the basis of the fundamental conception of nature which the physicists have formed in and through their original thematizing projection by means of which they in advance, a priori, clearly demarcated the domain of beings which would constitute the realm of their investigations. Thus the more the scientists are able to exactly project the basic conception of nature, the more they will be able to perform their experiments in an exact way.[43]

In Heidegger's opinion, it follows from all of this that it is not correct to call Roger Bacon the precurser of the modern experimenting scientists. It is certainly true that Roger Bacon did require *experimenta*, but his *experimenta* were not experiments in the sense of modern physics. Most medieval authors were concerned with faith and theology; the ultimate source of the truth in matters of faith and theology is the authoritative word of the Scriptures and human authorities and institutions proclaiming it. This preoccupation with faith and theology can explain why many authors gradually began to believe that in philosophy the authority of Plato and Aristotle is more important than evidence. Thus in investigations of natural phenomena Roger Bacon merely required an *argumentum ex re* instead of the commonly given *argumenta ex verbis*; in other words, Roger Bacon demanded observation in the sense of Aristotle's *empeiria* which was to take the place of the explanations of things commonly given on the basis of the opinions of the "authorities."[44]

c. NATURAL SCIENCE IS ENTERPRISE, SYSTEM, AND INSTITUTION

Heidegger next turns to a third element which in his view is characteristic for modern physics. He introduces his audience to this new theme to be considered by stipulating once more that each science, taken as research, is founded upon the projection of a carefully demarcated realm of objects and, therefore, is necessarily always this particular and individual science. In the subsequent unfolding of this original projection by means of the methodical procedures that are characteristic for each science, each individual science demarcates well-defined subfields of objects for special investigation. This process of specialization is by no means a fatal concomitant phenomenon of the continually increasing incalculability of the results of modern research in each case. Specialization is necessarily connected with the modern sciences insofar as they engage in research. Specialization is thus not the consequence but the ground of the progress in every form of research. Specialization furthermore does not proceed arbitrarily; it is oriented and guided by a third characteristic of modern science: modern science is *Betrieb*, it has become a complex enterprise or system.[45]

In one of the Appendixes Heidegger points out that the term "enterprise" is not used here in a pejorative sense. However, he says there, in view of the fact that science is essentially enterprise, there is always a real danger that it becomes a mere system and even "mere business." The scientific enterprise becomes mere system and mere business when, in its methodical procedures, it does not keep itself open and free by continually and creatively activating and renewing its original projection, and leaves this thematizing projection simply behind itself as a definitive achievement, a mere datum which does not require any further ascertainment, in order merely to focus on results and their further elaboration and application; in other words, science becomes mere business when, to use an expression coined by Kuhn, it enters the phase of "normal science." As Heidegger sees it, science must continually resist this danger.

He returns here to ideas which he had already suggested in *Being and Time* where he had written that "the real 'movement' of the sciences takes place when their basic concepts undergo a more or less radical revision which is transparent to itself. The level of [development] which a science has reached is determined by how far it is *capable* of a crisis in its basic concepts."[46] Science thus must continuously fight the danger of taking its original thematizing projection as a definitive accomplishment. Heidegger concludes this Appendix with the remark that in his view this situation of having continually to balance the essence and the unessence of science as research makes modern science, as well as our entire modern era, precisely something that is able to last and endure.

Be this as it may, when it is said that science is enterprise or system, then this does not at all mean that a science can be accepted as a genuine science only when it has come to the point where it is ready for the process of institutionalization. For research is not enterprise or system simply because its work is done in large institutes and institutions. It is rather the case that institutes and large institutions become necessary because science, taken as research, intrinsically has the character of becoming enterprise and system. The methodical procedures through which the individual realm of objects becomes "conquered," do not just pile up results. With the help of its own results, each individual science rather prepares itself for always new approaches which often imply basic changes in its fundamental assumptions. Its operations become confined in this way by its own results and these operations become also always more oriented toward the possibilities of progress which they themselves have first opened up. The fact that modern science must orient itself toward its own results, as toward ways and means of its own progressing operation and procedures, is the essence of the enterprise character that is typical for modern science.

It is in the ongoing activity of this enterprise that the thematizing projection that constitutes the relevant realm of objects, becomes built into the beings. All the arrangements which facilitate the integration of the methodical procedures that can be planned, obviously presuppose a proper distribution of "labor" and require reciprocal checking and a proper communication of the established results; thus these arrangements are by no means merely the extrinsic consequences of the fact that the work of research continuously grows and branches out. Research work rather becomes a sign that modern science is finally beginning to enter upon the decisive phase of its history; this sign is to a great extent still not fully understood. Only now does modern science begin to take possession of its own full essence.

In the expansion and consolidation of the institutionalization of modern science we find nothing less than the securing of the priority of method over those beings which become objectified in research. In this process modern science also secures for itself the solidarity and the unity that are appropriate for it. This is the reason that archeological or historiographic research that is carried out in an institutionalized fashion is essentially closer to research in physics, which is organized in a similar fashion, than it is to any other discipline which belongs to its own faculty of the *Geisteswissenschaften*, a faculty that is still bogged down in mere erudition instead of focussing on genuine research. The specialization of modern science, therefore, also creates a new kind of human being: the scholar is on the way out and the researcher who is part of a large research team, begins to come to the fore. A researcher needs no library at home; he constantly has to be in the laboratory with the other members of his team.

Furthermore, he is constantly on the move; he receives most of the information he needs during meetings and conferences. Finally, he only writes those books which his publisher asks him to write.[47]

In the third Appendix Heidegger observes that the publishing companies have become more and more important. Not only do they have a good ear for what the public needs, but they themselves have also become large enterprises that carefully plan production and marketing. This planning is oriented toward an effort to bring the world of science to the public in a manner that it can understand; and this is accomplished by means of the publication of collections, series, and pocketbooks. The authors obviously seldom object to this effort on the part of the publishers in view of the fact that their ideas in this way will be known much more quickly and much more widely.[48]

Because of all of this, the researcher finds himself moving ever closer to the technologist and the engineer, provided one takes both research and technicity here in an essential sense. This move keeps his research efficient and it guarantees the genuineness and relevance of this work for his own time. It is true that this development has not yet completely eliminated what formerly was called scholarship; and it is true also that not yet all universities have fallen victim to this development. Yet it cannot be denied that the function of the university has changed drastically in our era. The effective unity and true function of the university no longer lies in the intellectual power that is capable of bringing about a genuine unification of the sciences. The university has now become a large and complex enterprise and institution whose function consists rather in the fact that it makes the necessary specialization possible, justifies it, and makes it understandable. In view of the fact that the essential and characteristic forces of modern science become immediately and univocally effective in the research activities in which each science engages, it is understandable that whatever unity there still is among the sciences is brought about by research activities to the degree that they themselves predelineate and establish a characteristic unity with other related forms of research.

Heidegger is convinced that the genuine system of the sciences today consists in the fact that they, through continuous planning, continue to work together in their attitude and methodical approach as far as the objectivation of the beings is concerned. In other words, the systematization of the sciences does not consist in a contrived and fixed unity, which depends on an

TOWARD THE ESSENCE OF THE SCIENCES OF NATURE

inner relationship between their subject matters and contents, but rather in the greatest possible, free, but also regulated, flexibility as far as the change of existing or the introduction of new forms of research are concerned, in light of the tasks which at each time in a society appear to be dominant. Each modern science has systematically to follow its own research course and to engage in further specialization and further branching out wherever these appear to be necessary or desirable, if it wishes to remain what, according to its essence, it genuinely is. Specialization is a necessary condition which each science must fulfill, if it is to play its true part in modern society and its life. It is obvious, however, that in so doing each science also must return to the public anonymity which is characteristic of all work that is useful to society.[49]

Modern science is founded on a basic thematizing projection and, at the same time, it continues to branch out in the projection of ever new realms of objects. These objectivating projections unfold by means of the methodical procedures which correspond to these projections and are secured by the rigor that is characteristic for each science. The respective methodical procedures adapt and establish themselves at any given time in research activities. Thematizing projection, rigor, methodical procedure, and systematic research activities, which mutually require and determine each other, constitute the essence of modern science and make it research.[50]

Heidegger concludes this part of "The Era of the World as Picture" by briefly dealing with two basic questions which in his view are of the greatest importance if one is to understand the essence of modern science and to recognize its genuine "metaphysical ground." What conception of Being and what conception of truth ultimately underly and ground science that becomes research?

As Heidegger sees it, knowledge as research calls the beings to account for the question of how and how far they can be made available to man's proposing and positing presentation (*Vorstellung*). Research disposes of beings either when it is able to precalculate them in their future course, or when it is able to post-calculate the past. In this pre- and post-calculation nature and history become posited; they become the object of man's objectifying presentation which reckons on nature and reckons with history. Only that which in this manner becomes object, *is*, is considered to be a genuine being. Science becomes research whenever the Being of the beings is sought in such objectivity.

Thus science becomes research only when the Being of the beings comes to light by means of a pro-posing and positing presentation which aims at bringing each being before itself in such a way that calculating man can be sure and certain of it. In other words, we arrive for the first time at science as research when and only when truth has been changed into the certainty of man's pro-posing and positing presentation.

Heidegger then makes the important remark that this conception of the Being of the beings and of the truth has also dominated modern philosophy from Descartes to Nietzsche. This is one of the main reasons why modern metaphysics is to be transcended.[51] I shall return to this in section 23; yet first we must turn to another important aspect of the essence of modern science. For all objectivation notwithstanding, each science obviously is and remains a theory of the real.

21: MODERN NATURAL SCIENCE AS THE THEORY OF WHAT IS REAL

We are concerned here with modern science as we now know it, not with the Greek *episteme* or the medieval *scientia* or *doctrina*. For each of these conceptions of systematic knowledge on the basis of principles and methods has its own distinctive way of looking at, and asking about, "things," which in turn depend on their interpretation of the Being of things, their thingness.[52]

At first it seems not to be difficult to say what science really is. One can describe modern science and show how science began to have an important place in all organizational forms of modern life: industry, commerce, education, politics, journalism, war. Such a description is important, but it presupposes that we have first experienced that in which the mode of Being of science really consists. Perhaps one can express this experience in one concise statement: *science is the theory of what is actually real*.[53]

This statement is not just a definition or a handy formula, because it contains nothing but questions. These questions will emerge as soon as we try to clarify the meaning of the statement. Note first that the word "science" here refers exclusively to modern science. The statement holds neither for Greek nor for Medieval science. Yet it is true that the modern conception of science is grounded in the thinking of the Greeks, a thinking which Plato calls philosophy and which later was called metaphysics. By relating modern science to the Greek way of thinking

NATURAL SCIENCE AS THE THEORY OF WHAT IS REAL 163

we have in no way weakened the revolutionary character of modern science. Yet modern science needs the Greek way of thinking in order to become another kind of knowing which then can be placed over against Greek thinking.[54]

Our contemporary world is completely dominated by the desire to know that is inherent in modern science. Everyone who thinkingly reflects on modern science must keep in mind that modern science developed from the Greek way of knowing systematically and, thus, that our contemporary reflection must strike root into the ground of our historical existence. Such a dialogue with Greek thinkers and poets that is scarcely prepared for, obviously does not imply a kind of renaissance of Greek thought; nor does it consist in historiographical sophistication. That which was thought and sung at the dawn of Greek antiquity is still present in our Western world in such a manner that its genuine mode of Being is still hidden from itself, even though it encounters us and approaches us most of all where we least expect it, namely in the rule of modern technology. Technology in the modern sense was really foreign to Greek thought; and yet it nevertheless has its fundamental origin in it. In the statement "science is the theory of the actually real" there remains present what was originally thought and originally sent to us as a destiny.

Let us now turn to the issue itself and try to answer the following questions: what is meant by "what is actually real" and what is meant by "theory"? How do these two join together fundamentally?[55] We conceive of what is actually real as something that is intimately related to the active; what is actual and real brings to fulfillment some form of working or doing. Doing does not necessarily mean human activity only. Growing, i.e., the manner in which natural things abide among us, is also a manner of doing in this sense, a laying something before, placing it here, bringing it hither and forth, into its abiding presence. That which acts in this manner is that which works. The verb "to work" names one way in which something that is present, makes something be abidingly present. To work is to bring hither and forth, whether something brings itself forth into abiding presence, or whether the bringing forth is accomplished by man or some other being.

What is actually real is that which is worked and that which works: it is that which brings hither and forth into abiding presence, and that which, brought forth hither into abiding presence, lies in the open. Thus the basic characteristic of working and work (*ergon, Werk*) does not lie in the bringing about of an effect, but rather in that something comes to stand in nonconcealment. When Aristotle speaks about what later would be called the efficient cause, he never means the bringing forth of an effect. Ever since the time of Aristotle, however, what is actually real has been interpreted as something which is the result of an operation, which follows out of, and follows upon, an action, the outcome of an action, the consequence or the result. This consequence or result is brought about by that which precedes it, by its cause. What is actually real then appears as that which is brought about by causality, by some efficient cause. Even God is then presented in theology as first Cause. In the course of time the relationship between cause and effect was understood primarily in reference to common time; the following of the effect upon the working of the cause was then stressed.[56] Kant, too, recognizes causality primarily as a principle of temporal succession.[57] This conception is still found in contemporary physics. Under these influences that which is actually real is now taken in the sense of that which is factual, that which is the case as a fact, that which is certain and sure. We, therefore, say: it is certainly so, it is in fact so, it is really so. The real has come to mean the certain; and this did not happen by mere accident.[58]

That which is actually real in the sense of actually factual, constitutes now the opposite of that which does not stand firm as fully guaranteed, the opposite of mere appearance, of something that is only believed to be so. Yet in these various changes of the meaning of the "actually real" the most fundamental characteristic is still retained, even though it comes now less often and differently to the fore: that which is actually real makes itself be abidingly present, it sets itself forth from out of itself.

Today that which is actually real is taken predominantly as a consequence, as something that has come to abiding presence because something else gave it its secured stand. That which is actually real shows itself now as that which lies-or-stands-overagainst, as ob-ject. The typical characteristic of what we now call an object is often referred to by the term objectivity. How the objectivity (*Gegenständigkeit*) of what is abidingly present is brought to appearance, and how that which abides as present becomes an object for a placing-before (*Vorstellung*), a propositing presentation, will become clear only if we ask: what is the actually real in relation to theory?[59] Since science is the theory of what is actually real, and since the meaning of the expression "actually real" changed over time, the conception of

NATURAL SCIENCE AS THE THEORY OF WHAT IS REAL 165

theory underwent a corresponding shift. Our word "theory" comes from the Greek word "*theoria*" which grew out of the words *thea* and *horao*. *Thea* (connected with *theaomai*) is the outward look, the view, the aspect under which something shows itself. Plato calls this the *eidos*. To have seen such an aspect or view is to know (*eidenai*). *Horao* means to look at something attentively, to view it closely. Thus *theorein* means to look attentively at the outward appearance wherein that which is abidingly present becomes visible. *Theorein* was for the Greeks the highest way of doing; for them it was the reverent paying heed to the unconcealment of that which is abidingly present; it is the beholding that watches over truth.[60]

The Romans translated *theorein* by *contemplari*; this translation makes that which is essential in what the Greek words say vanish at a stroke. *Contemplari* (*templum*, from *temnein*, to cut, to divide) is to partition something off into separate sectors and enclose it in those sectors.[61] The original looking-at now becomes a looking that sunders apart and compartmentalizes. Originally, the English word "theory" was used in the same sense of both the Greek *theoria* and the Latin *contemplatio*, but today the word is very seldom used in this way. Since the 16th Century the word means either (1) conception or mental scheme of something to be done or the method of doing it (a systematic statement of rules or principles to be followed), or (2) a system of ideas or statements held as an explanation of a group of phenomena (a systematic set of hypotheses confirmed by observation or experiment), and various more technical meanings derived from this. A theory of what is actually real now means an elaboration or treatment of what is real which adjusts and secures.[62]

This conception of "theory" seems to run counter to what modern science tries to achieve; science does not adjust and change reality; it is purely theoretical and, thus, spurns every refining or adjustment of the real; it purely grasps what is, it does not encroach upon the real in order to change it. Pure science is totally disinterested.[63]

And yet modern science, taken as the theory of what is actually real, is a form of observation that strives after an adjustment and refinement of the actually real and encroaches uncannily upon it. It is precisely through this adjustment and refinement that science corresponds to a fundamental characteristic of the actually real taken in the modern sense. The actually real is that which is abidingly present as that which posits itself and exhibits itself in a manner which brings its being-present to a stand in objectivity. Science as theory corresponds to the holding-sway of the real's abiding in the form of objects, because it challenges forth the real to show itself in objectivity. Science posits the actually real by specifically aiming at its objectivity, so that an entire domain of real things may exhibit itself as a surveyable network of causes and effects. The refining pro-posing which secures everything in that objectivity which is capable of being followed up or followed out, is the fundamental characteristic of the pro-positing presentation through which modern science corresponds to what is actually real. The all-important work that this pro-positing presentation performs in every science consists in the refinement of the actually real which changes the real into objectivity by recasting each individual real thing in advance (a priori) into a diversity of inter-related objects about which certain knowledge can be secured. The fact that what is abidingly present (nature, life, man, language, history) sets itself forth as that which is real in its objectivity, and the fact that science is transformed into a theory which refines the real and secures it in its objectivity, would have been strange to medieval thinkers and dismaying to Greek thought.[64]

Thus modern science, as the theory of what is actually real, is not something self-evident. It is neither a mere construct of man, nor something systematically derived from the real. Science, as the pro-posing refinement of the real, becomes necessary the moment the actually real is to show itself in its objectivity. This moment is mysterious, as is every moment of its kind.[65]

Scientific theory makes actually real things its theme of investigation by refining them so that they become more tractable to its investigations. Primary and secondary qualities are distinguished from one another so that the ambiguities of appearance can be sifted out; in this way what is actually real is refined and adjusted so that it becomes a realm of fixed objects which can be handled in controlled experiments and measuring procedures. Science posits and projects its own object, placing it in a position in which it can be governed by scientific methods.[66]

The first step in the objectifying thematization is the delimitation of a region of real things which will constitute the object area of the science in question. The delimitation of this area determines the types of questions that may be asked. Every new phenomenon emerging within the object area of a science is first refined and adjusted to such a point that it fits into the prescriptive, objective coherence of the theory. This objective coherence may be changed from time to time, and the object area may

NATURAL SCIENCE AS THE THEORY OF WHAT IS REAL 167

be enlarged to encompass ever more new phenomena. But the typical objectivity as such remains unchanged in its fundamental characteristics.

That which is presented in advance as the determining basis for a strategy or a procedure, is what we call an end *(Zweck)*. If there is anything at all that is determined in advance by an end, then it is most certainly pure theory; for it is determined in advance by the objectivity of what is actually present. If one were to deny this, then there would no longer be science. This is the meaning of the assertion that modern atomic physics does not invalidate classical physics, but only narrows down its domain of application. But this narrowing down is at the same time a confirmation of the objectivity which is characteristic for the theory of nature, in accordance with which nature must present itself to be posited before man as a spatio-temporal coherence of motions, calculable in advance on the basis of mass and force.[67]

Since modern science is theory in the sense described, its method, i.e., its adjusting, refining, and securing procedures, has decisive superiority in science. Planck once observed that only that is real which can be measured.[68] This means that the decision about what may pass in physics for assured knowledge rests upon the measurability supplied by the objectivity of nature and upon the possibilities inherent in this type of measurability. Max Planck's statement is true, however, only because it articulates something which belongs to the very essence of all modern sciences, not only physics. For the method which implies refinement, adjustment, and securing, a method which is characteristic of all theories of what is actually real, is a form of calculation. Yet the expression "calculation" must not be taken here in a narrow sense of performing certain operations with numbers. Calculation is taken here in a very broad sense of taking something into account by setting it up as an object of expectation. All objectivation is a form of calculation, whether through causal explanations it pursues the consequences of certain causes, or whether it secures some coherence or order. Even in mathematics, calculation is not primarily a working with numbers, but rather an attempt at harmonizing all relations of order according to certain principles.[69]

Because modern science as the theory of what is actually real depends on its method, it must, in order to secure its object areas, delimit these areas over against one another, localize them in compartments, and thus compartmentalize them. The theory of what is actually real becomes compartmentalized into branches.

Research in a given object-area must in each case examine the specific characteristics of the objects belonging to that area. The examination of what in each case is specific transforms the methodical procedures of a branch of knowledge into specialized research. This specialization is not a deterioration due to some form of blindness on the part of man, or a sign of the decline of science; it is not even an unavoidable evil. Specialization is a necessary and positive consequence of the coming-to-presence of modern science. Yet the delimitation of object areas into special branches of learning and research, should not split the sciences off from one another. Rather it should lead to meaningful border traffic between them which precisely marks the boundaries and makes them meaningful. It is very often in these border areas that important new discoveries are made. There is something enigmatic and mysterious in this state of affairs, and it is as enigmatic as the entire mode of Being of modern science itself.[70]

Now that we have explained what is meant by "theory" and "what is actually real" in our provisional characterization of modern science as the theory of what is actually real, we must turn to the enigmatic character of modern science, to that which does not immediately show itself in the manner in which science abides among us. In so doing we shall take a particular example, namely physics, and focus on what is characteristic of the object-ness of this object area.[71]

Physics now includes macro- and micro-physics, astrophysics, and chemistry. They investigate nature insofar as it is inanimate, or insofar as it can be described in terms of mass, force, space, and time. In the form of the objectivity characteristic of physics' way of looking at nature, nature appears as a coherent whole of motions of elementary bodies in a space-time-framework. The elementary objects themselves and their coherence are represented in classical physics as moving particles related to one another by certain forces (point mechanics); in modern physics they are represented in terms of nucleus and field. In both cases it is assumed that matter is impenetrable, even though that which is now taken to be impenetrable may, if looked at from another point of view, consist of more elementary particles moving in regard to one another under the influence of certain forces. Accordingly, in classical physics it was assumed that the state of motion of every body that occupies space is at any time determinable and calculable in advance, and thus predictable, both with respect to position and velocity. Consequently, classical physics maintained that nature can be unequivocally and completely

NATURAL SCIENCE AS THE THEORY OF WHAT IS REAL

calculated in advance. On the other hand, contemporary physics only allows for the verification of an objective coherence which is of a statistical nature.[72]

It is important to note here that the objectivity of material nature in modern science shows characteristics that are completely different from those that it showed in classical physics. Yet classical physics can still somehow be incorporated into modern physics, whereas modern physics cannot be incorporated into classical physics. In other words, modern atomic physics is still genuine physics, a theory of what is actually real, i.e., a theory which presents the actually real things in their typical objectivity in order to secure them within the unity of this objectivity. For modern physics, too, it is a question of securing certain elementary objects of which all other objects of nature consist. The propositing presentation of modern science still aims at writing "one single fundamental equation from which all the properties of all elementary particles, thus the behavior of all material things, follow."[73]

This rough indication of the distinction between epochs within modern physics makes plain where the change from the one to the other takes place: in the experience and the determination of the objectivity in which what is actually real is made to show itself. That which does not change with the transition from classical to modern physics, is the fact that nature must set itself in place in advance for the objectifying and securing processes which science as the theory of what is actually real, accomplishes.[74]

But let us turn now to that aspect of modern science which as far as its mode of Being is concerned is inconspicuous. In order to deal with this concretely we begin again with modern physics. Physics makes inanimate nature into an object area of research. Yet nature itself continues to abide among us from itself, regardless of whether or not we engage in physical research. Nature makes itself be present to man in many ways; scientific research is only one of the ways in which nature is present to us, it is the one in which what presents itself of nature can be verified on the basis of direct or indirect experiences in which perception plays the important part. Even where, as in atomic physics, theory becomes the opposite of a direct seeing, its aim is to make particles exhibit themselves to sensory perception in an indirect manner which involves a multiplicity of technical devices and intermediary steps.

Yet scientific theory never exhausts nature which, independent of our scientific research, continues to abide among us, showing itself in many other ways. Physics' objectivation of nature remains oriented toward nature and man's theory can never make its way around nature. Physics may very well make present the most general and pervasive lawfulness of nature in the assumption of the identity of matter and energy. That which physics makes present in this way is indeed nature itself; but undeniably this is only nature as this particular object area whose objectivity has been first determined through the physical objectivation and thematization. Nature taken in the objectivity projected by modern physics is only one way in which that which as nature abides among us reveals itself and sets itself up for scientific research. Even if physics as an object area for scientific research is unitary and self-contained, its objectivity can never exhaust the fullness of what comes to presence as nature. Scientific thematization can never exhaustively encompass the coming to presence of nature, because the objectivity of nature is only one way in which nature shows itself. Nature itself thus remains for the science of physics that which cannot be gotten around completely, it is *das Unumgängliche*.[75]

This means two things: first, theory can never get around nature itself; it always remains oriented toward it; secondly, theory can never totally exhaust the fullness of nature as it abides among us. This is what haunted Goethe in his struggle with Newtonian physics.[76] Yet Goethe did not realize that even his "intuitive" presentation of nature still moves within the medium of objectivity, within the subject-object-opposition. His intuitive representation of nature was not basically different from modern physics and philosophically seen it, too, remained a form of physics. Scientific thematization itself can never determine whether its objectivation does not hide nature rather than bring to appearance the originally hidden fullness of nature's coming-to-presence. Science cannot even ask such questions. This is true for physics as well as for all other empirical sciences.[77]

Nature remains for the natural sciences that which is not to be gotten around in the two senses just distinguished, even though nature is made present in physics in its objectivity; physics remains oriented toward nature as that which in the fullness of its coming-to-presence it can never encompass exhaustively by means of its own manner of presenting it. The reason for this is not (as many scientists believe) the fact that our scientific research projects will always remain open-ended; it is

NATURAL SCIENCE AS THE THEORY OF WHAT IS REAL   171

grounded rather in the fact that in principle the objectivity in which nature shows itself, always itself remains only one kind of nature's coming-to-presence; in the thematizing projections of the sciences nature does indeed appear and show itself, but never in an exhaustive and all-encompassing manner. Thus it is false to assume that in principle physics will ultimately succeed in showing us the genuine and all encompassing truth about nature.[78]

For every empirical science it is true that there is something that is not to be gotten around. But this in itself is not yet the enigmatic state of affairs we just referred to. The object area of each science continues to refer to something beyond itself that in each science is not to be gotten around. One might thus expect that every science itself could find present within itself that which is not to be gotten around and, thus, could define it as such. But it is precisely this that is not and cannot be the case. Yet many scientists seem to assume that something like this is a real possibility when they claim that science tells us the truth about nature.

The reason why no science can ever define that which is not to be gotten around in it, is the fact that no science can present its own mode of Being. Physics as physics can make claims about objectified nature; but physics itself is not a possible object of physical research and experiment. This is true for all sciences, even though the contrary seems to be the case for historiography, where a historiography of historiography seems to be a genuine possibility. Yet it remains the case that the sciences are not in a position at any time to present themselves to themselves, to place themselves before themselves by means of their own type of theory and through the methods belonging to it. But if it is entirely denied to science as such to scientifically arrive at its objects' own mode of Being, then the sciences are utterly incapable of gaining access to that which is not to be gotten around and yet holds sway in their very mode of Being.

This is very disturbing and a genuinely enigmatic state of affairs; that which in each science is not at any time to be gotten around, is as that which is not to be gotten around, intractable, inaccessible for each science. Only when we pay heed to the inaccessibility of that which is not to be gotten around, does the state of affairs come into view as an enigmatic state of affairs which nonetheless holds complete sway throughout the very mode of Being of every science.[79]

One could in many ways object to calling this state of affairs enigmatic. First of all, one could say: look, you just have shown it to us; thus it is no longer enigmatic. One could also say that philosophy of science and the history of the sciences have made careful studies of what it means to engage in science; the very mode of Being of each science has already been determined in these investigations. Yet it is true also that what is inaccessible and not to be gotten around remains enigmatic, inconspicuous. The inconspicuousness of this state of affairs cannot lie in the fact that it does not astound us or that we did not notice it. The inconspicuousness of the state of affairs and its failure to shine forth is grounded in the fact that it itself does not come to appearance; that it continuously is passed over depends on itself as such. That which science is really concerned with and which holds sway throughout the very mode of Being of each science, throughout the entire theory of what is actually real, is itself that which is inaccessible and yet not to be gotten around. Physics wishes to reveal nature "as it is"; it reveals nature in its objectivity, nature itself is so passed over and yet constantly present as that which is not to be gotten around.

Our aim here merely is to point to this peculiar state of affairs in order that it itself might invite us to enter the region from out of which stems the very mode of Being of science itself. Through our pointing to the inconspicuous state of affairs (that physics attempts to show us the truth of nature by constantly hiding nature as it abides among us), we are directed onto the way that brings us before that which is worthy of being questioned. That which is worthy of being questioned gives us the impetus through which we are able to call near to us that which addresses itself to our own mode of Being. Travelling toward what is worthy of being questioned is not an adventure but a homecoming.[80]

To follow the direction and the way which something itself has already taken is called *sinnen*, to ponder about and search for meaning and sense (*Sinn*). To search for meaning is the very mode of Being of meditating reflection (*Besinnung*). This is not so much a peculiar way of being-conscious-of, but rather a self-possessed surrender to what is worthy of being questioned. Through this kind of reflection one arrives at the place where one has long been sojourning. This kind of reflection is neither science, nor education through instruction, but thinking in the authentic sense of the term.[81]

22: NATURAL SCIENCE AND TECHNOLOGY

The modern world convincingly shows the narrow bond that exists between the natural sciences and technology. Furthermore, the history of both shows clearly that their development has always been parallel. Technology has spread the natural sciences over the entire world and, at the same time, it has secured for them a central place in the preoccupation of today's thinkers. In the development of the past two hundred years, technology has constantly manifested itself as both a presupposition and as a consequence of the natural sciences. It is a presupposition insofar as the expansion and penetration of the natural sciences often depend on the technical refinement of the means of observation and experimentation. It is a consequence insofar as the technical utilization of natural forces is, generally speaking, possible only on the basis of a profound study of the relevant domain of experience.

The bond between the natural sciences and technology becomes even more manifest when one investigates more concretely in history how these two have always determined and complemented each other. The technology of the eighteenth and nineteenth centuries, for example, had to rely on the use of purely mechanical procedures, which ultimately reached their apex in the steam engine. The machines of that era did what man formerly had to do himself and they often even imitated man's way of handling tools. This form of technology was viewed therefore as a continuation and renewal of the old manual techniques. As soon, however, as electrotechnical processes began to develop, technology assumed a different character. There was then hardly any question of a bond between technology and manual crafts; it now became much more a utilization of natural forces that were largely unknown to man in his everyday life. Even today electrotechnical processes seem strange and somewhat frightening to many who, if they know how to use them in practice, still find them incomprehensible.

Chemical technology at first appeared to be closely allied to certain old types of craft, but modern chemical processes are again beyond comparison with familiar procedures of daily life. Finally, in atomic technology there is a question only of utilizing natural forces which are not even accessible to us from the world of ordinary experience. It is possible, of course, that we shall become as familiar with this kind of technology as we are now with electrotechnology, but it will never become a part of nature in the original sense of the term.[82]

The assertion that there exists an undeniable bond between physical science and technology does not tell us anything yet about the root of their interconnection. For, one could claim either that technology is applied natural science, or also that technology is the ultimate root of the natural scientist's theoretical study. Which of these two replies is correct will have to be determined by a study of the essence of technicity. While we are unable to develop this point here extensively, it may be useful to attempt briefly to indicate the standpoint of Heidegger in this matter.

The question of what the essence of technology is will remain a great mystery as long as one does not go beyond the technical phenomena taken as facts.[83] For asking what the essence of technology is, is asking what, properly speaking, technicity is. This question is usually answered by saying that technicity is a means to attain certain goals. Others have tried to define technicity as a special way of man's acting. Both of these aspects, obviously, are characteristic of technicity, for only man can set himself a purpose or goal. This attempt to define the essence of technicity could therefore be called the instrumental or anthropological description of technicity. It is hardly necessary to add that such a characterization of technicity is correct and applies not only to ancient forms of technical handling but also to contemporary technological processes.

The question, however, is whether such a reply indicates the essence of technicity. For, a correct reply is not always identical with the true reply in the philosophical sense of the term. On the other hand, it is possible that the instrumental description of technicity may lead to a definition of its essence. The first step in that direction should be a reflection on the proper meaning of instrumental causality.[84]

The famous doctrine of the four causes is, as everybody knows, of Aristotelian origin. The current interpretation of this doctrine, however, dates from later times and does not always do full justice to what Aristotle originally had in mind. For, the term *aition* used by Aristotle is usually interpreted as that which gives rise to something else. In its original sense, however, this term meant "to be guilty of, "to be responsible for," although one should keep in mind that in the present context the expression "to be guilty of" implies nothing pragmatical or ethical. Through the analysis of simple examples, Heidegger shows how the four

NATURAL SCIENCE AND TECHNOLOGY   175

causes in four different ways "are guilty of" the appearance and the being-in-itself of a utensil. Despite these differences the four causes have in common that they make present that which was not yet present; that they make it come forward, draw it from concealedness into non-concealment. Viewed in this way, cause is connected with *a-letheia*, a term that is usually translated as "truth."[85] For a clearer understanding of the matter, it will be useful to dwell briefly on this view of truth.

In the preceding sections we have seen already that Heidegger makes a distinction between the truth ascribed to judgments and a more fundamental sense that should be attached to the term "truth." The truth of judgments may be described with the Aristotelian tradition as "the agreement of the intellect with the thing." But even then one should not lose sight of the idea of intentionality. The "thing" of which there is question here, the real thing, is not some thing-in-itself but rather the thing *as it appears* to us in our encounter with it in the world. Alongside this "truth of judgment" there is a more fundamental form of truth which lies not primarily in a judgment but in the human eksistence itself insofar as it is as revealing. For the agreement of the judgment with the "real thing" presupposes that reality has already been drawn from concealedness in a more original way. But to draw real things from concealedness into non-concealment (*a-letheia*) requires a certain "light," a natural light, a *lumen naturale* to use the term of the tradition. This "light" is Dasein's eksistence itself, its Being-in-the-world from which originally all meaning draws its light.[86]

At first sight, it may seem that there is no clear connection between this idea of truth and the essence of technicity. On closer inspection, however, the two appear to be essentially related. For, *a-letheia*, as the original bringing to light, is the root of all other bringing-to-light, of all other discoveries and disclosures; on the other hand, the common element of the four causes, including the instrumental causality characterizing technicity, is precisely that they disclose and discover.

If these ideas are correct, then technicity should be conceived as a mode of bringing-to-light, of discovering, so that there exists a close connection between technicity and truth. Technicity discovers and discloses things which cannot disclose themselves. But, then the essence of technicity does not consist in making or using tools or instruments, but precisely in its own typical modality of bringing-to-light. If in the ancient handicraft this bringing-to-light was mainly a question of making things effectively, in modern technology the aspect of discovery and disclosure is more predominant. For today's technology forces nature to unlock its energy and to surrender its forces. It harnesses the forces of nature, transforms, accumulates, and conserves them; then it divides again what it has conserved and accumulated, to transform it again and use it. It is in this way that contemporary technicity brings things to light.[87]

We must now ask the question of precisely what is the character of the non-concealment proper to that which is brought to light through contemporary technology? It appears that the typical character of technicity's products must be sought in the fact that whatever is brought into being through modern technology has no other meaning than that of being ever ready to become part of an effective process in which man takes control over nature. An airplane, for example, stands ready on the runway of the airport to render secure the possibility of transportation for man and materials. This typical mode of Being of the product of modern technicity could be indicated by saying that it is always "in supply," but this expression does not do full justice to it. Heidegger, therefore, uses here the term "*Bestand*." His intention may perhaps be clarified in the following way. From our original Being-in-the-world, in which we deal with innerworldly beings around us through concern (*Besorgen*), we are able to pass to a different attitude toward these beings through a thematizing and objectivizing projection, so that henceforth these beings can appear to us as mere objects. In a similar way we are able, through a different but related change of attitude, to make the things of our daily concern appear to us henceforth only as *Bestand*, by pro-ducing them in such a way that they are now steadily at our disposal. Thus, that which stands before us as *Bestand*, as such, can no longer encounter us as a mere object.[88]

It is, of course, man himself who through his attitude toward the beings of the world makes innerworldly beings appear in the form of *Bestand*. But because of the essential intentionality existing between man and the world, man can do this only insofar as he himself is invited to "force" nature to "surrender" its energy. Now, since man is more originally invited by nature itself to make the innerworldly beings appear in the form of *Bestand*, of constant availability, than nature's own energy is forced by man to be readily at his disposal, man himself can never become *Bestand*. When man pursues technology, he simply pursues one of the many ways in which innerworldly beings can be "forced" to disclose themselves.[89]

It is important to note here that Heidegger in an earlier reflection, entitled "Overcoming Metaphysics," had argued that in the twentieth century modern technicity has driven man to the point where he thinks that he can make himself master of everything that is elemental. What modern man does not realize here is that he himself has become the most important raw material in this all-devouring process. "Man is the most important raw material because he remains the subject of all consumption. He does this in such a way that he lets his own will be unconditionally equated with this [purely technical] process . . ."[90]

But how exactly does technicity disclose innerworldly beings? Whenever Dasein does anything as Dasein in regard to innerworldly beings, Dasein itself is unconcealed and thus, in the truth. When Dasein investigates and examines nature with a theoretical gaze, then it uses a mode of bringing-to-light which invites it to encounter the object thus met also in a different but still related fashion. The object invites Dasein to make it appear also in the objectless realm of the constantly standing in reserve of the *Bestand* by means of technicity, so that it now will constantly stand unconcealed in a new way. But if this view is correct, then we cannot view technicity as a consequence of natural science, as is suggested by history, but rather natural science is a function of the essence of modern technicity; although science was first "in execution," technicity was first in a perhaps still unconscious intention.[91]

These brief reflections do not resolve all the questions that can be raised here. Nevertheless, I hope that they may serve to indicate the direction in which Heidegger looks for an answer to the question regarding the relationship between science and technology, i.e., the question about the ultimate motive which has driven modern man to thematize, objectivize, and control.

23: SCIENCE AND METAPHYSICS IN THE MODERN ERA. THE METAPHYSICAL MEANING OF THE MATHEMATICAL

We must now finally return to the question of what the metaphysical ground of modern science is, and what that which constitutes the metaphysical ground of science as research teaches us about the essence of the modern era.[92] One could perhaps say that the essence of the modern era consists in the fact that modern man has freed himself from all bonds imposed on him during the Middle Ages and, thus, has freed himself unto himself. This characterization of the modern era is correct; yet, as we shall see shortly, it is superficial and misleading. It is furthermore also true that man's vindication of his own freedom has led to subjectivism and individualism; yet it is just as certain that in no other epoch has one ever seen a form of objectivism and a form of collectivism that can be compared with that of the modern era. Even the statement that the interaction of subjectivism and objectivism determines the essence of the modern epoch does not yet go to the heart of the matter, as we shall see presently.[93]

As Heidegger sees it, the decisive factor in the constitution of the modern era is not so much the fact that man has freed himself from his previous obligations and, thus, freed himself onto himself, but rather the fact that the essence of man himself has changed. Man has changed from being a *zoion logon echon*, an *animal rationale*, a child of God, etc., into a subject. The term "subject" is derived from the Latin *subjectum* which as a technical term is the translation of the Greek term *hupokeimenon*. The latter term means that which lies before and underneath and, thus, that which as ground gathers everything toward itself. Taken in this sense, the term does not yet necessarily refer to human beings, and it certainly does not yet refer to a human *ego* or "I." Yet in the modern era, to say that man is the first and true subject becomes tantamount to saying that man is that being upon which all other entities are founded as far as their mode of Being and their truth are concerned. In this manner, man became the center of reference of the beings as such and taken as a whole; in this manner man became the measure of all things. But this, in truth, was possible only because the conception of the beings as such and taken as a whole no longer constituted the totality of all that emerges and abides (*west*), or the totality of all beings created by God, but rather the totality of all beings pro-posed to man as subject. In other words, opposed to man as subject and pro-posed (*vor-stellen*) and posited by him, the entire world of things has meaning from now on only in regard to him. In the modern era, the beings as such and taken as a whole are to be taken in such a manner that they are beings only insofar as they are posited by man's pro-posing presentation or by man's fabrication. Thus things are real to the degree that they can be pro-posed and posited by man. Thus what truly characterizes our modern epoch consists in the fact that being *is* merely insofar as it is objectified, *is* merely as posited pro-posedness.[94]

It is obvious that very important consequences follow from this decision about the "true" meaning of the beings. First of all, if the world appears merely as something that has meaning only in

SCIENCE AND METAPHYSICS

regard to man, then it becomes man's basic task to conquer the world. And man conquers the world mainly by means of objectifying projections, designs, calculations, and techniques. Moreover, anthropology as a basic philosophical discipline comes into being. The more the world of things is perceived as that which is to be conquered and, thus, the more objective all beings begin to appear, the more subjective the subject becomes and begins to claim priority, and the more a science of the world changes into a science of man. It is then also comprehensible why philosophical anthropology begins to propagate some modern form of humanism which, in the final analysis, is no more than a reflection on the aesthetic and moral dimensions of man. It is then understandable, also, why man begins to develop "pictures" of the world, world views, and, correspondingly, views of life. Let us not forget that in the nineteenth century the expression "world view" primarily meant "view of life." As Heidegger sees it, the fact that the expression "world view" was used predominantly, even though "world view" really meant "view of life," i.e., a view according to which man had placed himself at the privileged position in the midst of all that is, shows to what extent the world indeed had become a mere picture as soon as man, as *subjectum*, gave his own life the central position over all other possible centers of relationships. For this meant that whatever is, is considered to be only to the degree that it is taken as referring back to man's life and is experienced as such.

The fundamental event of the entire modern age is the conquest of the world as picture. Heidegger explains that the word "*Bild*" (picture) here receives the meaning of the systematic, structured totality (*Gebild*) of all the things which man posits, places before himself, and produces. In this positing and proposing production man tries to secure for himself that position in which he can be the being that gives the measure to everything else. In view of the fact that there are many forms of positing and producing, it is understandable that the modern relationship to that which is, leads to a confrontation of world views. "For the sake of this struggle of world views and in keeping with its meaning, man brings into play his unlimited power for the calculating, planning, and molding of all things." Science, taken in the sense of research, is an absolutely necessary form of man's effort to establish his own self in the world.[95]

From all of this it finally becomes understandable why people in the nineteenth century felt the need to begin to search for values. For the moment the beings become mere objects of man's own pro-posing and positing presentation, man has to compensate for the loss of their meaning by ascribing "values" to them, in such a way that these values can become the goals of all of man's interactions with things. These interactions with the beings are then no longer "natural," but they become understood as culture, values become cultural values and, thus, the goal of all human activities is placed in the service of man himself. Finally, these values themselves become again reduced to the level of mere objects that are pro-posed and posited by man himself as the goals which he needs in order to sustain his own activities in his efforts to establish his place in the world.[96]

In harmony with a widely-held view which, however, is questioned by some, Heidegger, too, adheres to the position that the origin of the entire modern era is to be sought in the philosophy of Descartes who, for the first time, made an effort to determine the metaphysical meaning of the mathematical. To fully understand Descartes' position in regard to both the metaphysical and the mathematical it is important to note that before the modern conception of the mathematical emerged, the authoritative source of the truth in the Western world was universally taken to be that of the Christian faith. If one wished to discover the truth about what is, one had to turn to the Scriptures and the tradition of the Church. In other words, one must realize that before the modern era there really was no worldly knowledge; the so-called natural knowledge which was not based on revelation, did not yet have its own form of intelligibility, nor its own independent ground, even though Albert the Great and Aquinas had already defended the independence of natural knowledge in principle. On the other hand, in the "essence of the mathematical," as this developed and was understood in the modern era, we find the specific will to a new foundation and self-grounding of man's knowledge as such. The detachment from revelation and the rejection of the tradition were only the negative consequences of the mathematical projection of what is. Furthermore, Heidegger continues, there was not only a liberation from dogma and tradition in this mathematical projection of what is, but also a completely new experience of freedom, i.e., a freedom which binds itself only to obligations that are self-imposed.

Now in view of the fact that natural science, modern mathematics, and modern metaphysics all emerged from the same root, and because of the fact that, of these three, metaphysics reaches farthest and deepest, it is the origin of modern metaphysics

SCIENCE AND METAPHYSICS

which will have to explain its own "mathematical" foundation and ground.[97]

Modern metaphysics, too, has its origin in the works of Descartes. Heidegger, therefore, turns to the philosophy of Descartes and first gives a brief description of the common interpretation of Descartes' thought. According to that view, during the Middle Ages philosophy was completely dominated by theology and gradually degenerated into a mere analysis of concepts and explanations of traditional opinions and theses. It gradually petrified and finally became a strictly academic knowledge which had no relevance for life; philosophy gradually became unable to enlighten the world as a whole. Descartes liberated philosophy from this disgraceful position. He introduced a new approach to philosophy that begins by doubting everything. Yet anyone who systematically tries to doubt everything is gradually led to the point where he encounters something that cannot possibly be doubted. For the doubting skeptic himself must be, and he must be present to himself, if he is to be able to doubt at all. Thus when I truly doubt, I still must admit that I am. The "I" in the "I am" is thus indubitable; the human subjectivity in this way came to be the center of all thought. Now in view of the fact that reflection upon man's knowledge is to be developed at the very beginning of the philosophical enterprise as a whole, a theory of knowledge must precede any theory of the world. Epistemology is to provide us with the foundations of philosophy and this conception constitutes the main difference between modern and medieval philosophy.[98]

According to Heidegger, this interpretation of Descartes' thought and significance is completely unacceptable. For the main work of Descartes is not his epistemology, but rather his *Meditations on First Philosophy* which, like Aristotle's *prote philosophia*, is concerned with the question concerning the Being of what is, concerning the thingness of the things. In trying to deal with this question Descartes accepted from the tradition that the proposition constitutes the guide for the question about the Being of the beings.[99]

Although Descartes tried to be an original thinker and although he suggested taking a very negative stance in regard to the tradition, he nevertheless was still deeply influenced by medieval philosophy and by Suarez' interpretation of Aristotle and of the entire medieval tradition in particular. In Heidegger's view, the title of his main work reflects "both his argument with this tradition and his will to take up anew the question about the

Being of what is," i.e., the question of the thingness of the things or the question of "substance."

But Descartes' philosophy developed during a period in which, for a century, mathematics had begun to emerge more and more as the true foundation of all thought. It was in this period that one tried to conquer reality in a new way by means of this free, mathematical projection of the world. But this new approach did not flow from some form of skepticism; nor did it stem from the desire to develop a subjectivist position. Rather the driving force of this new form of inquiry was to be found in the desire to bring to clarification and to unfold systematically the very essence of a fundamental position which at first was still dark and often misunderstood and, thus far, only had developed by fits and starts. In Heidegger's view, Descartes realized that the mathematical because of its own inner requirements "wills to ground itself" and "expressly intends to explicate itself as the standard of *all* thought . . ."[100] Thus he wholeheartedly participated in the reflection on the fundamental meaning of the mathematical. But in view of the fact that this kind of reflection was concerned with the totality of all that is as well as with man's knowledge of it, this reflection had to become a reflection on metaphysics. Thus what characterizes Descartes' position first and foremost is the fact that it was concerned with both the foundation of mathematics and a reflection on metaphysics.[101] As Heidegger sees it, one can see this most clearly in Descartes' early work, *Regulae ad directionem ingenii* which remained unfinished and appeared in print only posthumously in 1701.[102]

The term *"regulae"* here refers to "basic and guiding propositions in which mathematics submits itself to its own essence"; these basic propositions must lay the foundation of the mathematical in order that this, as a whole, can become the measure of all inquiry of the human mind. Thus in these reflections on the essence of mathematics Descartes attempted to formulate the idea of a universal science, to which every other inquiry must be directed and ordered as to the one and only authoritative science.[103]

To give the reader an idea of the aim and the spirit of the work Heidegger briefly discusses three of the twenty-one rules contained in the book, namely:

Rule III: "In the subjects we propose to investigate, our inquiries should be directed, not to what others have thought, nor to what we ourselves conjecture, but to what we can clearly and perspicuously behold and with

SCIENCE AND METAPHYSICS

Rule IV: certainty deduce; for knowledge is not won in any other way."

Rule IV: "There is need for a method for finding out the truth."

Rule V: "Method consists entirely in the order and disposition of the objects towards which our mental vision must be directed if we would find out any truth. We shall comply with it exactly if we reduce involved and obscure propositions step by step to those that are simpler, and then starting with the intuitive apprehension of all those that are absolutely simple, attempt to ascend to the knowledge of all others by precisely similar steps."[104]

In Heidegger's view, it is of prime importance that we fully understand how these reflections on the mathematical affect the argument with traditional metaphysics and how, starting from this, both the course and the form of modern philosophy is determined.

To see this, we have to return to an idea which we have already discussed earlier. There it was shown that the axiomatical, i.e., the formulation of the basic principles on which everything else is to be based in the proper order, belongs to the essence of the mathematical taken as a projection. In other words, if Descartes' *mathesis universalis* indeed is to give a foundation to all of man's knowledge, the formulation of special axioms is necessary and these axioms must be radically first, intuitively evident in themselves, and absolutely certain. In addition, these axioms must also establish *a priori*, with respect to the beings as such and taken as a whole, what truly is in being and above all what Being means; in other words, these axioms must establish *a priori* from where and how the thingness of the things is to be determined.

Descartes accepted from the tradition that the proposition has to play the central part here. Now the tradition had always taken the proposition to be the container of Being and assumed that the proposition, like all other things, is just present-at-hand. Yet Descartes fully realized that for a basically mathematical proposition there cannot be any pregiven things. The proposition in question must be a truly basic proposition which must itself be based only on itself, on its own foundation. It thus must be the basic principle in an absolute sense. We must thus try to find such a principle of all positing, i.e., a proposition in which that about which it says something (its *hupokeimenon*, its *subjectum*) is in no way taken from somewhere else. The underlying subject must emerge and be established for itself in this original proposition itself. For only in this manner can its *subjectum* be a *fundamentum absolutum et inconcussum*, i.e., something that is posited in and by the proposition as such and, thus, can be a basis that is indubitable and absolutely certain. But as soon as one sets the mathematical itself up as the principle of all knowledge, all knowledge that has come to us from our heritage and tradition must necessarily be put into question, regardless of whether it is tenable or not.[105]

Thus Descartes was not led to his universal, methodical doubt because he was a skeptic, but rather because he had posited the mathematical as the absolute ground of all human knowledge. He was not only concerned with finding a fundamental law for the realm of natural phenomena, but above all with discovering the highest principle for the Being of what is as such. Such an absolutely mathematical principle cannot have anything above it, under it, or in front of it; nor can it tolerate anything that might be given to it beforehand. The only thing that can be given here is the proposition itself as such, the positing itself, the thinking itself that asserts. Thus in the proposition the positing has only itself as that which can be posited. "Only where thinking thinks itself, is it absolutely mathematical, i.e., a taking cognizance of that which we already have." If this thinking positing directs itself to itself, it can rightly claim that, whatever else is asserted, the asserting of thinking itself is always an I think. Thinking is always *I*-think (*ego cogito*) and therein is implied that *I* am (*sum*). In other words, in the "I posit" the "I" as the positor is always co-posited and pre-posited as that which is already at hand, as being. Here the Being of the beings is determined out of the "I am" taken as the certainty of the positing.[106]

Descartes' formulation of the proposition, "Cogito ergo sum," suggests that there is here a question of an inference. Yet he himself explicitly stressed that no inference was meant. The "sum" is not the consequence of the thinking, but rather its foundation. In the essence of the thinking that posits lies the proposition: *I* posit. This proposition does not depend on something that is given beforehand. It gives to itself only what already lies within it; and in it we find that *I* posit; *I* am the one who thinks and posits. Thus this proposition has as its typical characteristic that it first posits that about which it makes an assertion, namely the *subjectum*, the "*I*." Thus it comes-to-pass that the "I" became the subject in a privileged sense, even though the specific character of the *ego* remained unspecified and unnoticed; the subjectivity of the subject is determined here only by the I-ness of the "I think." Heidegger stresses the point that this "I" which from now on is taken to be the privileged *subjectum*, is, in its meaning, nothing subjective at all, if the latter term is taken in its usual, modern sense; it becomes subjectivistic only when its essence is no longer properly understood.

Before Descartes' time everything that is present-at-hand for itself was said to be a *subjectum*. But as soon as the "I" became the privileged subject, i.e., that with respect to which all other things first became determined as such, things that formerly were said to be subjects, now became objects. For, mathematically "they first receive their thingness only through the founding relation to the 'subject' (the I)" and, as such, these things must now be taken to be that which lies over against the subject as its *objectum*.

The term *"objectum"* went through a corresponding change of meaning. For before the time of Descartes the term *"objectum"* referred to what was thrown up opposite one's mere imagination: I imagine a golden mountain. In other words, that which in the language of the Middle Ages was called an *objectum*, is, according to our modern language use, something that is merely "subjective"; for golden mountains do not exist "objectively" in the meaning of the modern language use.[107] Yet the fact that the meaning of the two words, *subjectum* and *objectum*, completely changed, is not just a question of language usage; rather it represents "a radical change of Dasein, i.e., of the clearing (*Lichtung*) of the Being of the beings, on the basis of the authoritative position granted to the mathematical. It is a stretch of the way of the true history which is necessarily hidden from the common eye, a history which always concerns the manifestness of Being--or nothing at all."[108]

From the time of Descartes on all certainty and truth has been based on the "I think." Thought (*logos*, assertion) is the guidance for the determination of the Being of the beings in the categories. The categories must be found by using the "I" as a guideline. At the same time, the "I" becomes part of the essential definition of man. Reason now becomes explicitly posited *according to its own demand* as the first ground of all knowledge and the guideline for the determination of the Being of things.

Aristotle already called man a rational living thing. For him, too, reason was the guideline for the determination of the categories, i.e., for the Being of what is. However the locus of this guideline was then not taken to be the subjectivity of the (finite) subject. Descartes sets reason forth explicitly in the form of "I think" as the highest court of appeal for all determinations of Being (=categories).[109]

The *cogito - sum* is the fundamental principle and axiom of all true and certain knowledge. Yet it is not the only principle. The positing in each case is such that what is posited in the concrete predicate may not speak against what lies in the subject. In the proposition as proposition, and accordingly also in the highest principle, there is co-posited, as equally basical and valid, the principle of the avoidance of contradiction. Both the I-principle and the principle of non-contradiction flow from the nature of finite thought. That is the reason why the principles which, in harmony with the fundamental mathematical character of thinking, spring solely from pure reason itself, become the principles of knowledge in the most proper sense, i.e., the principles of metaphysics, because the question about the Being of things is now anchored in pure, finite reason, i.e., the mathematical unfolding of reason's principles.[110]

To conclude these reflections let us briefly summarize Heidegger's position in regard to the main point under examination here: the root of the relationship between science and metaphysics in the modern era.

In his attempt to answer the question of what constitutes the essence of our modern era, Heidegger once pointed to the fact that in reflections on the modern era one is often concerned about our modern world-picture. In his view, the important question here is whether or not it is characteristic for every era to have a world-picture and to be concerned about it, or whether it is perhaps precisely typical for our own modern era to seek such world-pictures. This question leads to two other questions: What is meant here by world-picture? And if one conceives of world-pictures as pictures of the world, then one must also ask what is meant here by "world" and by "picture."

Heidegger explains that "world" stands here for the beings taken as a whole; thus world comprises nature, history, and the "world-ground." In the expression "world-picture" the word "picture" might make us think of a photo-copy. However, "world-picture" means more than just a photo or copy of the world. By world-picture one means the world itself conceived of as a totality of beings pro-posed and pro-posited by and to man as subject. Opposed to man as subject and pro-posed and posited by him, the world has meaning only in regard to him. In our modern era,

SCIENCE AND METAPHYSICS

when we speak about a world-picture, we imply that the beings taken as a whole are to be taken in such a way that they are beings only insofar as they are posited by man's pro-positing or fabrication. When a world-picture develops, then an essential decision is made in regard to that which the totality of beings is supposed to be. But all of this means that in the modern era things are only to the degree that they can be posited and proposed by man.

Wherever beings are thought of in another way, there a world-picture is excluded in principle. What characterizes our modern era, thus, and what distinguishes it from all others, consists in the fact that beings are merely as objectified, are merely in their pro-posedness.[111] The expression "our modern picture of the world" is thus really a pleonasm.

We must now try to answer the question of how the world-picture of our modern era really came to be and, secondly, also what conception of Being and truth genuine and authentic thinking has to offer in the place of that which is implied in the world-picture of our modern era. As far as the first question is concerned, Heidegger sees the origin of the modern era in Descartes' philosophy, as we have seen. In Descartes' philosophy we find that the main characteristic of modern man is found in the vindication of his own freedom whereby he frees himself from all ties which medieval Christianity had forced upon him; modern man frees himself onto himself.[112] Medieval man received all his certitudes from his faith.[113] By choosing independence in the name of freedom, modern man was thrown back upon himself so that he had to find certitude in and through himself.[114] The freedom which modern man chose was self-determination and, thus, the ground of all his certitudes was to be found in his own self-certitude. This means, among many other things, that modern man had to decide for himself what is knowable for him, what is genuine knowledge, and what is certitude. In attempting to find an answer for these three questions independent from faith Descartes realized that the ground of all his certitudes must itself be certain, and must be able to justify itself, and must be capable of being the ground of all other certitudes. As we have seen, for Descartes this *fundamentum inconcussum veritatis* which underlies (*hupo-keimenon, sub-jectum*) all other certitudes is to be found in the *cotito--sum*.[115]

In Descartes' view, Heidegger continues, the *cogito* is obviously itself certain because knowing is here known to conform with what is known, in that both knowing and what-is-known are simultaneously present to one another in one single act of knowledge. The *cogito* justifies itself because it is apodictically evident. And, finally, it is the ground of all other certitudes in that it is not only their model, but also a necessary and sufficient condition for all of them. For, to use a concise formulation of Sartre, "the necessary and sufficient condition for a knowing consciousness to be knowledge of its own objects, is that it be conscious of itself as being that knowledge."[116]

In Heidegger's opinion, all of this implies three very important theses. The first thesis is that knowledge is identical with a process of re-presentation (*re-praesentatio*) which pro-poses to itself what is known.[117] From this the second thesis follows immediately: the humanly knowable domain consists of whatever can be a term of a re-presenting and pro-posing process, that is, whatever can be objectified by such a process and, therefore, any "object."[118] The third thesis is connected with the second and states that certitude becomes understood as truth that is guaranteed by exact calculation, which itself is made possible by that process of objectivation.[119]

For Descartes, Heidegger concludes, being necessarily becomes being-as-object which is present to a subject, and its presence has necessarily to remain within the domain of the subject-object-relationship. That in addition to this there must be a much more fundamental form of presence, an emergence into non-concealment, is for Descartes unacceptable. But by excluding this primordial form of presence Descartes is necessarily driven into the epistemological problem, that is, the problem concerning a possible bridge between "consciousness" and "world."

What authentic thought has to say about this is explained by Heidegger by contrasting the Cartesian conception of re-presentative thought with the Pre-Socratic conception of *noein*. Referring to Parmenides' correlation of *noein* and *einai*, Heidegger claims that primordially to know does not mean to re-present and to pro-pose or posit; and, correlatively, that being does not necessarily mean "object." Heidegger interprets Parmenides' saying so as to mean that it belongs to Being, that is, that it is demanded and determined by Being, that beings be brought to light and how they will be brought to light. A being is that which emerges and opens itself up; and insofar as it comes to presence, it comes over a human being who likewise is coming-to-presence over himself in that he opens himself up unto what is coming to presence, inasmuch as he becomes aware of it (*vernehmen*). Thus a being is not a being insofar as a human being has perception of it, that

SCIENCE AND METAPHYSICS

is, has a re-presentation of it in the sense of a Cartesian *perceptio*. Man is rather looked-at (*angeschaut*) by beings in their Being; man is seized by the beings as they open themselves up in their Being. Man himself is gathered up in the process of coming-to-presence, he is drawn into the beings' openness where he is retained and sustained. However, man is not merely passive here; for, in order to bring his own essence to fulfillment he must gather together in his openness that which is opening itself up before him.[120] In other words, man, indeed, dwells with beings, but he is not just another being. He is the "mediation" between beings and Being, for he and he alone is *Da-sein*, that is the ekstatic domain of the revealing and concealing of Being.[121]

Chapter VI

HISTORY AND HISTORIOGRAPHY

HEIDEGGER'S UNDERSTANDING OF THE "GEISTESWISSENSCHAFTEN"

24: THE SCIENCE "HISTORY" WITHIN THE CONTEXT OF HERMENEUTIC PHENOMENOLOGY

In this chapter I wish to show that by interpreting *Verstehen* (understanding) as an eksistential of the Being of Dasein, Heidegger has laid the foundation on the basis of which the fundamental problems of the science "history" can receive an acceptable solution. In order to demonstrate this concretely we must return first to Heidegger's conception of understanding and explicitly relate it to the fundamental disposition or mood with which it is intimately connected.

In the introductory part of this book we have already seen that in Heidegger's opinion the fundamental disposition of *Befindlichkeit*, i.e., the disposition or mood on the basis of which Dasein always *finds itself* already to be there (*Da*), together with understanding and *logos* is constitutive of the luminosity of Dasein. What Heidegger indicated ontologically by the expression "*Befindlichkeit*," is ontically a very familiar phenomenon. In our everyday life we encounter this phenomenon in the form of moods, different forms of being-attuned-to. This is the reason why I wish to refer to this fundamental disposition with the term "moodness." Moodness communicates to Dasein something about its own mode of Being in relation to its world. In moodness each Dasein is aware of its own Being; its Being shows itself in moodness as a having-been-thrown.[1] Without wanting it, and without having chosen it, man is. He finds himself in a world which is not of his making, but in which his own Being is to be realized by himself as a task. In moodness man is thus aware of the fact that he is, and of the fact that he has to be. Man's thrownness thus implies that man who projects himself toward his own being-able-to-Be which as such lies in the future, must do so on the basis of his own already-having-been, so that all free projections are limited by the facticity of his own Being. Applied to the realm of concrete human phenomena this means that such phenomena in principle cannot be understood genuinely, except by understanding them within the framework of the tradition to which they themselves belong. Thus in trying to understand the meaning of concrete human phenomena the *Geisteswissenschaften* in general, and historiography in particular, cannot oppose themselves to the process of the tradition which itself precisely makes man's access to history possible. The concern of an interpretative human science, therefore, can no longer be to detach itself from that tradition in order to achieve the kind of objectivity which one finds in the natural sciences; for man essentially participates in that tradition. Tradition is that from which we come, from which we live, and which holds all of us together. That is why this tradition cannot be understood genuinely by approaching it with the help of empirical methods of the kind used in physics; for these methods precisely demand that we detach outselves from it. A tradition, thus, cannot be understood objectively; it must be methodically appropriated. A hermeneutic human science is nothing but an attempt to appropriate a tradition methodically by critically examining, clarifying, and giving a foundation to the presuppositions implied in our pre-scientific understanding of the world in which we live.

Man possesses the eksistential possibility of being always in a mood; his mode of Being is determined primordially by moodness.[2] However, his mode of Being is determined equiprimordially by his understanding (*Verstehen*). Original understanding has not so much reference to this or that concrete thing or situation as to the mode of Being which is characteristic of man as Being-in-the-world. In original understanding the mode of Being characteristic of man manifests itself as being-able-to-Be. And since man's Being is Being-in-the-world, his being-able-to-Be has reference to all the various ways of his being concerned for others and with things, and of his concern with the world. But in all this, man always realizes in one way or another his being-able-to-Be in regard to himself and for the sake of himself.

Original understanding always moves in a range of possibilities; it continuously endeavors to discover possibilities, because it possesses in itself the existential structure of a "project" (*Entwurf*).

Heidegger thus claims that Dasein is able to understand the Being of itself and the Being of other beings only insofar as its understanding has the character of a project. Richardson correctly observes here that the German verb *entwerfen* (to throw forward) is often used in the transferred sense so that its meaning implies that what is thrown forward is already somehow possessed by the one who throws it forward. Richardson explains this as follows: ". . . by this pre-possession, the structure of the project-ed precedes itself in the project-or; this preceding structure of the project-ed in the project-or is an anticipation; the anticipation is the bringing-to-pass of this precedent structure as precedent."[3]

As for Heidegger's interpretation of the meaning of *Entwurf*, Richardson mentions two different but related senses. The first one is discussed in connection with Kant's conception of *Entwurf*[4] where Heidegger writes: . . . "Accordingly, what makes comportment with beings (ontic knowledge) possible, is an antecedent understanding of the Being-structure, i.e., the ontological knowledge."[5]

The second sense is mentioned where Heidegger claims that the projection must "necessarily be a construction."[6] Richardson explains Heidegger's intention here as follows: *prior to* the encounter of Dasein and being, Dasein is so constituted as to seize by anticipation the structure of the being that is to be encountered; however, *during* the encounter, the seizure which was anticipated is now explicitly accomplished and achieved according to the predetermined plan as "dictated" by the primordial constitution of Dasein itself. "The achievement, then, is the actual process of discerning, the laying-in-the-open of the structure of the being-encountered, so that by the encounter the structure is 'built'."[7]

In original understanding man projects himself onto his ultimate "for the sake of which"; but this projection of self necessarily implies a projection of the world. In his original understanding man opens himself in the direction of his own Being but, at the same time, also in the direction of the world. That is why original understanding implies essentially an antecedent view, an anticipating "sighting" of man's own mode of Being and of his world. This anticipating "sighting" becomes articulated in interpretative explanation (*Auslegung*). In and through interpretative explanation man's understanding appropriates comprehendingly that which was already understood by it. Interpretative explanation is the development of the possibilities that in anticipation were projected in original understanding itself. Since in interpretative explanation each thing or event is to be taken as either this or as that, the hermeneutic *as* is the constitutive element of what is here called "interpretative understanding." If in interpretative explanation something is understood with the guiding clue "taking something as something," then such an explanation presupposes that what was understood in this way, was already implicitly contained in the original understanding of the world which is inherent in our Being-in-the-world as understanding. Thus we must say that the fact that we "*have*" intramundane things, that we *take* and *see* them as either this or as that, and therefore *conceive* of them in this way or in that way on the basis of our interpretative explanation of them, must be founded on an earlier "having," an earlier "seeing," and an earlier "conception" which are constitutive of our understanding as such. As we have seen, we can formulate this as follows: each concrete interpretative explanation takes place in a hermeneutic situation. In the first part of this book we have explained this as follows.

Thus we may say that all understanding in the final analysis is interpretation. The interpretation may be implicit as in our concernful dealing with things, or explicit as in our interpretative explanation and enunciation. The deepest root of the hermeneutic character of all human understanding is to be found in the fact that all understanding necessarily takes place in the *hermeneutic situation*. For man, understanding is impossible except on the basis of a fore-having, a fore-sight, and a fore-conception because of the fact that his eksistence is inherently finite and temporal. Anyone who tries to understand a human phenomenon, necessarily presupposes a totality of meaning or world within which in his view this phenomenon can appear as meaningful (fore-having). Secondly, he assumes a certain point of view which fixes that with regard to which what is to be understood, is to be interpreted (fore-sight). Finally, one tries to articulate one's understanding of that phenomenon with the help of concepts which are either drawn from the phenomenon itself, or are forced upon it as it were from the outside. In either case, the interpretative understanding has already decided for a definite way of conceiving of it (fore-conception).[8] It is of importance to note here that although an interpretation is never a presuppositionless apprehending of something presented to us, our interpretation obviously does not just freely constitute the meaning things and phenomena have for us. The only point argued for here is that the meaning of things receives its structure and articulation from our fore-having, fore-sight, and fore-conception.[9]

From the first page of *Being and Time* it is clear that Heidegger's basic concern is with the interpretation of Dasein in terms of temporality and the explanation of time as the transcendental horizon of the question of Being[10] A careful study of the Being of Dasein itself led to the insight that the Being of Dasein is to be found in care, whereas the meaning of care appears to consist in temporality.[11] Once it has been shown that man's Being is a being-able-to-Be which as such is always ahead of itself, whereas on the other hand any eksistential project must originate from a situation in which Dasein finds itself thrown into a world and being absorbed in what immediately manifests itself there, it becomes clear that Dasein's Being must consist in care. For care consists in the eksistentiality (having to be ahead of itself), facticity (finding oneself in a world which is already there), and fallenness (being referentially dependent upon and dragged down toward intramundane beings). Then it is clear also why care is radically made possible by temporality. For the ahead-of-itself of eksistentiality is grounded in the future; the being-already-in of facticity makes known our having-been; finally, the being-at of fallenness becomes possible in making-present.[12] Temporality is that basic "process" in and through which Dasein's Being becomes temporalized in three different directions; future, having-been, and present. These directions of time imply one another essentially and, nonetheless, they are mutually exclusive. For this reason they are called the ek-stases of primordial time.

If the meaning of care is temporality and temporality, in turn, constitutes the disclosedness of Dasein's *there*, whereas in the disclosedness of this *there* the world is disclosed along with it, then the world must likewise be grounded in temporality. The eksistential-temporal condition for the possibility of the world lies in the fact that temporality, taken as ek-static unity, implies directions or horizons. There belongs to each ek-stasis a typical kind of "whither" to which one is carried away. One could call the "whither" of each ek-stasis its horizonal schema. The schema then in which Dasein comes toward itself futurally is the "for the sake of which"; the schema in which Dasein is disclosed to itself in its thrownness is to be taken as that "in the face of which" it has been thrown and "to which" it has been abandoned; this is the horizonal schema of what has been. Finally the horizonal schema for the present is defined by the "in order to."

The unity of the horizonal schemata of future, present, and having-been, is thus grounded in the ek-static unity of temporality. The horizon of temporality as a whole determines that whereupon each eksisting being factically is disclosed. With its factical Being-there, a being-able-to-Be is projected into the horizon of the future, its having-been-already is disclosed in the horizon of having-been, and that with which Dasein concerns itself in each case is discovered in the horizon of the present. Thus the horizonal unity of the schemata of these ek-stases connects in a primordial way the relationships of the "in order to" and the "in face of which" with the "for the sake of which," so that on the basis of the horizonal constitution of the ek-static unity of temporality, there belongs to Dasein in each case a *world* that has been thus disclosed. Just as the present arises in the unity of the temporalizing of temporality out of the future and having-been, so in the same way the *horizon* of the present temporalizes itself equiprimordially with those of the future and the having-been. Thus, insofar as Dasein temporalizes itself, a world is.[13]

Since Dasein is ultimately a temporal being, it is essentially historical as well.[14] The analysis of Dasein's historicity is no more than an explicitation and further elaboration of what was already implied in our analysis of temporality. However, since the term "historical" connotes a reference to the past, our explicitation of temporality as historicity must pay special attention to the full meaning of the self to which Dasein comes in resolve.

We have seen that Dasein, as thrown, has been delivered over to itself and to its being-able-to-Be *as* Being-in-the-world. Thus, as thrown, it has been submitted to a world in which it eksists factically with others. Proximally and for the most part the self is then lost in the "they." In resolve Dasein comes back to itself. The resolve discloses current factical possibilities of *authentic* eksisting, and discloses them in terms of the heritage which that resolve takes over. In one's coming back to one's thrownness in resolve, there is hidden a handing down to oneself of the possibilities that have come down to us. The more authentically Dasein in resolve consents to be what it is in all its finitude, the more profoundly this heritage becomes its own in a freely chosen discovery of the possibilities of its eksistence. Dasein hands over to its self its own heritage, it expressly finds its potentiality all over again by retrieving it. Thus the retrieve is the explicit handing over of the heritage, i.e., Dasein's free return to possibilities that already have been made explicit.[15]

Yet it is not the retrieve of its own possibilities that makes Dasein historical. On the contrary, it is only because Dasein, as temporal is already historical that by retrieving its self, it can assume its own history. Furthermore, even though Dasein's historicity has its origin in the future (Dasein's coming to its self), still the fact that this implies a retrieving of the possibilities of the past and the assumption of a heritage, explains why an authentic interpretation of history must give a preponderance to the past. Finally, it should be noted that Dasein's Being includes a Being-with-others. Thus the coming-to-pass, structured by historicity, is achieved with other human beings, all of which together constitute a community, a people, a nation. This means that the heritage which Dasein assumes in authenticity, is not simply its individual history, but the heritage of the people with which Dasein is. It is the achieving of itself in and with its own generation that constitutes the full, authentic coming-to-pass of Dasein itself.[16]

Just as the temporality of Dasein entails the temporality of the world in which Dasein finds itself, so the inherent historicity of Dasein entails the historicity of the world. For, the historizing of history is the historizing of Dasein as Being-in-the-world. Now insofar as Dasein eksists factically, it already encounters that which has been discovered within the world. Thus all intramundane beings, whether present-at-hand or ready-to-hand, have already, in each case, been incorporated into the history of the world. Equipment and work have their destiny; buildings and institutions have their "history." Since the historicity of intramundane beings presupposes the historicity of Dasein's world, we can call their being, "world-historical." It is important to note here that the world-historical is, in each case, already really there in the historizing of eksisting Being-in-the-world, without and antecedent to being grasped historiologically by the science "history."[17]

25: THE EKSISTENTIAL SOURCE OF HISTORIOLOGY IN DASEIN'S HISTORICITY.[18]

The science of history, like any other science, at each time depends factically on the prevailing conception of world. Furthermore, if Dasein's mode of Being is in principle historical, then historiology, like any other science, remains always and manifestly in the grip of Dasein's own historizing. Yet, it must be noted that Dasein's historicity is a necessary presupposition for

HISTORIOLOGY AND DASEIN'S HISTORICITY

historiology in a sense which is markedly different from that found in the natural sciences, for instance. For historiology is the science of Dasein's history and thus it must presuppose as its possible subject matter a being which is primordially historical. However, history must not only be, in order that historical entities may become accessible scientifically. Furthermore, historiological knowledge is not only historical because it is itself a historizing way in which Dasein may manifest itself. For these negative remarks do not yet lead us to the root of the issue at stake here. For taken as such, they do not yet show us why and how Dasein's historicity is the *source* of historiology. In order to accomplish these tasks one must show that the ontological structure of historiology is such that in itself the historiological disclosure of history has its roots in the historicity of Dasein itself, i.e., that the idea of historiology must be projected ontologically in terms of Dasein's historicity.

In order to discover the *idea* of historiology, one cannot turn to the way things are factically done in the historical disciplines today. For there is no a priori guarantee that the idea of historiology which one can discover in this way, will be properly representative of historiology in its primordial and authentic possibilities. On the contrary, one can discover this idea only on the basis of a clarification of the thematization which is characteristic for historiology as such. It is obviously true that the idea of historiology as a science implies that the specific task which historiology has set for itself consists in the disclosure of historical phenomena. However, one must realize that phenomena are historical only insofar as they have been projected as historical. To explain this point which is vital for a genuine understanding of the idea of historiology we must dwell for a moment on the thematization characteristic of historiology.

Every science is constituted primarily by a fundamental thematization in which what was already familiar prescientifically in Dasein itself taken as disclosed Being-in-the-world, becomes projected upon that mode of Being which is characteristic of it. With this projection, the realm of entities to be examined is bounded off. Furthermore, the thematizing projection predelineates the methodological access to these entities, as well as the conceptual structure for interpreting them scientifically. If we now assume (as is done generally), that historiology's task is to disclose the past, then the historiological thematization of history is possible only if the past has, in each case, already been disclosed. For it is impossible to go back to the past historiologically, if the way to it were not to be open to it.

In the analytic of Dasein's Being it was shown that this way is in general prepared for the thematization of the past in and by historiology, insofar as Dasein's Being is inherently historical and, thus, insofar as by reason of its ek-statico-horizonal temporality it is open in its character of "having-been." Furthermore, since it has been shown there, also, that Dasein, and only Dasein, is primordially historical, that which the thematization of historiology presents as a possible subject matter of research, must have the kind of Being which is typical for Dasein as having-been-there, i.e., Dasein insofar as it has-been-there, the world of Dasein that has-been-there, and all entities which functioned in that world.

The latter may still be present in our world today as the things which belong to a world that has-been-there. Thus relics, monuments, and records, that are still present-at-hand, are possible material for the disclosure of that Dasein which has-been-there. These things can turn into historiological material because, in harmony with their own mode of Being, they have a world-historical character. Thus they are capable of becoming such material only when they have been understood in advance with regard to their within-the-worldness. From this insight it becomes understandable why the world that has already been projected in this way as a world that has-been-there, can then be given its definite and articulate character through an interpretation of the world-historical material we have received "from the past."

Our going back to the past does not originate from the acquisition, the selection, and the critical justification of such material; for these activities necessarily presuppose the historicity of the historian's own mode of Being. It is from the historicity of Dasein itself, thus, that one must try to determine what the subject matter of historiology precisely and really is. In other words, the determination of the primordial theme of historiology must be carried through in conformity with the character of the authentic historicity of what-has-been there, i.e., with retrieve (*Wiederhohlung*) taken as this form of disclosure. In such retrieve the Dasein that has-been-there can be understood in its authentic possibility which has-been. Thus when the claim is made that the eksistential foundation of historiology as a science is to be found in Dasein's historicity, this really means that when the historian takes the historiological object as his primary theme, he is

HISTORIOLOGY AND DASEIN'S HISTORICITY

projecting the Dasein that has-been-there upon its ownmost possibility of Being.

This point is of the greatest importance for our proper understanding of the scientificity of historiology as a science. It is often said that historiology attempts to understand "the facts," i.e., the individual historical happenings in a chronological sequence; other philosophers have argued that history is concerned primarily with the laws that somehow govern these "facts." It is not difficult to show that both these views are mistaken. The theme of historiology is not that which has happened, taken as that which happened just once and for all. Neither is this theme something universal that somehow floats above these facts. The genuine theme of historiology is the *possibility* that has been factically eksistent. For one must realize here that Dasein's facticity is constituted precisely by its own resolute projection of itself upon a chosen being-able-to-Be. That which has-been-there factically is Dasein's existentiell possibility in which fate (for the individual), destiny (for a society), and world-history (for the given constellation of intramundane things) have been determined factically. Thus because in each case eksistence is only as factically thrown in a world which only then can be its world, historiology will disclose the gentle "force" of the *possible* with greater penetration, the more concretely it understands Dasein's having-been-there in terms of its possibilities only.

It has often been argued that historiology should be concerned with the universal in what has been once and for all. This is then often explained in such a way that the task of historiology would be to show what has-been-there in some supratemporal mode. From the preceding reflections, however, it is clear that this, too, cannot possibly be the task of historiology. Historiology is not concerned with passively re-presenting or merely repeating the events of the past, but rather with retrieving what has-been-there in such a manner that in this retrieve the "force" of the *possible* gets struck home into the historian's factical eksistence, i.e., that it comes towards this eksistence in its *futural* character. For Dasein's historicity does not originate from the present, i.e., from what is actually only today, in order then to grope its way back from there to something that is past. Only a being which, as *futural*, is equiprimordially in the process of *having-been*, can, by handing down to itself the possibilities it has inherited, take over its own thrownness and momentarily be for 'its' time.[19] That is, the historiological disclosure must temporalize itself in terms of the future. The selection of what is to become a possible theme for historiology has already been met with in the factical, existentiell choice of Dasein's historicity in which, as we have seen, genuine historiology originates and in which alone it is.

From this it follows that in historiology objectivity cannot be determined by reference to the universal validity of standards and rules. Historiology is objective if its research is regulated primarily in terms of whether it can confront us with that being which belongs to it as its theme, and can bring it, uncovered in the primordiality of its Being, to our understanding. Historiology must obviously take its orientation from the "facts"; but one must realize here that the central theme of historiology is the *possibility* of eksistence which has-been-there in a given world.

It is of importance to note here also that each given world consists of a great number of beings and events which may be worthy of historiological research. Accordingly, this research factically has many branches and can take as its basic theme the history of equipment and technology, the history of work, of culture, of art, of the "spirit," and of ideas. From this it follows that history (*Geschichte*), as handing itself down to the historian, is in itself at the same time and in each case mentioned always in an interpretedness and explicit articulatedness. This articulatedness has in each case a history of its own. Finally, it follows that historiology penetrates to what has-been-there for the most part only through the history which hands itself down in this articulated manner. It is this complexity that explains why in historiology we can distinguish various, relatively independent branches, and why each concrete historiological research can achieve in each case a varying degree of closeness to its authentic theme.

But regardless of whether historiology focuses on the conception of world that was typical and characteristic for an era, or on a relatively independent realm in such a world, or even merely on the critical edition of "original" sources, the actual research itself must be such that it contributes to the authentic historicity of the historian and his contemporaries. Historiology is authentic only to the degree that in it the threefold character of Dasein's historicity itself is materialized. For Dasein eksists authentically *as futural* in resolutely disclosing a possibility which it has chosen. Coming back resolutely to itself in historiology, Dasein is by retrieve open for the possibilities of human eksistence. Furthermore, since Dasein is in the process of having-been (*als Gewesendes*), it has been delivered over to its own thrownness.

When the possible is made its own by retrieve, there is adumbrated at the same time the possibility of reverently preserving the eksistence that has-been there. Finally, Dasein temporalizes itself in the way that future and having-been are united in the authentic present. This present discloses what is the case today in an authentic manner. But if historiology interprets what is the case today in terms of understanding a possibility of eksistence which has been seized upon in the sense that it retrieves what has-been-there in a futural manner, authentic historiology becomes a way in which the inauthentic present becomes deprived of the inauthentic character it always has in the publicness of the "they." Thus authentic historiology is necessarily a critique of the inauthentic present.

From this it follows at once that authentic historiology can never go beyond the hermeneutic situation. Authentic historiology is inherently hermeneutical in that the historical thematization is no more than a cultivation of the hermeneutical situation, which, once a historically eksisting Dasein has made its resolution, opens itself to the retrieving disclosure of what has-been-there.

26: TOWARD A COMPREHENSIVE THEORY OF OUR KNOWLEDGE OF HISTORY

It seems to me that the preceding pages contain sufficient evidence to justify the claim that Heidegger has been able to give us an acceptable solution for some problems pertaining to our knowledge of history, which have remained unanswered in the vast literature on the subject.

Heidegger has made a great effort to deal adequately with the philosophically important question concerning the conditions of both history and our scientific knowledge of history. Both history and our scientific knowledge of history have their ontological roots in the radical finitude of man, in the essential temporality and historicity of man, his world, and of Being itself; in the communality of man, particularly as evidenced in the happening of the tradition; and finally in language taken in a broad sense as essentially related to man's finite articulating interpretation. In other words, a philosophy of history does not go to the root and source of all issues if it does not explicitly focus on the finite, i.e., the revealing and concealing, character of the coming-to-pass of the truth of Being in regard to finite man as well as on the radical finitude of any articulating interpretation through language in the broad sense. Furthermore, a philosophy which refrains from dealing with these basic issues will be unable to give a justifiable answer to a great number of other questions which may legitimately be asked in regard to both history and our scientific knowledge of history.

On the basis of a careful explanation and justification of these basic issues it is understandable why our scientific knowledge of history cannot be defined as the systematic and methodical knowledge of past events. It may be true that historians in some sense are primarily concerned with events that have taken place in mankind's past; yet very little is said about the meaning and function of this kind of knowledge by just pointing to this undeniably true insight. One must realize here that the good historian is not primarily concerned with the historical facts taken in their factual *Einmaligkeit*. Recording facts one by one in a temporal sequence has as such still very little to do with genuine historical knowledge. Just as in physics the physical fact is co-constituted by a physical theory and, thus, must be shown to be projected as such in the light of universal laws or principles, so the historian will have to show the historical facts as genuine possibilities of man's eksistence in a world which he shares with others. But such a projection of the facts cannot be achieved except on the basis of fundamental insights which are implicitly or explicitly contained in an ontological conception of man. Once the historical projection of past events has been clarified and justified in the light of an ontological conception of man and world, it is at once possible to understand the typical universality which is characteristic of historical research. For what is to be retrieved scientifically is the historic fact in its "eidetic generality"; i.e., as a *universal* possibility for man's eksistence. That which happened in the past and was handed down to us by our heritage in some form or other, is then shown to contain genuine possibilities for our own future. The past events obviously do not determine contemporary man; they are merely constitutive components of the situation in which contemporary man finds himself and which in that sense make him free. For what is handed down by our heritage is that which we live from in order to live away from it in freedom.

These reflections lead us at once to another issue of great importance: the question concerning the meaning of history and of historical knowledge. From this perspective it is clear that once the idea that man is capable of knowing absolutes is given up, except those which he creates in an artificial manner, the augustinian question concerning the meaning of history, is no longer a legitimate philosophical question. For on the level of our radically finite knowledge we do not really understand that question, nor do we know how to go about answering it, except by dogmatic claims or by an appeal to unjustifiable absolutes. If the question concerning the meaning of history is a legitimate question at all, it is a religious issue that should be discussed in theology.

In this same general perspective it is also possible to find an acceptable solution for another issue often discussed in the literature. Our historical knowledge has no immediate access to the events that happened in the past. We are still able to know them today because of the "traces" they have left behind. Thus one can say that the very subject matter of our historical knowledge consists in the "traces" of past events which are still available to us. It seems to me, however, that at least three remarks should be added to these statements if one wishes to avoid basic misunderstanding. First of all one must realize that most traces left behind in our tradition have the character of being interpretations of the events of which they are the traces. One must note here that not all events have left traces; also, as far as the most important sources of our historical knowledge are concerned the existence of "traces" has implied at one time a deliberate selection on the part of the one who wrote about the event, eternalized it in a work of art, etc. Secondly, traces are not just found in our world today. We project certain texts, relics, monuments, etc., as traces. Finally, it seems to be incorrect to argue that the subject matter of our historical knowledge consists merely in the traces which the science history itself has left behind.

The question as to how traces are projected in our historical research leads us to a whole cluster of problems, all of which are related to the very scientificity of our scientific knowledge of history. It would seem that Heidegger's idea that each individual scientific research effort originates in a thematizing project contains the elements necessary to answer the most important, relevant questions. In his view, as we have seen, true scientific research limits itself in its procedures to a clearly delineated realm of beings. The expression "procedures" used here does not mean merely "methods" or modes of proceeding, because such a methodical way of proceeding presupposes that there is already an open realm in which one can move. The opening up of such a realm is precisely the fundamental operation of any form of thematization. The delineation of a definite realm of beings is brought about by a projection (*Entwurf*) by means of which a certain aspect of things is taken as the exclusive theme of investigation.

It is by such a projection that the realm of beings characteristic of a particular discipline is clearly demarcated, the access to that domain acquires its methodical direction, and the structure of the conceptual and discursive explanation acquires its first orientation.

It seems to me that in *Being and Time*, Heidegger has been able to clarify the thematizing project which underlies all forms of historical research. Yet in 1927 there were important problems which must have puzzled the careful reader. First of all, we have seen that Heidegger's conception of the thematizing project was clarified in *Being and Time* for the first time in connection with the natural sciences only.[20] There it is explicitly stated that the thematizing project, as found in the natural sciences, is inherently objectifying. In the section devoted to historiology, Heidegger does not make the claim that historical research is also objectifying; yet the fact that no explicit claim to the contrary is made either, must originally have been a source of possible misunderstanding. From Heidegger's later work it is clear that not every thematizing project is objectifying, and that particularly in the case of history, no objectivation is involved.

Speaking about the thematization which is at the root of the natural sciences Heidegger writes in *Being and Time*: "Its aim is to free the entities we encounter within the world and to free them in such a way that they can 'throw themselves against' a pure discovering--that is, that they become 'objects.' Thematizing objectifies."[21] From this text one might derive the view that in Heidegger's conception any scientific thematization is objectifying. With the help of the hints found in his later work, however, it can be made perfectly clear that already in 1927 Heidegger was convinced that not all thematization is objectifying and, secondly, that this particularly is not the case for our historical research. Only where the thematization implies a transition from the ready-to-hand to the present-at-hand and, thus, only where the thematization implies a demundanization, is the thematizing project objectifying. However, where the ready-to-hand is made a theme of scientific investigation and, a fortiori, when man himself or his world is made a subject of scientific research, no objectivation can take place because no demundanization is necessary or even possible.[22]

Being and Time contains only a few passing remarks in regard to the question concerning what the consequences of the scientific thematization in history are for its methodical direction and the structure of the conceptual and discursive explanation.

TOWARD A COMPREHENSIVE THEORY OF HISTORY

Heidegger merely limits himself to the remark that "the main point is the cultivation of the hermeneutical situation which . . . opens itself to the repetitive disclosure of what has-been-there . . . Since the basic concepts of the historical sciences . . . are concepts of eksistence, the theory of the *Geisteswissenschaften* presupposes an eksistential interpretation of the theme of the historicity of Dasein."[23] In the preceding pages I have added the elements Heidegger refers to here. For the necessary concepts I have selected some relevant passages of *Being and Time* itself. Once all of this is put into proper perspective it is clear that there is a radical difference between the natural sciences and our scientific knowledge of history and that the latter contrary to the former is not objectifying. Doing so will make it clear also why a causal explanation of historical events is not desirable, if not impossible altogether, even though "research" is not completely excluded in the domain of historical phenomena.

There is finally one more problem which, although in my view it is of prime importance, has not yet been dealt with explicitly until now. Almost all authors speak about the science of history, historiology, historiography, etc., as if there is one such "thing" that in all cases is guided by the same "cognitive interest," aiming at one basic goal to be achieved in all investigations of this kind, on the basis of one fundamental set of methodological principles, and using a type of conceptualization which is identical or at least similar in all cases. To formulate the problem in another way, one may ask the question as to whether or not the thematizing projection which is at the root of all historical investigations is in all cases of essentially the same character and, thus, whether the methodological principles and the scientific conceptualizing relevant in each case are essentially of the same nature? We have just seen that by thematization we understand the process in which the demarcation of a determinate region of beings or entities is brought about and the aspect under which these entities will be conceived of, becomes established. One could say that the domain projected by the science "history" is to be found in the phenomena that have been handed down by a given tradition. Yet, one must realize here that not all historians are concerned with the same types of phenomena that have been handed down by our tradition. A historian of religion is concerned with religious phenomena, a historian of the sciences is concerned with the scientifically relevant data of the past, a historian of art is concerned with aesthetic phenomena, etc. Thus it seems to me uncritical to assume without any further investigation that although the concrete thematizations are different in each given case, nonetheless the same stipulations are to be made in regard to the methods to be used in studying the entities of the domain in question, as well as the typical concepts to be employed.

In order to be able to approach the issue in a systematic fashion a few introductory remarks are necessary. First a few distinctions seem to be in order.

When we speak about historiology in order to attempt to determine its scientificity, we must first make a distinction between auxiliary disciplines and perhaps some "sub-disciplines" on the one hand, and historiology proper on the other. Collecting manuscripts, examining their "paper" and "ink," subjecting them to complicated chemical and physical experiments, determining their chronology and authenticity, ordering them, etc., all of this is work historians sometimes do. Yet, this kind of work is totally different from the work they do when they try to explain the origin of a war, the shift in the relationship between two nations at a given moment in time, or the gradual development of the Reformation in 15th and 16th century Christianity. It seems obvious to me that the scientificity of the "auxiliary" disciplines is inherently different from the scientificity of historiology taken in the strict sense.

In these "auxiliary" disciplines there is ample room for scientific research. Once speaking about modern research experiments in the natural sciences, Heidegger said that the function of experiments in physical research is analogous to the function of, for instance, "source critique" in the historical disciplines, provided the expression "source critique" be understood in a very broad sense, so as to include the whole of discovering, screening, verifying, evaluating, preserving, and the interpretative explanation of sources.

Wherever the historian engages in this kind of research and tries to give a scientific explanation of a state of affairs, he must begin with some form of objectifying thematization. Thus even though in historiology proper objectivation in the sense in which this is employed in the natural sciences is excluded in principle, some form of objectivation is a necessary condition for the research in what I have called the "auxiliary" disciplines. But even then, Heidegger sets limits to the analogy between the natural and the historical sciences. In his view, it is important to observe that historical explanation does not lead to rules and laws; on the other hand, such an explanation does not limit itself to a mere reporting of facts either. The historical sciences, just as does mathematical physics, try in this case to present something permanent; and this can be done only by an objectifying historiology. But history obviously can be objectified only after it has already passed by. That which is permanent in what has passed by, that is to say that in terms of which our historical explanation tries to evaluate happenings that occur only once, is that which always has been there already; and, as such, it can in each case be compared with the actual state of affairs. By continuously comparing everything with everything, it is possible to lay bare that which is understandable in history and to verify it as the basic outline of history. The realm of historical phenomena with which historical *research* is concerned extends only so far as our historical *explanation* can reach. This is the reason why the unique, that which occurs only once, the simple, briefly, that which is genuinely great in history, is never self-evident and, thus, must remain outside the domain of that which can be explained. Historical research obviously never denies what was great in history; yet it must conceive of it as being an exception. In Heidegger's view, there is no other form of historical explanation possible as long as explanation means: the reduction of what is not yet intelligible to that which is already intelligible, that is to say, as long as historiography remains research. It is important to note that in this kind of explanation the great is always measured against the common and the average.

Because historiology, taken as research and as an effort to explain historical phenomena, must project and objectify the past, in order to make it an explainable and surveyable network of actions and their consequences, it requires source critique as one of its instruments of objectivation. Yet historiology in the proper sense of the term, in its effort to understand the past, goes far beyond historical research even though it obviously must presuppose its scientific explanation and critique. It is thus important to stress that the conception of historiology which Heidegger tries to unfold, does not at all exclude the possibility of empirical research in the domain of historical phenomena. He merely claims that historiology proper in addition to explanation must concern itself with interpretation and critique.[24]

Yet even this distinction does not bring us much closer to a solution of the basic problem under consideration here. For we have still made the assumption that historiology proper is one homogeneous science. Yet it is precisely this assumption which seems to be illegitimate. One must realize that there seem to be as many relatively independent historiologies as there are relatively independent forms of man's orientation toward the world. To clarify this point, let me make a list of some important forms of historiology. Quite generally one speaks of history of religion, history of moral systems or views, art history (history of the literary forms of art, of music, of the visual arts, etc.), history of philosophy, history of the sciences (of mathematics, physics, chemistry, biology, etc.), history of historiology, history of the social, economic, and political *praxis*, history of technology, not to mention the history of the art of cooking, making clothes, riding horses, weaving materials, etc. It is clear to me that not all of these forms of historical research flow from the same type of thematization which, in turn, would entail the same kind of conceptualization.

One will obviously object here that what we usually call "historiology proper" is the harmonious totality of all these possibilities. One could say that just as physics deals with fluids, solids, and gaseous entities, with things, forces, fields, magnetism, electricity, nuclear particles and forces, etc., so history proper must deal with all human forms of man's behavior and their intentional correlates with the intention of finding out critically how all of this came to be the way it did. Yet, it seems to me that such a view is first of all contradicted by the actual facts, and secondly rests upon an arbitrary analogy.

First of all, it should be pointed out here that in actual fact, research in the realm of the history of science is most often done by historians who are also scientists, history of religion and theology is almost always one of the basic concerns of theologians, history of philosophy is an essential component of the work of any good philosopher. Similar remarks could be made for the arts, moral systems, etc. In other words, in actual fact there are certain types of historical investigations which are generally assumed not to belong to the specific concern of the historian *tout court*. One could also point here to the fact that this situation is reflected in what is actually practiced in almost all institutions of higher education: history of religion is taught in divinity colleges, art history is taught in the college of the arts, history of education is taught in the college of education, history of science is taught either in the college of science or in the department of philosophy, not or seldom in the department of history proper. But secondly, it is obvious to me that the thematization and the conceptualization that flows from it, which are characteristic of history of religion, for instance, are basically different from the thematization and conceptualization typical for the history of science.

It is not my intention to claim that there are as many forms of historiology as there are examples one could quote similar to those listed above. Yet it seems to me that some basic forms of historiology can and should be distinguished, and that in each case the question is to be asked as to the nature of the underlying thematizing projection and the typical conceptualization flowing from it. Without advocating the making of exhaustive distinctions, I suggest that at least the following types of historiology should be distinguished: (1) history of religion and morality, (2) history of the arts, (3) history of national and international social, economic, and political events, (4) history of the formal and empirical science, (5) history of philosophy, (6) history of various forms of technologies, (7) history of law and legal systems.

Although Heidegger has never explicitly focused on this issue, there are nevertheless several indications which lead one to believe that in principle he would have agreed with the suggestions made here. First of all, it is well known that Heidegger has explicitly defended the thesis that although philosophical questions are inherently historical questions, philosophy itself is nonetheless essentially different from the historical sciences.[25]

Secondly, speaking about historiology in *Being and Time*, Heidegger explicitly stipulates that historiology has factically many branches which are to be characterized by means of the realms of beings they select as the immediate subject matter of research: equipment, work, culture, spirit, ideas, etc. This suggestion is not further developed there. However, in a lecture on theology written at the same time (1927) Heidegger defended the thesis that theology is a very special historical science, the scientificity of which is to be determined by means of a careful analysis of the way theology thematizes its subject matter, namely the Christianness of Christianity.[26]

We may thus conclude, I think, that Heidegger subscribed to the view that in the domain of historiology proper, it is important to make a distinction between different, relatively independent historiologies, each with its own relatively independent thematization, concepts, and methodical techniques.

CHAPTER VII

HERMENEUTIC PHENOMENOLOGY AND THE HUMAN SCIENCES

27: WHY DID HEIDEGGER NOT EXPLICITLY FOCUS ON THE HUMAN SCIENCES?

In the sections to follow I shall make an effort to answer the question of how Heidegger's thought about the sciences perhaps can be made relevant to philosophical reflections on the behavioral and the social sciences. As far as the human sciences are concerned, we find ourselves in a situation that is quite different from the one we encountered in the preceding chapters. Until now we could always rely on texts in which Heidegger himself has formulated his views on some important issues which he has discussed in his philosophical reflections on the various sciences. For the human sciences this is no longer the case.

We have seen that Heidegger grew up in an educational and philosophical climate in which one commonly made a distinction between the natural and the historical sciences.[1] When the term *"Geisteswissenschaften"* was introduced in the second half of the 19th century it responded to an actual state of affairs in the domain of the sciences. Today this is no longer the case. Formerly, the term referred to all the known sciences that are neither philosophical sciences in the strict sense, nor natural sciences. Since sociology, anthropology, political science, etc., at that time were still considered to be philosophical disciplines, one could then thus state that the *Geisteswissenschaften* were historical sciences, so that Heidegger, following many other authors, could simply identify the *Geisteswissenschaften* with the science of culture or the science of the objective spirit. The reason why this conception no longer holds is not so much the fact that the subject matters of the different human sciences do not have a

WHY DID HEIDEGGER NOT FOCUS ON HUMAN SCIENCES?

historical dimension that is to be examined in one of the historical sciences or the sciences of culture, but rather the fact that since 1875 different types of empirical sciences have developed which concern themselves with aspects of human phenomena, and which before that time had not yet been explicitly anticipated. For, as we shall see shortly, in each realm of human phenomena there is indeed room for several approaches: empirical, historical, descriptive, interpretative, critical, etc.

At any rate, what we now call the behavioral and the social sciences does not easily fit into the scheme of the distinction commonly made in the 19th century between the sciences of nature and the *Geisteswissenschaften*. It is true that at first some authors were convinced that the behavioral sciences belong among the natural sciences, whereas at a later stage of the development, the social sciences for some perhaps could have found a place among the *Geisteswissenschaften*. Yet, in my view, it is clear that such a solution, in light of the actual situation confronting us today, is not without very serious difficulties. I think that currently many people would object to calling empirical psychology simply a natural science; furthermore, methodologically it is very difficult to make economics and sociology simply historical sciences or sciences of culture.

Another reason why Heidegger himself never discussed the implications of hermeneutic phenomenology for the sciences of man, can perhaps be found in the fact that he never really studied empirical psychology, sociology, anthropology, economics, political science, etc., in a systematic fashion. What we today understand by the behavioral sciences and by such social sciences as anthropology, economics, political science, and sociology did not yet exist as such within the structure of the German university during the first quarter of this century. "Departments" and institutes for most of the individual social sciences did not originate as a rule before the end of World War II. There may have been schools and institutions in Germany where one could engage in a study of social phenomena, but in most cases such a study was more philosophical than empirical in orientation.

One may be inclined to draw the conclusion from these facts that it then perhaps would be better not to raise the question of the relevance of Heidegger's hermeneutic phenomenology for the behavioral and the social sciences. Yet, on the other hand, we find a number of reasons that suggest that the issues are to be raised. First of all, it seems to be very important explicitly to ask the question of whether and to what extent the human reality can be made the subject of scientific research, i.e., whether and to what degree the human reality can be studied with the help of empirical methods. Furthermore, Heidegger does explicitly admit the importance of a scientific psychology and sociology among the "positive" sciences, as we shall see shortly. He also shared Husserl's view on the meaning and function of regional ontologies.[2] He thus must have been convinced that it is possible and also important to develop regional ontologies for the domain of psychic phenomena and for the realm of social phenomena. Finally, several authors have, each in his own way, shown that and how Heidegger's hermeneutic phenomenology can be made relevant to philosophical reflections on the human sciences.[3]

In light of all of this it thus seems to be a legitimate project to examine the question of the relevance of Heidegger's hermeneutic phenomenology for philosophical reflections on the behavioral and social sciences, even though there are no explicit texts by Heidegger himself that could be cited to justify the theses to be developed.

Furthermore, in an effort to deal with the relevant issues, it is not correct, it seems to me, to just limit the discussion to the *quaestio juris*; we shall also have to ask how methodologically the human reality is to be made a subject of empirical research and what kinds of limitations and restrictions one will have to place on this kind of research.

The thesis that the human reality is a valid subject matter for biological research has not been doubted seriously since the time of the Greeks. In most cases this research was "validated" by the enormous contribution that this kind of research can make to medicine. The thesis that man is also a valid subject matter for empirical research in the human sciences has not yet found universal approval, as we shall see.[4]

It is perhaps fair to say that psychology, sociology, anthropology, economics, political science, etc., are of recent origin and that they developed as empirical sciences in the 19th and the 20th centuries, although they developed from a tradition that is much older and in which, at first, philosophy played the leading part. Each of these sciences is now a well-established "professional institution" with its societies, journals, departments, national and international meetings and conferences, etc. In each case there is a relatively clear awareness of the extent of the research domain, of what does and what does not belong to the subject matter of the different sciences, a relatively clear conception of the methods to be used in studying the relevant phenomena, some agreement on basic theoretical assumptions, a relatively clear distinction between what is already known scientifically and what is still to be examined, etc.

Yet there are still philosophers and scientists who deplore the actual development and the current state of affairs in the domain of the human sciences, from sociobiology to anthropology and political science. Some of them believe that what actually developed under the guise of the conception of empirical science, as we now know it in physics and chemistry, is unacceptable in that it is no more than a form of control and domination over human beings. In their view, the ideal of what is meant by calling a form of research empirical, implies explanation, prediction, and possible control. Now it can easily be shown on moral grounds, these people argue, that in the study of man there cannot possibly be a place for a kind of research that tries to predict and to control human behavior. If man indeed is free and also an autonomous moral agent then every form of manipulation, control, and enslavement is to be rejected definitively and in principle.

There are others who adopt a less radical position, but nonetheless still claim that empirical human sciences are simply impossible. The reason for this, in their view, is that such sciences cannot account for the human meaning of a man's actions, although they can perhaps deal with the physiological aspects or conditions of these actions. Furthermore, it is said there, that man's behavior is not governed by uniformity and law, because of the fact that it is essentially intentional, purposive, free, temporal, historical, and reflective.

There are still other authors who do not deny that empirical sciences of man perhaps could be possible, but who are convinced that such sciences do not yet really exist. As they see it, in the domain of the human sciences we are today still in a "pre-paradigm" state. The human sciences still find themselves at this moment in a state of "foundational crisis"; there is no common agreement on the basic theoretical assumptions and principles upon which empirical research in each case is to rest.

Finally, there are many philosophers and scientists who agree that it is indeed the case that empirical research in the domain of the human sciences often leads to domination, control, and enslavement; yet, as they see it, this need not be the case, in view of the fact that domination and control are not intrinsic to empirical research. The negative consequences mentioned are merely due to the positivist interpretation of what it means to engage in empirical research. If one were to examine more carefully what is essential to empirical research as such, these authors claim, it would become clear at once that empirical psychology, empirical sociology, and empirical political science need not at all lead to domination and abuse.

Many of the issues underlying these convictions have been discussed in the literature time and again over the past forty years or so, and most scholars today prefer to forget about the entire debate in order "to go on with important and urgent research." In my own view, indeed it makes little sense to rehash one more time the whole debate about what attitude to adopt in regard to the so-called "separatist thesis."[5] Yet before returning to Heidegger's position in regard to the human sciences it is perhaps important to indicate briefly where Heidegger's own efforts are to be located in this debate and what reasons one can give for the position that he appears to have taken.

It is clear that Heidegger was strongly opposed to any empirical science that concerns itself with a study of human beings in such a manner that its research remains completely separated from every effort on the part of philosophy to come to a better understanding of the human reality. In other words, Heidegger certainly rejected a complete separation of science and philosophy, even though he always defended a radical difference between philosophy and science, and fully realized the depth of the gap that exists between them.[6]

It is clear also that Heidegger strongly objected to every form of domination and control over human beings on the part of the human sciences. In his own opinion there is a close connection between these two views inasmuch as a genuine effort to bridge the gap between philosophy and science will decrease the danger that empirical research will be abused.[7]

On the other hand, Heidegger explicitly accepted the possibility and the legitimacy of empirical research in the domain of human phenomena. For just as in his view there is room for research in the domain of historical phenomena, so is there equally room for research in the domain of the phenomena studied by the sciences of man. Furthermore, he did not think it to be the task of philosophy in its critical reflections on the sciences to tell the scientists what as scientists they should or should not do. In his view hermeneutic phenomenology is rather an effort to understand the meaning and function of the sciences. Thus Heidegger's reflections on the sciences are oriented not so much toward the sciences themselves as toward developing a possible

WHY DID HEIDEGGER NOT FOCUS ON HUMAN SCIENCES?

interpretation of the meaning and function of these sciences. Moreover, Heidegger was convinced also that in reflections on methodology the concern of the philosopher is not primarily oriented toward an explanation of what scientists should do from a purely methodical point of view; Heidegger rather wished to understand what a scientist does when he employs methods, and what his assumptions really are when he does so. Usually a careful and critical reflection on such assumptions leads to the point where new possibilities can be seen and where options can be shown to exist, even though they were never seriously considered before. To be specific, Heidegger was convinced that in his reflections on phenomenological psychology Husserl had discovered important possibilities and options that most empirical psychologists of his time had not yet fully realized.[8] The same can be said about new perspectives opened up by hermeneutic phenomenology for the social sciences when one began to realize the analogy between human action and text.

In the preceding reflections the claim was made that even though Heidegger never engaged in philosophical reflections which explicitly focus on the behavioral and social sciences, he nevertheless was fully familiar with the main issues. It is of some importance to provide evidence for this latter claim.

Heidegger often uses the term "psychology." Sometimes the term is employed to refer to the philosophical or "rational" psychology that had been known in the tradition since the time of Aristotle. Sometimes he uses the term in the sense of Dilthey's descriptive and analytic psychology (*die beschreibende und zergliedernde Psychologie*). Sometimes the term refers to the phenomenological psychology of Karl Jaspers. Yet there are also instances in which he mentions scientific psychology explicitly.[9] By "scientific psychology" Heidegger then understands what we now call empirical psychology. The term "sociology" is used only occasionally, but it is always taken in the sense of scientific or "empirical" sociology and not for one of the philosophical disciplines.[10]

Furthermore, in *Being and Time*[11] Heidegger explicitly states that for each research domain of the "positive" sciences, there is to be a regional ontology that concerns itself with the mode of Being of the entities examined in that science. Among such areas of research Heidegger mentions history, nature, space, time, life, Dasein, language, and the like.[12] There he also writes, anticipating some contemporary ideas used in the history and sociology of science: "And although research may always lean toward this positive approach, its real progress comes not so much from collecting results and storing them away in 'manuals' as from inquiring into the ways in which each particular area is basically constituted . . . The level which a science has reached is determined by how far it is capable of a crisis in its basic concepts . . ."[13]

Heidegger also explicitly described efforts to put research on new foundations in mathematics,[14] physics,[15] biology,[16] the *Geisteswissenschaften*,[17] and theology.[18] Psychology and sociology are not mentioned there, but they are not excluded either. The reasons why these two sciences are not mentioned explicitly may have been those given already (these sciences did not yet exist within the educational framework in which Heidegger grew up, and he never studied them as such); yet the reason may also have been connected in part with the neo-Kantian distinction between the natural and the historical sciences, a distinction under which neither empirical psychology nor sociology easily fits, and partly with the fact that Heidegger perhaps was of the opinion that both the behavioral and the social sciences must receive their ultimate foundations from a regional ontology that concerns itself with Dasein, taken as Being-in-the-world, and not just from a regional ontology that concerns itself exclusively with the "psychic" and the "social."[19]

For our present purposes it is important to keep in mind here that Heidegger thus was convinced that the human reality, too, can be projected upon various, a priori domains of meaning, and that on the basis of these projections, legitimate empirical sciences of man can be developed. It is, therefore, a legitimate question to ask precisely how these various thematizing projections are to be articulated in which for each discipline a domain of phenomena becomes delineated, the formal aspect under which these phenomena are to be studied becomes determined, the conceptual framework and the proper language becomes established, etc. Furthermore, in view of the fact that human phenomena are inherently meaningful phenomena, and in view of the fact that all meaning is inherently finite, temporal, and historical, we shall also have to take the actions of human beings as "texts" that are to be interpreted and considered critically. Thus in this regard the human sciences are completely different from the natural sciences, insofar as the phenomena studied in the natural sciences do not have meaning of themselves. At any rate, it is clear that for Heidegger laying the foundation of a science is not just a question of formal logic; rather it is the task of a "productive"

WHY DID HEIDEGGER NOT FOCUS ON HUMAN SCIENCES?

logic and, in the final analysis, one of a "transcendental logic" which concerns itself with the Being of the relevant beings.[20]

Thus even though Heidegger did not explicitly focus on the implications of hermeneutic phenomenology for the human sciences, we can nonetheless safely make the following claims. Heidegger did accept the idea, first developed by Husserl in this form, that regional ontologies are to be developed which are to bridge the gap between the empirical sciences and fundamental ontology. For Heidegger, these regional ontologies are "philosophical" disciplines insofar as they are concerned with investigations about the mode of Being of the entities which constitute a certain research domain. For Husserl, on the other hand, regional ontologies are not philosophical disciplines because these disciplines do not practice the so-called transcendental reduction. Regional ontologies must mediate between the effort on the part of each science to lay its own foundations and the "ultimate" foundation which only ontology can provide.[21] Both Husserl and Heidegger thus assume that in each empirical science, assumptions are made that usually remain implicit and which only ontological investigations can justify thematically.

What each regional ontology has to explain is the typical objectifying thematization which in each empirical discipline delineates the field of study, establishes the aspect under which the entities that belong to the relevant research domain are to be studied, determines the proper methodical procedures and techniques to be used, stipulates guidelines for the use of language, etc. It is assumed that there is an overarching theoretical framework, projected by the relevant thematization, which holds for all phenomena of the respective field of study. This thematization inherently implies abstraction, idealization, and formalization. It is assumed further that in a given science there may be "subfields" for which more specialized thematizations may be necessary. In that case the various thematizations that belong to one science must obviously to some degree be in agreement with one another.[22]

Finally, we must keep in mind here that Heidegger was completely familiar with Husserl's ideas about the regional ontology for psychic phenomena, although we know from his observations on the first drafts of Husserl's article on phenomenology for the 1928 edition of the *Encyclopaedia Brittannica* that Heidegger did not completely accept Husserl's position in this regard. In Heidegger's view, the regional ontologies for the somatological and psychological disciplines are to be founded ultimately, not upon transcendental phenomenology, but rather on a fundamental ontology that concerns itself with the concrete totality of man and determines the mode of Being characteristic of man taken as Dasein.[23] Although in this context Heidegger does not explicitly mention the social sciences, I am convinced that similar remarks can be made for these sciences also.

We must thus try to give an account of the regional ontologies for the human sciences and explain both their descriptive and interpretative dimensions. For, as we shall see, in each human science there really are two basic issues. The first issue is concerned with the manner in which in each discipline the realms of meaning are constituted from which the scientists in each case perceive and conceive the relevant phenomena. To be specific, the question must be asked of precisely how the realm of meaning is constituted from which in psychology in each given domain of research, one conceives of the relevant phenomena, asks questions, and tries to answer them, and of how, in sociology for instance, the realms of meaning are constituted from which structuralists, functionalists, ethnomethodologists, neo-positivists, ecologists, symbolic interactionists, etc., approach the pertinent phenomena, raise questions, answer them, and justify their answers. To answer the question of precisely how such realms of meaning become constituted (thematization), careful descriptive analyses are necessary. It is in this area where according to Husserl and Heidegger there is an important task for descriptive, phenomenological analyses. These analyses must show: (a) the precise significance and function of these realms of meaning; (b) how relevant these realms in each case really are in regard to the phenomena to be studied empirically; (c) what limits must be placed on the corresponding empirical research because of the limitations inherent in most of these realms of meaning; and (d) how the different realms of meaning developed for each discipline relate to one another.

Secondly, one must try to bridge the gap that exists between the meaning which the agents attribute to their own actions, and the meaning which these actions have according to the view of the scientists. Here there is room for hermeneutic and critical methods in view of the fact that one appears to have one "text" for which more than one interpretation can be given. Thus we must ask the question concerning the "validity" of these interpretations: what is the precise significance of both, and how are they to be related to each other. In the reflections to follow it is obviously not my intention to develop such descriptive, interpretative, and critical components for each science of man in detail. This is the work of those scientists who in each case concern themselves with the "foundations" of their own discipline. My task will only be one of showing what hermeneutic phenomenology has to say about such efforts and about their methodological implications. This also explains why I have decided not to devote separate chapters to the behavioral and to the social sciences, respectively.

To prevent misunderstanding a few additional observations are in order here. First, it is of the greatest importance to stress once more that the argument in favor of descriptive and hermeneutic components for the human sciences is not to be taken as a rejection or even a criticism of *empirical* research in the domain of human phenomena; nor does this argument make *philosophical* reflections on human phenomena superfluous. Hermeneutic and descriptive investigations must be developed if the foundations of empirical research are to be properly understood and justified. Furthermore, a philosophical anthropology and, above all, also a transcendental analytic of Dasein remain essential if the foundational investigations of the scientists in each field are to be justified "radically," i.e., in "transcendental," ontological reflections. Finally, it should be obvious also that the argument developed here leaves ample room for historical investigations of human phenomena and human institutions.

Secondly, it should be noted once more also that if all understanding is hermeneutical, then descriptive and interpretative research is also hermeneutic, just as empirical research itself is hermeneutic in that sense. Yet empirical research, descriptive analysis, interpretation, and critique are, for that very reason, *methodologically* not yet to be reduced to what in the first part of this book was called "hermeneutic phenomenology" or to historical investigations. In the empirical component of each human science we use common empirical (statistical) methods; in the descriptive component we use common descriptive ("phenomenological") methods; in the interpretative and critical component of a human science we use the common methods of *scientific* hermeneutics and criticism; finally, only for the philosophical disciplines mentioned do we suggest that one use the hermeneutico-phenomenological method. Yet it is true that taken in a deep sense, all these methods and every effort at understanding are and remain forms of interpretation in light of the essential temporality and historicity of all human endeavors.[24]

In view of the fact that elsewhere I have already discussed a number of issues that are immediately relevant to these regional ontologies for the behavioral and social sciences, I shall limit myself here to what I take to be essential to show the implications of Heidegger's hermeneutic phenomenology and his transcendental analytic of Dasein for the sciences of man.[25]

28: OBJECTIFYING THEMATIZATION IN THE HUMAN SCIENCES

In his important book, *Radical Reflection*, Calvin Schrag has recently concerned himself with the question about the possibility, i.e., the true origin, of the human sciences and of philosophical anthropology.[26] In his view such an examination is necessary in view of the current crisis in the sciences of man as well as in philosophical anthropology. The fact that there is such a crisis in these disciplines is acknowledged by many, scientists and philosophers alike. Yet there is no agreement on the nature and the origin of the crisis, and of the factors that have occasioned. it. Our understanding of the nature of the crisis is complicated by the fact that each individual human science is in a crisis of its own. In psychology, sociology, anthropology, political science, economics, and history this crisis was in part the consequence of a reductionist and naturalistic attitude adopted by many scientists in these fields. The crisis shows itself there equally in the proliferation of various models and conceptions of man. Schrag does not see the source of the crisis in specialization, the increasing preoccupation with quantification and formalization, or even the claim that the sciences of man have become technological with respect to both procedures and goals. In his view, to identify the root of the crisis, a more fundamental disproportion is to be articulated. Some authors have sought the source of the crisis in the proliferation of "philosophies" in our contemporary world. Schrag rejects this line of thought also, and concludes that what is needed is a move to a more radical form of reflection that antedates the conceptualization and typification that is already at work in the formalization of both philosophy and science.[27]

It seems to me that the radical form of reflection which Schrag refers to here can be found in Heidegger's fundamental ontology and the general ontology on which it itself is to be founded. The implications of Heidegger's philosophy for the human sciences, implications which, as we have seen, Heidegger himself has never drawn explicitly, have already been discussed by Gadamer and Ricoeur.[28] Yet there are still two important

OBJECTIFYING THEMATIZATION IN THE HUMAN SCIENCES

problems which in the hermeneutic tradition have not yet received much attention. First of all there is the problem concerning the projecting thematization in the human sciences; secondly there is the problem of methodology.

We have seen that Heidegger did agree with Husserl that special regional ontologies are to be developed; according to Heidegger these ontologies have to mediate between the empirical sciences and the hermeneutic phenomenology developed concretely in his analytic of Dasein. We have seen also that Heidegger explicitly leaves room for a strictly scientific study of the human phenomena (in empirical psychology, sociology, anthropology, economics, etc.). The question now is first one of how in each human science an a priori framework of meaning is to be projected and developed in order that the relevant human phenomena can be properly thematized. Secondly, the question must be asked of precisely what kinds of methods are to be used in these regional ontologies of the human sciences. It is with these two questions that I shall be concerned in this section and the next. To give these reflections a sharper focus I shall refer mainly to psychology and sociology because of the fact that they occupy a privileged position in the domain of the behavioral and social sciences, respectively.

To explain the projection of an a priori framework of meaning in the human sciences we must focus first on the fact that each empirical human science that has developed in history deals with a determinate realm of phenomena which in each human science is to be taken from a specific point of view. One should note here that there are many human sciences and their number is still increasing. Each science is concerned with a certain aspect of the human reality and the human world. When a psychologist looks at human beings and their world then he often "sees" psychological problems, where a sociologist or an economist will "see" social or economic problems. In the final analysis the difference in this way of perceiving human phenomena is in each case due to some framework of meaning from which these scientists have learned to perceive human beings and their world. This framework of meaning is called a priori in the sense that the scientist must already have it at his disposal before he can perceive the phenomena as he actually does. In some sense this framework of meaning is constitutive for the relevant phenomena as such. At any rate, the framework of meaning "precedes," and is independent of, the phenomena which with its help are to be explained empirically. In other words, the term "a priori" does not have here the technical meaning which it has in Kant's first *Critique*, where it means "independent of experience and even of all impressions of the senses."[29] The framework of meaning under discussion is seldom explicitly articulated; yet its basic concepts and principles can be made explicit by means of descriptive analyses. The latter is one of the basic tasks of the relevant regional ontology in each case.

Each human science must, thus, delineate its own realm of investigation and project the formal ontological framework from which all entities or events to be studied are to be taken and viewed. Once this decision has been made on good grounds, the basic concepts to be used in the science are determined in principle, and a fundamental choice is made in regard to the methods to be employed.

Such a determination of the formal aspect under which the things that belong to a certain region of entities or events are to be investigated, necessarily comprises some form of idealization, formalization, and functionalization. Formalization means the description of things or events with respect to some of their formal ontological characteristics only. Functionalization refers to the consideration of the phenomena which are already so formalized, in terms of other formalized phenomena, according to the general scheme "if p then q," or any further development of this "causal" scheme. Formalization and functionalization give the scientist the possibility of explaining the phenomena with the help of scientific theories. It is evident that when these procedures are applied to the original phenomena, the latter become reduced to more or less ideal entities which are abstract in comparison with the original phenomena.

In this sense one can then say that without the projection of a formal ontological framework, without concepts and principles that are a priori in regard to the phenomena to be explained, no empirical science can ever be developed. There must be some a priori framework of reference, a perspective from which things to be studied in an empirical science are to be taken. As we have seen already, psychologically these concepts and principles are not (as Kant thought) independent of all experience; rather they are often implicitly derived from our experiences in which tradition, philosophical reflection and observation, and knowledge of the research field in question may go hand in hand. The framework itself is no more than an idealization of some aspects of a much larger and less articulated framework of meaning from which we usually perceive, think, and act.

From the preceding reflections it will be clear that the question of whether or not an empirical science of the human reality is possible, and if so within what limits, is not primarily one of whether the statements of the human sciences can be systematically related to one another in a determinate way, but is connected rather with the problem of whether man's actions and institutions allow for a thematization which essentially implies idealization and formalization.[30] The question of whether or not one is to allow for mathematization in this context is a derivative one and can perhaps be answered most easily by conceiving of mathematics in a sufficiently broad manner. As far as the first question is concerned, it is apparent that, when applied to human phenomena, idealization and formalization necessarily imply that some part or aspect of the meaning of these phenomena will have to be left out of consideration. This is not to say, however, that consequently an empirical science of the human reality is impossible, but merely that such a science has meaning within certain limits only, thus leaving room for other approaches to man's actions and institutions.

Many leading scientists have made an explicit effort to develop an a priori framework of meaning for the empirical study of human phenomena. In both the behavioral and the human sciences one finds scholars who have concerned themselves primarily with the very foundations of their own science. In many cases it is the work of these scholars that is discussed primarily in the history of the human sciences. Yet it seems to me that the basic problem of our contemporary human sciences, as Schrag has suggested, consists in the fact that none of these theoretical frameworks has been accepted universally. The very fact that today we still make a distinction between a dozen or so different schools and trends in psychology and sociology justifies this claim. A careful analysis of the most important frameworks developed thus far shows why none of them was capable of playing a role comparable to that played by Newton's framework in classical physics. For in many cases, it is not clear at all how these scholars gradually developed their frame of reference. It seems to me that, all semblance notwithstanding, in no case was the frame of reference directly derived from the human phenomena themselves on the basis of universally acceptable methodological principles. Furthermore, in all of these conceptual frameworks we find an a priori association with metaphysical conceptions. In making these remarks, it is not my intention to criticize the contributions to the behavioral and social sciences which many leading scholars in these fields have made with so much effort and diligence, but merely to focus once more on the need, felt by many, to develop a universally acceptable framework of meaning on which in each science the human phenomena can be projected. The development of such a universally acceptable framework of meaning obviously need not exclude the development of more limited realms of meaning in each science.

In the natural sciences it was not too difficult to derive the a priori framework from the natural things themselves, insofar as Newton and his contemporaries were familiar with them. Perhaps it did not really matter too much whence this framework of meaning ultimately came, as long as it was adequate for the purposes at hand. In the human sciences, on the other hand, the issue is much more complex and complicated because of the layer of meaning which is constitutive for the human phenomena as such. Thus the constitution of the a priori framework from which the originally given human phenomena are to be re-interpreted in order to make them a legitimate subject matter of empirical research must make certain not only that verifiable predictions can be derived from the resulting framework, but also (and this constitutes the basic difference between the natural and the human sciences) that the explanations and predictions derived from it are indeed pertinent to the relevant phenomena as human. The latter is all the more important in view of the fact that, as we have seen, all scientific projection implies with necessity idealization and formalization and, thus, also some kind of demundanization of the original phenomena.

As an empirical discipline, each human science makes and must make assumptions which, as this particular science, it cannot examine and which yet play an essential part in its research and its results. At the root of these assumptions is the constitution of a framework of meaning which in regard to the phenomena to be explained by each human science is *a priori*, and upon which the phenomena are to be projected if they are to become a legitimate subject matter for empirical research. If in each human science there were no a priori synthesis, i.e., no ideal framework of meaning constituted in advance of the scientific research in this field, there would be no possibility of methodical research in regard to human phenomena. Anyone who denies this thesis, will either try to work from the perspective of our prescientific framework of meaning, so that his work and its achievements will basically be uncritical and imply relativism, or from the perspective of an ideology whose origin is either religious, philosophical, or political; but in that case his work and its results would be merely dogmatic.

It is obvious that such an a priori framework cannot be that of Newton's *Principia*, because his mechanics is concerned with material entities which are taken to have no characteristics other than those defined in its a priori framework, i.e., mass, force, space and time determinations; the human meaning with which the sciences of man are concerned is not one of them. Secondly, it is obvious also that the commonly accepted logic of science cannot provide us with such a framework. For a conceptual framework which would merely fulfill the conditions stipulated by logic of science, would for that reason alone not yet be adequate to explain and predict human phenomena. As Popper correctly pointed out, these logical reflections are concerned only with those conditions which must be fulfilled, if our empirical research in a human science is to be systematic and, thus, both logically and epistemologically acceptable, but they cannot account for its relevance. Finally, it seems obvious that such a framework cannot be just derived from one of the many philosophical "systems" that happen to be available. It seems to me that Comte was correct in demanding that positive research should not be built upon "metaphysical" speculation. In other words, it would not be correct for a scientist to argue: In view of the fact that I happen to be familiar with the works of Marx or Peirce, I am entitled to constitute a Marxian or Peircean framework upon which I shall then project the human phenomena to be examined. Fear of metaphysics, however legitimate in empirical research, seems to have been the reason why some people have tried to understand human phenomena by reducing them to physiological processes. Yet these people did not realize that the thesis according to which human phenomena can be adequately understood by reducing them to physiological processes, is itself just a metaphysical claim of the type Comte precisely tried to overcome.[31] But again this claim does not at all exclude the possibility that some form of reduction might not be a good heuristic maxim.

If there is to be a framework of meaning constituted in advance upon which then all human phenomena are to be projected so that they can become the legitimate subject matter for empirical research, it has to take into account that all human phenomena contain a realm of meaning of their own. This realm of meaning is co-determined by human institutions constituted in a tradition within the general framework of the culture of a given society. All of this together predelineates how any member of that community is to take any given phenomenon. In view of the fact that we know that many of these overall frameworks or worlds are possible, in principle one cannot claim that one of these worlds taken as such should or could have a privileged position. Thus a human science, if it is to be a universal science of human phenomena, is in need of an overarching a priori framework which is not identical with any one given world and yet is constituted in such a way that from that framework all relevant human phenomena occurring in concrete worlds can be investigated empirically.

Secondly, the framework of meaning that is to be projected in advance should not focus on either human actions, or human institutions, each taken in isolation. The framework must be such that it makes possible our understanding of human actions as relating directly or indirectly to human institutions, and of the institutions themselves as relating to possible human actions. Institutions to which no one any longer refers in his actions are dead; on the other hand, an action which is not at least indirectly related to a human institution is either not human or un-understandable.

Thirdly, the framework must be such that no explicit distinction is made between an economic, social, political, or religious world, because genuine actions occur in worlds in which these realms of meaning are intimately interwoven. Obviously, this remark should not be construed to mean that more limited frameworks of meaning cannot and should not be developed, or that the different sciences corresponding to them should not be distinguished from one another and developed in relative independence.

At first sight, it may seem that such an overarching framework cannot be universal in the sense that it could apply to all people at all times. Yet upon closer investigation, it appears that this is not necessarily the case. For the framework *upon* which all human phenomena are to be projected so that they can become the subject matter of empirical research, is obviously not the framework of meaning *from* which they will be ultimately explained. A given human science if it is to understand a man's actions in regard to relevant social institutions, obviously cannot do so without having to take into consideration the institutions and the entire world in which these actions actually occurred. What is to be understood is precisely this man's actions in regard to the institutions of the society to which he belongs. These institutions as well as the worlds in which they function do, indeed, differ from place to place and from time to time. Thus it follows that an explanation given in one case cannot be extrapolated to other

OBJECTIFYING THEMATIZATION IN THE HUMAN SCIENCES

cases occurring in different societies or in the same society at different moments in time. What is to be studied is, in Popper's words, social problems; they occur in given societies with their respective institutions. If one succeeds in explaining these actions scientifically in regard to the given institutions, the explanation is perfectly legitimate and respectable.[32] The a priori framework of meaning, however, upon which all human phenomena are to be projected, is of a much more formal nature. The function of this framework is merely to make it possible to determine: (a) What will and what will not be a legitimate subject matter of empirical research, (b) which characteristics and relations of the human phenomena to be considered will be relevant in each case and which will not be, (c) the research methods to be used in the explanation of these phenomena, and (d) the linguistic means adequate for the precise formulation of problems and solutions, both in terms of the formal framework and the relevant world. It is obvious that the a priori framework of meaning must be such that it is not in conflict with the concrete worlds of any actual or possible human society or community.

Thus the constitution of the a priori framework necessarily presupposes that the social theorist already has some knowledge of the essential structures of concrete societies, their institutions, and the possible human actions pertaining to them. This type of knowledge must be provided by history, anthropology, philosophy, by the critical evaluation of the data thus collected, and finally by a descriptive human science. On the other hand, the application of the a priori framework to concrete human phenomena presupposes that the abstractness of the a priori framework and the concreteness of a given world be mediated in each case. As far as this mediation is concerned, it seems to me that Weber's ideal types will have to play an important part.

One might be inclined to argue that the constitution of an a priori framework is superfluous in the human sciences, in that from that perspective it suffices that the scientists take a real problem and study it with the help of situational logic, while making certain that every possible hypothesis formulated in this way as a possible answer to this problem be made subject to critical discussion. Yet what one would then overlook is the fact that it is not at all clear which problems formulated from the perspective of our everyday knowledge of society would be legitimate problems for empirical research. To take an example: The divorce rate is a real problem in contemporary American society. Everyone in this country will see this as a problem and yet very few people are capable of formulating this problem in such a way that psychology or sociology can actually deal with it. The formulation of a problem as well as the anticipation of what could in principle be an acceptable hypothesis to explain this problem is precisely the work of the scientist who in so doing must first project the pre-scientifically experienced problem upon the general perspective of the a priori framework of meaning, in order to see what "variables" might be brought into the discussion to find a reasonable hypothesis. One will argue that these reflections still do not show the necessity of constituting an a priori framework, in that the scientist derives all he has to know to formulate a relevant problem and an acceptable hypothesis from his knowledge of society and from the knowledge of his own field. Yet it seems to me that in arguing along these lines one misses the real point at stake here. For in the preceding pages the claim was made that the constitution of what is called here the field of meaning that is characteristic for every human science, *necessarily* implies the constitution of an a priori framework and that, if the latter framework is not constituted according to justifiable principles, the entire effort of the scientist will be merely dogmatic or relativistic.

29: DESCRIPTIVE AND INTERPRETATIVE HUMAN SCIENCES. ON THE METHODS TO BE EMPLOYED IN THE DESCRIPTIVE COMPONENT OF EACH HUMAN SCIENCE

In the preceding reflections it was implied that it is important in each human science to make a distinction between three different but closely related components, an empirical component, a descriptive component, and an interpretative component. The empirical component is concerned with the explanation and prediction of human phenomena; the descriptive component tries to articulate the theoretical framework of meaning upon which in each case the phenomena are to be projected, whereas the interpretative component is concerned with an effort to understand the full human meaning of these phenomena. Before we can turn to methodological reflections we must first explain briefly what is to be understood by the descriptive and the interpretative components of each empirical science of man.

To answer the question of exactly what the expression "descriptive science of man" stands for we can turn to Husserl's view on the meaning and function of regional ontologies, whose position Heidegger shared. For Husserl a regional ontology is an

ON THE METHOD OF DESCRIPTIVE HUMAN SCIENCES

aprioric, eidetic, intuitive, and purely descriptive science of the basic structures of the phenomena that belong to a certain region of beings. Since each regional ontology is a science to be carried out within the realm of the natural attitude, for Husserl regional ontologies are not philosophical disciplines.[33]

As we have seen, Husserl defended the necessity of regional ontologies by pointing to the fact that there is a gap to be filled between the empirical sciences and philosophy. Regional ontologies presuppose the existence of the corresponding empirical sciences in the order of time, but they are not founded upon these sciences or on their results. The fundamental principles of regional ontologies are--on the contrary--to be brought to light by an accurate reflection, analysis, and description of the very essence of the phenomena belonging to a certain region.[34] Because the extension of the different regions cannot be determined a priori and, on the other hand, because the precise delineation of the different regions cannot be the task of the empirical sciences which precisely presuppose this delineation, the different "regional ontologies" have to take their starting point in a "general ontology of the world of our immediate experience." It is clear that in Husserl's view the "regional ontologies" must find their ultimate and radical foundation in transcendental phenomenology, because without transcendental phenomenology the "regional ontology of the world of our immediate experience" is left in suspension as far as its foundations are concerned.[35]

Taking the foregoing into consideration, one sees that a hermeneutic-phenomenological view on science does not exclude regional ontologies. On the contrary, it even seems to require such "additional" sciences, although it is true that hermeneutic phenomenology describes the meaning and function of these ontologies in a different way.

For, if we realize that notwithstanding the results obtained in them, time and again in the empirical sciences of man (to which we wish to limit ourselves here), important problems arise which cannot be solved with the help of the empirical methods as such, we can see that there is not only room, but even a certain need for these "additional" sciences, focusing all their attention on those aspects of man's orientation toward the world which the empirical sciences had to leave out of consideration because of limitations essentially connected with the methods employed. The difference between such a descriptive science and the correlative empirical sciences consists in that, whereas the empirical sciences focus attention on "facts, the descriptive sciences must first and foremost be faithful to the general and necessary structures of the phenomena to which these facts refer.

Provisionally we may say then that in this context the expression "the descriptive component of a human science" means that regional ontology which in each case tries to bring to light descriptively the essential and necessary structures of all the various modes of being which are characteristic of the phenomena that belong to the region which constitutes the subject matter of the corresponding empirical science.

In the ideas just presented I have repeatedly used the expression "the descriptive science of man" or, more accurately, "the descriptive component of a human science." The meaning of these expressions has been indicated there only in very general terms and in a rather indirect way. Referring to Husserl's conception of regional ontologies, I pointed out that what Husserl intended by these expressions seems to be very important and that, indeed, there is a need for such descriptive sciences of man which can fill the gap between philosophy and the empirical sciences of man. In order to make our conception of the descriptive component of a science of man more concrete we must now focus our attention on the problem of the methods which such a science must employ in order to reach its goal. In so doing I shall again take my starting point in Husserl's view and try to indicate briefly in what sense I think this view is to be re-interpreted.

We have seen that Husserl defines a regional ontology as an aprioric, eidetic, intuitive, descriptive study of certain phenomena which--although it is to be carried out within the realm of the natural attitude--nonetheless presupposes some kind of phenomenological reduction. The most important methods to be used in this science are according to Husserl "the method of free variation" and "intentional analysis."[36]

From what has been said it is clear that Heidegger agrees with Husserl regarding the function and subject matter of the science in question. The difference between Husserl's and Heidegger's conception on these matters is mainly a matter of the philosophical view from which the conception is defended. However, as I said before, the difference in philosophical orientation and the difference in terminology which is the necessary consequence of it, by no means immediately affects the essential structure and function of the science in question. Although there is a great difference in motivation and terminology, what is intended in both points of view is, as far as its essential structure and function are concerned, the same.

ON THE METHOD OF INTERPRETATIVE SCIENCES OF MAN 231

In my opinion an analogous point of view is to be adopted in regard to the methods to be used in such a descriptive science. As we have seen, Husserl held that the method of free variation is essential to every regional ontology. This method is to be used in connection with intentional analysis and both these methods are to be carried out in regard to phenomena which must be taken as "unities of meaning."

From Heidegger's criticism of Husserl's phenomenology it will be clear that in the view defended here, there is no room for a reduction in Husserl's sense. What is to be brought to light are the essential structures of the fundamental modes of man's orientation toward the world as they are immediately "lived" in our Being-in-the-world. With respect to the procedures which are to be used in doing so, a phenomenological reduction is superfluous.

But what about Husserl's intentional analysis and his "method of free variation"? We have seen already that Heidegger had high regard for three basic components of Husserl's phenomenology: his conception of intentionality, his view on categorial intuition, and his interpretation of the meaning of the a priori.[37] Yet Heidegger made it quite clear that Husserl's conceptions concerning these matters were to be re-interpreted so as to bring them into harmony with the basic "principles" of his own hermeneutic phenomenology. For all practical purposes this means that the method to be used in the descriptive sciences of man must be that which Heidegger has outlined in section 7 of *Being and Time*.

30: INTERPRETATIVE SCIENCES OF MAN AND THE METHODS TO BE USED THERE

We must now turn to a brief reflection on the methods to be used in the interpretative sciences of man. But before we can turn to methodological reflections we must again first explain once more precisely what is to be understood here by the interpretative component of the various sciences of man, and to the question of how the interpretative component in each case is to be related to the relevant empirical and descriptive components of the same science. It will not be possible here to deal with all the problems involved in these issues; yet I hope to be able to indicate briefly how most of these problems can be resolved in principle. Instead of focussing predominantly on philosophical issues to which the problems referred to are related, I wish to deal mainly with methodological issues. Yet a few introductory remarks of a more philosophical nature appear to be necessary.

The subject matter of the *interpretative* component of a human science consists in the totality of all human phenomena which function in a meaningful way in our human world (or the world of a given society, as the case may be). In the interpretative component of a human science one is not interested in the factual occurrences of these phenomena, nor in the way these phenomena can be "explained" by relating them to one another. This would be the task of the empirical component of the same science. In the interpretative component of a human science one is not interested either in discovering invariable structures which are found in human phenomena of a certain kind. For this would be the task of the corresponding *descriptive* component. In the interpretative part of a human science one focusses his attention on an attempt to understand the human meaning of these phenomena, i.e., the meaning which these phenomena have in our (or as the case may be, in a given) world.[38] It will be clear that in an interpretative science one is not interested in discovering the meaning which a private individual or a group of individuals who happen to be concerned with, or involved in, these phenomena, may attach to them, nor in the meaning which human beings "deep in their hearts" may attach to certain actions they perform. Interpretative science is concerned only with discovering the human meaning which a community that shares a common world attaches to certain phenomena and certain patterns of social behavior. Although this meaning is never "objective" in the sense in which this term is used in the natural sciences (for this meaning is by no means the result of a process of objectivation), nonetheless this meaning is in no sense of the term "subjective" either. This meaning is intersubjectively shared by the members of a community and thus intersubjectively accessible, so that a community of scholars in principle can achieve an intersubjectively acceptable understanding of the meaning of these institutions, phenomena, patterns of behavior, etc.

In trying to understand the meaning of human phenomena, institutions, and actions, the interpretative component of a human science employs *hermeneutic methods*. Before we can turn to a more detailed description of these methods, it should be noted that the expression "interpretative understanding" (*Verstehen*) has nothing at all in common with empathy, "subjective feeling," "private conception," "personal conviction," etc. The term is taken here in the sense in which the members of a nation that has been in a war and finally has reached peace, can say that they understand what war and peace mean; or also in the sense

ON THE METHOD OF INTERPRETATIVE SCIENCES OF MAN

in which adults who have children of their own can say that they understand what it means to take care of a family. Although this type of understanding has relatively little in common with the understanding of a mathematician who says that he understands the proof for a certain theorem of geometry, nonetheless it should be pointed out that this type of understanding is by no means necessarily subjective in any sense of the term. Furthermore, it should be noted that in employing this type of understanding the interpretative part of a human science binds itself to hermeneutic rules whose goal it is to achieve intersubjective validity in regard to the results obtained via this type of understanding. Thus, contrary to Dilthey's view, such a systematic attempt which binds itself to rules, does not lead to, or in any way involve, relativism. It is true that the understanding of the meaning of human phenomena, institutions, and actions which can be achieved in this way, will not always have validity for all peoples of all times; nonetheless it certainly, in principle, can have intersubjective validity for all those who are members of a given community at a given moment in time. This fact has been one of the reasons why Weber tried to combine the method of *Verstehen* with empirical methods, in order through this combination to reach a higher degree of "objectivity." It is obviously true that if one employs empirical methods in the study of human phenomena, methods which imply abstraction, formalization, and idealization, one can in many cases discover insights which transcend the limitations of place and time. This is due to the fact that the processes mentioned precisely place the phenomena under consideration outside the historical process in which they developed and in which they have the meaning the members of a community actually attach to them. But it is equally true that if one precisely is interested in understanding the meaning of these phenomena as they actually occur, the results have validity only for the community under consideration taken in a given epoch. However, this does not mean that this latter type of knowledge is inferior or, in any sense of the term, subjective or unscientific. This does mean that the interpretative part of a human science is to some degree a historical science. For it is clear that the meaning of human phenomena cannot be understood genuinely if it is not studied as the meaning of a historic event, process, or institution whose origin goes back far into the life of a community or individual.

Yet there is a difference between history and the interpretative component of a human science. In the past it has been said that the sciences of man in general are the sciences of the present, whereas history is the science of the past. Whatever one thinks about this characterization of the distinction between human science and history, it becomes clear here that the human sciences certainly are continuous with history. The interpretative component of a human science tries to understand the *historical situation* in which human phenomena arise and to show how they are incorporated in the context of a living tradition in which each individual of a society forms his or her identity. Thus it must study traditions with the intention of displaying alternatives and instigating changes; in other words the interpretative part of a human science is interested in the past because it is concerned with the future.[39]

This brings us to a last point that must be clarified before we can turn to the canons which each interpretative component of a human science has to employ in order to achieve intersubjective validity. One will recall that both Dilthey and Weber have claimed that the human sciences should be value-free, i.e., the human sciences must be "scientifically objective" and avoid all reference to practical affairs. Human phenomena must be studied in as value-neutral a way as possible. No claims to normative bonds can be made and the interpretation must progressively objectify the meaning of the human phenomena under consideration, through abstracting from a decision about the credibility of assertions and about the acceptability of norms and values. The interpreter is not permitted to take any responsibility with respect to the truth claims of the conceptions held about these phenomena, or to formulate prescriptions concerning what should be done about them.

It is to be observed here first that the discussion concerning the distinction to be made between "fact" and "value" gained importance the moment empirical methods were applied to human phenomena. For originally it was believed that in order to achieve objectivity and intersubjective validity the empirical sciences had to abstract from all value aspects of the phenomena to be considered in that they were said to be inherently subjective and thus beyond the possible concern of science. However, it is now quite generally assumed that this view is in error and that phenomena which have value can be brought within the compass of empirical research without any such explicit abstraction. Secondly one should realize that although some individuals may indeed have a highly subjective conception of the value of these phenomena, the values themselves are by no means subjective.

Furthermore, the terms "fact" and "value" are very vague and confusing, unless they are taken in the sense given to these expressions in the various value-theories which have been developed between Lotze and Nicolai Hartmann, and unless in Weber's case the distinction is to be understood from the viewpoint of Rickert's neo-Kantianism. However, if these terms are taken in that philosophical perspective, the question must be asked as to whether or not philosophy of value is an acceptable form of philosophy. Elsewhere I have tried to explain why Heidegger is convinced that any value-theory rests upon a basic misunderstanding which in the final analysis has its roots in a scientific interpretation of the meaning and function of empirical science. Let me briefly summarize the conclusions reached in that essay.[40]

In objecting to any form of value philosophy it was not Heidegger's intention to state that there are no values, nor that philosophy should not be concerned with them. Philosophy must certainly be concerned with the values things and events have for us, but in so doing it should not separate from one another ontology (dealing with what is) and axiology (dealing with what ought to be). For one must realize that the distinction between facts and values rests upon an abstraction and that in the "real" world there are no bare facts nor mere values. On the level of our pre-philosophical and pre-scientific life we never experience things without values, nor do we ever experience values which are not the values of things or events. Anyone who begins his reflection on values by isolating "that which ought to be" from "that which is," will find himself confronted with pseudo-problems. From an epistemological point of view the problem is: how do we know values?; and from the ontological perspective the question is: how can values be? It can be shown that (once this distinction between fact and value has been made) anyone who is able to find an adequate solution for the epistemological problem will find himself confronted with a mystery as far as the ontological problem is concerned. For if we are able to know values, then these values must be human, temporal, and historical; however from an ontological point of view merely relative values are incapable of solving the problems they were supposed to solve. On the other hand, if values are to fulfill the function for which they have been suggested in the various axiologies, they must be absolutes of some kind, but in that case they obviously cannot be known by man. However, on the level of our immediate experience upon which philosophy must reflect, it is undeniable that there are values, that we do know them, and that we know them as the values which things and events have for us.

As soon as the distinction between separated facts and separated values has been replaced by the conception of meaning (*Sinn*) as found in hermeneutic phenomenology, it is clear at once that the interpretative component of a human science cannot possibly be value-neutral or value-free, if by this is meant that this type of social science should try to establish facts without having an option about their value or meaning. However, there is a great difference between an attempt to understand the meaning of human phenomena by means of interpretation, and to formulate a set of ethical standards or norms with which the human meaning of these phenomena can be evaluated. Whereas the former is, indeed, the main concern of the interpretative component of a human science, the latter is the task of social philosophy and ethics. Let us turn now to some methodological reflections which follow from these basic insights.

31: THE CANONS OF HERMENEUTICS AND INTERPRETATIVE SOCIAL SCIENCE

The interpretative part of every human science tries to understand the meaning of human phenomena by interpreting these phenomena according to the canons of hermeneutics which, in principle at least, are to guarantee the intersubjective validity of the interpretation. These canons have nothing in common with the rules developed in formal logic for considering valid syllogisms or for checking the validity of arguments. For the rules of logic, if correctly applied to the proper subject matter, "automatically" lead to the desired result. The canons of hermeneutics, on the other hand, cannot be applied to a subject matter as it were "from the outside"; for interpretation and critique presuppose that one knows the subject matter already, at least to some degree. In other words, in the case of hermeneutic interpretation it is assumed that before the interpretation can be developed, the interpreter *knows* the phenomena he wishes to *understand* and has at least some knowledge of the context of meaning in which these phenomena appear and to which they belong. It is assumed, also, that to some degree he knows the world in which these phenomena occur. The task of hermeneutic interpretation is to critically examine this fore-knowledge of the world and of the phenomena we encounter there, with the intention of coming to a deeper comprehension of these phenomena and, thus, to a type of understanding (*Verstehen*) which leads to an intersubjectively acceptable result. In other words, the canons have no other

CANONS OF HERMENEUTICS IN SOCIAL SCIENCE

function than to help us make explicit systematically what implicitly was already there before us. It is in that sense that one could say that that to which one wishes to "apply" the canons of hermeneutics determines, from the very start and in its entirety, the effective and concrete content of the understanding itself.

Furthermore, hermeneutic interpretation is inherently oriented toward historical understanding and historical understanding cannot be modeled after the objective knowledge found in the empirical sciences, because this understanding itself is a process which has all the characteristics of a historic event. Even as historians we are and remain members of a community in which (through an uninterrupted chain) the past addresses itself to us. In other words, the historicity of the historian's interpretation is one of the necessary pre-conditions of his hermeneutic understanding. Only a person who himself stands in history can hope to understand history.[41] But let us now turn to a brief reflection of some important canons and explain their meaning in the light of the preceding considerations.[42]

A *first* canon states that the meaning of a phenomenon cannot be projected into that phenomenon, but must be derived from this phenomenon itself. *The canon of the "autonomy of the object"* thus states that one must understand a phenomenon from within itself; the phenomenon itself is the primary and final source of, as well as the criterion for, the legitimacy of the interpretation. The canon obviously does not demand that the human phenomenon be taken in isolation; for the phenomenon is what it is precisely in the context to which it harmoniously belongs; nor does it require a passive adherence to the meaning which is already articulated and expressed in our advance knowledge of it. The canon merely tries to prevent that insights and conceptions extraneous to the phenomenon itself will be forced upon it, or that the phenomenon will be articulated by concepts which themselves do not flow from a careful analysis of the phenomenon itself. In the human sciences we are often inclined to clarify human phenomena with ideas which really have their origin in certain philosophical prejudices, rather than in the phenomena themselves. Someone interested in the question of why college students become alienated from the church communities to which they originally belonged may be inclined to take the concept of alienation as found in either Hegel or Marx, or in the sense given to it in psychoanalysis, without carefully trying to understand this very typical form of alienation from the phenomenon itself, taken in the concrete context in which we encounter it today in our world.

Obviously this does not mean that these determinations of the phenomenon of alienation as given by philosophers and scientists may not be used as hints pointing to what one should "look for," because we may assume that these authors themselves derived their views from analogous phenomena they experienced or observed. Yet, in a hermeneutic interpretation, the source and criterion of the articulated meaning is and remains the phenomenon itself.

A *second canon* states that one must search for an interpretation which makes *the phenomenon maximally reasonable*, or in our case perhaps better: maximally human. In order to understand the meaning of this canon one must realize that many human phenomena are so complex and so richly structured, so deeply rooted in the past of a community that their genuine meaning often cannot be made explicit on the basis of the phenomena as they actually manifest themselves at a certain moment in time. In many instances the original, and often the genuine, meaning of patterns of human behavior, types of action, the adherence to social institutions, and the institutions themselves, may have been covered up by secondary and tertiary layers of meaning so that those actually involved in these actions or confronted with these institutions no longer explicitly realize their original meaning. Anyone who has made a serious study of institutions as well as of social customs will have encountered this fact on many occasions. In that case the interpreter must complement the phenomena as they immediately manifest themselves with suitable assumptions so as to make these phenomena maximally reasonable or human. So it is that the interpreter tries to understand the relevant phenomena "better" and more "deeply" than those who are actually involved in, or confronted with, them. The second canon obviously must be counterbalanced by the first, and the assumptions mentioned should be chosen in such a way that they are inherently connected with the given phenomena. The question as to whether or not a given assumption is, indeed, inherently connected with a phenomenon can often be solved only by careful, historical research.

In all of this it is presupposed that the interpreter bring himself into a harmonious relationship with the phenomena to be interpreted. Thus a *third canon* states that the interpreter must try to achieve *the greatest possible familiarity* with the phenomenon whose meaning he wishes to understand interpretatively. In the older school of hermeneutics (Schleiermacher, Dilthey), it was often said that the interpreter should empathize with the agents

CANONS OF HERMENEUTICS IN SOCIAL SCIENCE 239

involved in these phenomena. Imaginative re-enactment as well as the placing of oneself in the situation of the agents may, psychologically, have a heuristic value in the first explorative stages of the process, but this is most certainly not what the third canon attempts to accomplish. If one wishes at all to speak of imagining oneself in the place of some other person, he must realize that it is *not* with the other's thoughts that he should be concerned, but with *what* these thoughts are about, i.e., the human meaning of the phenomena under consideration. Since hermeneutics is really concerned with the mediation of traditions, the interpreter has to familiarize himself with the phenomena in their historical origin, with the various components of meaning which have been gradually attached to the original meaning in a long historical process, and with the various traditions themselves which influenced the origin and the further development of the phenomena.

The most important canon, however, is to be found in the *hermeneutic circle*. Before discussing this all-important canon in detail, I wish first to give a brief description of the meaning of this canon for the interpretative component of a human science and to relate it to a last canon according to which one must show the meaning of human phenomena for one's own situation.

The hermeneutic circle is essentially a very general mode of the development of all human knowledge, namely the development through dialectic procedures. In the canon it is assumed that there cannot be any genuine development of knowledge without some fore-knowledge. The anticipation of the global meaning of an action, of a form of life, of a social institution, etc., becomes articulated through a dialectic process in which the meaning of the "parts" or components is determined by the fore-knowledge of the "whole," whereas our knowledge of the "whole" is continuously corrected and deepened by the increase of our knowledge of the components. The hermeneutic circle involves four different aspects. For, the part-whole-relationship holds first for the phenomenon taken as a whole and all of its constituent parts or elements. Furthermore, this relationship also holds between this particular phenomenon and all other related phenomena from which, in the final analysis, it derives (part of) its meaning. Then, this relationship holds between the human agents insofar as they are involved in this phenomenon and the world in which they live. Finally, this relationship holds between our Western civilization taken as a whole and the particular phenomenon taken as appearing in the agents' world as a constitutive part of this civilization. It is because of all of these circular and spiral relationships that a definitive and all-encompassing interpretation can never be achieved. The "dialectic" process is quasi-infinite, both on the side of our knowledge of the relevant "wholes" and on the side of their "parts." However, in most instances an interpretation can be reached which genuinely can be said to be adequate in regard to the phenomena under consideration.

A final canon to be mentioned here, is that which states that in all of these steps the interpreter must try to show the meaning of a phenomenon for his own situation. No one is really interested in understanding something that is totally irrelevant for himself and the world in which he lives. Thus, after trying to understand a phenomenon in its historical origin and further development he must try to come to a view which states the meaning of all of this for his own situation. This cannot be done except on the basis of certain pre-judgments which in many cases may appear to be mere prejudices and often are inherent in the situation itself in which the interpreter finds himself. One of the main tasks of hermeneutic interpretation is to carefully stipulate these pre-judgments and to examine them critically for their inner human meaning.

After this brief summary of the most important canons to be used in hermeneutic interpretation, I wish now to return to a more detailed discussion of the last two canons listed, in that they not only are essential to any acceptable interpretation, but also lead to a number of significant problems.

In our attempt to determine more concretely the structure of the interpretative understanding which is constitutive for all hermeneutic endeavors, we must stress once more that this type of understanding essentially implies an affinity with the tradition of the phenomena to be understood. Hermeneutic interpretation tries to bring about a mediation of traditions in that it tries to understand all human phenomena as inherently historical. With this reminder let us turn now to a careful examination of the basic rule of hermeneutics: the circular relationship between the whole and its parts. The anticipated understanding of the whole is to be complemented and deepened by means of a better understanding of the parts; and yet, it is only within the light of the whole that the parts can play their clarifying roles. This can easily be explained by considering the example of working with a foreign language. When one begins to translate a text written in a foreign language, he starts by structuring the text provisionally on the basis of a global understanding of its content or subject matter (as suggested by its title, subheadings, the overall context to

CANONS OF HERMENEUTICS IN SOCIAL SCIENCE 241

which the text belongs, similar or analogous texts, etc.). This is true not only for the text taken as a whole, but also for its major parts, and ultimately even for the paragraphs and sentences of which it consists. During the process of translation this global idea guides our translation, but it will be rectified, corrected, or even rejected on the basis of the more careful study of its parts. What every translator aims at is the complete coherence of this global meaning with the "final" meaning; for this is the most important criterion for his own correct understanding of the text. What is said here about translating a text holds analogously for our understanding of an inherently historical phenomenon, and thus for all human phenomena.

Schleiermacher and Dilthey, speaking about the hermeneutic circle, made a distinction between a subjective and an objective interpretation. "The art [of interpretation] can develop its rules only from a positive formula, namely: the historical and divinatory, objective and subjective, reconstructing of a given utterance" or phenomenon.[43] The goal of the subjective interpretation is to discover the mental experiences of the author of a text or the agents involved in social phenomena and to reconstruct their thoughts, intentions, feelings, etc. On the other hand, the aim of the objective interpretation is to come to an understanding of the meaning of the text or the historical phenomenon as it presents itself to the interpreter. In making this distinction both Schleiermacher and Dilthey were guided by the historicist prejudice that even in history no genuine scientific insight can be achieved if the final result does not possess a kind of "objectivity" which is somehow comparable to that found in the natural sciences. In order to achieve this, Schleiermacher and Dilthey tried to separate two realms, one in which genuine objectivity can be achieved, and one in which this objectivity cannot be achieved, but which nonetheless is of great heuristic value in regard to the first. In Heidegger's view this distinction was a very unfortunate one; it led to a great number of quasi-problems and was an easy target for criticism, particularly from the neo-positivist point of view. The goal of hermeneutic interpretation is not to be found in the interpreter's re-living of the experiences of those involved in the phenomenon to be understood; the interpreter does not wish to place himself in the position of someone else (the agents) and to penetrate their "mental" activities. He wishes merely to understand the meaning of the phenomenon in question as it has been handed down to us by our tradition. Thus the goal of interpretation is to unveil the "miracle" of the mediation of traditions, and not the mysterious communication between "souls." Interpretative understanding is a typical kind of participation in something that in principle can be "seen" by everybody. What is typical for this kind of participation is that it is critical and binds itself to methodical rules and principles.

As for the objective aspect of the hermeneutic circle as explained by Schleiermacher and Dilthey, it should be noted that the type of objectivity they wished to achieve is impossible and, even if it were possible, would be undesirable. One has to realize that what determines our anticipation and fore-knowledge and what guides us in our understanding of a phenomenon, is precisely that which we have in common with that tradition insofar as this manifests itself in the phenomenon under consideration. Thus it is impossible to tear oneself completely away from that tradition, to adopt a "neutral" and "objective" attitude, and, in this way, to achieve an "authentic" understanding. The intention of the interpreter is rather to mediate between the phenomenon and the tradition which is pre-understood in that phenomenon.[44] I shall return to this problematic shortly.

In order to understand the genuine meaning of the hermeneutic circle, let us turn once more to a text of Heidegger. Speaking about the implications of the circle for the analytic of man's Being he writes: "But if we see this circle as a vicious one and look out for ways of avoiding it, even if we just 'sense' it as an inevitable imperfection, then the act of understanding has been misunderstood from the ground up . . . What is decisive is not to get out of the circle but to come into it in the right way. This circle of understanding is not an orbit in which any random kind of knowledge may move; it is the expression of the existential fore-structure of Dasein itself. It is not to be reduced to the level of a vicious circle, or even of a circle which is merely tolerated. In the circle is hidden a positive possibility of the most primordial kind of knowing. To be sure, we genuinely take hold of this possibility only when, in our interpretation, we have understood that our first, last, and constant task is never to allow our fore-having, fore-sight, and fore-conception to be presented to us by fancies and popular conceptions, but rather to make the scientific theme secure by working out these fore-structures in terms of the 'things themselves.'"[45]

It is clear that here in this text the positive, ontological meaning of the circle is stressed for the first time. This dimension was still lacking in Schleiermacher as well as in Dilthey. Anyone who wishes to understand something should adhere to

CANONS OF HERMENEUTICS IN SOCIAL SCIENCE

"the things themselves" and try to overcome his prejudices, regardless of whether they have their origin in his personal life or in the tradition to which he belongs. For what is to be discovered by means of the interpretation, is what has been the case, not what should have been the case, or what I and other people would have liked to have been the case.

Let us take a historical document as an example to illustrate what is meant here. As soon as the interpreter has found some elements he thinks he understands, he projects a provisional conception concerning the meaning of the whole text. But this first understanding of some of its parts has been motivated not only by the statements found in the text, but also by the general context in which, in his view, such statements should fit. To understand the "thing itself" that in this way begins to emerge before him, means to project a provisional conception of the whole which is to be corrected as his reading of the document proceeds. Eventually he will have to adopt another point of view in regard to the document and its overall meaning; but this new perspective, too, is perhaps still to be broadened, changed, specified. In all of this the "thing itself" as it emerges for him in the process of "decyphering," keeps guiding him. It is this perpetual oscillation of our interpretative conceptions which Heidegger tried to describe in the text just quoted: namely our comprehension of something in terms of a process in which an anticipated understanding is to be examined critically on the basis of ever new projects, as long as the situation requires it, i.e., until finally the "thing itself" begins to manifest itself.

Anyone who tries to do this, continuously runs the risk of getting entangled in his own prejudices and of finding that the conceptions he has projected in anticipation appear not to conform with the "thing itself" as it emerges there before him. That is why it is the interpreter's continuous task to elaborate ever new projects and to examine critically the pre-judgments which they imply, until he reaches the point where his anticipated understanding appears to be "authentic" in that it is proportionate to the thing to be brought to light. The only form of "objectivity" which is found in such a process consists in the fact that my anticipation is gradually confirmed when (in studying the various elements and aspects involved) I try to test this anticipation time and again on the "thing" which emerges before me in so doing. Thus each interpretation of a phenomenon must be begun with a reflection by the interpreter on his own preconceived ideas which necessarily result from the "hermeneutic situation" in which he finds himself. He must try to justify them, i.e., to clarify their origin and meaning.

From this it follows that the hermeneutic task as Heidegger conceives of it, does not consist merely in recommending a method for studying historical documents. We have seen that he tried to radicalize that type of understanding which everyone attempts to accomplish when he genuinely tries to comprehend something. What we encounter in our attempt to understand a text or document is already found in all forms of our understanding, provided the subject matter of our understanding is something intrinsically human, and for that reason essentially historical. That is why Heidegger's ideas are particularly relevant for reflections on the methods of the interpretative component of human sciences. For in all the cases in which man tries to understand something inherently human, he has to follow the "same" procedure. He begins by assuming that such and such is the meaning of the phenomenon under consideration. In this pre-conception of the meaning of the phenomenon many factors play a part: his personal outlook on the world, his moral standards, his religious convictions, the tradition to which he belongs and from which he lives, his knowledge of the field connected with the phenomenon, his interest, etc. Obviously, his main guide in forming his pre-conception is that which here and now already shows itself, however partially this may be. Hermeneutics does not demand that one give up the "subjective" co-determinants of our pre-conceptions. It does not require either that one try to come to an "objective neutrality" in regard to the "phenomena," for such neutrality is excluded in principle. The hermeneutic attitude asks merely that one be willing to qualify prejudices as prejudices, and to take mere opinions as opinions, and to give them up the moment the phenomenon, i.e., the thing itself, appears to be incompatible with them. It is only when one adopts this "critical" attitude that he gives a phenomenon, an institution, a document, a thing the possibility of manifesting itself in its being-different, i.e., to show its truth against the preconceived ideas which originally we tried to substitute for it.[46]

Another element of the circle that has become manifest through Heidegger's investigations is the fact that the hermeneutic circle does not have a merely formal character. Schleiermacher and Dilthey speak only about a formal relationship between a whole and its parts; they speak of a dialectic between the "guessing" concerning the meaning of the whole and its later explanation by means of the parts. In this romantic conception of the circle, the circular movement is nothing but a deficient, although necessary, form of investigation. Schleiermacher suggests that once we have gone through the circle we finally reach certainty. At that moment our circular form of understanding is no longer necessary; our original pre-conception has then been verified (or falsified) and, thus, is no longer needed as such. Heidegger, on the contrary, defends the thesis that our comprehension of human phenomena never ceases to be determined by the anticipatory impetus of our pre-conception.

But there is more. We have just said that all comprehension must be characterized as a totality of circular relationships between a whole and its parts. Now we have to add to this that these circular relationships themselves must be characterized by our anticipation of a "*perfect coherence*." This means that in the final analysis only an interpretation which is intrinsically coherent in itself as well as with all of its parts can be admitted. This requirement could still be understood in a purely formal way. However, if one reflects on the meaning of this requirement it becomes clear that the coherence we assume to be present in a series of phenomena transcends this series in that this coherence is also assumed to be referring to what happens to be the truth, thus to the things themselves re-presented by them. In other words, when I claim that a text must be coherent in order to be understandable, I make this claim because I am convinced that this coherence is a necessary condition for the text's describing the truth, and thus for my finding the truth via a historico-critical analysis of the text. What I am ultimately interested in are the things themselves, not the way in which they have been handed down to me. In other words, finally, the anticipation of perfect coherence presupposes not only that the text is an adequate expression of an idea, but also that this idea corresponds with what is the case. If we apply this requirement to our attempt to understand the human phenomena with which the interpretative component of a human science is primarily concerned, it will obviously have to be mitigated in that in this realm a perfect coherence can very seldom be achieved due to the fact that human beings are not always consistent in their activities. And yet even here hermeneutic interpretation tends toward the "things themselves" and thus cannot rest until all inconsistencies are explained, if not in harmony with the laws of a rigorous logic, then at least in the light of a typically human "logic."

These reflections also explain in what sense the interpreter is related to the tradition through affinity in his hermeneutic interpretation of historical phenomena. Hermeneutics takes its point of departure in the conviction that to comprehend means to be in direct relation with the "things themselves" while at the same time being related to the tradition from which these "things" address themselves to us. Interpretation is necessary here precisely because there is a tension between what is familiar to us in the present and that which has become strange to us in the relevant tradition. But this tension is not merely psychological in character (Schleiermacher); it constitutes precisely the meaning and structure of man's historicity. Thus what hermeneutic interpretation takes as its subject matter of investigation is not the psychic states of actors, agents, and interpreters, but the "things themselves" as they have been handed down by a tradition which is no longer genuinely mine.[47]

What has been said previously about the "hermeneutic situation" sheds light on another important element of all hermeneutic interpretation, namely the genuine meaning and function of *temporal distance* in any attempt to understand historical phenomena. "Temporal distance" has nothing in common with a distance one can travel through. This was one of the basic, but naive, prejudices of historicism. It was assumed there that it is possible to reach historic objectivity by going back and placing oneself within the perspective of an earlier epoch and re-thinking the facts in terms of conceptions characteristic of that time. In truth, however, one must try to conceive of temporal distance as an essential element and a positive and productive possibility of hermeneutic interpretation and comprehension. Thus, temporal distance is not a distance to be travelled through, but a living continuity of elements which as links in a chain constitute the tradition which, taken as a whole, functions as the light in which everything with which we are confronted, i.e., which is now being handed down to us, precisely can appear as that which it really is. The reason why it is difficult to genuinely appreciate contemporary works of art or contemporary changes in our social structure is to be found in the lack of temporal distance which purifies and separates the universally valuable from the non-universally valuable.

Obviously one can make the remark that if one approaches human phenomena in this way, many prejudices necessarily must be at work in any attempt to interpret their meaning. However, one must realize again that hermeneutics does not deny that there are prejudices. It itself, by means of its critical methods and careful application of the canons of hermeneutics, precisely tries to separate true from false pre-judgments, i.e., pre-judgments

CANONS OF HERMENEUTICS IN SOCIAL SCIENCE

which clarify from pre-judgments which obscure. Prejudices are dangerous merely as long as one does not recognize them as such. But in order for us to be able to recognize them, they must have been at work. It is true that unobserved prejudices have determined the opinion of people concerning a great number of things. In critically looking back upon the course of history, it is often possible to unmask false prejudices. But this again is possible only after one has been provoked by them and this, in turn, is possible only by returning to a tradition by means of a renewed contact with it and by critically examining the motives of its beliefs.[48]

This brings us finally to a last aspect of the hermeneutic approach to human phenomena. Let us suppose that in trying to explain the meaning of a human phenomenon one becomes aware of having used a pre-judgment which appears to be a mere prejudice. Let us assume also that he substitutes another pre-judgment in the place of the former. In that case the second pre-judgment obviously cannot be conceived of as being the "definitive" truth, for that would again mean a return to the naive thesis of objectivist historicism. Such a conception forgets that the prejudice which was denounced and the pre-judgment which was substituted for it both belong to an uninterrupted chain of events of which both are members. In other words, one must realize here that the original prejudice continues to play an important part, even though this part is different from that played before. Everyone knows how difficult it is to give up a prejudice and to substitute a new conviction in its place. The reason for this is that the new conviction can never be presented as the eternal truth. And what is more, the new conviction can never be specified adequately except in connection with the original prejudice whose part it now plays. It is by dialectic opposition that convictions become evaluated.

Thus we are led here to a new element, namely *the dialectic between old and new*. The original, implicit prejudice which was not yet understood as a prejudice, functioned within the overall conception concerning a set of phenomena. My new conviction is not in harmony with the original overall-conception. Adopting a new conviction means to give up part of my original overall understanding of those phenomena. Thus a dialectic process begins to take place between what is mine but appears to be inauthentic, and what is authentic but is not yet mine. Our interrogation which is the universal mediator of this dialectic will never reach a point where it becomes impossible to replace an implicit prejudice by a new conception which is still alien to me but which I shall have to make mine if I am really willing to comprehend the relevant set of phenomena.

In other words, what naive, objectivist historicism has never understood is that the process of interpretation is itself inherently a finite process that in itself is as historical as the historical phenomena which it tries to explain. For historicism there is a kind of historicity that is found in all objects of historical investigation, but this historicity is ultimately an illusion that can be overcome. At the end there will be a veritable object which is no longer historical. Thus for naive historicism the "historical object" is a kind of mixture of an in-itself and a for-us, a mixture of an a-historical veritable object and our historic illusion. However, a more careful examination of historical phenomena which includes a careful examination of all the pre-judgments inherent in the methodical procedures we employ while studying these phenomena systematically, shows that such a conception of the "historic object" is unacceptable and that it, finally, leads either to complete subjectivism (the in-itself is a pole which never can be reached), or to radical objectivism (the for-us seems to be mere appearance). According to the hermeneutic conception of the "historic object" the historic reality itself and our historic understanding of that reality can never be separated. What we call the "historic object" is the affinity, the dialectical relationship which necessarily exists between these two poles, poles which in reality do not exist in separation.[49]

EPILOGUE

1. TWO FORMS OF THINKING. THOUGHTLESSNESS THE DOMINANT CHARACTERISTICS OF OUR EPOCH

According to Heidegger, all of us, even those who claim to think professionally, such as the philosophers and the scientists, are often thought-poor today and far too easily thoughtless. Thoughtlessness is found everywhere in today's world. Today we take in everything in the quickest and the cheapest way; and we forget it just as quickly. But even though we are often thoughtless, we do not give up our capacity to think. Most of the time we use this capacity only in an implicit manner; most of the time we let it lie fallow. Still only that can lie fallow that in itself has a ground for growth.

The growing thoughtlessness springs from a process that gnaws at the very marrow of man today; today man is in flight from thinking. Part of this flight is that man will neither see nor admit it. He even flatly denies this flight from thinking. In his view, there never was a time that there were more far-reaching plans, so many inquiries in so many areas, and so much research carried on as passionately as today. In Heidegger's view, this is true, and this display of ingenuity and deliberation certainly has its great usefulness; it is even indispensable. Yet is is true also that this form of thinking is a thinking of a very special kind. We often call it a form of "instrumental rationality."

In all these ways of thinking, Heidegger continues, we always reckon with conditions that are given. We take them into account with the calculated intention of their serving some specific purpose. This calculation is the mark of all thinking that plans and engages in research. Such thinking remains calculating thinking, even if it never works with numbers or never uses computers. Calculating thinking inherently computes. It computes ever more promising and ever new economical possibilities. It races from one project to another; it never stops and never collects itself. It is not meditative thinking that contemplates the meaning that reigns in everything that is.

Thus there are two modes of thinking, calculative and meditative thinking, and each is justified in its own way. When we say that contemporary man is in flight from thinking, we mean meditative thinking. Many people will say that this form of thinking serves no meaningful purpose; it is worthless for dealing with real issues. Furthermore, it is above the reach of ordinary understanding. It does not just happen by itself; it demands practice; it requires a great effort; and it is in need of even more delicate care than any other form of thinking or even any craft.

Whether all of this is correct or not, it is nonetheless a fact that anyone can follow the path of meditative thinking in his own manner and within his own limits, because man is indeed a thinking, i.e., a meditating being. Meditative thinking need not be high-flown; it is enough that we dwell on what lies close and meditate on what concerns us here and now. This is modern science.[1]

2. THE THREAT OF NIHILISM

There are two basic forms of thinking. Modern man is concerned predominantly with calculative thinking only. This is the form of thinking that is employed in the sciences. The sciences, in manifold ways, claim to present the fundamental form of knowing and of the knowable. Yet to the degree that modern man is in flight from meditative thinking, he exposes himself to the dangers of nihilism.

For Nietzsche, nihilism, taken in its essence, is the fundamental movement of the history of the West since the 16th century. Many people conceive of nihilism in a purely negative manner. In their view nihilism shows such great profundity that its unfolding today can have nothing but catastrophes as its consequence.

For Nietzsche nihilism means the becoming valueless of all established values. Yet for him this is not only a phenomenon of

CALCULATIVE AND MEDITATIVE THINKING 251

decay; nihilism, rather, as the fundamental event of Western history, the world-historical movement of the peoples of the earth who have been drawn into the power of the modern age, simultaneously and above all is the intrinsic law of that history. True, the former values have become valueless; but this merely means that new values are to be posited, Nietzsche believes. Thus in his view a revaluing of all values has to take place.

For value is value only insofar as it counts. It counts only insofar as it is posited as that which matters. It is so posited through an aiming-at and a looking-toward an end that has to be reckoned with. This aim is the preservation and enhancement of life as the highest value. According to Nietzsche, when all suprasensible values advocated by Plato as well as by Christianity have become valueless and God himself and all gods are dead, the will to power is deliberately willed as the principle of all positing of the conditions that govern all that is.[2]

For Heidegger, however, nihilism is something completely different. Provisionally one could perhaps describe nihilism briefly as follows. For modern man all that is, is either what is actual and real, taken in the sense of object, or that which brings about the actual and the real. The latter objectifies the actual and the real; it is that within which the objectivity of the object takes place. Objectifying thought, in its pro-positing presentation, places things before man and delivers up the things as objects to man, taken as the *ego cogito*. In this delivering up, the *ego* proves to be that which underlies its own activity; in this way it proves to be the genuine *sub-jectum*. The subject is ultimately subject for itself. The essence of the subject is self-consciousness. Everything that is, is therefore either the object of the subject or the subject of the object. Everywhere the Being of whatever is, consists in placing itself before itself or in placing something else before the subject. Man, within the subjectness belonging to whatever is, rises up into the subjectivity which is nothing but the positing subjectivity. At the same time the world changes into an object. In this revolutionary objectifying of everything that is, the earth, that which first of all must be put at the disposal of the pro-posing presentation, moves into the midst of the human positing. The earth can show itself as the object of an assault that, in man's will to power, establishes itself as unconditioned objectification. Nature appears everywhere exclusively as the object of modern science and technicity.

The doing-away with all that is suprasensible and with all that is "in itself" has been completed and is accomplished by the making secure of the constant reserve by means of which modern man makes secure for himself all resources, material as well as spiritual, and this for the sake of his own security which wills nothing but dominion over all that is, in order that all that is will fully correspond to his will to power. From now on to be for each thing and each being means nothing but to be mastered, controlled, at someone's disposal, to stand-reserve as part of a carefully positioned stock. In his blind desire to guarantee the stability of what is so posited, controlled, and finally used up, man himself is also drawn into this process. He now becomes the most important raw material, insofar as he remains the subject of all consumption. At the same time our world has become an unworld.[3]

3. THE DANGER OF THE ATOMIC AGE

The age in which we live is often called the atomic age. Atomic energy was once used for destructive purposes during World War II. Now nuclear physicists everywhere are very busy with vast plans to implement peaceful uses of atomic energy and develop it into a gigantic business. And because of this a new era of prosperity and happiness is envisioned. Some time ago eighteen Nobel Prize winners proclaimed that modern natural science is the road to a happier human life.

Yet, Heidegger continues, we must ask: does this statement spring from reflection, from meditative thinking? Does it ponder on the meaning of the atomic age? No; for if we rest content with the statements of science and technology, we remain as far as possible from meditating thinking, and from the reflective insights into the meaning of our own age. For then we forget to ask: precisely what is the ground that enabled modern science and technology to discover and set free new energies in nature?

This ground is connected with a revolution in the leading concepts that has been going on for several centuries and by which man is placed in a totally different world. This radical resolution in outlook has come about in modern philosophy, and it has led us to a completely new relation to the universe and our place in it. The world from then on began to appear as an object of the attacks of calculative thinking, attacks that nothing is believed able to resist any longer. Nature becomes a gigantic energy resource for modern technology and industry. This basically technical relation of man to the world developed in Western Europe after the 17th Century and remained for a long time

CALCULATIVE AND MEDITATIVE THINKING

unknown to other continents. And it is totally alien to former ages and histories.

The power hidden in modern science and technology determines man's relation to all that is, it rules the entire earth and today even part of outer space. Such gigantic resources of power have become known recently through the discovery of atomic energy and it is now believed that in the foreseeable future the world's demand for energy will be ensured for ever; an abundance of energy will from now on be available to every nation. The question now no longer is: where do we find enough energy? The decisive question now is: in what way can we tame the inexhaustible amounts of energy and so secure mankind against the danger that the atomic energy suddenly will destroy everything.

If the taming of atomic energy is successful, and it is assumed that it will be successful, then a totally new era of technical development will begin. What we now know as the technology of today is only a crude start of the radical changes to come. The consequence of this development will be that in all areas of his being man will be encircled ever more tightly by the forces of technology. And since man did not make these incredible forces, they have moved along since beyond his will and have outgrown his capacity for decision. And this, too, is characteristic of the new world of science and technology, just as the fact that today technology's accomplishments come most speedily to be known by everybody and admired publicly.

In the last decade even life has been placed in the hands of scientists who will be able to synthesize, split, and change living substances at will. We all admire these daring research projects without, however, thinking about it. We do not dare to consider that a new attack with technological means is being prepared on the life and nature of man, compared with which the hydrogen bomb means relatively little.

Yet it is not the fact that the world is becoming ever more scientific and technical which is really uncanny. For most uncanny is the fact that we are not prepared for this change and are unable to confront meditatively what is really dawning in this age. No single man and no group of men, no government, industry, or science can brake or direct the progress of history in the atomic age; no human organization is capable of gaining control over it.

Is man, then, a defenseless victim at the mercy of the irresistible power of modern science and technology? He would be if man were to abandon any intention of balancing merely calculative thinking with meditative thinking, instrumental rationality with genuinely human rationality.

Can a new ground or foundation be granted to man, a foundation out of which man's Being and all his works may flourish in a new way in our atomic age? The answer to this question lies at hand, so near that we all too easily overlook it. This way is the way of meditative thinking. Let us see how this form of thinking can be beneficial to us today.

All the things that modern science and technology have created are to a greater or lesser extent indispensable. We cannot attack science and technology blindly, and try to do away with them. This, too, would be self-destructive. It is foolish to condemn science and technology as the work of the devil. Yet suddenly and unaware of what is really going on we find ourselves firmly shackled to our scientific and technical devices and realize that we have fallen into bondage to them. Yet, in Heidegger's view, we also can act otherwise. We can use scientific and technical devices properly and keep ourselves free from them in such a way that we may let go of them any time. We can affirm the unavoidable use of these devices and at the same time deny them the right to dominate us and lay waste our very own Being.

This ambivalent attitude in regard to modern science and technology, which says at the same time yes and no, corresponds to the two modes of thinking we have referred to earlier. Calculative thinking will help us to use our resources effectively; meditative thinking will help us in making certain that technicity will not overpower us. Meditative thinking will thus make it possible for us to come to a freedom in regard to things that lets beings be (*Gelassenheit*), by maintaining an openness to the mystery that is hidden in modern technicity.

As Heidegger sees it, *Gelassenheit* in regard to beings and openness to the mystery belong together. By means of them, thought can grant us in principle the possibility of dwelling in the world in a new way. They promise us a new foundation upon which we can stand and from which we can endure in the world of technicity without being periled by it. Yet for the time being, man finds himself still in a very perilous situation. For the danger remains that the approaching tide of the technological revolution will captivate and beguile us, because calculative thinking is still quite universally accepted and practiced as the *only* way of thinking. To overcome this thoughtlessness and avoid that man will have to give up and throw away what genuinely makes him human, we must try to keep meditative thinking alive.

CALCULATIVE AND MEDITATIVE THINKING

We must try to prepare for this thinking by engaging in a more careful meditation about the meaning of modern science and technicity.[4]

ABBREVIATIONS

EM	*Einführung in die Metaphysik*
FD	*Die Frage nach dem Ding*
G	*Gelassenheit*
GP	*Die Grundprobleme der Phänomenologie*
HB	*Brief über den "Humanismus"*
HW	*Holzwege*
ID	*Identität und Differenz*
KPM	*Kant und das Problem der Metaphysik*
LFW	*Logik. Die Frage nach der Wahrheit*
N	*Nietzsche*, 2 vols.
PG	*Prolegomena zur Geschichte des Zeitbegriffs*
PI	*Phänomenologische Interpretation von Kants Kritik der reinen Vernunft*
SD	*Zur Sache des Denkens*
SZ	*Sein und Zeit*
TuK	*Die Technik und die Kehre*
US	*Unterwegs zur Sprache*
VA	*Vorträge und Aufsätze*
W	*Wegmarken*
WD	*Was heisst Denken?*
WG	*Vom Wesen des Grundes*
WM	*Was ist Metaphysik?*
WW	*Vom Wesen der Wahrheit*

NOTES

PREFACE

1. Cf. Joachim Wach, *Das Verstehen. Grundzüge einer Geschichte der hermeneutischen Theorie im 19. Jahrhundert*, 3 vols. Tübingen: Mohr, 1926-1933; Richard E. Palmer, *Hermeneutics: Interpretation Theory in Schleiermacher, Dilthey, Heidegger, and Gadamer*. Evanston: Northwestern University Press, 1969.
2. Cf. Arion L. Kelkel, *La legende de l'etre. Langage et poesie chez Heidegger*. Paris: Vrin, 1980.
3. Cf. Thomas A. Fay, *Heidegger: The Critique of Logic*. The Hague: Nijhoff, 1977; Joseph J. Kockelmans, ed., *On Heidegger and Language*. Evanston: Northwestern University Press, 1972; Arion L. Kelkel, *La legende de l'etre*, pp. 21-154.

INTRODUCTION

1. For what follows see Joseph J. Kockelmans, *The World in Science and Philosophy*. Milwaukee: The Bruce Publishing Company, 1969; "Phenomenology and the Critique of the Scientific Tradition," in Lester E. Embree, ed., *Essays in Memory of Aron Gurwitsch*. Washington, D.C.: University Press of America, 1984; "The Foundations of Morality and the Human Sciences," in A.-T. Tymieniecka and C. O. Schrag, eds., *Analecta Husserliana*, vol. 15 (1983), pp. 369-386; Calvin O. Schrag, *Radical Reflection and the Origin of the Human Sciences*. West Lafayette, Ind.: Purdue University Press, 1980; Thomas McCarthy, *The Critical Theory of Jürgen Habermas*. Cambridge, Mass.: The MIT Press, 1978, pp. 1-16; Jürgen Habermas, *Theory and Practice*, trans. John Viertel. Boston: Beacon Press, 1980.
2. Section 2 of this introduction is a revised version of a passage from my essay, "Science and Discipline. Some Historical and Critical Reflections," in Joseph J. Kockelmans, ed., *Interdisciplinarity and Higher Education*. University Park, Pa.: The Pennsylvania State University Press, 1979, pp. 17-24. For what follows cf. Jean Ladriere, "Sciences et discours rationnel," in

Encyclopedia Universalis, vol. 14. Paris, 1972, pp. 754-767; *Les limitations internes des formalismes*. Louvain: Nauwelaerts, 1957; "Mathematics in a Philosophy of the Sciences," trans. Theodore J. Kisiel, in Joseph J. Kockelmans and Theodore J. Kisiel, eds., *Phenomenology and the Natural Sciences*. Evanston: Northwestern University Press, 1970, pp. 443-465; "Mathematics and Formalism," trans. Theodore J. Kisiel, eds., *Phenomenology and the Natural Sciences*. Evanston: Northwestern University Press, 1970, pp. 443-465; "Mathematics and Formalism," trans. Theodore J. Kisiel, in *Phenomenology and the Natural Sciences*, pp. 466-499; Jean Cavailles, "On Logic and the Theory of Science," trans. Theodore J. Kisiel, in *Phenomenology and the Natural Sciences*, pp. 353-409; Wolfgang Stegmüller, *Probleme und Resultate der wissenschaftliche und analytische Philosophie*, 4 vols. Berlin: Springer Verlag, 1969-1975. To the best of my knowledge these four volumes contain the most comprehensive discussion of the basic ideas developed by Carnap, Braithwaite, Oppenheim, Hempel, Nagel, Campbell, Hanson, Scheffler, Toulmin, Popper, Lakatos, Suppes, Goodman, etc. Cf. also Wolfgang Stegmüller, *The Structure and Dynamics of Theories*, trans. W. Wohlhueter. New York: Springer Verlag, 1976. This book contains a thorough discussion of the ideas proposed by Kuhn, Lakatos, Musgrave, Sneed, et al. Finally also see Kurt Hübner, *Critique of Scientific Reason*, trans. Paul R. Dixon and Hollis M. Dixon. Chicago: University of Chicago Press, 1983; Frederick Suppe, ed., *The Structure of Scientific Theories*. Urbana: University of Illinois Press, 1977.

3. Sections 3, 4, and 5 of this introduction are taken from "Phenomenology and the Critique of the Scientific Tradition" (with some minor changes).

4. Cf. the "Introduction" to the Cambridge Colloquium in "The Ideological and Theological Debate About Science," in *Anticipation*, 25(1979), pp. 4-11; the passage quoted can be found on p. 5. Cf. also *Revolutions and Reconstructions in the Philosophy of Science*. Bloomington: Indiana University Press, 1980, pp. vii-xxvi, and passim.

5. Ibid.

6. Cf. Max Jammer, "A Reconsideration of the Philosophical Implications of the New Physics," in G. Radnitzky and G. Andersson, eds., *The Structure and Development of Science*. Dordrecht: Reidel, 1979, pp. 41-61. Cf. Sir E. T. Whittaker, *From Euclid to Eddington*. Cambridge: University Press, 1949; A. Einstein and

NOTES TO INTRODUCTION

L. Infeld, *The Evolution in Physics*. New York: Simon and Schuster, 1961.

7. Sir Karl Popper, *The Logic of Scientific Discovery*. New York: Basic Books, 1959; *Conjectures and Refutations: The Growth of Scientific Knowledge*. London: Routledge and Kegan Paul, 1963.

8. Thomas Kuhn, *The Structure of Scientific Revolutions*. Chicago: University of Chicago Press, 1970; *The Essential Tension*. Chicago: University of Chicago Press, 1977.

9. Cf. I. Lakatos and A. Musgrave, eds., *Criticism and the Growth of Knowledge*. Cambridge: University Press, 1974.

10. J. Sneed, *The Logical Structure of Mathematical Physics*. Dordrecht: Reidel, 1971; W. Stegmüller, *The Structure and Dynamics of Theories*; R. E. Butts and J. Hintikka, eds., *Historical and Philosophical Dimensions of Logic, Methodology, and Philosophy of Science*. Dordrecht: Reidel, 1975, pp. 245-309; G. Radnitzky and G. Andersson, eds., *Progress and Rationality: The Structure and Development of Science*, pp. 151-256; W. Stegmüller, *The Structuralist View of Theories*. New York: Springer Verlag, 1979.

11. Kurt Hübner, *Critique of Scientific Reason*, part 2.

12. For bibliographical information on the works of the authors mentioned in this section see Frederick Suppe, ed., *The Structure of Scientific Theories*, pp. 731-767.

13. Cf. Joseph J. Kockelmans and Theodore J. Kisiel, eds., *Phenomenology and the Natural Sciences*. For Merleau-Ponty's criticism of the behavioral and social sciences see Remy C. Kwant, *The Phenomenological Philosophy of Merleau-Ponty*. Pittsburgh,: Duquesne University Press, 1963; *From Phenomenology to Metaphysics: An Inquiry Into the Last Period of Merleau-Ponty's Philosophy*. Pittsburgh: Duquesne University Press, 1966.

14. Joseph J. Kockelmans, *A First Introduction to Husserl's Phenomenology*. Pittsburgh: Duquesne University Press, 1967, pp. xv-xvii; *Edmund Husserl's Phenomenological Psychology*. Pittsburgh: Duquesne University Press, 1967, pp. 17-26, and passim.

15. Cf. Maurice Merleau-Ponty, *Consciousness and the Acquisition of Language*, trans. H. J. Silverman. Evanston: Northwestern University Press, 1973; "Translator's Preface," ibid., pp. xxxiii-xl.

16. Joseph J. Kockelmans, ed., *Philosophy of Science: The Historical Background*. New York: The Free Press, 1969.

17. Cf. Carl F. von Weizsäcker, *Der Garten des Menschlichen. Beiträge zur geschichtlichen Anthropologie*. Munich: Carl Hanser, 1977, pp. 404-431.

18. William J. Richardson, "Heidegger's Critique of Science," in *The New Scholasticism*, 42(1968), 511-536, p. 511.

19. Hans Seigfried, "Heidegger's Longest Day: 'Being and Time' and the Sciences," in *Philosophy Today*, 22(1978), 319-331, p. 319.

CHAPTER I

1. For what follows cf. Martin Heidegger, "My Way to Phenomenology," in *On Time and Being*, trans. Joan Stambaugh. New York: Harper and Row, 1972, pp. 74-82; Thomas Sheehan, "Heidegger's Early Years: Fragments for a Philosophical Biography," in Thomas Sheehan, ed., *Heidegger: The Man and the Thinker*. Chicago: Precedent Publishing, 1981, pp. 3-19, and the literature quoted there.

2. Hans Seigfried, "Martin Heidegger: A Recollection (1957)," in Thomas Sheehan, ed. *Heidegger*, p. 21.

3. Franz Brentano, *On the Several Senses of Being in Aristotle*, trans. Rolf George. Berkeley: University of California Press, 1975.

4. Martin Heidegger, "Das Realitätsproblem in der modernen Philosophie," in *Philosophisches Jahrbuch der Görres-Gesellschaft*, 25(1912), pp. 353-363.

5. Martin Heidegger, *Die Lehre vom Urteil im Psychologismus*. Leipzig: Barth, 1914.

6. Martin Heidegger, *Die Kategorien- und Bedeutungslehre des Duns Scotus*. Tübingen: Mohr, 1916.

7. Edmund Husserl, *Logische Untersuchungen*, 2 vols. Halle: Niemeyer, 1900-1901. English translation of the revised edition by J. N. Findlay, *Logical Investigations*. 2 vols. New York: Humanities Press, 1970.

8. Thomas Sheehan, "Heidegger's Early Years," p. 5.

9. Ibid.

10. Carl Braig, *Vom Sein. Abriss der Ontologie* (Grundzüge der Philosophie). Freiburg i.Br.: Herder, 1896. Cf. *On Time and Bring*, pp. 74-75.

11. Martin Heidegger, *Wegmarken*, ed. Fr.-W. von Herrmann. Frankfurt: Klostermann, 1976, pp. 1-44.

12. Frankfurt: Klostermann, 1979. The lecture course was edited by Petra Jaeger.

13. Martin Heidegger, *Sein und Zeit* (1927). Tübingen: Niemeyer, 1953. English translation by John Macquarrie and Edward Robinson, *Being and Time*. London: SCM Press, 1962. In the pages to follow I shall always refer to the German edition; the page numbers of this edition are also included in the margin in the English translation. Cf. for the remarks made in the text: SZ, p. 38; see also, pp. 47, 50, 51, 77, 218, 244, and 363.
14. Wilhelm Dilthey, *Gesammelte Schriften*, vol. V, 1, edited by Georg Misch. Göttingen: Vandenhoeck & Ruprecht, 1924, pp. 90ff.
15. SZ, p. 205.
16. SZ, p. 209.
17. Ibid.
18. SZ, pp. 209-210.
19. SZ, p. 249n.
20. SZ, p. 377.
21. SZ, p. 385.
22. SZ, p. 397.
23. SZ, p. 398.
24. SZ, p. 404.
25. SZ, pp. 46-47.
26. Martin Heidegger, *Prolegomena zur Geschichte des Zeitbegriffs*, ed. Petra Jaeger. Frankfurt: Kostermann, 1979, chapter I.
27. PGZ, pp. 10-12.
28. PGZ, p. 11; cf. pp. 13-180.
29. PGZ, pp. 13-33.
30. PGZ, p. 6.
31. PGZ, p. 6.
32. PGZ, p. 1.
33. PGZ, p. 7.
34. PGZ, p. 34.
35. Ibid.
36. PGZ, pp. 8-10.
37. PGZ, p. 18.
38. PGZ, p. 19.
39. Ibid.
40. Ibid.
41. PGZ, p. 1.
42. PGZ, pp. 20-21.
43. PGZ, pp. 23-28.
44. PGZ, pp. 28-32.
45. PGZ, pp. 32-33.

46. Edmund Husserl, *Ideen zu einer reinen Phänomenologie und phänomenologischen Philosophie*, vol. I (1913), ed. Walter Biemel. The Hague: Nijhoff, 1950. English translation by F. Kersten: *Ideas Pertaining to a Pure Phenomenology and to a Phenomenological Philosophy*. The Hague: Nijhoff, 1982.
47. PGZ, pp. 34-36.
48. PGZ, pp. 36-40.
49. PGZ, pp. 40-46.
50. PGZ, pp. 46-51.
51. PGZ, pp. 52-58.
52. PGZ, pp. 58-63; cf. section 9 below.
53. PGZ, pp. 63-65.
54. Cf. Martin Heidegger, *Logik. Die Frage nach der Wahrheit*, ed. Walter Biemel. Frankfurt: Kostermann, 1976, pp. 127-195. Cf. Joseph J. Kockelmans, "Being-True as the Fundamental and Basic Determination of Being," paper presented at the 17th annual meeting of the Heidegger conference in New Hampshire, May 13-15, 1983.
55. PGZ, pp. 54-75. Cf. SZ, sect. 44; *Vom Wesen der Wahrheit*. Frankfurt: Klostermann, 1961; English translation by John Sallis in David Farrell Krell, ed., *Martin Heidegger: Basic Writings*. New York: Harper and Row, 1977, pp. 117-141.
56. Edmund Husserl, *Logical Investigations*, vol. II, 2, pp. 667-834.
57. PGZ, pp. 74-85, 85-90, 90-99.
58. PGZ, p. 98; cf. pp. 97-99.
59. PGZ, pp. 99-103; GP, section 5 and 22; cf. Joseph J. Kockelmans, "Heidegger's Fundamental Ontology and Kant's Transcendental Doctrine of Method," in *Kant and Phenomenology*, ed. Thomas M. Seebohn and Joseph J. Kockelmans. Washington, D.C.: University Press of America, 1984, pp. 161-183.
60. GP, section 7-9.
61. Edmund Husserl, *Ideas*, p. 171.
62. PGZ, p. 158.
63. Edmund Husserl, *Ideas*, p. 114-115.
64. PGZ, p. 158.
65. Ibid.
66. PGZ, p. 159.
67. PGZ, pp. 159-160.
68. PGZ, p. 161.
69. Wilhelm Dilthey, *Die geistige Welt: Einleitung in die Philosophie des Lebens. Erste Hälfte: Abhandlungen zur*

Grundlegung der Geisteswissenschaften, ed. Georg Misch. Göttingen: Vandenhoeck & Ruprecht, 1957.
70. Wilhelm Dilthey, Der Aufbau der geschichtlichen Welt in den Geisteswissenschaften, ed. Bernard Groethuysen. Göttingen: Vandenhoeck & Ruprecht, 1958.
71. PGZ, pp. 163-164.
72. Edmund Husserl, "Philosophie als strenge Wissenschaft," in Logos, 1(1910-1911), pp. 289-341; English translation by Quentin Lauer, "Philosophy as Rigorous Science," in Quentin Lauer, ed., Edmund Husserl: Phenomenology and the Crisis of Philosophy. New York: Harper & Row, 1965.
73. PGZ, pp. 162-163.
74. PGZ, pp. 163-165; cf. Edmund Husserl, "Philosophie als strenge Wissenschaft," pp. 319-320 (English: pp. 117-118).
75. Edmund Husserl, Ideen. Zweites Buch: Phänomenologische Untersuchungen zur Konstitution, ed. Marly Biemel. The Hague: Nijhoff, 1952. I assume that we may take it for granted that Heidegger was one of these students.
76. PGZ, p. 167; cf. Edmund Husserl, Phänomenologische Psychologie, ed. Walter Biemel. The Hague: Nijhoff, 1962. It thus appears here that Heidegger, after he had left for Marburg, still remained in close contact with Husserl. The relationship between the two thinkers would soon come to an end. A first clear sign of a basic disagreement can be found in the fact that Husserl and Heidegger appeared to be unable to cooperate on an article on phenomenology for the Encyclopaedia Britannica; cf. Walter Biemel, "Husserl's Encyclopaedia Britannica Article and Heidegger's Remarks Thereon," in Frederick Elliston and Peter McCormick, eds., Husserl: Expositions and Appraisals. Notre Dame: University of Notre Dame Press, 1977, pp. 286-303.
77. PGZ, pp. 167-168.
78. PGZ, pp. 171-173; cf. pp. 168-171.
79. PGZ, pp. 173-174.
80. PGZ, p. 180.
81. PGZ, pp. 174-178; cf. pp. 178-182.
82. For what follows see Manfred Riedel, "Geisteswissenschaften--Grundlagenkrise und Grundlagenstreit," in Meyers Enzyklopädisches Lexikon. Mannheim: Bibliographisches Institut, 1973, vol. 9, pp. 838-844; J. Ritter, Die Aufgabe der Geisteswissenschaften in der modernen Gesellschaft. Münster: Aschendorff, 1963; Theodore Litt, Das Allgemeine im Aufbau der geisteswissenschaftlichen Erkenntnis. Groningen: Wolters, 1959; A. Diemer, "Die Differenzierung der Wissenschaften in die Natur- und die

Geisteswissenschaften und die Begründung der Geisteswissenschaften als Wissenschaften," in A. Diemer, ed., *Beiträge zur Entwicklung der Wissenschaftstheorie im 19. Jahrhundert.* Meisenheim am Glan: Hain, 1968, pp. 174-223; cf. also "Geisteswissenschaften," in *Historisches Wörterbuch der Philosophie,* ed. J. Ritter (Stuttgart: Schwabe, 1971ff.), vol. 3, col. 211-215.

83. Cf. Hans-Georg Gadamer, *Truth und Method.* New York: The Seabury Press, 1975, pp. 5-10, 192-234, 460-491; E. Betti, *Die Hermeneutik als allgemeine Methodik der Geisteswissenschaften.* Tübingen: Mohr, 1962; E. Betti, *Allgemeine Auslegungslehre als Methodik der Geisteswissenschaften.* Tübingen: Mohr, 1967; Erich Rothacker, *Einleitung in die Geisteswissenschaften.* Tübingen: Mohr, 1930.

CHAPTER II

1. Sz, pp. 27-29.
2. Cf. PGZ, pp. 103-122; GP, pp. 1-32, and passim.
3. PGZ, pp. 13-182; cf. section 2 above.
4. Cf. Joseph J. Kockelmans, "World-Constitution. Reflections on Husserl's Transcendental Idealism," in *Analecta Husserliana,* vol. I, ed. A.-T. Tymieniecka. Dordrecht: Reidel, 1972, pp. 11-35.
5. Cf. SZ, p. 38 and 38n; cf. section 2 above.
6. Martin Heidegger, *Unterwegs zur Sprache.* Pfullingen: Neske, 1960, pp. 85-99; English translation by Peter D. Hertz: *On the Way to Language.* New York: Harper & Row, 1971, pp. 1-12.
7. Cf. O. Schnübbe, *Der Existenzbegriff in der Theologie Bultmanns.* Göttingen: Vandenhoeck & Ruprecht, 1955; Otto Pöggeler, ed., *Heidegger: Perspektiven zur Deutung seines Werkes.* Cologne: Kiepenheuer & Witsch, 1969, pp. 11ff., 54ff., 169ff., 179ff.; Joseph J. Kockelmans, "Heidegger on Theology," in *The Southwestern Journal of Philosophy,* 4(1973), pp. 85-108, cf. pp. 86-89 in particular.
8. Martin Heidegger, *Was heisst Denken?* Tübingen: Niemeyer, 1961, p. 20; English translation by Fred D. Wieck and J. Glenn Gray: *What is Called Thinking?* New York: Harper & Row, 1968, p. 50.
9. SZ, pp. 2-4.
10. SZ, pp. 5-8.
11. SZ, pp. 7-8.
12. SZ, pp. 152-153.

13. SZ, pp. 362-363.
14. Immanuel Kant, *Critique of Pure Reason*, pp. B 735 - B 884. Section 5 is a slightly revised version of the first two parts of my article, "Destructive Retrieve and Hermeneutic Phenomenology," which appeared in *Research in Phenomenology*, 7(1977), pp. 106-137.
15. Cf. Carl-Friedrich Gethmann, *Verstehen und Auglegung. Das Methodenproblem in der Philosophie Heideggers*. Bonn: Bouvier Verlag, 1974, pp. 14-21, and passim. (Hereafter: GVA).
16. SZ, p. 202.
17. SZ, pp. 28, 38, 357; GP, pp. 26-33.
18. Rene Descartes, *Rules for the Direction of the Mind*, Rule IV, in *The Philosophical Works of Descartes*, trans. E. S. Haldane and G. R. T. Ross, 2 vols. New York: Dover, 1931, vol. I, p. 9.
19. Ibid., Rule III, *The Philosophical Works*, vol. I, p. 5.
20. Rene Descartes, *Discourse on the Method of Rightly Conducting the Reason and Seeking for Truth in the Sciences*, Part I, in *The Philosophical Works*, vol. I, pp. 85-87; *Meditations on First Philosophy*, Meditation I, ibid., pp. 144ff. Cf. Immanuel Kant, *Prolegomena to Any Future Metaphysics*, trans. Lewis White Beck. New York: The Bobbs-Merrill Company, 1950, pp. 3ff.; Edmund Husserl, "Philosophy as a Rigorous Science," pp. 71ff.; *Ideas*, vol. I, Chapter II. Cf. also SZ, p. 22.
21. SZ, pp. 15ff., 152f., 314f. Cf. G. F. W. Hegel, *Phenomenology of Mind*, trans. J. Baillie. London: Allen & Unwin, 1964, "Introduction," pp. 131ff.
22. GP, sections 1 and 4.
23. SZ, pp. 37-38. Cf. *Kant und das Problem der Metaphysik*. Frankfurt: Kostermann, 1951, pp. 185-122; English translation by James S. Churchill: *Kant and the Problem of Metaphysics*. Bloomington, Ind.: Indiana University Press, 1962, pp. 211-255.
24. SZ, p. 22; cf GP, pp. 31-32.
25. SZ, p. 303.
26. SZ, pp. 356-364.
27. SZ, pp. 15ff.
28. SZ, pp. 27-28.
29. SZ, p. 303, pp. 15ff.
30. SZ, pp. 5-8, 152ff., 314f., 436f.
31. Immanuel Kant, *Critique of Pure Reason*, p. B xii.
32. Ibid., p. B xiii.
33. Ibid., pp. B 735-736.

34. Gethmann, GVA, pp. 14-21.
35. This has become evident after the publication of the *Prolegomena zur Geschichte des Zeitbegriffs*; cf. PGZ, pp. 13-182, pp. 123-182 in particular; cf. also section 2 above.
36. GP, pp. 1-3.
37. GP, pp. 3-5, 5-14; cf. Immanuel Kant, *Werke*, ed. Cassirer, vol. 8, pp. 342ff.; *Critique of Pure Reason*, pp. B 833, B 844, B 868.
38. GP, pp. 15-19.
39. SZ, p. 15. Section 6 is in part a slightly revised version of the third part of my essay, "Destructive Retrieve and Hermeneutic Phenomenology," mentioned in note 14 above.
40. SZ, p. 16.
41. SZ, pp. 17ff.
42. SZ, pp. 19-20; cf. pp. 372ff.
43. SZ, pp. 20-23.
44. KPM, p. 185 (211).
45. GP, pp. 30-32.
46. SZ, p. 153.
47. GP, pp. 26-32.
48. SZ, pp. 27-28. For what follows also see my article, "Destructive Retrieve and Hermeneutic Phenomenology," mentioned in note 14 above.
49. SZ, p. 28.
50. SZ, p. 28.
51. SZ, pp. 28-31.
52. SZ, p. 32.
53. SZ, pp. 32-34.
54. SZ, pp. 34-35.
55. SZ, pp. 35-36.
56. SZ, pp. 36-37.
57. William J. Richardson, *Heidegger: Through Phenomenology to Thought*. The Hague: Nijhoff, 1963, p. 47.
58. SZ, pp. 37-38.
59. SZ, pp. 151-153, 313-316.
60. SZ, p. 38.
61. Edmund Husserl, *Phänomenologische Psychologie*, pp. 600-602.
62. William J. Richardson, *Heidegger*, pp. *viii-xvii*.
63. Ibid., pp. *x-xiv*
64. Ibid., pp. *xiv-xvi*.
65. Ibid., pp. 46-47, 630-633.
66. Edmund Husserl, *Phänomenologische Psychologie*, p. 601.

67. Ibid.
68. Ibid., pp. 601-602.
69. Martin Heidegger, *Unterwegs zur Sprache*, pp. 97-100 (11-13).
70. Gethmann, GVA, p. 29.
71. Joseph J. Kockelmans, "Destructive Retrieve and Hermeneutic Phenomenology," pp. 136-137.

CHAPTER III

1. SZ, pp. 5-8; KPM, p. 207 (237-238).
2. KPM, p. 205 (234-235).
3. KPM, p. 206 (235-236).
4. KPM, pp. 205-207 (234-237).
5. *Vom Wesen des Grundes*. Halle: Niemeyer, 1929, p. 18; English translation by Terrence Malick: *The Essence of Reasons*. Evanston: Northwestern University Press, 1969, pp. 32-36.
6. KPM, p. 212 (243-244).
7. KPM, pp. 205-206 (234-235).
8. William J. Richardson, *Heidegger*, pp. 33-41.
9. SZ, pp. 57-59.
10. SZ, pp. 59-62.
11. SZ, pp. 63-88.
12. SZ, pp. 134-140.
13. SZ, pp. 142-148; KPM, pp. 210-212 (241-244).
14. SZ, pp. 148-149.
15. SZ, p. 149.
16. SZ, pp. 149-150; 231-232.
17. SZ, pp. 150-152.
18. SZ, pp. 153-157.
19. SZ, pp. 157-160.
20. SZ, pp. 231-232.
21. Cf. Hans-Georg Gadamer, "Vom Zirkel des Verstehens," in *Martin Heidegger zum siebzigsten Geburtstag* (Festschrift), ed. Günther Neske. Pfullingen: Neske, 1959; Erasmus Schöfer, "Heidegger's Language: Metalogical Forms of Thought and Grammatical Specialties," in Joseph J. Kockelmans, *On Heidegger and Language*. Evanston: Northwestern University Press, 1972, pp. 281-287.
22. SZ, pp. 7-8.
23. SZ, p. 8.
24. SZ, pp. 149-151.
25. SZ, pp. 151-152, 231-232.

26. SZ, pp. 315-316, with several minor changes.
27. SZ, p. 201. Section 12 is a slightly revised version of the first part of chapter eight of my book, *Martin Heidegger: A First Introduction to His Philosophy*. Pittsburgh: Duquesne University Press, 1965.
28. SZ, p. 202.
29. SZ, p. 62.
30. SZ, pp. 202-203.
31. SZ, pp. 203-206.
32. SZ, pp. 206-208.
33. SZ, pp. 208-209.
34. Ibid.
35. Martin Heidegger, *Vom Wesen der Wahrheit*. Frankfurt: Klosterman, 1961; English translation by John Sallis, in David Farrell Krell, ed., *Martin Heidegger: Basic Writings*. New York: Harper & Row, 1977, pp. 117-144. Section 13 is in part a revised version of the second part of chapter eight of my book, *Martin Heidegger*, quoted in note 27 above.
36. Martin Heidegger, *Identität und Differenz*. Pfullingen: Neske, 1957, p. 47; English translation by Joan Stambaugh: *Identity and Difference*. New York: Harper & Row, 1969, p. 51.
37. Martin Heidegger, *Platons Lehre von der Wahrheit. Mit einem Brief über den 'Humanismus'*. Bern: Francke Verlag, 1947; English translation by Frank A. Capuzzi and J. Glenn Gray, in David Farrell Krell, ed., *Basic Writings*, pp. 193-242.
38. This is true at least for the lecture which Heidegger delivered in 1930. The first paragraph of the concluding note was added in 1949, whereas the first edition appeared in 1943. Cf. William J. Richardson, *Heidegger*, p. 212, note.
39. SZ, p. 213.
40. SZ, pp. 212-213.
41. Edmund Husserl, *Logical Investigations*, vol. II, Investigations VI, sect. 36-39.
42. WW, p. 5 (17).
43. Cf. Joseph J. Kockelmans, "Bring-True as the Fundamental and Basic Determination of Being"; paper presented during the 17th annual meeting of the Heidegger Conference in New Hampshire, May, 13-15, 1983.
44. WW, pp. 5-8 (118-121).
45. WW, pp. 8-9 (121).
46. WW, p. 9 (121-122).
47. WW, pp. 10-11 (122-124).
48. WW, pp. 11-12 (124-125).

49. SZ, pp. 212-220.
50. SZ, pp. 220-227.
51. SZ, p. 219.
52. SZ, pp. 133, 170; cf. pp. 220-221.
53. SZ, p. 221.
54. SZ, pp. 221-222.
55. SZ, p. 223.
56. SZ, pp. 223-224.
57. WW, p. 11 (213).
58. WW, p. 11 (123-124).
59. Ibid.
60. WW, p. 12 (125).
61. WW, pp. 12-13 (125-126).
62. WW, p. 15 (128).
63. WW, pp. 15-16 (128-129).
64. WW, pp. 6-9 (118-122).
65. SZ, p. 221.
66. SZ, p. 133.
67. SZ, p. 221.
68. SZ, p. 220.
69. SZ, p. 218.
70. SZ, p. 220.
71. SZ, p. 222.
72. SZ, p. 226.
73. SZ, p. 227.
74. SZ, p. 218.
75. WW, pp. 14-15 (126-128).
76. WW, p. 15 (128).
77. WW, pp. 18-19 (130-133).
78. SZ, p. 11.
79. Edmund Husserl, *Ideas*, pp. 15-20, 137-139, 161-164, 366-370, and passim.
80. Edmund Husserl, *Logical Investigations*, vol. II, pp. 435-489.
81. Edmund Husserl, *Ideen*. Drittes Buch: *Die Phänomenologie und die Fundamente der Wissenschaften*, ed. Marly Biemel. The Hague: Nijhoff, 1952, pp. 21-105, and passim; cf. *Ideas*, vol. I, pp. 67-69, 171-181; Joseph J. Kockelmans, *A First Introduction to Husserl's Phenomenology*. Pittsburgh: Duquesne University Press, 1967, pp. 99-105.
82. Joseph J. Kockelmans, *A First Introduction*, pp. 99-105.
83. Edmund Husserl, *Phänomenologische Psychologie*, pp. 87-89.

84. Ibid., pp. 55-64.
85. Edmund Husserl, *The Crisis of European Sciences and Transcendental Phenomenology*, trans. David Carr. Evanston: Northwestern University Press, 1970, pp. 103-189.
86. Ludwig Landgrebe, "Seinsregionen und regionale Ontologien in Husserl's Phänomenologie," in *Studium Generale*, 9(1956), pp. 313-324.
87. Edmund Husserl, *The Idea of Phenomenology*, trans. William P. Alston and George Nakhnikian. The Hague: Nijhoff, 1964, pp. 14-15.
88. Edmund Husserl, *Die Idee der Phänomenologie*, ed. Walter Biemel. The Hague: Nijhoff, 1950, p. 79 (this passage is not included in the English translation).
89. Edmund Husserl, *Ideas*, p. 32.
90. *Ideas*, pp. 135-139; cf. also E. Levinas, *Theorie de l'intuition dans la phenomenologie de Husserl*. Paris: J. Vrin, 1963, pp. 21-22.
91. *Ideas*, p. 138.
92. Edmund Husserl, *Ideen*, vol. II: "Einleitung des Herausgebers," p. xvi.
93. Edmund Husserl, *Ideen*, vol. III, pp. 79-85.
94. Ibid., pp. 79-80.
95. Ibid., pp. 80-81.
96. Ibid., p. 84.
97. Ibid., p. 83.
98. Ibid., pp. 84-85, 88.
99. Cf. Edmund Husserl, *Ideas*, pp. 18-20; *Ideen*, vol. III, pp. 23-24.
100. Edmund Husserl, *Crisis*, pp. 103-189.
101. Edmund Husserl, *Phänomenologische Psychologie*, pp. 57, 111.
102. Ibid., p. 57.
103. Ibid., p. 111.
104. H. Drüe, *Edmund Husserls System der phänomenologischen Psychologie*. Berlin: de Gruyter, 1963, pp. 72-81.
105. Edmund Husserl, *Crisis*, pp. 143-157. Cf. Joseph J. Kockelmans, *Edmund Husserl's Phenomenological Psychology*. Pittsburgh: Duquesne University Press, 1967, pp. 274-301.
106. Edmund Husserl, *Crisis*, pp. 135-148, 151-153, 173-174.
107. Ludwig Langrebe, "Seinsregionen und regionale Ontologien," pp. 313-314.
108. Edmund Husserl, *Ideas*, pp. 17-18, 161-164; Ludwig Landgrebe, "Seinsregionen," p. 315.

NOTES TO CHAPTER IV 271

109. *Ideas*, pp. 20-21.
110. Ibid.
111. Ibid.
112. Ibid.
113. C. Lannoy, "Phenomenologie, ontologie en psychologie in het werk van Edmund Husserl," in *Tijdschrift voor Philosophie*, 11 (1949), pp. 391-416; cf. pp. 406-408 in particular.
114. Edmund Husserl, *Ideas*, pp. 20-21.
115. Ibid., pp. 24-27; cf. E. Levinas, *Theorie de l'intuition*, p. 21.
116. SZ, p. 11.

CHAPTER IV

1. Cf. SZ, sections 13 and 69. For what follows see also: Martin Heidegger, *Phänomenologische Interpretation von Kants Kritik der reinen Vernunft*, ed. Ingtraud Görland. Frankfurt: Klostermann, 1977, section 2; *Die Frage nach dem Ding*. Tübingen: Niemeyer, 1962, section B, I, 5; English translation by W. B. Barton and Vera Deutsch: *What is a Thing?* Chicago: Henry Regnery, 1967; *Nietzsche*, 2 vols. Pfullingen: Neske, 1961, vol. I, pp. 520-525, and passim; *Gelassenheit*. Pfullingen: Neske, 1959; English translation by John M. Anderson and E. Hans Freund: *Discourse on Thinking*. New York: Harper & Row, 1966; *Vorträge und Aufsätze*. Pfullingen: Neske, 1954, pp. 1-100; *Holzwege*. Frankfurt: Klostermann, 1963, pp. 69-104, 193-247; *Was heisst Denken?* Tübingen: Niemeyer, 1961; English translation by Fred D. Wieck and J. Glenn Gray: *What is Called Thinking?* New York: Harper & Row, 1968. An English translation of the essays relevant to science and technology which are contained in *Vorträge und Aufsätze* and *Holzwege* can be found in *The Question Concerning Technology and Other Essays*, trans. William Lovitt. New York: Harper & Row, 1977.
2. Cf. the autobiographical sketch in Martin Heidegger, *Die Lehre vom Urteil im Psychologismus*. Leipzig: Barth, 1914. Cf. also *Frühe Schriften*, ed. Fr.-W. von Hermann. Frankfurt: Klostermann, 1978, pp. ix-xi.
3. Martin Heidegger, *Phänomenologische Interpretation von Kants Kritik der reinen Vernunft*, ed. Ingtraud Görland. Frankfurt: Klostermann, 1977, pp. 9-39.
4. Ibid., pp. 23-24. Section 15 is a revised version of the first two sections of chapter nine of my book, *Martin Heidegger:*

A First Introduction to His Philosophy. Pittsburgh: Duquesne University Press, 1965.
    5. Martin Heidegger, *Phänomenologische Interpretation*, p. 25; cf. pp. 23-25.
    6. SZ, pp. 153-160, 356-362.
    7. SZ, p. 62.
    8. SZ, p. 359.
    9. Ibid.
    10. SZ, p. 360.
    11. SZ, p. 362.
    12. SZ, pp. 155-156.
    13. HW, pp. 71-76; VA, pp. 55-59, and passim.
    14. SZ, p. 363. Section 16 is a revised version of the third section of chapter nine of my book, *Martin Heidegger*, quoted in note 4.
    15. SZ, pp. 59-62, 364.
    16. SZ, pp. 153-160, 356-364.
    17. SZ, pp. 364-366.
    18. PI, p. 26.
    19. PI, pp. 26-27.
    20. PI, pp. 27-29.
    21. SZ, pp. 363-364.
    22. SZ, p. 363.
    23. PI, pp. 32-33.
    24. PI, pp. 33-34.
    25. PI, pp. 34-35.
    26. PI, p. 35.
    27. PI, p. 36.
    28. PI, pp. 36-37.
    29. PI, pp. 38-39.
    30. PI, p. 30.
    31. For the most important issues discussed in the secondary literature cf. Joseph J. Kockelmans, "Heidegger on the Essential Difference and Necessary Relationship Between Philosophy and Science," in *Phenomenology and the Natural Sciences*, ed. Joseph J. Kockelmans and Theodore J. Kisiel. Evanston: Northwestern University Press, 1970, pp. 147-166; Theodore J. Kisiel, "Science, Phenomenology, and the Thinking of Being," ibid., pp. 167-183; Joseph J. Kockelmans, "The Era of the World-as-Picture," ibid., pp. 184-201; William J. Richardson, "Heidegger's Critique of Science," in *New Scholasticism*, 42(1968), pp. 511-536; Karlfried Gründer, "Heidegger's Critique of Science," in *Philosophy Today*, 7(1963), pp. 15-32; Karlfried Gründer, "Martin

Heideggers Wissenschaftskritik in ihren geschichtlichen Zusammenhangen," in *Archiv für Philosophie*, 11(1961), pp. 312-335; John C. Sallis, "Towards the Movement of Reversal: Science, Technology, and the Language of Homecoming," in *Heidegger and the Path of Thinking*, ed. J. Sallis. Pittsburgh: Duquesne University Press, 1970, pp. 138-168; Theodore J. Kisiel, "Heidegger and the New Image of Science, in *Research in Phenomenology*, 7(1977), pp. 162-181; P. Chiodi, *Heideggers Einfluss auf die Wissenschaften*. Bern: Francke Verlag, 1949; Hans Seigfried, "Heidegger's Longest Day: 'Being and Time' and the Sciences," in *Philosophy Today*, 22(1978), pp. 319-331. Cf. HW, pp. 69-70.

32. WD, pp. 4-5 (7-8). Cf. Joseph J. Kockelmans, "Heidegger and the Essential Difference," pp. 147-148.
33. WD, pp. 53, 57, 155 (22-23, 32-33, 132-133).
34. WD, p. 57 (32-33).
35. SZ, pp. 357-364.
36. N I, pp. 520-525.
37. FD, pp. 139-140 (177-179); VA, p. 65 (176-177).
38. VA, p. 70 (181-182); VA, p. 51 (67).
39. VA, pp. 45-46 (155-157).
40. G, pp. 13-14 (45).
41. G, p. 14 (46).
42. G, pp. 25-26 (54-55); cf. *Zur Sache des Denkens*. Tübingen: Niemeyer, 1969, pp. 61-65 (English translation in *Basic Writings*, pp. 374ff.).
43. Cf. Joseph J. Kockelmans, "Reflections on Lakatos' Methodology of Scientific Research Programs," in *The Structure and Development of Science*, ed. G. Radnitzky and G. Andersson. Dordrecht: Reidel, 1979, pp. 196-202.

CHAPTER V

1. Martin Heidegger, *Die Frage nach dem Ding*. Tübingen: Niemeyer, 1962, pp. 49-83; English translation by W. B. Barton Jr. and Vera Deutsch: *What is a Thing?* Chicago: Henry Regnery, 1967, pp. 65-108; HW, pp. 69-104 (115-154); VA, pp. 45-70 (155-182); *Die Technik und die Kehre*. Pfullingen: Neske, 1962 (cf. VA, 13-44 and the English translation of this essay by Lovitt in *The Question Concerning Technology*, pp. 3-35); *Gelassenheit (Discourse on Thinking)*, passim; *Was heisst Denken?* Tübingen: Niemeyer, 1961; English translation by Fred D. Wieck and J. Glenn Gray: *What is Called Thinking?* New York: Harper & Row, 1968, passim. The issues discussed in this chapter have

been treated in a somewhat different manner in chapter 10 of my book, *On the Truth of Being. Reflections on Heidegger's Later Philosophy*. Bloomington, Indiana University Press, 1984, pp. 209-225.

2. HW, p. 70 (117).
3. HW, 70-71 (117-118).
4. FD, pp. 50-53 (66-69).
5. FD, pp. 50-51 (66-67).
6. FD, pp. 51-52 (67-68).
7. FD, p. 51 (68).
8. FD, p. 52 (68). Cf. Immanuel Kant, "Preface" to the *Metaphysical Foundations of Natural Science*, trans. Belfort Bax. London: Bell & Sons, 1883, pp. 137-149 (the quotation is from p. 140).
9. FD, pp. 52-53 (68-69).
10. FD, p. 53 (69-70).
11. FD, pp. 54-59 (70-76).
12. HW, pp. 71-72 (118-119); cf. Joseph J. Kockelmans, "The Era of the World-as-Picture," p. 188.
13. FD, p. 59 (76).
14. FD, pp. 59-60 (76-77).
15. FD, p. 60 (77-78).
16. Cf. Isaac Newton, *Mathematical Principles of Natural Philosophy and the System of the World*, trans. A. Motte (1729), revised trans. by Florian Cajori. Berkeley: University of California Press, 1946, p. 13.
17. Ibid., p. xxii.
18. FD, pp. 60-61 (78).
19. FD, pp. 60-61 (78-79).
20. Aristotle, *De Caelo*, Γ, 7, 306a6 and 306a16-17.
21. Isaac Newton, *Mathematical Principles*, Book III, Rule IV.
22. FD, p. 63 (82).
23. Aristotle, *De Caelo*, A, 8, 277b6; cf. 269b69.
24. FD, pp. 63-66 (82-85).
25. FD, pp. 66-68 (85-88).
26. FD, p. 69 (89).
27. FD, pp. 69-70 (90).
28. FD, p. 70 (90).
29. FD, p. 70 (91).
30. FD, pp. 70-71 (91).
31. FD, p. 71 (91-92).
32. Aristotle, *Physics*, B, 1, 192b21-22.

NOTES TO CHAPTER V

33. HW, pp. 72-73 (118-120); FD, p. 71 (92).
34. FD, p. 71 (92-93).
35. FD, pp. 71-72 (93-94).
36. FD, pp. 72-73 (94-95).
37. HW, pp. 69-70 (115-117). For what follows here also see my essay, "The Era of the World-as-Picture," in *Phenomenology and the Natural Sciences*, pp. 184-201.
38. Cf. my book *On the Truth of Being, Reflections on Heidegger's Later Philosophy*. Bloomington, IN: Indiana University Press, 1984, chapter 10.
39. HW, pp. 70-71 (117-118).
40. HW, p. 71 (118).
41. HW, pp. 71-73 (118-120).
42. HW, pp. 73-74 (120-121).
43. HW, pp. 74-75 (121-122).
44. HW, p. 75 (122).
45. HW, pp. 76-77 (122-124).
46. SZ, p. 9; cf. HW, p. 90 (138).
47. HW, pp. 77-78 (123-125).
48. HW, pp. 90-91 (139).
49. HW, pp. 78-79 (125-126).
50. HW, pp. 79-80 (126-127).
51. HW, p. 80 (127), pp. 90-92 (139-140).
52. VA, pp. 46-59 (156-170); FD, pp. 50-53 (66-69). For what follows cf. Theodore J. Kisiel, "Science, Phenomenology, and the Thinking of Being," pp. 177-183.
53. VA, p. 46 (156-157).
54. VA, p. 47 (157).
55. VA, pp. 47-48 (157-159); VA, pp. 20-22 (294-296), 177-183 (178-185).
56. VA, pp. 50-51 (159-161). Note that the etymological relation between *Wirklichkeit* and *wirken, Werk, ergon*, does not show up in the English translation.
57. VA, p. 51 (161); HW, p. 69 (115-116).
58. VA, p. 51 (161-162).
59. VA, pp. 51-52 (162-163).
60. VA, pp. 52-54 (163-165).
61. VA, p. 53 (165-166); cf. HW, p. 286 (132).
62. VA, pp. 53-55 (166-167).
63. VA, p. 56 (167).
64. VA, pp. 56-57 (167-168).
65. VA, p. 57 (168).

66. Cf. Joseph J. Kockelmans, "Heidegger on the Essential Difference," pp. 157-164.
67. VA, pp. 57-58 (168-169); cf. SZ, pp. 365-366; Kockelmans, ibid.
68. VA, p. 58 (169).
69. VA, pp. 58-59 (169-170).
70. VA, p. 59 (170-171).
71. VA, pp. 59-60 (171).
72. VA, p. 60 (171-172).
73. VA, pp. 60-61 (172); cf. Werner Heisenberg, *Wandlungen in den Grundlagen der Naturwissenschaften*. Berlin: de Gruyter, 1949, p. 98.
74. VA, 61 (172-173).
75. VA, 61-62 (173-174).
76. VA, 62 (174).
77. VA, 62-63 (174).
78. VA, 63-64 (174-176).
79. VA, 64-66 (176-177).
80. VA, 66-68 (177-180).
81. VA, 68-70 (180-182).
82. Werner Heisenberg, *Das Naturbild der heutigen Physik*. Hamburg: Rowohlt, 1956, pp. 12-15.
83. VA, pp. 13-44; cf. my book *On the Truth of Being*, Chapter 11.
84. VA, pp. 13-15 (3-5).
85. VA, pp. 15-20 (5-12).
86. WW, pp. 9-19 (122-123); SZ, pp. 212-230. Cf. section 13 above.
87. VA, pp. 20-24 (12-17).
88. VA, pp. 24-25 (17-18).
89. VA, pp. 25-27 (18-19).
90. VA, pp. 71-100; the passage referred to can be found on pp. 91-92; English translation in *The End of Philosophy*, trans. Joan Stambaugh. New York: Harper & Row, pp. 103-104.
91. VA, pp. 27-31 (19-23).
92. Cf. my book *On the Truth of Being*, chapter 11.
93. HW, pp. 80-81 (127-128).
94. HW, pp. 82-84 (128-132).
95. HW, pp. 85-87 (132-135).
96. HW, pp. 93-94 (141-143).
97. FD, pp. 74-76 (96-98).
98. FD, pp. 76-77 (98-99).
99. FD, p. 77 (99).

100. FD, p. 78 (100).
101. FD, p. 78 (100).
102. FD, pp. 77-78 (99-100).
103. FD, p. 78 (101).
104. FD, pp. 78-79 (101-102). Cf. Rene Descartes, *Oeuvres*, vol. X, p. 501; *Rules for the Direction of the Mind*, p. 8.
105. FD, p. 80 (103).
106. FD, pp. 80-81 (103-104).
107. FD, pp. 81-82 (105-106).
108. FD, p. 82 (106).
109. FD, pp. 82-83 (106-107).
110. FD, p. 83 (107-108).
111. HW, pp. 82-84 (129-131).
112. HW, p. 81 (128).
113. HW, p. 75 (121-122); cf. p. 81 (127-128).
114. HW, p. 99 (148-149).
115. HW, pp. 98-99 (147-148).
116. J.-P. Sartre, *Being and Nothingness*, trans. Hazel Barnes. New York: Philosophical Library, 1956, p. *lii*.
117. HW, p. 100 (149-150).
118. HW, p. 101 (150-151).
119. HW, p. 100 (149-150). Cf. William J. Richardson, *Heidegger*, pp. 321-323.
120. HW, pp. 83-84 (130-132).
121. HW, p. 88 (135-136); cf. p. 104 (153-154); Richardson, *Heidegger*, pp. 419-421.

CHAPTER VI

1. SZ, pp. 134-142. This chapter is a revised version of part of an essay, "Hermeneutic Phenomenology and the Science of History," which appeared in *Phänomenologische Forschungen*, pp. 130-179.
2. SZ, pp. 142-153.
3. William J. Richardson, *Heidegger*, p. 60, note 91.
4. Immanuel Kant, *Critique of Pure Reason*, p. B xiii.
5. KPM, p. 20 (15).
6. KPM, p. 210 (240-241).
7. Richardson, *Heidegger*, p. 61.
8. SZ, pp. 149-151.
9. SZ, pp. 151-2, 231-232.
10. SZ, p. 1, 39.
11. SZ, pp. 180-181, 324.

12. SZ, p. 327.
13. SZ, p. 364-366.
14. SZ, p. 376.
15. SZ, pp. 382-385.
16. SZ, pp. 385-387.
17. SZ, pp. 388-389.
18. SZ, pp. 392-397.
19. SZ, p. 385.
20. SZ, pp. 350-366.
21. SZ, pp. 362-363.
22. SZ, pp. 361-362.
23. SZ, p. 397.
24. HW, pp. 74-76 (122-123).
25. SZ, pp. 392-397. Cf. Martin Heidegger, *Einführung in die Metaphysik*. Tübingen: Niemeyer, 1953, p. 33, 35-36; English translation by Ralph Manheim: *An Introduction to Metaphysics*. Garden City: Doubleday, 1961, pp. 35-36, 38-39. VA, pp. 48, 63-64, 69 (158-159, 174-175, 180-181); WD, pp. 90-91, 104 (131-132, 138); US, p. 80 (196-197). Cf. Hans-Georg Gadamer, *Truth and Method*. New York: The Seabury Press, 1975, pp. xi-xxvi, 343-447.
26. Martin Heidegger, *Phänomenologie und Theologie*. Frankfurt: Klostermann, 1970, pp. 21-27, 44-46.

CHAPTER VII

1. Cf. section 2 above.
2. Cf. section 14 above.
3. Cf. Hans-Georg Gadamer, *Truth and Method*. New York: The Seabury Press, 1975; *Philosophical Hermeneutics*, trans. David E. Linge. Berkeley: University of California Press, 1977; "Hermeneutics and Social Science," in *Cultural Hermeneutics*, 2(1975), pp. 307-316; "Practical Philosophy as a Model of the Human Sciences," in *Research in Phenomenology*, 9(1979), pp. 74-86; Paul Ricoeur, "Phenomenology and the Social Sciences," in *Annals of Phenomenological Sociology*, 1(1977), pp. 145-159; *Hermeneutics and the Human Sciences*, ed. John B. Thompson. New York: Cambridge University Press, 1981; "Expliquer et comprendre: sur quelques connexions remarquables entre la theorie du texte et la theorie de l'action," in *Revue Philosophique de Louvain*, 75 (1977), pp. 126-147; "The Model of the Text: Meaningful Action Considered as a Text," in *Social Research*, 38 (1971), pp. 529-562; Joseph J. Kockelmans, ed., *Phenomenology*.

The Philosophy of Edmund Husserl and Its Interpretation. Garden City: Doubleday, 1967, pp. 533-555; "Phenomenology and Psychology: Theoretical Problems in Phenomenological Psychology," in M. Natanson, ed., *Phenomenology and the Social Sciences*, 2 vols. Evanston: Northwestern University Press, 1973, pp. 225-280; "Empirische und hermeneutische Psychologie. Gedanken zu einer mehrdimensionalen Bestimmung des Problems der Psychologie," in A. Metraux, ed., *Versuche über Erfahrung*. Bern: Hans Huber, 1976, pp. 35-49; "Toward an Interpretative or Hermeneutic Social Science," in *Graduate Faculty Philosophical Journal*, 5(1975), pp. 73-96; "Reflections on Social Theory," in *Human Studies*, 1(1978), pp. 1-15; "Some Reflections on the Meaning and Function of Interpretative Sociology," in *Tijdschrift voor Filosofie*, 42(1980), pp. 294-324; Josef Bleicher, ed., *Contemporary Hermeneutics: Hermeneutics as Method, Philosophy, and Critique*. London: Routledge and Kegan Paul, 1980.

4. Stephan Strasser, *Phenomenology and the Human Sciences*. Pittsburgh: Duquesne University Press, 1963; Georg Henrik von Wright, *Explanation and Understanding*. Ithaca: Cornell University Press, 1971; Karl-Otto Apel, *Analytic Philosophy of Language and the Geisteswissenschaften*. Dordrecht: Reidel, 1967; Rudiger Bubner, Konrad Cramer, and Reiner Wiehl, eds., *Hermeneutik und Dialektik*, 2 vols. Tübingen: Mohr, 1970; Richard S. Rudner, *Philosophy of Social Science*. Englewood Cliffs: Prentice-Hall, 1966; Michael Oakeshott, *Rationalism in Politics and Other Essays*. London: Methuen and Co., 1962; Peter Winch, *The Idea of Social Science*. New York: Oxford University Press, 1958; R. G. Collingwood, *The Idea of History*. New York: Oxford University Press, 1964; Charles Taylor, *The Explanation of Behavior*. London: Routledge and Kegan Paul, 1964; G. Radnitzky, *Contemporary Schools of Metascience*, 2 vols. Gothenburg: Akademiförlaget, 1968; Jürgen Habermas, *Zur Logik der Sozialwissenschaften*. Tübingen: Mohr, 1967; etc.

5. For an extensive bibliography on the issues raised here see: Leonard I. Krimerman, ed., *The Nature and Scope of Social Science: A Critical Anthology*. New York: Appleton-Century-Crofts, 1969, pp. 759-780.

6. Cf. WD, pp. 1-8, 48-52 (3-18).

7. Cf. Martin Heidegger, "Overcoming Metaphysics," in VA, pp. 77-99 (English translation in *The End of Philosophy*, pp. 84-110).

8. Cf. Walter Biemel, Husserl's *Encyclopaedia Britannica* Article and Heidegger's Remarks Thereon," in Frederick Elliston

and Peter McCormick, eds. *Husserl: Expositions and Appraisals*. Notre Dame: Notre Dame University Press, 1977, pp. 286-303.

9. SZ, pp. 16, 45-51, 134, 138, 163, 209, 247ff., 301, 338, 394-399.

10. SZ, pp. 28, 51, 272.

11. SZ, p. 9.

12. Ibid.

13. Ibid.

14. Ibid.

15. SZ, pp. 9-10.

16. SZ, p. 10.

17. Ibid.

18. Ibid.

19. Cf. Walter Biemel, "Husserl's *Encyclopaedia Britannica* Article," pp. 299-300.

20. SZ, p. 10. Cf. Martin Heidegger, *Phänomenologische Interpretation von Kants Kritik der reinen Vernunft*, pp. 9-39.

21. Martin Heidegger, *Phänomenologische Interpretation*, p. 39.

22. Ibid., pp. 17-39; SZ, pp. 356-364.

23. Walter Biemel, "Husserl's *Encyclopaedia Britannica* Article," pp. 299-303.

24. This dimension of the Sciences has been discussed particularly by Theodore J. Kisiel and Patrick Heelan. Cf. Theodore J. Kisiel, "Zu einer Hermeneutik naturwissenschaftlicher Entdeckung," in *Zeitschrift für allgemeine Wissenschaftstheorie*, 2(1971), pp. 195-221; "The Rationality of Scientific Discovery," in Theodore F. Geraets, ed., *Rationality To-Day*. Ottawa: The University of Ottawa Press, 1979, pp. 401-411; Patrick Heelan, "Natural Science as a Hermeneutic of Instrumentation," in *Philosophy of Science*, 50(1983), pp. 181-204; *Space-Perception and the Philosophy of Science*. Berkeley: University of California Press, 1982.

25. Cf. the publications mentioned in note 3 above.

26. Calvin O. Schrag, *Radical Reflection and the Origin of the Human Sciences*. West Lafayette, Ind.: Purdue University Press, 1980. -- Section 28 is a revised version of my essays: "Reflections on Social Theory" and "Some Reflections on the Meaning and Function of Interpretative Sociology," quoted in note 3 above.

27. Calvin O. Schrag, *Radical Reflection*, pp. 1-27.

28. Cf. the literature quoted in note 3 above.

29. Immanuel Kant, *Critique of Pure Reason*, p. B 2.

30. Cf. the publications by Gadamer and Ricoeur quoted in note 3 above.
31. Cf. Rudolf Carnap, "Logical Foundations of the Unity of Science," in Leonard I. Krimerman, *The Nature of Scope of Social Science*, pp. 362-373.
32. Karl R. Popper, "The Logic of the Social Sciences," in Theodore W. Adorno et al., *The Positivist Dispute in German Sociology*, trans. by Glyn Adey and David Frisby. New York: Harper & Row, 1976, pp. 87-104.
33. Edmund Husserl, *Phänomenologische Psychologie*, pp. 46-52. -- Section 29 is a revised version of one part of my essay, "Phenomenology and Psychology" quoted in note 3 above.
34. Cf. section 14 above.
35. Edmund Husserl, *Ideas*, vol. I, pp. 17-33, 135-139, 161-164.
36. Edmund Husserl, *Phänomenologische Psychologie*, pp. 46-51, 72-87.
37. Cf. section 2 above.
38. Section 30 is a revised version of the second part of my essay, "Toward an Interpretative or Hermeneutical Social Science," quoted in note 3 above. The term "interpretative social science" or "interpretative sociology" was suggested by Alfred Schutz. The expression "empirical social science" as well as the terms "descriptive social science" and "interpretative social science" do not refer to three different sciences or disciplines, but rather to three different basic possibilities in each social science. For the distinction between the empirical, descriptive, and interpretative components of every human discipline, see Joseph J. Kockelmans, "Theoretical Problems in Phenomenological Psychology" and "Reflections on Social Theory," quoted in note 3 above.
39. Gerard Radnitzky, *Continental Schools of Metascience*, vol. II, pp. 147-153, and the literature quoted there.
40. Joseph J. Kockelmans, "Metaphysics and Values," in *The Future of Metaphysics*, ed. Robert E. Wood. Chicago: Quadrangle Books, 1970, pp. 246-249.
41. Hans-Georg Gadamer, *Le probleme de la conscience historique*. Louvain: Publications Universitaires, 1963, pp. 65-67. -- Section 31 is a slightly revised version of the third and fourth parts of my essay, "Toward an Interpretative or Hermeneutic Social Science," quoted in note 3 above.
42. For what follows see: E. Betti, *Allgemeine Auslegungslehre*. Tübigen: Mohr, 1967, pp. 211ff.; Thomas M. Seebohn, *Zur*

Kritik der hermeneutischen Vernunft. Bonn: Bouvier, 1972, pp. 7-43; Gerard Radnitzky, *Continental Schools*, vol. II, pp. 19-40.

43. F. Schleiermacher, *Hermeneutik*, ed. H. Kimmerle. Heidelberg: Winter, 1959, p. 87.
44. Hans-Georg Gadamer, *Le probleme*, pp. 67-69; Gerard Radnitzky, *Continental Schools*, p. 27.
45. SZ, pp. 151-153.
46. Hans-Georg Gadamer, *Le probleme*, pp. 70-76.
47. Ibid., pp. 76-80.
48. Ibid., pp. 81-83.
49. Ibid., pp. 83-87.

EPILOGUE

1. G, pp. 12-15 (44-47); cf. WD, pp. 1-8 (3-12).
2. HW, pp. 193-247 (53-112); cf. N II, pp. 31-203 (passim).
3. VA, pp. 91-99 (103-110); cf. HW, pp. 194-195 (55), 235-236 (100), and pp. 241-242 (107).
4. G, pp. 17-28 (48-57).

BIBLIOGRAPHY

This bibliography is limited to the publications which I have used in writing this book. For an extensive bibliography of works by Heidegger and of publications on his thinking I refer the reader to the one prepared by Hans-Martin Sass (*Martin Heidegger: Bibliography*. Bowling Green: Philosophy Documentation Center, 1982).

This bibliography is divided into four sections:
I. Works by Heidegger in chronological order with English translations.
II. Books and articles on Heidegger's philosophy and his conception of the sciences.
III. Collections of essays on Heidegger's thinking.
IV. Other publications quoted, or used in writing this book.

I. WORKS BY HEIDEGGER IN CHRONOLOGICAL ORDER WITH ENGLISH TRANSLATIONS

Sein und Zeit (1927) Tübingen: Niemeyer, 1953.
    Being and Time, trans. John Macquarrie and Edward Robinson. London: SCM Press, 1962.
Kant und das Problem der Metaphysik (1927). Frankfurt: Klostermann, 1951.
    Kant and the Problem of Metaphysics, trans. James S. Churchill. Bloomington: Indiana University Press, 1962.
Vom Wesen des Grundes (1928). Frankfurt: Klostermann, 1928.
    The Essence of Reasons, trans. Terrence Malick. Northwestern University Press, 1969.
Was ist Metaphysik? Frankfurt: Klostermann, 1955.
(Postscript added to 4th edition in 1943; Introduction added to 5th edition in 1949)
    What is Metaphysics? trans. David Farrell Krell in Martin Heidegger, *Basic Writings*, ed. David Farrell Krell. New York: Harper & Row, 1977, 95-116.

"Postscript" to *What is Metaphysics?*, trans. R. F. C. Hull and Alan Crick in Werner Brock, *Existence and Being*. Chicago: Regnery, 1949, 349-361.
"Introduction" to *What is Metaphysics?*, trans. W. Kaufmann, in W. Kaufmann, ed., *Existentialism from Dostoevsky to Sartre*. New York: New American Library, 1975, 265-279.

Vom Wesen der Wahrheit (1930, 1943). Frankfurt: Klostermann, 1961.
   On the Essence of Truth, trans. John Sallis, in *Basic Writings*, 117-141.

Einführung in die Metaphysik (1935). Tübingen: Niemeyer, 1953.
   An Introduction to Metaphysics, trans. Ralph Manheim. New Haven: Yale University Press, 1959.

Holzwege (1936-1946). Frankfurt: Klostermann, 1950.
The book contains six essays whose English translations appeared in different collections:

"Der Ursprung des Kunstwerkes," *Holzwege*, 1-68.
   "The Origin of the Work of Art," in Martin Heidegger, *Poetry, Language, Thought*, trans. Albert Hofstadter. New York: Harper and Row, 1971, 7-87.

"Die Zeit des Weltbildes," *Holzwege*, 69-104.
   "The Age of the World Picture," in Martin Heidegger, *The Question Concerning Technology and Other Essays*, trans. William Lovitt. New York: Harper & Row, 1977, 115-154.

"Hegels Begriff der Erfahrung," *Holzwege*, 105-192.
   Hegel's Concept of Experience, trans. J. Glenn Gray. New York: Harper & Row, 1970.

"Nietzsches Wort 'Gott ist tot'," *Holzwege*, 193-247.
   "The Word of Nietzsche: 'Got Is Dead'," in Martin Heidegger, *The Question Concerning Technology and Other Essays*, trans. William Lovitt, 53-112.

"Wozu Dichter?" *Holzwege*, 248=295.
   "What Are Poets For?" in Martin Heidegger, *Poetry, Language, Thought*, trans. Albert Hofstadter, 91-142.

"Der Spruch des Anaximander," *Holzwege*, 296-343.
   "The Anaximander Fragment," in Martin Heidegger, *Early Greek Thinking*, trans. David Farrell Krell and Frank A. Capuzzi. New York: Harper & Row, 1975, 13-58.

Nietzsche (1936-1946), 2 vols. Pfullingen: Neske, 1961.
   Nietzsche, vol. I: *The Will to Power as Art*, trans. David Farrell Krell. New York: Harper & Row, 1979.
   Nietzsche, vol. IV: *Nihilism*, trans. Frank A. Capuzzi and David Farrell Krell. New York: Harper & Row, 1982.

Vorträge und Aufsätze (1943-1954). Pfullingen: Neske, 1961.
The collection contains eleven essays which were translated by different people for different occasions:
"Die Frage nach der Technik," VA, 13-44.
  "The Question Concerning Technology," in Martin Heidegger, *The Question Concerning Technology and Other Essays*, trans. by William Lovitt, 3-35.
"Wissenschaft und Besinning," VA, 45-70.
  "Science and Reflection," in Martin Heidegger, *The Question Concerning Technology and Other Essays*, trans. by William Lovitt, 155-182.
"Überwindung der Metaphysik," VA 71-99.
  "Overcoming Metaphysics," in Martin Heidegger, *The End of Philosophy*, trans. Joan Stambaugh. New York: Harper & Row, 1973, 84-110.
"Wer ist Nietzsches Zarathustra?," VA, 101-126.
  "Who Is Nietzsche's Zarathustra?," trans. Bernd Magnus in *Review of Metaphysics*, 20 (1967), 411-431.
"Was heisst Denken?," VA, 129-143.
  This lecture is practically speaking identical with the first two lectures of the lecture series with the same title; cf. below.
"Bauen, Wohnen, Denken," VA, 145-162.
  "Building Dwelling Thinking," trans. Albert Hofstadter, in *Basic Writings*, 323-339.
"Das Ding," VA, 163-185.
  "The Thing," in Martin Heidegger, *Poetry, Language, Thought*, trans. Albert Hofstadter, 165-186.
"...dichterisch wohnet der Mensch...", VA, 187-204.
  "...Poetically Man Dwells...", in Martin Heidegger, *Poetry, Language, Thought*, trans. Albert Hofstadter, 213-229.
"*Logos* (Heraklit, Fragment 50)," VA, 207-229.
  "*Logos* (Heraclitus, Fragment B 50)," in Martin Heidegger, *Early Greek Thinking*, trans. David Farrell Krell, 59-78.
"*Moira* (Parmenides VIII, 34-41)," VA, 231-256.
  "*Moira* (Parmenides VIII, 34-41)," in Martin Heidegger, *Early Greek Thinking*, trans. Frank A. Capuzzi, 79-101.
"*Aletheia* (Heraklit, Fragment 16)," VA, 257-282.
  "*Aletheia* (Heraclitus, Fragment B 16), in Martin Heidegger, *Early Greek Thinking*, trans. Frank A. Capuzzi, 102-123.
Platons Lehre von der Wahrheit (1942). *Mit einem Brief über den "Humanismus"* (1946). Bern: Francke, 1947.

"Plato's Doctrine of Truth," trans. John Barlow, in *Philosophy in the Twentieth Century II*, W. Barrett et al., eds. New York: Random House, 1962, 251-270.
"Letter on Humanism" trans. Frank A. Capuzzi and J. Glenn Gray, in *Basic Writings*, 193-242.
Was heisst Denken? (1951-1952). Tübingen: Niemeyer, 1954.
What is Called Thinking? trans. Fred D. Wieck and J. Glenn Gray. New York: Harper & Row, 1968.
Identität und Differenz (1957). Pfullingen: Neske, 1957.
Identity and Difference, trans. Joan Stambaugh. New York: Harper & Row, 1969.
Zur Sache des Denkens. Tübingen: Niemeyer, 1969.
On Time and Being, trans. Joan Stambaugh. New York: Harper & Row, 1972.
Unterwegs zur Sprache (1950-1959). Pfullingen: Neske, 1957.
On the Way to Language, trans. Peter D. Hertz and Joan Stambaugh. New York: Harper & Row, 1966.
The first essay of US, namely "Die Sprache," was translated by Albert Hofstadter and appeared in *Poetry, Language, Thought*, 189-210.
Gelassenheit (1962). Pfullingen: Neske, 1959.
Discourse on Thinking, trans. John M. Anderson and E. Hans Freund. New York: Harper & Row, 1966.
Die Technik und die Kehre (1962). Pfullingen: Neske, 1962.
"The Question Concerning Technology," trans. William Lovitt, in *The Question Concerning Technology and Other Essays*, 3-35.
"The Turning," trans. William Lovitt, in *The Question*, 36-49.
Wegmarken (1967). Frankfurt: Klostermann, 1978.
Die Grundprobleme der Phänomenologie (1927), ed. F.-W. von Hermann. Frankfurt: Klostermann, 1975.
The Basic Problems of Phenomenology, trans. Albert Hofstadter. Bloomington: Indiana University Press, 1982.
Logik. Die Frage nach der Wahrheit (1925-1926), ed. Walter Biemel. Frankfurt: Klostermann, 1976.
Prolegomena zur Geschichte des Zeitbegriffs (1925), ed. Petra Jaeger. Frankfurt: Klostermann, 1976.

II. BOOKS AND ARTICLES ON HEIDEGGER"S PHILOSOPHY AND HIS CONCEPTION OF THE SCIENCES

Ahlers, Rolf. "Technologie und Wissenschaft bei Heidegger und Marcuse," in *Zeitschrift für philosophische Forschung*, 25 (1971), pp. 575-590.

Alderman, Harold G. "Heidegger's Critique of Science and Technology," in *Heidegger and Modern Philosophy. Critical Essays*, ed. Michael Murray. New Haven: Yale University Press, 1971, pp. 35-50.

Apel, Karl-Otto. *Dasein und Erkennen. Eine erkenntnistheoretische Interpretation der Philosophie Martin Heideggers*. Bonn, 1950.

———. "Wissenschaft als Emanzipation?" in *Zeitschrift für allgemeine Wissenschaftstheorie*, 1 (1970), pp. 173-195.

Astrada, Carlos, et al. *Martin Heideggers Einfluss auf die Wissenschaften aus Anlass seines 60. Geburtstages*. Bern: A. Francke, 1949.

Ballard, Edward G. "Heidegger's View and Evaluation of Nature and Natural Science," in *Heidegger and the Path of Thinking*, ed. John C. Sallis. Pittsburgh: Duquesne University Press, 1970, pp. 37-64.

Beaufret, Jean. *Dialogue avec Heidegger*, 3 vols. Paris: Minuit, 1973-1974.

———. "Heidegger et le probleme de la verite," in *Fontaine*, 63 (1947), pp. 758-785.

Biemel, Walter. *Heidegger. An Illustrated Study*, trans. J. L. Mehta. New York: Harcourt, Brace, Jovanovich, 1976.

Birault, Henri. "Existence et verite d'apres Heidegger," in *Revue de Metaphysique et de Morale*, 56 (1950), pp. 35-87.

———. *Heidegger et l'experience de la pensee*. Paris: Gallimard, 1978.

Bretschneider, Willy. *Sein und Wahrheit. Uber die Zusammengehörigkeit von Sein und Wahrheit im Denken Martin Heideggers*. Meisenheim am Glan: Hain, 1965.

Chapelle, A. *L'Ontologie phenomenologique de Heidegger*. Paris: Editions Universitaires, 1962.

Gethmann, Carl Friedrich. *Verstehen und Auslegung. Das Methodenproblem in der Philosophie Martin Heideggers*. Bonn: Bouvier, 1974.

———. "Zu Heideggers Wahrheitsfrage," in *Kantstudien*, 65 (1974), pp. 186-200.

Giroux, Laurent. "L'Historialite chez Heidegger et son rapport a la philosophie de Wilhelm Dilthey," in *Dialogue*, 15(1976), pp. 583-594.
Gründer, Karlfried. "Heidegger's Critique of Science," in *Philosophy Today*, 7 (1963), pp. 15-32.
———. "Martin Heideggers Wissenschaftskritik in ihren geschichtlichen Zusammenhängen," in *Archiv für Philosophie*, 11 (1961), pp. 312-335.
Kelkel, Arion L. *La legende de l'etre. Langage et poesie chez Heidegger*. Paris: Vrin, 1980.
Kisiel, Theodore J. "Heidegger and the New Image of Science," in *Research in Phenomenology*, 7 (1977), 162-181.
———. "On the Dimensions of a Phenomenology of Science in Husserl and the Young Doctor Heidegger," in *Journal of the British Society for Phenomenology*, 4 (1973), pp. 217-234.
———. "Science, Phenomenology, and the Thinking of Being," in *Phenomenology and the Natural Sciences*, ed. Joseph J. Kockelmans and Theodore J. Kisiel. Evanston: Northwestern University Press, 1970, pp. 167-183.
Kockelmans, Joseph J. "Being-True as the Fundamental and Basic Determination of Being," paper presented at the 17th annual meeting of the Heidegger Conference in New Hampshire, May, 13-15, 1983.
———. "Destructive Retrieve and Hermeneutic Phenomenology in 'Being and Time'," in *Research in Phenomenology*, 7 (1977), pp. 106-137.
———. "Heidegger on the Essential Difference and Necessary Relationship Between Philosophy and Science," in *Phenomenology and the Natural Sciences*, ed. Joseph J. Kockelmans and Theodore J. Kisiel. Evanston: Northwestern University Press, 1970, pp. 147-166.
———. "Heidegger on Theology," in *The Southwestern Journal of Philosophy*, 4 (1973), pp. 85-108.
———. *Martin Heidegger. A First Introduction to His Philosophy*. Pittsburgh: Duquesne University Press, 1965.
———. "Heidegger's Fundamental Ontology and Kant's Transcendental Doctrine of Method," in *Kant and Phenomenology*, ed. Thomas M. Seebohm and Joseph J. Kockelmans. Washington, D.C.: University Press of America, 1984.
———. *On the Truth of Being. Reflections on Heidegger's Later Philosophy*. Bloomington, Ind.: Indiana University Press, 1984.
———. "The Era of the World-as-Picture," in *Phenomenology and the Natural Sciences*, ed. Joseph J. Kockelmans and Theodore

J. Kisiel. Evanston: Northwestern University Press, 1970, pp. 184-201.

Maurer, Reinhart. "From Heidegger to Practical Philosophy," in *Idealistic Studies*, 3 (1973), pp. 133-162.

Mehta, Jarava Lal. *Martin Heidegger: The Way and the Vision*. Honolulu: University of Hawaii Press, 1976.

———. *The Philosophy of Martin Heidegger*. New York: Harper & Row, 1971.

Pöggeler, Otto. *Der Denkweg Martin Heideggers*. Pfullingen: Neske, 1963.

———. "'Historicity' in Heidegger's Late Work," in *The Southwestern Journal of Philosophy*, 4 (1973), pp. 53-73.

Richardson, William J. "Heidegger's Critique of Science," in *The New Scholasticism*, 42 (1968), pp. 511-536.

———. *Heidegger. Through Phenomenology to Thought*. The Hague: Nijhoff, 1963.

Sallis, John C. "Towards the Movement of Reversal: Science, Technology, and the Language of Homecoming," in *Heidegger and the Path of Thinking*, ed. John C. Sallis. Pittsburgh: Duquesne University Press, 1970, pp. 138-168.

Schöfer, Erasmus. "Heidegger's Language: Metalogical Forms of Thought and Grammatical Specialties," in *On Heidegger and Language*, ed. Joseph J. Kockelmans. Evanston: Northwestern University Press, 1972, pp. 281-287.

Schrag, Calvin O. "Heidegger on Repetition and Historical Understanding," in *Philosophy East and West*, 20 (1970), pp. 287-295.

———. "Phenomenology, Ontology, and History in the Philosophy of Martin Heidegger, in *Revue Internationale de Philosophie*, 12 (1958), pp. 117-132.

Seigfried, Hans. "Descriptive Phenomenology and Constructivism," in *Philosophy and Phenomenological Research*, 37 (1976), pp. 248-261.

———. "Heidegger's Longest Day: 'Being and Time' and the Sciences," in *Philosophy Today*, 22 (1978), pp. 319-331.

Sheehan, Thomas. "Heidegger's Early Years: Fragments for a Philosophical Biography," in *Heidegger: The Man and the Thinker*, ed. Thomas Sheehan. Chicago: Precedent Publishing, 1981, pp. 3-19.

Watson, James R. "Heidegger's Hermeneutic Phenomenology," in *Philosophy Today*, 15 (1971), pp. 30-43.

Wiplinger, Fr. *Wahrheit und Geschichtlichkeit*. Freiburg: Alber, 1961.

III. COLLECTIONS OF ESSAYS ON HEIDEGGER'S THOUGHT

Ballard, Edward G. and Charles E. Scott, eds. *Martin Heidegger: In Europe and America*. The Hague: Nijhoff, 1973.
Frings, Manfred S., ed. *Heidegger and the Quest for Truth*. Chicago: Quadrangle Books, 1968.
Gadamer, H. G., W. Marx, C. F. von Weizsäcker, eds. *Heidegger: Freiburger Universitätsvorträge zu seinem Gedenken*. Freiburg: Alber, 1977.
Guzzoni, Ute, ed. *Nachdenken über Heidegger*. Hildesheim: Gerstenberg Verlag, 1980.
Kockelmans, Joseph J., ed. *On Heidegger and Language*. Evanston: Northwestern University Press, 1972.
Murray, Michael, ed. *Heidegger and Modern Philosophy: Critical Essays*. New Haven: Yale University Press, 1978.
Pöggeler, Otto, ed. *Heidegger: Perspektiven zur Deutung seines Werkes*. Cologne: Kiepenheuer und Witsch, 1969.
Sallis, John C., ed. *Heidegger and the Path of Thinking*. Pittsburgh: Duquesne University Press, 1970.
Sheehan, Thomas, ed. *Heidegger: The Man and the Thinker*. Chicago: Precedent Publishing, Inc., 1981.
Anteile. Martin Heidegger zum 60. Geburtstag. Frankfurt: Klostermann, 1970.
Durchblicke. Martin Heidegger zum 80. Geburtstag. Frankfurt: Klostermann, 1970.
Martin Heidegger zum siebzigsten Geburstag. Pfullingen: Neske, 1959.

IV. OTHER PUBLICATIONS QUOTED OR USED IN WRITING THIS BOOK

Apel, Karl-Otto. *Analytic Philosophy of Language and the Geisteswissenschaften*. Dordrecht: Reidel, 1967.
Betti, Emilio. *Allgemeine Auslegungslehre als Methodik der Geisteswissenschaften*. Tübingen: Mohr, 1967.
———. *Die Hermeneutik als allgemeine Methodik der Geisteswissenschaften*. Tübingen: Mohr, 1962.
———. *Zur Grundlegung einer allgemeinen Auslegungslehre*. Tübingen: Mohr, 1967.
Biemel, Walter. "Husserl's *Encyclopaedia Britannica* Article and Heidegger's Remarks Thereon," in *Husserl: Expositions and Appraisals*, ed. Frederick Elliston and Peter McCormick. Notre Dame: University of Notre Dame Press, 1977, pp. 286-303.

BIBLIOGRAPHY

Bleicher, Josef, ed. *Contemporary Hermeneutics: Hermeneutics as Method, Philosophy, and Critique*. London: Routledge and Kegan Paul, 1980.

Braig, Carl. *Vom Sein. Abriss der Ontologie*. Freiburg: Herder, 1896.

Bretano, Franz. *On the Several Senses of Being in Aristotle*, trans. Rolf George. Berkeley: University of California Press, 1975.

Bubner, Rüdiger, Konrad Cramer, and Reiner Wiehl, eds., *Hermeneutik und Dialektik*, 2 vols. Tübingen: Mohr, 1970.

Butts, R. E. and J. Hintikka, *Historical and Philosophical Dimensions of Logic, Methodology, and Philosophy of Science*. Dordrecht: Reidel, 1975.

Carnap, Rudolf. *Philosophical Foundations of Physics*. New York: Macmillan, 1966.

Cavailles, Jean. "On Logic and the Theory of Science," trans. Theodore J. Kisiel, in *Phenomenology and the Natural Sciences*, ed. Joseph J. Kockelmans and Theodore J. Kisiel. Evanston: Northwestern University Press, 1970, pp. 353-409.

Collingwood, R. G., *The Idea of History*. New York: Oxford University Press, 1964.

Descartes, Rene. *Rules for the Direction of the Mind*, in *Philosophical Works of Descartes*, trans. E.S. Haldane and G.T.R. Ross. New York: Dover Publications, 1931.

Diemer, Alwin. "Die Differenzierung der Wissenschaften in die Natur- und Geisteswissenschaften und die Begründung der Geisteswissenschaften als Wissenschaften," in *Beiträge zur Entwicklung der Wissenschaftstheorie im 19. Jahrhundert*, ed. A. Diemer. Meisenheim am Glan: Hain, 1968, pp. 174-223.

Diltehy, Wilhelm. *Gesammelte Schriften*, 17 vols. Göttingen: Vandenhoeck & Ruprecht, 1914-1974. Vol. V. *Die geistige Welt: Einleitung in die Philosophie des Lebens*. Erste Hälfte: *Abhandlungen zur Grundlegung der Geisteswissenschaften*, ed. Georg Mish (1924). Vol. VII. *Der Aufbau der geschichtlichen Welt in den Geisteswissenschaften*, ed. Bernard Groethuysen (1927).

Drüe, Hermann. *Edmund Husserls System der phänomenologischen Psychologie*. Berlin: de Gruyter, 1963.

Einstein, Albert and L. Infeld. *The Evolution in Physics*. New York: Simon & Schuster, 1961.

Gadamer, Hans-Georg. "The Continuity of History and the Existential Moment," in *Philosophy Today*, 16 (1972), pp. 230-240.

———. "Hermeneutics and Social Science," in *Cultural Hermenetics*, 2 (1975), pp. 307-316.
———. "Hermeneutik als theoretische und praktische Aufgabe," in *Revue Internationale de Philosophie*, 33 (1979), pp. 239-259.
———. "Hermeneutik und Historismus," in *Philosophische Rundschau*, 9 (1962), pp. 241-276.
———. "The Historicity of Understanding as Hermeneutic Principle," in *Heidegger and Modern Philosophy. Critical Essays*, ed. M. Murray. New Haven: Yale University Press, 1978, pp. 161-183.
———. *Kleine Schriften*, 4 vols. Tübingen: Mohr, 1967ff.
———. *Philosophical Hermeneutics*, trans. David E. Linge. Berkeley: University of California Press, 1976.
———. "Practical Philosophy as a Model of the Human Sciences," in *Research in Phenomenology*, 9 (1979), pp. 74-86.
———. "Le probleme hermeneutique," in *Archives de Philosophie*, 33 (1970), pp. 5-15.
———. Le probleme de la conscience historique. Louvain: Publications Universitaires de Louvain, 1963.
———. "The Problem of Historical Consciousness," in *Graduate Faculty Philosophical Journal*, 5 (1975), pp. 8-52.
———. *Truth and Method*, trans. Garrett Barden and John Cummings. New York: The Seabury Press, 1975.
———. "Die Universalität des hermeneutischen Problems," in *Philosophisches Jahrbuch*, 73 (1966), pp. 215-225.
———. "Vom Zirkel des Verstehens," in *Martin Heidegger zum siebzigsten Geburtstag*, ed. Günther Neske. Pfullingen: Neske, 1959, pp. 24-34.
Habermasn, Jürgen. *Theory and Practice*, trans. John Viertel. Boston: Beacon Press, 1980.
———. *Zur Logik der Sozialwissenschaften*. Tübingen: Mohr, 1967.
Heelan, Patrick, "Natural Science as a Hermeneutic of Instrumentation," in *Philosophy of Science*, 50 (1983), pp. 181-204.
———. *Space-Perception and the Philosophy of Science*. Berkeley: University of California Press, 1982.
Hegel, Georg, Friedrich, Wilhelm. *Phenomenology of Mind*, trans. J. Baillie. London: Allen & Unwin, 1964.
Heisenberg, Werner, *Das Naturbild der heutigen Physik*. Hamburg: Rowohlt, 1956.
———. *Wandlungen in den Grundlagen der Naturwissenschaften*. Berlin: de Gruyter, 1949.

BIBLIOGRAPHY

Hempel, Carl. *Aspects of Scientific Explanation and Other Essays in the Philosophy of Science.* New York: The Free Press, 1965.

Hesse, Mary. *Revolutions and Reconstructions in the Philosophy of Science.* Bloomington, Ind.: Indiana University Press, 1980.

Hübner, Kurt. *Critique of Scientific Reason,* trans. Paul R. Dixon and Hollis M. Dixon. Chicago: University of Chicago Press, 1983.

Husserl, Edmund. *Die Idee der Phänomenologie,* ed. Walter Biemel. The Hague: Nijhoff, 1950. English translation by William P. Alston and George Nakhnikian, *The Idea of Phenomenology.* The Hague: Nijhoff, 1964.

———. *Ideen zu einer reinen Phänomenologie und phänomenologischen Philosophie,* vol. I (1913), ed. Walter Biemel. The Hague: Nijhoff, 1950. English translation by F. Kersten, *Ideas Pertaining to a Pure Phenomenology and to a Phenomenological Philosophy.* The Hague: Nijhoff, 1982.

———. *Ideen.* Zweites Buch: *Phänomenologische Untersuchungen zur Konstitution,* ed. Marly Biemel. The Hague: Nijhoff, 1952.

———. *Ideen.* Drittes Buch: *Die Phänomenologie und die Fundamente der Wissenschaften,* ed. Marly Biemel. The Hague: Nijhoff, 1952.

———. *Die Krisis der europäischen Wissenschaften und die transzendentale Phänomenologie. Eine Einleitung in die phänomenologische Philosophie,* ed. Walter Biemel. The Hague: Nijhoff, 1954. English translation by David Carr, *The Crisis of European Sciences.* Evanston: Northwestern University Press, 1970.

———. *Logische Untersuchungen* (1900-1901), 3 vols. Halle a.S.: Max Niemeyer, 1921-1922. English translation by J. N. Findlay, *Logical Investigations,* 2 vols. New York: Humanities Press, 1970.

———. *Phänomenologische Psychologie,* ed. Walter Biemel. The Hague: Nijhoff, 1962.

———. "Philosophie als strenge Wissenschaft," in *Logos,* 1 (1910-1911), pp. 289-341. English translation by Quentin Lauer, "Philosophy as Rigorous Science," in Edmund Husserl, *Phenomenology and the Crisis of Philosophy.* New York: Harper and Row, 1965.

Kant, Immanuel. *Critique of Pure Reason,* trans. Norman Kemp Smith. New York: St. Martin's Press, 1965.

———. *Prolegomena to Any Future Metaphysics,* trans. Lewis Beck. New York: The Bobbs-Merrill Company, 1950.

Kisiel, Theodore J. "The Rationality of Scientific Discovery," in Theodore F. Geraets, ed., *Rationality To-Day*. Ottawa: The University of Ottawa Press, 1979, pp. 401-411.

―――. "Zu einer Hermeneutik naturwissenschaftlicher Entdeckung," in *Zeitschrift für allgemeine Wissenschaftstheorie*, 2(1979), pp. 195-221.

Kockelmans, Joseph J. *A First Introduction to Husserl's Phenomenology*. Pittsburgh: Duquesne University Press, 1967.

―――. *Edmund Husserl's Phenomenological Psychology*. Pittsburgh: Duquesne University Press, 1967.

―――. "Empirische und hermeneutische Psychologie. Gedanken zu einer mehrdimensionalen Bestimmung des Problems der Psychologie," in *Versuche über Erfahrung*, ed. A. Metraux. Bern: Hans Huber, 1976, pp. 35-49.

―――. "The Foundations of Morality and the Human Sciences," in *Analecta Husserliana*, ed. A.-T. Tymieniecka and Calvin O. Schrag, vol. 15 (1983), pp. 369-386.

―――. "Hermeneutic Phenomenology and the Science of History," in *Phänomenologische Forschungen*, 2 (1976), pp. 130-179.

―――. "L'Objectivite des sciences positives d'apres le point de vue de la phenomenologie," in *Archives de Philosophie*, 27 (1964), pp. 339-355.

―――. "On the Meaning of Scientific Revolutions," in *Philosophy Forum* 11 (1972), pp. 243-264.

―――. "Phenomenology and the Critique of the Scientific Tradition," in *Essays in Memory of Aron Gurwitsch*, ed. Lester E. Embree. Washington, D.C.; University Press of America, 1984.

―――. *Phenomenology and Physical Science*. Pittsburgh: Duquesne University Press, 1966.

―――. "Phenomenology and Psychology: Theoretical Problems in Phenomenological Psychology," in *Phenomenology and the Social Sciences*, ed. Maurice Natanson. Evanston: Northwestern University Press, 1973, vol. I, pp. 225-280.

―――, ed. *Phenomenology. The Philosophy of Edmund Husserl and Its Interpretation*. Garden City: Doubleday, 1967.

―――, ed. *Philosophy of Science: The Historical Background*. New York: The Free Press, 1969.

―――. "Reflections on Lakatos' Methodology of Scientific Research Programs," in *The Structure and Development of Science*, ed. G. Radnitzky and G. Andersson. Dordrecht: Reidel, 1979, pp. 196-202.

―――. "Reflections on Social Theory," in *Human Studies*, 1 (1978), pp. 1-15.

———. "Science and Discipline. Some Historical and Critical Reflections," in *Interdisciplinarity and Higher Education*, ed. Joseph J. Kockelmans. University Park, PA: The Pennsylvania State University Press, 1979, pp. 17-24.

———. "Some Reflections on the Meaning and Function of Interpretative Science," in *Tijdschrift voor Filosofie*, 42 (1980), pp. 294-324.

———. "Toward an Interpretative or Hermeneutic Social Science," in *Graduate Faculty Philosophical Journal*, 5 (1975), pp. 73-96.

———. "World-Constitution. Reflections on Husserl's Transcendental Idealism," in *Analecta Husserliana*, ed. A.-T. Tymieniecka, vol. I (1972), pp. 11-35.

———. *The World in Science and Philosophy*. Milwaukee: The Bruce Publishing Company, 1969.

Kockelmans, Joseph J. and Theodore J. Kisiel, eds., *Phenomenology and the Natural Sciences: Essays and Translations*. Evanston: Northwestern University Press, 1970.

Krimerman, Leonard I., ed., *The Natura and Scope of Social Science: A Critical Anthology*. New York: Appleton-Century-Crofts, 1969.

Kuhn, Thomas. *The Essential Tension*. Chicago: University of Chicago Press, 1977.

———. *The Structure of Scientific Revolutions*. Chicago: University of Chicago Press, 1970.

Kwant, Remy C. *From Phenomenology to Metaphysics: An Inquiry into the Last Period of Merleau-Ponty's Philosophy*. Pittsburgh: Duquesne University Press, 1966.

———. *The Phenomenology of Merleau-Ponty*. Pittsburgh: Duquesne University Press, 1963.

Ladriere, Jean. *Les limites internes des formalismes*. Louvain: Nauwelaerts, 1957.

———. "Mathematics in a Philosophy of Science," trans. Theodore J. Kisiel, in *Phenomenology and the Natural Sciences*, ed. Joseph J. Kockelmans and Theodore J. Kisiel. Evanston: Northwestern University Press, 1970, pp. 466-499.

———. "Sciences et discours rationnel," in *Encyclopedia Universalis*, Paris, 1972, vol. 14, pp. 754-767.

Lakatos, I. and A. Musgrave, eds., *Criticism and the Growth of Knowledge*. Cambridge: University Press, 1974.

Landgrebe, Ludwig, "Seinsregionen und regionale Ontologien in Husserls Phänomenologie," in *Studium Generale*, 9 (1956), pp. 313-324.

Levinas, Emmanuel. *Theorie de l'intuition dans la phenomenologie de Husserl.* Paris: Vrin, 1963.
Litt, Theodor. *Das Allgemeine im Aufbau der geisteswissenschaftlichen Erkenntnis.* Groningen: Wolters, 1959.
McCarthy, Thomas. *The Critical Theory of Jürgen Habermas.* Cambridge, Mass.: The MIT Press, 1978.
Merleau-Ponty, Maurice. *Consciousness and the Acquisition of Language,* trans. Hugh J. Silverman. Evanston: Northwestern University Press, 1973.
Nagel, Ernst. *The Structure of Science. Problems in the Logic of Scientific Explanation.* London: Routledge and Kegan Paul, 1961.
Newton, Isaac. *Mathematical Principles of Natural Philosophy and the System of the World,* trans. A. Motte (1729), revised translation by Florian Cajori. Berkeley: University of California Press, 1946.
Oakeshott, Michael. *Rationalism in Politics and Other Essays.* London: Methuen and Company, 1962.
Palmer, Richard. *Hermeneutics: Interpretation Theory in Schleiermacher, Dilthey, Heidegger, and Gadamer.* Evanston: Northwestern University Press, 1969.
Polanyi, M. *Personel Knowledge. Towards a Post-Critical Philosophy.* New York: Harper & Row, 1964.
Popper, Sir Karl. *Conjectures and Refutations.* London: Routledge and Kegan Paul, 1963.
―――. *The Logic of Scientific Discovery.* New York: Harper & Row, 1965.
―――. "The Logic of the Social Sciences," in *The Positivist Dispute in German Sociology,* ed. Theodore W. Adorno, et al. New York: Harper & Row, 1976, pp. 87-104.
Radnitzky, Gerard. *Contemporary Schools in Metascience,* 2 vols. Göteborg: Akademiförlaget, 1970.
Radnitzky, G. and G. Andersson, eds., *Progress and Rationality: The Structure and Development of Science.* Dordrecht: Reidel, 1979.
Ricoeur, Paul. *The Conflict of Interpretations. Essays in Hermeneutics,* ed. Don Ihde. Evanston: Northwestern University Press, 1974.
―――. "Expliquer et comprendre: sur quelques connexions remarquables entre la theorie du texte et la theorie de l'action," in *Revue Philosophique de Louvain,* 75 (1977), pp. 126-147.
―――. "The Hermeneutical Function of Distanciation," in *Philosophy Today,* 17 (1973), pp. 129-141.

———. *Hermeneutics and the Human Sciences*, ed. John B. Thompson. New York: Cambridge University Press, 1981.
———. "History and Hermeneutics," in *Journal of Philosophy*, 73 (1976), pp. 683-694.
———. *History and Truth*, trans. C. A. Kelbley. Evanston: Northwestern University Press, 1965.
———. *Interpretation Theory: Discourse and the Surplus of Meaning*. Fort Worth: Texas Christian University Press, 1976.
———. "The Model of the Text: Meaningful Action Considered as a Text," in *Social Research*, 38 (1971), pp. 529-562.
———. "Phenomenologie et hermeneutique," in *Man and World*, 7 (1974), pp. 223-253.
———. "Phenomenology and the Social Sciences," in *Annals of Phenomenological Sociology*, 1 (1973), pp. 145-159.
Rothacker, Erich. *Einleitung in die Geisteswissenschaften*. Tübingen: Mohr, 1930.
Rudner, Richard S. *Philosophy of Social Science*. Englewood Cliffs: Prentice Hall, 1966.
Riedel, Manfred. "Geisteswissenschaften -- Grundlagenkrise und Grundlagenstreit," in *Meyers Enzyklopädisches Lexikon*. Mannheim: Bibliographisches Institut, 1973, vol. 9, pp. 838-844.
Ritter, Joachim, *Die Aufgabe der Geisteswissenschaften in der modernen Gesellschaft*. Münster: Aschendorff, 1963.
Sartre, Jean-Paul. *Being and Nothingness*, trans. Hazel Barnes. New York: Philosophical Library, 1956.
Scheffler, L. *The Anatomy of Inquiry: Philosophical Studies in the Theory of Science*. New York: Alfred Knopf, 1963.
Schleiermacher, F. *Hermeneutik*, ed. H. Kimmerle. Heidelberg: Winter, 1959.
Schnübbe, O. *Der Existenzbegriff in der Theologie Bultmanns*. Göttingen: Vandenhoeck & Ruprecht, 1955.
Schrag, Calvin O. *Radical Reflection and the Origin of the Human Sciences*. West Lafayette, Ind.: Purdue University Press, 1980.
Seebohm, Thomas M. *Zur Kritik der hermeneutischen Vernunft*. Bonn: Bouvier, 1972.
Sneed, Joseph. *The Logical Structure of Mathematical Physics*. Dordrecht: Reidel, 1971.
Stegmüller, Wolfgang. *Probleme und Resultate der Wissenschaftstheorie und analytischen Philosophie*, 4 vols. Berlin: Springer Verlag, 1969-1975.
———. *The Structuralist View of Theories*. New York: Springer Verlag, 1979.

―――. *The Structure and Dynamics of Theories*, trans W. Wohlhuetter. New York: Springer Verlag, 1976.
Strasser, Stephen. *Phenomenology and the Human Sciences*. Pittsburgh: Duquesne University Press, 1963.
Suppe, Frederick. *The Structure of Scientific Theories*. Urbana: University of Illinois Press, 1977.
Taylor, Charles. *The Explanation of Behavior*. London: Routledge and Kegan Paul, 1964.
Wach, Joachim. *Das Verstehen. Grundzüge einer Geschichte der hermeneutischen Theorie im 19. Jahrhundert*, 3 vols. Tübingen: Mohr, 1926-1933.
Weizsäcker, Carl von. *Der Garten des Menschlichen. Beiträge zur geschichtlichen Anthropologie*. Munich: Carl Hanser, 1977.
Whittaker, E. T. *From Euclid to Eddington*. Cambridge: University Press, 1949.
Winch, Peter. *The Idea of Social Science*. New York: Oxford University Press, 1958.
Wright, Georg Henrik von. *Explanation and Understanding*. Ithaca: Cornell University Press, 1971.

INDEX OF NAMES

Adorno, Theodor, 12
Agricola, Georgius, 143
Albert the Great, Saint, 156, 180
Apel, Karl-Otto, 13
Aristotle, *xi*, 22, 23, 24, 28, 64, 65, 91, 94, 145, 146, 147, 148, 149, 150, 153, 156, 157, 164, 174, 175, 181, 185, 215
Augustine, Saint, 23

Balliani, Giovanni Battista, 144
Bergson, Henri, 26, 28, 40
Biemel, Marly, 105
Blondel, Maurice, 23
Boeckh, August, 46
Bohr, Niels, 137, 141
Braig, Carl, 23
Brentano, Frantz, 14, 22, 23, 27, 28, 30, 31, 32, 37
Bultmann, Rudolf, 50

Calinich, Ernst, Adolf, Edward, 41
Carnap, Rudolf, 6, 9, 12
Cohen, Hermann, 46
Comte, Auguste, 44, 46, 225
Copernicus, Nicolaus, 143, 145
Cotes, Roger, 144

Dahrendorf Rolf, 12

Descartes, Rene, 23, 54, 55, 56, 61, 69, 78, 90, 94, 144, 151, 162, 180, 181, 182, 183, 184, 185, 187, 188
Dilthey, Wilhelm, *xi*, 13, 22, 24, 25, 26, 27, 28, 29, 30, 37, 38, 39, 40, 42, 43, 46, 47, 48, 50, 155, 215, 233, 234, 238, 241, 242, 244
Dostoevsky, Fedor, 23
Droysen, Johann, 46
Drue, Hermann, 108
Duhem, Pierre, 8
Dumery, Henri, 23

Einstein, Albert, 8, 137
Ellul, Jacques, 13
Eudoxus, 146

Feyerabend, Paul, 12, 18
Fichte, Johann, Gottlieb, 23, 57, 69

Gadamer, Hans-Georg, 47, 220
Galilei, 144, 148, 149, 150, 153
George, Stefan, 23
Gethmann, Carl-Friedrich, 70
Geyser, Joseph, 22
Goethe, Wolfgang, 170
Grabmann, Martin, 22
Gröber, Conrad, 22

INDEX OF NAMES

Habermas, Jürgen, 12, 13
Hanson, N.R., 18
Hartmann, Nicholai, 235
Hegel, Georg, Friedrich, Wilhelm, 23, 43, 45, 55, 57, 61, 62, 95, 237
Heisenberg, Werner, 17, 137, 141
Hempel, Carl, 12
Heraclitus, 97
Herschel, John, 16
Hertz, Heinrich, 8
Hölderlin Friedrich, 21
Hübner, Kurt, 9, 13
Husserl, Edmund, *xi*, 12, 14, 16, 17, 22, 23, 24, 26, 27, 28, 30, 31, 32, 33, 34, 35, 36, 37, 38, 39, 40, 47, 48, 49, 50, 54, 57, 61, 62, 69, 70, 71, 94, 95, 96, 97, 103, 104, 107, 108, 109, 110, 111, 112, 113, 215, 217, 221, 228, 229, 230, 231, 263n.

Isaac Israeli, 94

Jaspers, Karl, 215
Johannes Duns Scotus, 22

Kant, Immanuel, *xi*, 12, 13, 15, 16, 23, 25, 27, 28, 29, 34, 35, 47, 53, 54, 56, 57, 58, 61, 64, 69, 71, 78, 91, 92, 94, 95, 112, 145, 192, 222
Kepler, Johann, 143
Kierkegaard, Søren, 22
Kuhn, Thomas, 8, 9, 12, 13, 18, 158
Külpe, Oswald, 22

Lakatos, Imre, 9, 12, 13
Landgrebe, Ludwig, 104
Lask, Emil, 34
Leibniz, Gottfried, Wilhelm, 144, 151
Lipps, Theodor, 30
Lotze, Hermann, 44, 235

Marx, Karl, 225, 237
Maxwell, James, 8
Merleau-Ponty, Maurice, 12, 14
Merton, Robert, 13
Messer, August, 22
Meyerson, Émile, 8
Mill, John Stuart, 16, 29, 42
Misch, Georg, 26
Mumford, Lewis, 13
Musgrave, Alan, 13

Nagel, Ernest, 12
Natorp, Paul, 46
Newton, Isaac, 8, 28, 137, 143, 144, 145, 146, 147, 148, 149, 150, 151, 223, 224, 225
Nietzsche, Friedrich, Wilhelm, 22, 44, 162, 250, 251

Paracelsus, 143
Parmenides, 23, 94, 188
Pascal, Blaise, 46
Paul, Saint, 23
Paulsen, Friedrich, 14, 30
Peirce, Charles, 225
Planck, Max, 167
Plato, *xi*, 34, 54, 64, 142, 145, 146, 157, 162, 251
Polanyi, Michael, 18
Popper, Karl, 8, 9, 12, 13, 225, 227
Ptolemy, 145

INDEX OF NAMES

Radnitzky, Gerard, 12, 13
Ravaisson, Félix, 23
Richardson, William, 18, 69, 192
Rickert, Heinrich, xi, 22, 28, 30, 32, 46, 235
Ricoeur, Paul, 47, 220
Rilke, Rainer Maria, 23
Roger Bacon, 16
Russell, Bertrand, 16

Scheler, Max, 26, 27, 28, 34, 35, 37, 40, 47
Schelling, Friedrich, Wilhelm, Joseph, 23
Schiel, J., 42
Schleiermacher, Friedrich, Ernst, Daniel, 50, 86, 238, 241, 242, 244, 245, 246
Schneider, Arthur, Carl, August, 22
Schrag, Calvin O., 220, 223
Schutz, Alfred, 281n.
Seigfried, Hans, 18
Sheehan, Thomas, 23
Stegmüller, Wolfgang, 9, 12
Stumpf, Carl, 14, 30
Sneed, Joseph, 9, 12
Suarez, 181

Thomas Aquinas, Saint, 180
Thomas von Ehrfurt, 22
Toulmin, Stephen, 13
Trakl, Georg, 23

Vico, Giovanni Battista, 43, 45, 46

Weber, Max, 13, 227, 233, 234, 235
Weierstrass, Karl, Theodor, Wilhelm, 30

Weinberg, Alvin, 12
Weizsäcker, Carl von, 17
Weizsäcker, Victor von, 13
Whewell, William, 16
Windelband, Wilhelm, 28, 30, 46
Wittgenstein, Ludwig, 16
Wundt, Wilhelm, 14

Yorck von Wartenburg, Paul, Graf, 26, 47

INDEX OF TOPICS

Abschattungen (perspectives), 32
Aletheia, as non-concealment, 65, 73. See Truth
Acceleration, 148
Analytic geometry, 151
Analytic of Dasein, 27-40, 48-49, 53, 59, 66-67. See Fundamental ontology
Ancient science, vs. modern, 140-42, 145-48, 156-57, 162
Anthropology (philosophical), 40, 178-79
Appearance (mere), 63-64
A priori (in phenomenology), 34-35
A priori framework of meaning in human sciences, 221-28; and relativism, 224; formal ontological framework, 222-23; projection of, 221-23; two kinds of, 226-27
Argumentum ex re, 157
Argumentum ex verbis, 157
As, apophantic vs. hermeneutic, 81-82, 98, 193
Atomic age, 252-55; and science and technology, 253; dangers of, 252-55
Axiology, 44, 235; problem of, 235
Axiomata, 150

Being, 53; absolute, 35-36; as pure consciousness, 36; immanent, 35; meaning of, 35-36, 53; priority of question of, 49-53; pure, 35; transcendent, 36; truth of, 53
Being, as being an object for a subject, 188
Being-in-the-world, 73, 74-75
Being-true, 97; as uncovered, 97-98; as uncovering, 97-98
Besinnung (reflection), 172
Bestand, 176-77; as constant availability, 176
Bildung (formation, education), 46-47

Calculation, 141, 167
Calculus, 151
Canons of hermeneutics, 236-48; canon of autonomy of object, 237-38; of optimal interpretation, 238; of relevance, 240; of the greatest familiarity with the phenomena, 239-40; function of, 236-37; hermeneutic circle, 239-40
Care (*Sorge*), 92-93; and eksistentiality, 194; and facticity, 194; and fallenness, 194

INDEX OF TOPICS

Categorial Intuition, 33-34
Cause, Aristotle's theory of, 174-75
Certainty, 34. See Truth
Chremata, 142
Circumspection, 119-21; and perception, 120-21
Concern (Besorgen), 75; and theoretical knowledge, 74-78, 118-19; 176
Concernfully dealing with (praxis), 118-24; and theory, 118-24
Conformity, and truth, 94-96. See Truth
Consciousness (pure), in Husserl's phenomenology, 35-40
Criterion of empirical significance, 6-7
Culture, 133

Dasein, 73, 72-74; and Being, 189
Descriptive human science, 227-31; and empirical human science, 229-30; and general ontology of the world of immediate experience, 229; and intentional analysis, 230-31; and method of free variation, 230-31; and phenomenological reduction, 230-31; as regional ontology, 228-29
Descriptive social science, 227-31; 281n.
Destructive retrieve, 54-55; and hermeneutic phenomenology, 59-62

Dialectic between old and new, 247-48
Dialectic process, and hermeneutic circle, 239-40
Disclosedness (Erschlossenheit), 98
Discovery, 101

Education (Bildung), 46-47
Empirical science, 1-3; 117-38; and modern world, 1-3; importance of, 2-3
Eksistence, 73-74; and transcendence, 73-74
Eksistential, 78-79
Ekstasis, 194-95
Exactitude of science, 154-55
Experience, 61; of nature in ancient and modern science, 145-48; pre-predicative, 94
Experiment, 141; vs. empeiria and experientia, 148-49, 151, 156-57
Evidence, 34; and truth, 94

Facticity, 194
Facts, vs. values, 234-36
Fallenness, 74, 75, 134
Force, 147-48; gravitational, 147; impressed, 147
Fore-conception, 85, 87, 193-94, 242, 244, 245
Fore-having, 85, 87, 193-4, 242
Fore-knowledge, 236, 239, 242
Fore-sight, 85, 87, 193-194, 242
Fore-structure, 242
Formalization, 112, 222-24

Foundational research, 130-33; and fundamental ontology, 132-33; and philosophy, 130-32; and regional ontology, 131-33; vs. philosophy of science, 3-7

Freedom, 99-102, 254; and openness, 100; and modern metaphysics, 180-81; and the open (=world), 99; and truth, 99-102

Free fall, 148-52

Fulfillment, 32-33

Functionalization, 222-23

Fundamental ontology, 53; as analytic of Dasein, 53, 59, 66-67

Fundamentum inconcussum, 183, 187-88

General ontology of world of immediate experience, 229

Generalization, 112; and specialization, 112

Geisteswissenschaften, 30, 41-47, 210-11

Gelassenheit, 254. See Letting-be

Hermeneutic *as*, 81-82, 84, 92, 98, 193; and apophantic *as*, 81-82, 84-85, 98

Hermeneutic circle, 1, 52-53, 82, 85-88, 239-40; and dialectic, 244; and interpretative understanding, 85; and subjective and objective interpretation, 241-42

Hermeneutic phenomenology, 69-71; vs. transcendental phenomenology, 69-71

Hermeneutic situation, 82, 85, 86-88, 193, 201, 205, 243, 246; and fore-conception, 85, 87; and fore-having, 85, 87; and fore-sight, 85, 87

Hermeneutics, 50-67

Historicism, 246-48

Historicity, 59-60, 195-96, 248; and historiology, 196-197; of world, 196

Historiology, 196-201; and eidetic generality of facts, 202; and explanation, 207; and objectivation, 200; and research, 206-207; and thematization, 197; authentic, 201; essence of, 202-209; genuine theme of, 100; idea of, 197; scientificity of, 199; various branches of, 200-01; various forms of, 208

History, 202-03

Horizonal schema, 194-95

Humanism (modern), 179

Human sciences, 210-20; and fundamental ontology, 220-21; and *Geisteswissenschaften*, 210-11; and hermeneutic and critical methods, 218-19; and philosophical anthropology, 219-20; and philosophy, 214-15; and regional ontology, 217-18, 219-20, 221-22; and transcendental analytic of Dasein, 219; crisis of, 220-221; descriptive component of, 219, 228, 231-32; different components of, 219-20; empirical component of, 219, 228, 231-32; thematization of, 216-18, 220-28

Idealism, 89, 92-93
Idealization, 222, 223-24
Ideation (*Wesensschau*), 34, 113
Identification, 33; and evidence, 33-34; and truth, 33-34
Induction, 6, 146
Isotropy, 154
Inspectio sui, 39-40
Instrumental rationality, 249, 253-54
Intentional analysis, 113
Intentionality, 31-33
Interpretative human science, 228, 231-36, 245-48; and canons of hermeneutics, 236-48; and hermeneutic methods, 232-33; and historicism, 246-48; and history, 233-34; value free?, 234-36
Interpretative sociology, 281n.
Interpretative social science, 281n.

Law, 155
Law of inertia, 145
Law of motion (first), 143-45, 147-50
Learning, 142-43
Letting-be (*Gelassenheit*), 101-102, 254
Life-world, 108-09

Logos, 64-65, 78; and truth, 65; as *apophansis*, 83
Lumen naturale (Dasein), 97-98; 100-101, 175

Mathemata, 142
Mathematical, as absolute ground of all knowledge, 184; essence of, 142-44, 150-152, 154, 156, 180; metaphysical meaning of, 180, 182-83
Mathematical physics, 129
Mathematical projection of nature, 150-52
Mathematics, 143-44
Mathematization, 222-23
Meaning (*Sinn*), 82-83
Mediation of traditions, 240-42
Measurement, 141, 167
Method, 53-58; analytic, 56; and compartmentalization, 167; and specialization, 167-68; and subject matter, 54; and truth in science, 7-8, 10; deductive, 56; empirical, 56; transcendental, 53, 56; transcendental doctrine of, 53
Methodology, ontological vs. transcendental, 53-54
Modern era, 177-89; and certitude, 187-88; and proposing positing presentation, 186-87; and world as picture, 186-87; characterization of, 177-81; essence of, 186
Modern metaphysics, 177-89; and epistemology, 181; and

INDEX OF TOPICS

mathematical projection of nature, 182; and *mathesis universalis*, 183; origin of, 180-85

Modern science, 140, 145, 168-71; enigmatic character of, 168, 170-71; mathematical character of, 143-45; vs. ancient and medieval science, 140-42, 145-48, 156-57, 162

Moodness (*Befindlichkeit*), 78-79, 190-91; and thrownness, 191

Motion, 146-48; in ancient vs. modern science, 146-48; natural vs. forced motion, 147-48

Natural science, 139-89; and the Greek way of thinking, 162-63; and technology, 163, 173-77; as a function of the essence of technology, 177; as theory of what is real, 162-72; vs. ancient science of nature, 140-42, 145-48, 156-57, 162

Nihilism, 44, 250-52; and proposing, positing presentation, 251; and will-to-power, 251-52; in Heidegger, 251-52; in Nietzsche, 250-51

Noein, 188

Non-concealment (*aletheia*, truth), 65, 73. See Truth

Objectifying thematization, 165-67; in modern physics, 165-67, 170-72; in the human sciences, 220-28

Objectum vs. *subjectum*, 185-86

Objectivation, 123-29; and thematization, 124-29; essence of, 128; in the natural sciences, 123-24

Ontologies, 102-13; formal, 105-107, 111-12; material, 105-107, 111-13; regional, 102-13

Ontology, scientific character of, 53-55

Ontology of the world of immediate experience, 107-109; and general ontology of the life-world, 108

Open (=world), 99

Openness to the mystery, 138, 254

Part-whole relationships, 239-40

Perception, 31-33, 120-21

Perspectives (*Abschattungen*), 32

Phenomenological psychology, 103

Phenomenology, 57-67; and fundamental ontology, 66-67; and psychology, 36-39; as descriptive psychology, 30-31; as ontology, 66-67; as the method of scientific philosophy, 57-58; as the science of Being, 66; definition of, 65-66; hermeneutic phenomenology, 66-68; hermeneutic vs. transcen-

dental phenomenology, 57-58; meaning of term, 62-66; origin of, 27-39
Phenomenon, 63; in the ordinary sense, 64; in the phenomenological sense, 64; vs. mere appearance, 63; vs. semblance, 63
Philosophy, and empirical science, 134-38; and *Weltanschauung*, 58; as the science of Being, 49-53, 58-59; as universal phenomenological ontology, 68; scientific character of, 53-58
Philosophy of science, 3-17; and hermeneutic phenomenology, 14-17; leading trends of, 10-14; recent developments in, 7-10; vs. foundational research, 3-7
Phusika, 142
Physics, classical vs. atomic, 168-69; privileged position of, 6. See natural science
Picture, 179, 187
Place, 147
Poioumata, 142
Positivism, 14-15, 141
Possible, as theme of historiology, 199, 200, 202; as gentle force, 199
Prejudice, 242-44, 246-48
Presuppositionlessness, 62
Project (*Entwurf*), 82, 87-88; and possibilities, 82
Projection (mathematical), and physics, 129; (metaphysical), and the thingness of the things, 142

Pro-posing and positing presentation (*Vor-Stellung*), 161-62, 178; and modern metaphysics, 162, 178
Proposition, and positing presentation, 184-86; and principle of non-contradiction, 186
Psychic phenomena, vs. natural things, 38-39
Psychology, 38-39, 215-16; and phenomenology, 36-39; and regional ontologies, 215-16; in Heidegger, 215; naturalistic vs. personalistic, 37-39

Question, 51-52

Real, 163-64; and mere appearance, 164; and positing presentation, 164
Realism, 88-92
Reality, 89-93; of the world, 25
Region, 109-110; and regional categories, 110
Regional ontology, 102-13; and empirical sciences, 104, 109-12; and transcendental phenomenology, 106; formal vs. material ontologies, 105; Heidegger's conception of, 113; Husserl's conception of, 102-109
Releasement, 138
Representation, 188-89
Research, 153-55
Researcher, 159-60

Resolve, 195; and authenticity, 195-96; and heritage, 195-96; and retrieve of possibilities, 195-96
Retrieve (*Wiederhohlung*), 195-96; 198-99
Rule, 155

Scholar, 159-60
Science, 1-7, 133-38; and metaphysics, 136-38; and other forms of rational discourse, 133-38; and philosophy, 134-38; as business, 158; empirical science, 1-3; institutionalization of, 158-59; natural vs. historical, *xi-xii*, 28-30; natural vs. social, *xi*; science vs. philosophy, 4-7. See Natural science, Human science
Science of nature (modern), 139-89; and metaphysics, 152, 177-89; and method, 155-57; and modern era, 152; and research, 153-55; as enterprise, 157-62; as institution, 157-62; as system, 157-62; essence of, 152-62. See Natural science
Scientism, 14
Scientization, 3
Semblance, 63-64
Situational logic, 227
Social science, See Human science
Source critique, 206
Specialization, 112, 157-58; and generalization, 112; and unification of the sciences, 160-61

Subject, 178, 181, 184-86
Subject-object-opposition, 75-78, 188; and epistemological problem, 188

Technicity, essence of, 175-77
Technology, 173-77; and natural science, 173-77; and truth as non-concealment, 175; as applied science, 174; atomic, 173-74, chemical, 173; electrotechnical, 173; essence of, 174-77
Temporal distance, 246
Temporality, 59-60, 194; and care, 194-95; and historicity, 195-96
Temporalization, 122
Thematization, 124-29; and demundanization, 204; and laws, 206-207; and objectivation, 124-29; and research, 207; in historiology, 197-98, 203-208; in human sciences, 220-28
Thematizing projection, 153-55, 159, 161, 170-72; and objectivation, 176
Theoretical knowledge, 74-78; and concern, 74-77; and subject-object-opposition, 75; and traditional epistemology, 75-78
Theory, 164-65; and concern, 118-24; modern conception of, 165-67, cf. 9-10
Thing (*res*), 89, 92
Thinking, 134-36, 172; calculative, 250, 253-54; meditative, 250, 252-54; vs.

science, 134-36; two forms of, 249-50
Thoughtlessness (in modern era), 138, 249-50, 254-55
Thrownness, 74, 191, 195, 199
Traces, 203-204
Tradition, 60; and destructive retrieve, 60-61
Transcendence, 73-74
Transcendental idealism, 49-50
Transcendental phenomenology, vs. hermeneutic phenomenology, 69-71
Transcendental philosophy, 57, 53-58
Truth, 33-34, 93-102; and evidence, 94; and freedom, 98-102; and presence, 94; and semblance, 98, 101; and untruth, 98, 101; as *aletheia*, 65, 97; as certitude, 188; as conformity, 175; as nonconcealment, 175-76; as uncovering, 97-99; classical definition of, 93-97; essence of, 93; Heidegger's conception of, 97-102; Husserl's conception of, 95-97; logical vs. ontological truth, 95-96
Truth of Being, as transcendental horizon, 53

Uncoveredness (*Entdecktheit*), 98
Understanding (*Verstehen*), 78-85, 190-193, 236; and being-able-to-be, 191; and enunciation (*Aussage*), 81; and explanation, 192; and interpretation, 192-93; and interpretative explanation (*Auslegung*), 81; and possibilities (for Dasein), 80, 191-92; and project (*Entwurf*), 80, 191-93
Unification of the sciences and specialization, 160-61
Unumgängliche, 170

Values, 234-36; and philosophy of values, 235; vs. facts, 234, 236

Wesensschau (ideation), 34, 113
World, 78; as the open, 99-101; problem of the existence of the external world, 89-93; vs. unworld, 252